# A Tone Parallel to Duke Ellington

American Made
Music Series

ADVISORY BOARD

David Evans, General Editor
Barry Jean Ancelet
Edward A. Berlin
Joyce J. Bolden
Rob Bowman
Curtis Ellison
William Ferris
John Edward Hasse
Kip Lornell
Bill Malone
Eddie S. Meadows
Manuel H. Peña
Wayne D. Shirley
Robert Walser

# A Tone Parallel to Duke Ellington

## The Man in the Music

Jack Chambers

University Press of Mississippi / Jackson

The University Press of Mississippi is the scholarly publishing agency of the Mississippi Institutions of Higher Learning: Alcorn State University, Delta State University, Jackson State University, Mississippi State University, Mississippi University for Women, Mississippi Valley State University, University of Mississippi, and University of Southern Mississippi.

www.upress.state.ms.us

The University Press of Mississippi is a member of the Association of University Presses.

Copyright © 2025 by University Press of Mississippi
All rights reserved
Manufactured in the United States of America

∞

Library of Congress Cataloging-in-Publication Data

Names: Chambers, J. K., author.
Title: A tone parallel to Duke Ellington : the man in the music / Jack Chambers.
Other titles: American made music series.
Description: Jackson : University Press of Mississippi, 2025. | Series: American made music series | Includes bibliographical references and index.
Identifiers: LCCN 2024055933 (print) | LCCN 2024055934 (ebook) | ISBN 9781496855701 (hardback) | ISBN 9781496855749 (trade paperback) | ISBN 9781496855756 (epub) | ISBN 9781496855763 (epub) | ISBN 9781496855770 (pdf) | ISBN 9781496855787 (pdf)
Subjects: LCSH: Ellington, Duke, 1899–1974. | Ellington, Duke, 1899–1974—Criticism and interpretation. | African American jazz musicians—Biography. | Jazz musicians—United States—Biography. | African American composers—Biography. | Pianists—United States—Biography. | BISAC: MUSIC / History & Criticism | HISTORY /African American & Black Classification: LCC ML410.E44 C43 2025 (print) | LCC ML410.E44 (ebook) | DDC 781.65092—dc23/20250106
LC record available at https://lccn.loc.gov/2024055933
LC ebook record available at https://lccn.loc.gov/2024055934

British Library Cataloging-in-Publication Data available

# Contents

Acknowledgments . . . . . . . . . . . . . . . . . . . . . . . . . vii
Introduction . . . . . . . . . . . . . . . . . . . . . . . . . . . . ix
Abbreviations . . . . . . . . . . . . . . . . . . . . . . . . . . . xi

Chapter 1. Echoes of Harlem . . . . . . . . . . . . . . . . . . . 3
    Appendix: Ellington's Harlem Songs . . . . . . . . . . . . . . . 20
Chapter 2. Forty-Eight Years with the Duke on Trains. . . . . . . . 24
    Appendix: The Duke on Trains—The Complete Discography . . . . 39

**Interlude 1—First Impressions of Duke Ellington
Worlds and Years Apart** . . . . . . . . . . . . . . . . . . . . . 42

Chapter 3. The Piano Player. . . . . . . . . . . . . . . . . . . . 44
    Appendix: Piano Recitals Annotated . . . . . . . . . . . . . . . 65
Chapter 4. Wordless Articulation . . . . . . . . . . . . . . . . . 68
Chapter 5. Ellington's Music with Words . . . . . . . . . . . . . . 88

**Interlude 2—Musicians' Impressions of Duke Ellington
Years and Genres Apart** . . . . . . . . . . . . . . . . . . . . 112

Chapter 6. The Lotus Eaters. . . . . . . . . . . . . . . . . . . 114
Chapter 7. Accidental Suites: Duke Ellington's Hollywood Scores . . . 135
Chapter 8. Ellington in the Global Village. . . . . . . . . . . . . 157

**Interlude 3—Poets' Impressions of Duke Ellington
Ages and Styles Apart** . . . . . . . . . . . . . . . . . . . . . 174

Chapter 9. Diamonds in a Glittering Heap . . . . . . . . . . . . 176
Chapter 10. A Final Masterpiece, Reluctantly. . . . . . . . . . . 188

Chapter 11. The Missing Last Act of an American Composer . . . . . . 209

Works Cited . . . . . . . . . . . . . . . . . . . . . . . . . . . . . 235
Index of People and Places . . . . . . . . . . . . . . . . . . . . . 243
Index of Compositions and Songs . . . . . . . . . . . . . . . . . . 255

# Acknowledgments

This book is a gleaning from a much larger project that resulted from the COVID-19 pandemic of 2020 to 2023, when teaching was shut down and conferencing became remote. I have sought out the high points of that project, some of them well known and some new and novel, in hopes of making what my editor Craig Gill at UPM calls "a deep dive into the works of Duke Ellington." It has been a pleasure working with Craig and coeditor Katie Turner on our common ambition for bringing fresh insights into Ellington's voluminous works for well-versed listeners and especially for music lovers who may have found Ellington's sheer volume daunting.

The MS was read with a critical eye by Steve Bowie and Ian Bradley. I am grateful for the attention of such exacting, patient, and knowledgeable colleagues. Because of them, the book is better in matters both large and small.

My first debt is to the members of the Toronto Duke Ellington Society (TDES), who were the first audience for several of the themes. I have listened to the music of Duke Ellington since my early teens, and I began writing about his music soon after that. Writing about it led to invitations to present talks. The themes in this book—and many others—were first aired in annual talks to the TDES over more than twenty years. When the prospect of mounting a university course on Ellington arose, I wrote sketches of the nine themes I was going to present to the class, some of them based on my previously published articles. Thanks to a grant from the TDES, I self-published them under the title *Sweet Thunder* (2019, out of print). Those sketches found their way beyond my classroom, mainly via the international network of Duke Ellington Societies in New York, Washington, Southern California, the United Kingdom, and Sweden as well as Toronto. The response of the members was gratifying, as was the response of my students. I was encouraged to develop the themes further and add new ones for a deeper look into the prodigious works of this master musician.

Acknowledgments to colleagues who provided specific materials are listed as they arise in the chapters.

# Introduction

> What I'm involved in is a continuing autobiography, a continuing record
> of the people I meet, the places I see and then see change.
> —DUKE ELLINGTON TO NAT HENTOFF (1976, 36)

This book explores Edward Kennedy "Duke" Ellington's music thematically, collating topics, motifs, memes, and predilections that caught his attention and inspired his restless muse. In presenting Ellington's music linked by themes, as I do here, the music is embedded in the context in which it was created—historical, political, musical, biographic, personal, and, at best, immersed in the give-and-take of popular and critical tastes at the moment of their creation and beyond. It offers, I hope, a novel kind of accessibility.

Ellington's music presents a daunting task because of its sheer volume. The numbers defy credulity: Ellington wrote more than two thousand compositions in numerous genres, including jazz and blues, pop songs, big-band swing, revues, hymns, tone poems, soundtracks, suites, ballets, concertos, and symphonies. He wrote music almost every day, on trains, buses, ocean liners, and in recording studios, green rooms, and hotel suites. For fifty years, until his death in 1974, his band performed almost nightly and recorded almost weekly. The soundtrack of his life is more fully preserved than perhaps any composer. Even his most devoted listeners continually discover novel gems in it.

For anyone who might be enticed to delve into it, where does one start? The themes in this book make very manageable entry points. The organization into themes will, I hope, bring new insights to listeners who already know Ellington's music. Most of all, I hope it will provide entry points for relative newcomers to Ellington's fifty-year creative journey.

Ellington's music is grounded in times and places and situations more or less familiar to us and yet sublimated so that we see them freshly, as if for the first time. Looking at the man through the prism of his music provides a "tone parallel," a phrase that Ellington favored, to the elusive composer himself. His music has its roots in dance-band rhythms, blues harmonies, and pop song melodies, but it is, at its best, so much more than any of those things. It quite literally rose out of them.

Though the emphasis is on the music, the life and times of the composer are woven into it in a particularly intimate way. For Ellington, music was grounded in the world. "We see an old man walking along the street," Ellington told an unidentified interviewer in 1945 (254), "we play a song that goes with the man." Instead of conservatory titles like "Prelude in C Minor," he chose "Prelude to a Kiss"; not "Concerto for Cello and Orchestra" but "Concerto for Cootie"; not "C Sharp Étude" but "C Jam Blues." That was Ellington's way. His first biographer, Barry Ulanov, summed up his sensibility this way (1960, 168): "He has never failed to take compass points, wherever he has been, in a new city, a new country, a redecorated nightclub, to make his own observations and to translate these into fanciful narratives." One of the delights of listening to his music comes from gathering impressions of the personal, social, and historical circumstances that drew it forth.

The themes provide the context in which the music came into being with enough biography to satisfy most music lovers, even those who come to the book knowing very little about Ellington's life. Each chapter is more or less self-contained with its own playlist as a guide to the music discussed in it, and, in some cases, fuller listings for readers who might want to pursue a topic further. The themes naturally interact, and the order of the chapters is not arbitrary. Earlier themes cover fairly long stretches of Ellington's fifty-year creative span, thus charting movements and events and developments that shed some light on the trajectory of his career. Later chapters sometimes cover more specific themes, some of them from his last decades, which are less well studied but no less rewarding in the music that resulted. The "continuing autobiography" that was Duke Ellington's music covers many themes. This book explores some of the most enticing.

# Abbreviations

| | |
|---|---|
| as | alto saxophone |
| b | bass, string bass |
| bcl | bass clarinet |
| bjo | banjo |
| bs | baritone saxophone |
| CBC | Canadian Broadcasting Corporation |
| CBS | Columbia Broadcasting System |
| CJRT | Toronto radio station |
| cl | clarinet |
| Cm-sax | C-melody saxophone |
| cor | cornet |
| d | drums |
| DE | Duke Ellington |
| DEMS | Duke Ellington Music Society |
| DESS | Duke Ellington Society of Sweden |
| DESUK | Duke Ellington Society United Kingdom |
| dir | director |
| el-p | electric piano |
| flt | flute |
| flugl | flugelhorn |
| Fr | France |
| frh | French horn |
| g | guitar |
| IAJRC | International Association of Record Collectors |
| LP | long-play record, 33 1/3 rpm, usually vinyl |
| *MiMM* | *Music is My Mistress* (1973 memoir by Ellington) |

| | |
|---|---|
| mvts | movements |
| NAACP | National Association for the Advancement of Colored People |
| NYC | New York City |
| org | organ |
| ORTF | *Office de Radiodiffusion-Télévision Française* (National Broadcast Corporation of France) |
| p | piano |
| tb | trombone |
| TDES | Toronto Duke Ellington Society |
| tp | trumpet |
| ts | tenor saxophone |
| VOA | Voice of America, radio broadcasts for Europe |
| vln | violin |
| voc | vocal |

# A Tone Parallel to Duke Ellington

Chapter 1

# Echoes of Harlem

> The octoroon choruses at the Lafayette, the black sheiks at Small's, the expert amateur dancing to be seen at the Savoy, the Curb Market along the 8th Avenue L, with its strange West Indian roots and flare of tropical fruits.... Harlem was ... a cosmopolitan delight.
> —JOSEPHINE COGDELL, HARLEM DIARY 1927

When Duke Ellington arrived in Harlem in 1923, he was simply dazzled. In that, he was by no means alone. The poet Langston Hughes arrived two years before him, age twenty-one, to attend Columbia University but mainly in hopes of finding his niche in what he called the Harlem "love-nights." "I was in love with Harlem long before I got there," he said (quoted by Taylor 2019, 39–40). He rhapsodized about the bustle, about "Harlem and ... its cabarets and casinos, its dark, warm bodies. The thundering subways, the arch of the bridges, the mighty rivers. ... I become dizzy dancing to the jazz-tuned nights, ecstasy-wearied in the towered days. The fascination of this city is upon me, burning like a fire in the blood."

So dazzling was the atmosphere that it was dubbed a "renaissance"— the Harlem Renaissance, by analogy with the revered Italian Renaissance, though, tragically, this one would be measured in decades rather than centuries. All these sights and sounds and smells and schemes Duke Ellington would capture in his music, in a lifelong homage to the milieu that crystallized his creative gifts.

Not that he was a bumpkin by any means—he was twenty-four when he arrived, and back home in Washington, DC, he was a hotshot well beyond his years, a contractor of dance bands for all occasions, often their leader and piano player, the best-dressed man at any gathering, a pool shark, a "world champion drinker" (as he would later fancy himself years after he had lost interest in the charms of alcohol), a husband and father at the age of nineteen, and a redoubtable lady's man who cruised the nightspots in his Chandler town car, "going nowhere," he said, "as fast as we could" (Nicholson 1999, 18). But to Ellington, Harlem represented a higher league altogether. "It was New York that filled our imagination," he recalled fifty years later. "We were awed by the never-ending roll of great talents there, talents in so many fields, in society music and blues, in vaudeville and songwriting, in jazz and theatre, in dancing and comedy.... Harlem, to our minds, did indeed have the world's most glamorous atmosphere. We had to go there" (*MiMM* 35–36).

Harlem, the upper Manhattan neighborhood whose stately brownstones were built by the Knickerbockers and other Dutch American gentry in the nineteenth century, was named by them for Haarlem, the stately port city in North Holland. The uptown Manhattan Harlem was, by the 1920s, almost exclusively African American. It was the epicenter for the "blasting pressures," in novelist Ralph Ellison's kinetic imagery, "which in a scant eighty years have sent the Negro people hurtling, without a clearly defined trajectory, from slavery to emancipation, from log cabin to city tenement, from the white folks' fields and kitchens to factory assembly lines" (1945, 105).

Conspicuous among Harlem's citizens was an upstart class of cultural bellwethers, "the never-ending roll of great talents," as Ellington called them, including political theorists W. E. B. Du Bois (1868–1963) and Marcus Garvey (1887–1940); composer and conductor William Grant Still (1895–1978); poets and novelists Zora Neale Hurston (1891–1960) and Countee Cullen (1903–1946), whose ranks Langston Hughes (1902–1967) would join; artists Aaron Douglas (1899–1979) and Romare Bearden (1911–1988); contralto Marian Anderson (1897–1993); Broadway orchestrator Will Vodery (1885–1951); hit songwriters Eubie Blake (1883–1983), Noble Sissle (1895–1975), Andy Razaf (1895–1973) and Henry Creamer (1879–1930); piano virtuoso and composer James P. Johnson (1894–1955); tap dancer and movie star Bill "Bojangles" Robinson (1878–1949); singer/dancer and entrepreneur Ada "Bricktop" Smith (1894–1984); world heavyweight boxing champion Jack Johnson (1878–1946); and star athlete, actor, and operatic baritone Paul Robeson (1898–1976), among others. It was a teeming meritocracy, bringing amazing vigor to American culture scarcely two generations after Abraham Lincoln's Emancipation Proclamation.

Duke Ellington would quickly carve out his own space among these bellwethers. Like him, they came from some other corner of the country. He could match their swagger from the start and, most importantly, he quickly learned to emulate their strivings. "In Harlem," Ellington wrote in 1931, "we have what is practically our own city; we have our own newspapers and social services, and although not segregated, we have almost achieved our own civilization." In his program notes, sadly unused, for *Black, Brown and Beige*, his 1943 "tone parallel to the American Negro," he rhapsodized about its music (Peress 2004, 186)—

> Harlem! Black Metropolis!
> Land of mirth!
> Your music has flung
> The story of Hot Harlem
> To the four corners
> Of the earth!

Langston Hughes soon added Ellington, the architect of what Hughes memorialized as Harlem's "jazz-tuned nights," to the panoply of stalwarts. "The sheer dark size of Harlem intrigued me," Hughes wrote, "and the fact that poets and writers like James Weldon Johnson and Jessie Fauser lived there, and Bert Williams, Duke Ellington, Ethel Waters, and Walter White too."

Harlem was the focus of his orchestra's theme song from 1940 onward, its theme stated in composer/arranger Billy Strayhorn's opening verse—

> Hurry hurry hurry, take the "A" Train,
> You'll find it's the quickest way to get to Harlem.
> If you should take the "A" Train,
> You'll get where you're going in a hurry.

How to get to Harlem was the first of many lessons Strayhorn, the young provincial from Pittsburgh, learned from Ellington, directing him to the subway line that would take him to the place where he would hang his hat for the rest of his days as Ellington's associate composer. By the time Strayhorn wrote his one and only tribute to Harlem in 1940, Ellington had already written no fewer than fourteen compositions with "Harlem" in the title. There would be seventeen in all, culminating in 1951 with *A Tone Parallel to Harlem*, widely recognized as the pinnacle of Ellington's extended compositions. His Harlem songs leading up to that pinnacle run the gamut from trite to terrific, and because of that, they make an entertaining and occasionally enlightening preamble to the majestic *Tone Parallel to Harlem*. (Ellington's "Harlem" songs with discographic details are listed at the end of the chapter.)

## "The Cotton Club, the Aristocrat of Harlem"

It took a couple of years for young Duke Ellington to gain street-corner status in the Harlem pantheon. He may have been a local hero in DC, but when he arrived in New York, he had to develop the street smarts to get him into the nightspots run by mobsters and the moxie to get past the "we'll-call-you" indifference of bookers and agents. As always, his impeccable grooming and decorous manners, lifelong accoutrements of his genteel upbringing, helped him win the kinds of friends who could get him in the front door. One of his early champions was Willie "the Lion" Smith (*née* William Henry Joseph Bonaparte Bertholf Smith), the piano wizard who welcomed him into his Harlem nightspot, the Capitol Palace, where he could rub shoulders with the established New York crowd. Another was the singer/dancer/vaudevillian Bricktop (*née* Ada Beatrice Louise Virginia Smith), who got Ellington's band, the Washingtonians, some exposure by touting its virtues to the mobsters who ran Barron's Club, where she performed. The Broadway orchestrator Will Vodery agreed to answer Ellington's importunate questions on composing and arranging. "He used to give me valuable lectures in orchestration," Ellington wrote (*MiMM* 98), and he would use those lectures as starting points for his own unique soundscape.

"Ellington did not know or care about the textbooks," Gunther Schuller noted. "His own piano playing gave him the most immediately accessible answer to voice-leading questions" (1968, 342). And his self-reliance guided him beyond musical acumen. Otto Hardwick, who grew up with Ellington in Washington and played saxophone in his bands until 1946, saw it firsthand. "The amazing thing about him is that the language, the slant, everything, didn't rub off from someone else, and it wasn't a legacy, either," he said. "He went inside himself to find it. He's an *only*, that's for sure" (reported by Balliett 1988, 522).

Ellington's mother had told him, "Edward, you are blessed," and he never doubted her in this or anything else.

He soon took over the leadership of the Washingtonians, replacing banjo player Elmer Snowden in 1924. Two years after that, their records came out with his name attached as "Duke Ellington and His Washingtonians," and a year after that, in 1927, it was simply "Duke Ellington and His Orchestra." It would take a few more years, until 1929, for the first records under the name "Duke Ellington and His *Famous* Orchestra."

The big break came in April 1927, when the Duke Ellington Orchestra won the job as house band of the Cotton Club. Ellington characteristically turned this crucial career move into a self-deprecating anecdote (*MiMM*

75–76). The band was slated for an audition, but the call went out for eleven pieces and the Washingtonians were making do with six at the Kentucky Club where they were working. "The audition was set for noon, but by the time I had scraped up eleven men it was two or three o'clock," he wrote. "We played for them and got the job. The reason for that was that the boss, Harry Block, didn't get there till late either, and didn't hear the others! That's a classic example of being in the right place at the right time with the right thing before the right people."

Rightly so, but we know now that his great good fortune started even earlier, when circumstances conspired to make an audition possible for his relatively unsung band. The Cotton Club engagement was originally offered to the Sam Wooding Orchestra, returning at that moment from a triumphant tour of Europe with an African American revue called *Chocolate Kiddies* (that included five songs by Ellington and lyricist Jo Trent). According to Garvin Bushell (1990, 73), who played clarinet and other reed instruments in Wooding's orchestra, Wooding received a telegram offering him the Cotton Club job for a very generous $1,100 a week. Wooding turned it down, saying, "No, I'm not coming back to Harlem. We started in Harlem, and we've been playing on Broadway and for the royalty of the world. We don't come back to Harlem." Bushell notes, "It was the biggest mistake he ever made. Duke Ellington took the job, he got that radio hookup two or three nights a week, and the rest is history."

Ellington's expanded band accompanied the song and dance numbers in the nightly revues at the Cotton Club by the songwriting team Dorothy Fields and Jimmy McHugh and also played for interludes of dancing by the all-white audience in the segregated setting. McHugh quickly recognized that Ellington's arrangements lent unique timbres to their music and encouraged him to contribute specialty numbers to the revues as well. It was a challenge that the young bandleader accepted readily. His skills flourished, honed by the disparate challenges of supplying music for dramatic entertainments and providing rhythms for couples gliding across the dance floor. The breadth was uncommon, and Ellington's music was quickly recognized for its unique voicings and memorable melodies.

The dance music was broadcast on network radio. The show music beguiled Jascha Heifetz, Leopold Stokowski, and dozens of other downtown celebrities who frequented the club, as well as the hundreds who bought the records. Ellington's ascendancy was celebrated by the entertainment reporter Archie Seale, writing in the *New York Age* in 1935. He dubbed the Cotton Club "the aristocrat of Harlem," and gave Duke Ellington full credit for its nobility. "When Duke Ellington wrote 'Black and Tan Fantasy,' little did he realize that this was the beginning of country-wide recognition for himself and the Cotton Club," Seale wrote. "The Cotton Club then began to entice the silk hats and ermines—the class people of Park Avenue and Riverside Drive."

### Park Avenue and Riverside Drive Come to Harlem

Inevitably, Ellington would memorialize the nightly excursions of midtown Manhattanites to the Cotton Club—"the silk hats and ermines"—in song, but that would take a few more years in these busy times. "Black and Tan Fantasy," Ellington's early breakout composition, was first recorded in April 1927, one month after "East St. Louis Toodle-Oo," its companion in harmonic sophistication. (Both compositions would stay in Ellington's repertoire for the rest of his career—forty-seven years—though none of their predecessors did.) By then, Ellington had already tried his hand at exalting Harlem with the first of his seventeen "Harlem" titles. He called that first piece "A Night in Harlem," and we can imagine that a composition about a night in Harlem must have been raucous in its own right. Unfortunately, we will never know. The record was never issued. Ellington recorded it in November 1926, and that same date produced the incipient brilliance of "East St. Louis Toodle-Oo" and "Birmingham Breakdown."

The disappearance of "A Night in Harlem" meant that the real inauguration of Ellington's Harlem tributes came a few months later, after the orchestra established itself as the heartbeat of the uptown community at the Cotton Club. It was called "Harlem River Quiver," a jittery little number by Dorothy Fields and Jimmy McHugh, with Ellington's arrangement. It was written for the first Cotton Club show that Ellington accompanied and designed as a showcase for the kickline of beautiful young dancers (which may account for its alternate title, "Brown Berries"). Steven Lasker (1991) quotes a contemporary review from *Variety*, the show biz bible of the day, which provides a glimpse of the bawdy delights that charmed the downtown sophisticates at the uptown hotspot. The exuberant reviewer writes: "One choocher, a boyish bobbed hoyden, said to be specially imported from Chicago for her Annapolis proclivities, does the *Harlem River Quiver* like no self-respecting body of water. The teasin'est torso tossing yet, and how!" *Variety*'s argot, then and now, begs for translation. Suffice it to say that the "Annapolis proclivities" referred to the hyperactive dancer's (the "choocher's") more than ample hips by a metaphoric chain that invokes the US Naval Academy at Annapolis, Maryland, and circuitously a street-corner ditty that extols a woman with "a pair of hips

/ Just like two battleships." (The refrain that follows says, "Oh boy, that's where my money goes.") Titillating, obviously, for gentlefolk of the 1920s who wore starch collars to the office and full-length costumes on the tennis court.

Suddenly at the Cotton Club, those genteel folks found themselves immersed in the Jazz Age. As Hsio Wen Shih says, in an early history, the allure of Harlem was a mixed blessing. "The vogue for Negro entertainment spread among the white public, who saw Harlem as a black Arcadia, a reservation of hedonists" (1959, 177). Ellington's scores for the revues were dubbed with the unflattering misnomer "jungle music." As Shih noted, "It was all a misunderstanding, of course, at least where the music was concerned: Ellington's style of the 1920s has rightly been called the papier-maché jungle. But the white public was fooled, and the urbane Ellington was forced by public demand to be the mock-primitive." Indeed, Ellington appropriated the name in several of his song titles, including one of his most spirited Harlem tunes, "Jungle Nights in Harlem," recorded in 1930.

## Taxi Uptown

While it lasted, the nightly rush of midtown A-listers was a social phenomenon, and Ellington, with his unerring instincts, wrote a piece that caught the derring-do of the slumming fur coats and white ties. "Drop Me Off at Harlem" is a foxtrot with a sinuous lope as its rhythm. Ellington's arrangement of his composition leaves the infectious melody unadorned all through with smooth trombonist Lawrence Brown stating the A melody and equally smooth trumpeter Arthur Whetsol the bridge. When Ellington jazzes up the piece in the second chorus, he does it conservatively by having the orchestra reprise the melody with tasteful embellishments by Cootie Williams on muted trumpet and Barney Bigard on clarinet. With the instincts of a hit maker, Ellington never lets the simple pop-style melody recede.

"Drop Me Off at Harlem" practically cried out for a lyric, and it soon got one. Nick Kenny, popular columnist for the *New York Daily Mirror* and an occasional contributor of light verse, adorned Ellington's melody with plainspoken hyperbole:

> Drop me off in Harlem,
> Any place in Harlem,
> There's someone waiting there
> Who makes it seem like Heaven up in Harlem

Legend has it that Kenny and Ellington shared a taxi and the song title came into being when Ellington announced his drop-off point to the driver (Lawrence 2001, 189). Kenny took Ellington's drop-off point as his starting point.

## Concertos for Cootie

Ellington's compositional genius has its roots, as everyone agrees, in his sensitivity to the individuality of his soloists and in his ability to enfold their personal sounds into settings that are imprinted with the personality of both soloist and composer.

Cootie Williams blossomed under Ellington's baton. He joined the band in 1929, in the efflorescence that came with the Cotton Club tenure, and quickly became an integral part of it. He was recruited as an emergency replacement for Bubber Miley, Ellington's first star soloist and also the co-composer of his first great compositions. Miley appeared to be indispensable in the first flowering of the band, but he was a binge drinker who soon began missing more engagements than he showed up for. Ellington suffered Miley's erratic behavior with characteristic patience until finally, in 1929, he had no choice. He hired Cootie Williams (given name Charles, but never called that except by his mother, who died when he was eight), a southerner who had made his way to New York with an obscure band in 1928 when he was seventeen, and impressed all the city slickers with his rich, confident trumpet sound in the manner of the nonpareil Louis Armstrong.

Williams was not hired because he could fill Miley's role but simply because he was the best young trumpet player available. Ellington recalled, "Cootie had been playing open horn all that time, and when the guys heard about the change he was making [by joining Ellington's band], he got kidded a lot. . . . Everybody told him he'd have to use the plunger and growl all night long [as Miley had done]. How was he going to make out, they all wanted to know. But he didn't pay them any mind. He caught onto a lot from Tricky Sam [Nanton, the band's plunger specialist on trombone], and before you knew it everyone was saying nobody could work with a plunger like Cootie" (Shapiro 1955, 215). One of Miley's ardent admirers, Vic Bellerby, soon found himself waxing poetic about his successor. Cootie Williams, he declared, "brought to the band a sweeping majesty of the growl phrase, and injected shivers of intensity to the most powerful of ensembles" (1962, 145).

Williams takes center stage in two of Ellington's Harlem tributes. "The Boys from Harlem" provides a handsome workout for Williams's dexterous open trumpet, and "Echoes of Harlem," one of Ellington's masterworks, an inevitable entry on anyone's list of his twenty or thirty greatest compositions, showcases his mastery of the plunger mute.

"The Boys from Harlem" was recorded by an octet from the Ellington band called Cootie Williams and His Rug Cutters, one of a series of small-band spin-offs intended to keep an entrepreneurial foot in the more modest side of the record-buying market. It is a lively, jive-worthy confection. In an unexpected treat, Williams's long turns at the opening and the closing are separated by a two-chorus interlude composed by Ellington for two deep-throated reeds playing rapidly in unison. The horns are baritone saxophone (Harry Carney) and bass saxophone (Otto Hardwick). It is a strangely guttural combination, but Ellington gives it life. It is a short (forty-six seconds!) but joyful sign of Ellington's inventive spirit that he would insert such an ingenious segment into an otherwise straightforward toe-tapping piece. "The Boys from Harlem" is a plainspoken demonstration of Cootie Williams's bold control on the open trumpet that just happens to include a gee-whiz duet in the middle like the jelly in a donut.

"Echoes of Harlem," the other Harlem title that Ellington composed for Cootie Williams,[1] is arguably the pinnacle of Williams's trumpet artistry, though there are many contenders. It was first recorded in 1936, a debut that was impressive but uncharacteristically tentative compared to many of its later recordings. Admittedly, "tentative" is a relative term when it comes to Williams; his style reflected his physical presence, a broad-shouldered, firm-footed bravado that seemed to epitomize his ebullience, an inseparable trait of his commanding presence. Happily, there are many versions to choose from because the number was a fixture in Ellington's repertoire from 1934 until 1940, when Williams left the band.

Of its many iterations, the masterwork (in my hearing) survives on a radio broadcast from a downtown club deceptively called the Cotton Club. The original Cotton Club, the Harlem aristocrat where Ellington honed his art, closed in February 1936, but some entrepreneurs opened a club with that famous name seven months later (September 1936) on Broadway in the Theater District. This downtown Cotton Club would fade away in 1940, but in its first year, it was a boon for Ellington, because in an attempt to recreate its Harlem glory, the owners installed the Duke Ellington orchestra on its bandstand fairly regularly from May 1937 to May 1938.

---

1. "Echoes of Harlem" was sometimes called "Cootie's Concerto," though that title is too easily confused with "Concerto for Cootie," a later composition that became well known as "Do Nothin' till You Hear from Me" when lyrics were added to it.

As Ellington begins the piano vamp that sets the stage for Williams's grand entry on this masterful version of Cootie's concerto at the downtown Cotton Club, it elicits a ripple of applause from the well-versed audience. Williams crafts the beautiful blues melody plaintively at first, carefully placing his notes in syncopation with the vamp. After the first chorus, Williams rests as the saxophone section takes over with a handsome interlude (an interpolation from a minor 1932 composition called "Blue Mood"). In this live performance, Williams intones colorful phrases on top of the ensemble as if he is impatient to get on with his starring role. Then the piano vamp returns and sets the mood for Williams's climactic variation on the theme, now more heated and assertive. Williams is assertive with or without the mute, as befits his stevedore frame, but beneath this gruff exterior, he expresses a kind of melancholy that he seemingly cannot hide.

When a reporter asked Ellington about the sources of his inspiration, Ellington said, "You look at the same melancholy again and again from a different perspective" (Boyer 1944, 234). Readers might have assumed Ellington's invocation of melancholy was poetic license in a man who exuded such easygoing, apparently insouciant charm. His music, habitually, reveals the deeper side. "Echoes of Harlem" frames that melancholy in a rare kind of perfection, even more so because it is a seamless meeting of the minds of the composer and his soloist, a striking instance of their symbiosis.

Cootie Williams left the Ellington orchestra in 1940 and, in a stunning reversal, returned twenty-two years later. His departure from Ellington's front line in November 1940, at the crest of the Swing Era, had made news in the entertainment pages of every major American newspaper; his return in late 1962, with the Swing Era a distant memory, may have received a column inch in the jazz press but was otherwise unheralded. Like so many Ellingtonians, Williams's successes in his years away from the band were few. He left to join the popular Benny Goodman Orchestra as featured soloist (with Ellington's blessing), and after a year with Goodman, fronted a dance band under his own name at the Savoy Ballroom. He became a trivia answer among devoted beboppers when he was listed as co-composer with Thelonious Monk on the great jazz standard "Round Midnight," taking credit for adding an eight-bar interlude on his 1944 recording that predates Monk's first recording of it by three years; Williams's credit abides, though no one else plays his interlude (Kelley 2009, 567–68). As the dance bands waned, Williams traveled with a quartet, and in the end, found himself playing with local rhythm sections in small cities when the opportunities arose.

On his return to Ellington after twenty-two years, Williams must have wondered why he had waited so long. Ellington celebrated his return by reviving "Echoes of Harlem" with an arrangement that was sparser and the melancholy more evident. To Ellington's audience, young and old, as to Ellington himself, Cootie Williams was still the star soloist he had been when he left. At an outstanding concert in Paris in 1963, soon after Williams's return, Ellington starts the piano vamp that signals the introduction to "Echoes of Harlem" and the audience erupts. The twenty-two-year gap seems to be wiped away in an instant. In this Paris rendition and other revivals, Ellington extends the vamp, perhaps allowing for the time it takes for the fifty-two-year-old to wend his way from the back riser, where the trumpet section sits, to the microphone on the proscenium. Or perhaps Ellington slows the vamp to give the soloist time to reacquaint himself with phrases he had not played for decades. Whatever the reason, the slower tempo has the salutary effect of allowing this mellow veteran to wring out the melancholy that was always there and which has now, in this incarnation, become the focus of Cootie's concerto. In this new arrangement, the saxophone interlude (the "Blue Mood" interpolation) has disappeared; most of the saxophone players who had played it in the 1930s were still present in the band and could no doubt have revived it, so its absence is deliberate.

This "Echoes of Harlem" reveals a seasoned Cootie Williams, somewhat quieter though far from taciturn, somewhat less intense on the high notes though still hitting them, and somewhat pensive, maybe musing about the bygone days when it all seemed so easy. Decades after the composer and the soloist first played these notes, they are still perfectly in sync. Here is perfection on a different scale.

## "Essence of Harlem in an Air Shaft"

One of the first pieces by Ellington that reflected with his delight in Harlem's exuberance came in March 1929, two years into his five-year tenure at the Cotton Club. He called it "Harlem Flat Blues," and it was his first attempt at evoking the rhythms and harmonies of tenement life. Ellington had spent his Washington youth in spacious surroundings, and he seemed to be fascinated by the vertical swirl of humanity all around him in Harlem's crowded apartment blocks. The profusion of humanity in these Harlem flats would eventually become an urban problem with overcrowding, but in these halcyon early days, Ellington simply saw it as a swirl of human energy, an ultramodern cityscape. Harlem was a magnet not only for musicians and poets, but for thousands of African Americans from smaller cities and especially for workers from the southern states seeking opportunities in the big city.

From 1899, when Ellington was born, until 1923, when he first set foot in Harlem, the population of this seven-square-mile neighborhood increased by 150 percent, from 60,000 to 150,000 (Lawrence 2001, 37).

"Harlem Flat Blues" captures the urban bustle by spotlighting the reed section for eight bars and then the brass section with plungers for eight more, evoking a symmetry for ensemble and soloists. It is a theme Ellington would imprint more indelibly in later compositions "Harlem Air Shaft" and *A Tone Parallel to Harlem*. The progression from "Harlem Flat Blues" in 1929 to the polytonal swing of "Harlem Air Shaft" in 1940 and the self-assured concert grandeur of the *Tone Parallel* in 1951 provide easy landmarks for Ellington's musical evolution.

"Harlem Air Shaft" burst forth in one of the creative peaks for Duke Ellington's orchestra, 1939 to 1942, with an aggregation of musicians who had been with him for a decade or more and a couple of newcomers who injected new spirit into the band. The newcomers were bassist Jimmie Blanton, only twenty when he joined in late 1939, and tenor saxophone player Ben Webster. This version of the orchestra is often called "the Blanton–Webster band" in homage to their presence.

Although Harlem's mystique was waning by the time he gathered the Blanton–Webster band together, Ellington obviously found its rhythms hard to resist. He built a monument to those rhythms in a composition he called "Harlem Air Shaft," a striking example of what we might call reckless precision, an oxymoronic combination that thrived in the Blanton–Webster band.

"Harlem Air Shaft" gained further distinction because it was accorded a rhapsodic description of its content—or, more accurately, of its composer's *intent*—in an interview with Richard O. Boyer for a two-part profile that appeared in the *New Yorker* in 1944. An "air shaft," also known architecturally as a ventilation shaft, is an enclosed opening that runs the height of a tall building and allows air flow (ventilation) into otherwise enclosed spaces. Air shafts have fallen out of use with the invention of air conditioning and other technologies. They were a feature of many of Harlem's overcrowded tenements (though not, of course, Ellington's expansive West Harlem penthouse). Asked by Boyer about his fanciful title, Ellington explained that he saw the air shafts as "one great big loudspeaker" in which all the vitality of the community could be captured. Here is Ellington's remarkable description:

> So much goes on in a Harlem air shaft. You get the full essence of Harlem in an air shaft. You hear fights, you smell dinner, you hear people making love. You hear intimate gossip floating down. You

hear the radio. An air shaft is one great big loudspeaker. You see your neighbor's laundry. You hear the janitor's dogs. The man upstairs' aerial falls down and breaks your window. You smell coffee. A wonderful smell, that smell. The air shaft has got every contrast. One guy is cooking dried fish and rice and another guy's got a great big turkey. Guy-with-fish's wife is a terrific cooker but the guy's wife with the turkey is doing a sad job. You hear people praying, fighting, snoring. Jitterbugs are jumping up and down always over you, never below you. That's the funny thing about jitterbugs. They're always above you.

"I tried to put all that in 'Harlem Air Shaft,'" Ellington said.

It is a tall order, obviously, but the time was right. With Ellington's compositional skills at their peak and his orchestra seemingly sensitive to every nuance he set down, "Harlem Air Shaft" managed to slot a hundred impressions into its three-minute space.

Numerous commentators have noted that Ellington's composition actually invokes no obvious sound parallels to his verbal description—no barking dogs, no "praying, fighting, snoring" humans or any other mundane sounds. Does it matter? "Rather than ponder the meaning of the title," says Mark Tucker (1986), annotating the definitive Blanton–Webster compilation, "it's much more enjoyable to be swept away by the sheer exuberance of the Ellington orchestra." The rhythm is an insistent thump in straightforward quarter time. The composition is built on an equally insistent riff, a phrase repeated over and over, serving as the underpinning for ensemble statements by the trumpets on one iteration and by the reeds on another. Adding yet another layer to the complex orchestration are soaring solo statements played over the riff by Tricky Sam Nanton on trombone, Cootie Williams on trumpet, and Barney Bigard on clarinet. The master's touch, adding yet another fillip to the rich texture, is seen when the tune's powerful forward motion—its swing—is stopped dead at the end of each thirty-two-bar chorus while the reeds fill with an out-of-time two-bar phrase.

"Harlem Air Shaft" may have been constructed for acrobatic dancers in the first place—the "jitterbugs" Ellington mentions prominently at the end of his verbal description. It is easy to imagine those jitterbugs catching their breath in the two-bar interludes before resuming their acrobatics.

But for Ellington's inspired title, air shafts might be completely forgotten. The composition occupies a special niche for its exuberant invocation the "glamorous atmosphere" Ellington found on his arrival, the Harlem of the bygone days of the Cotton Club, the all-night rent parties, and the artistic flowering of the Harlem Renaissance—all of which were fading by the 1940s.

"Harlem Air Shaft" reimagines that exuberance. As Ellington himself said, recalling the "rich, special folklore" of his early impressions, "It's gone now." Harlem was suffering through hard times, and after "Harlem Air Shaft," it seemed as if Ellington had given up on it as a musical stimulus. "Harlem Air Shaft" might have been a worthy consummation of Ellington's long infatuation with his adopted home. But unpredictable as he always was, the consummation was still to come in a grand final bow to the Harlem that, by then, existed only in his imagination.

## A "Kaleidoscopic, Marvelously Descriptive Tour"

Eleven years after "Harlem Air Shaft," in 1951, Duke Ellington visited his Harlem theme one last time. He was fifty-two, and the epic composition that resulted, called *A Tone Parallel to Harlem*, recaptures the vigor and joy and pride he felt when he arrived there in his twenties and thrived there in his thirties. *A Tone Parallel to Harlem* is long, almost fourteen minutes. It was conceived as a symphony and exists as such, but it works at least as well in the big band version. Paradoxically, this consummation, this celebration of "the world's most glamorous atmosphere," was conceived and performed at the very moment that Harlem was going through the most desolate and dispiriting time in its history.

Harlem was already overcrowded when the Great Depression hit in 1929. The influx of African American immigrants from the Dust Bowl South and smaller northern cities multiplied as the economy foundered, with men and women seeking work where there was almost none to be had. Housing, employment, education, sanitation, welfare, and other services practically collapsed under the weight. Many people thought, with abundant evidence, that the situation was made worse by a lack of will among politicians to address the problems because of the monochromatic racial complexion of the place. Poverty increased, the crime rate soared, and policing became brutal. Civil rights protests sometimes ended in riots and looting, with the spiraling of violent retaliation. By the 1940s, the streets were inhospitable places for people who appeared affluent and dangerous for non-Blacks, affluent or not. East Harlem became a ghetto. West Harlem, where the Ellingtons lived, may have felt the tensions less forcibly, but even there, they were inescapable. They hit close to home in 1954, when Billy Strayhorn was mugged on leaving a taxi late at night; his wallet was stolen after he was punched in the face, kicked in the ribs, and shoved into a sandpile at a construction site (Hajdu 1996, 149–50). Ellington took to carrying a pistol in the 1940s, "a .38 snubnose," according to his manager Al Celley, "in case he got on the elevator at his home in Harlem and was threatened by an intruder" (Cohen 2010, 454).

None of these tensions found their way into the *Tone Parallel*. It was an artistic decision on Ellington's part, not naïveté. Ellington was well aware of what was happening. Civil rights protesters, among others, were singled out in his description of the urban landscape he was seeking to capture, and the first performance of the work, a gala event at the Metropolitan Opera House in January 1951, was a benefit concert for the National Association for the Advancement of Colored People (NAACP). For all that, he was not writing protest music. Ellington presumably knew, as his exact contemporary Ernest Hemingway knew, that sociopolitical problems of the day have no place in art. "All you can be sure about in a political-minded writer," said Hemingway, "is that if his work should last you will have to skip the politics when you read it."[2] The Harlem that Ellington captured in his music was the one imprinted in his mind, not the one smoldering on the streets below. All these years later, with Harlem's equilibrium restored, his conception is fully justified. The music, as Ellington knew, would outlive the turmoil.

Ellington seems to have gone to some lengths to invest this composition with romantic trappings that removed it further from the contemporary distress. In *Music Is My Mistress* (189), he talks about composing it on the Île de France, the transatlantic luxury liner, as he was returning with the members of the orchestra from a European tour. It was commissioned, he says, as "a concerto grosso for our band and the symphony" by the NBC Symphony Orchestra when Arturo Toscanini was its conductor. Ellington introduced it on the occasion of its 1951 premiere with lengthy remarks about the Harlem he was portraying musically. He wrote, in part,

> We would now like to take you on a tour of this place called Harlem. It has always had more churches than cabarets. It is Sunday morning. We are strolling from 110th Street up Seventh Avenue, heading north through the Spanish and West Indian neighborhood towards the 125th

---

2. Hemingway was born three months after Ellington in 1899, and the two men filled comparable spaces in American culture as standard bearers of American fiction and American music, respectively. They never met, and indeed their personal styles were so different—Ellington coy and devious, Hemingway blunt and direct—it might not have been gratifying if they had, but they shared an esthetic (a term neither was likely to use), starting with a disdain for analytics. Hemingway said, "It is hard enough to write books and stories without being asked to explain them as well," akin to Ellington's "If you're busy analyzing, you can't listen." It is a romantic mantra they share with the Romantic patriarch, Wordsworth: "Our meddling intellect / Mis-shapes the beauteous forms of things: / We murder to dissect" (*Lyrical Ballads*, 1798).

Street business area. Everybody is nicely dressed, and on their way to or from church. Everybody is in a friendly mood. Greetings are polite and pleasant, and on the opposite side of the street, standing under a street lamp, is a real hip chick. She, too, is in a friendly mood. You may hear a parade go by, or a funeral, or you may recognize the passage of those who are making Civil Rights demands.

The Sunday church procession that Ellington takes as his unifying image was an emblem of Harlem in its cultural heyday. Two decades earlier, in 1932, the novelist Rudolph Fisher evoked it in *The Conjure-Man Dies*, describing "the flocks that flowed out of the innumerable churches" as "the colorful variety of this weekly promenade: the women . . . with costumes, individually and collectively, running the range of the rainbow; the men with derbies, high collars, spats, and a dignity peculiar to doormen, chauffeurs, and headwaiters."[3] Fisher, like Ellington years later, fastens on the street scene for the vibrancy of its setting. Somehow, Ellington manages to get it all in—the decorum of Sunday churchgoers, the dash of Spanish rhythm, the glimpse of the earthy hipster, the passing funeral—in "this kaleidoscopic, marvelously descriptive tour of Harlem" (as his biographer Hasse aptly puts it, 323).

*A Tone Parallel to Harlem* is built around two short motifs. The first is a two-note phrase stated at the opening on trumpet (by Ray Nance) that sounds like a sing-song version of the word "Harlem."

The second motif, a kind of hymn, is introduced later by a solo trombone, and recurs with different voicings, most notably by a clarinet trio grounded magisterially by Harry Carney's bass clarinet. The climax melds the two motifs over an insistent rhythmic crescendo that leaves the impression of chest-beating pride and confidence.

Ellington brings in his two motifs repeatedly, but they are always nuanced and fresh. (In the second studio recording by the band in 1951, generally reckoned to be the most inspired among many wonderful performances, I counted sixteen repetitions of the "Harlem" motif in the first half, about seven minutes, but the count is hardly definitive when its guises are so bountiful.)

---

3. Rudolph Fisher (1897–1934) was a medical doctor who wrote two novels and a handful of short stories while practicing medicine as a specialist in radiology (then called roentgenology). His stature as a Harlem Renaissance writer was largely forgotten after his early death from radiation exposure at thirty-seven. *The Conjure-Man Dies* is a brilliant adaptation of Agatha Christie's then-fresh methods to a totally different cultural milieu. Fisher includes a couple of low-comedy characters, considered essential in his day though mildly embarrassing now (but no more so than in the work of his lauded contemporaries). The main characters, by contrast, are intelligent and articulate, and the Harlem setting is vibrant.

Har - lem.

The opening notes, played on trumpet, sound like a singsong "Harlem," and the motif is repeated throughout.

The contexts in which the motifs recur are so rich in texture and varied in instrumentation that there is no sense in which they seem excessive. On the contrary, they unify the composition, providing the listener with melodic touchstones as Ellington's longer works did not always succeed in doing.

Ellington performed *A Tone Parallel to Harlem* frequently with the band for the rest of his days, often springing it on the musicians at concerts whenever he received a request and watching them scramble to unearth their complex scores in the playbook. He recorded the big band version in studios five times, including what might be considered the definitive version in December 1951 and a lively, more spontaneous concert version in 1963 (both listed below). He also recorded it twice with symphony orchestras (also in the Playlist). Since his death, it has been performed by symphony orchestras all over the world (http://musicsalesclassical.com/composer/work/2311/27667).

## "American music undiluted"

Ellington's sensitivity to the plight that had overtaken Harlem in the decades after his arrival in 1923 becomes clear in a revealing incident at the time (reported by John Edward Hasse 1993, 297). Ellington autographed a score of *A Tone Parallel to Harlem* and had it delivered to President Harry S. Truman in 1950 with a note about the upcoming NAACP benefit concert. In the note, Ellington expressed his hope that the proceeds from the concert "will be used to help fight for your civil rights program—to stamp out segregation, discrimination, bigotry and a variety of other intolerances in our American society." Ellington also asked if Margaret Truman, the president's daughter and a classical singer, might serve as chairwoman of the event.

He never received a reply. The note, discovered by Hasse in the Truman archives, shows that "somebody wrote an emphatic 'No!' in inch-high letters, underlined twice."

Though the glory days of Harlem had been overwhelmed by social issues of many kinds by the time Ellington composed his consummate tone parallel to it, Harlem's half-century as the nurturing ground of African American—nay, of distinctively American—music, dance, literature, entertainment, athletics, civil rights, and political debate continued to inspire him. If its abrasive present obliterated any recognition of the creative pinnacle that preceded it, for Duke Ellington's contemporaries, the generation that witnessed its glory days and reveled in them, Harlem's nurturing role was simply a matter of fact. One of those contemporaries, George F. Frazier, reflecting in 1933 on Ellington's impact on his European audiences, said, "The British and the French publics realized that here was American music undiluted, music unblemished by foreign tinctures, music that had come many generations past from Africa to New Orleans and Harlem" (1933, 126–27).

Frazier's genealogy gives due prominence to Harlem alongside New Orleans. Harlem, after all, was the place where New Orleans rhythms and inventiveness were invested with the harmonic depth and formal extensions that turned them into a music that could be admired internationally and, ultimately, globally. All jazz histories, the best and the worst, maintain New Orleans's primacy, but Harlem has been largely undervalued for its role in its upward mobility. Harlem today, decades after reconciling the most pressing social and political issues that briefly made it a forbidding place, still awaits historical restitution. For a moment in time, it really was, as one of its many gifted habitués put it, "the world's most glamorous atmosphere."

## Acknowledgments

Thanks to Jim Northover, archivist of the Toronto Duke Ellington Society and super-sleuth of the internet, for turning up the 1935 article by Archie Seale on the Cotton Club, among many other treasures. The transcription of the Harlem motif from the *Tone Parallel to Harlem* is by Martin Loomer.

## Appendix: Ellington's "Harlem" Songs

Original recordings from 1926 to 1951 plus later recordings cited in the text. Duke Ellington is the composer unless otherwise noted.

| | |
|---|---|
| 1926 | "A Night in Harlem," November 29, 1926, Vocalion unissued. Duke Ellington and His Kentucky Club Orchestra. Bubber Miley, Louis Metcalf tp, Joe Nanton tb, probably Prince Robinson cl; Otto Hardwick ss, as, bs; unknown cl, as, bs, Duke Ellington p, Fred Guy bjo, Mack Shaw tuba, Sonny Greer d. |
| 1927 | "Harlem River Quiver," 2:41 (a.k.a. "Brown Berries," comp Dorothy Fields and Jimmy McHugh), December 19, 1927. Bubber Miley, Louis Metcalf tp, Joe Nanton tb, Rudy Jackson cl, Otto Hardwick ss, as, bass sax, Harry Carney cl, as, bs, Duke Ellington p, Fred Guy bjo, Wellman Braud b, Sonny Greer d. Solos: Nanton, Hardwick bass sax, Metcalf. |
| 1928 | "Harlem Twist," 3:15, (= "East St. Louis Toodle-Oo") January 18, 1928, Okeh Records. Same as "Harlem River Quiver" except Barney Bigard cl replaces Rudy Jackson. Solos: Nanton, Carney, Jenkins, Bigard. |
| 1929 | "Harlemania" (comp Jimmy McHugh and Dorothy Fields), February 18, 1929. Arthur Whetsol, Freddy Jenkins tp, Joe Nanton tb, Barney Bigard cl, Johnny Hodges, Harry Carney reeds, DE p, Fred Guy bj, Wellman Braud b, Sonny Greer d. (Note: This record is often said to mark the debut of Cootie Williams as Bubber Miley's replacement, but he is not present.) Solos: Nanton, Ellington, Carney, Jenkins, Hodges, Bigard. |
| 1929 | "Harlem Flat Blues," 3:07, March 1, 1929, *Early Ellington* Decca GRP. Same as "Harlemania" but add Cootie Williams, tp. Solos: Nanton, Bigard. |
| 1930 | "Jungle Nights in Harlem," June 4, 1930. Cootie Williams, Arthur Whetsol, Freddy Jenkins tp, Joe Nanton, Juan Tizol tb, Barney Bigard cl, Johnny Hodges, Harry Carney reeds, DE p, Fred Guy bj, Wellman Braud b, Sonny Greer d. Solos: Ellington, Jenkins, Bigard. |
| 1932 | "Blue Harlem" May 16, 1932. Cootie Williams, Arthur Whetsol, Freddy Jenkins tp, Joe Nanton, Juan Tizol, Lawrence Brown tb, Barney Bigard cl, Johnny Hodges, Otto Hardwick, Harry Carney reeds, DE p, Fred Guy g, Wellman Braud b, Sonny Greer d. Solos: Nanton, Ellington, Carney, Jenkins, Hodges, Bigard. |
| 1932 | "Harlem Romance" (usually "Clouds in My Heart") May 18, 1932. Same as "Blue Harlem." Solos: Ellington, Bigard, Nanton. |
| 1933 | "Drop Me Off at Harlem" 3:06 February 17, 1933. *Original Masters 1932–1939* Arthur Whetsol, Cootie Williams, Freddie Jenkins tp, Joe Nanton, Juan Tizol, Lawrence Brown tb; Barney Bigard cl, Johnny Hodges, Otto Hardwick, Harry Carney reeds, DE p, Fred Guy g, Wellman Braud b, Sonny Greer d. Solos: Brown, Whetsol, Williams, Bigard. |
| 1933 | "Harlem Speaks" (take 1) 3:14 July 13, 1933. Chenil Galleries, London. *The British Connexion 1933–1940* (Jazz Unlimited 1999). Arthur Whetsol, Cootie Williams, Freddie Jenkins tp, Joe Nanton, Juan Tizol, Lawrence Brown tb, Barney Bigard cl, Johnny Hodges, Otto Hardwick, Harry Carney reeds, DE p, Fred Guy g, Wellman Braud b, Sonny Greer d. Solos: Williams, Hodges, Braud, Jenkins, Carney, Nanton (muted), Brown (open), Nanton again (plunger-muted). |
| 1934 | "Harlem Rhythm" (from *Symphony in Black*, a.k.a. "Merry Go Round") December 1934. Same as "Harlem Speaks." |

## APPENDIX: ELLINGTON'S "HARLEM" SONGS

1936   "Echoes of Harlem" 3:00 (a.k.a. "Cootie's Concerto") February 27, 1936. *The Chronological Duke Ellington 1935–1936*. Classics 659. Arthur Whetsol, Cootie Williams, Rex Stewart tp, Tricky Sam Nanton, Lawrence Brown, Juan Tizol tb, Barney Bigard cl, Johnny Hodges, ss, as, Harry Carney cl, bs, DE p, Fred Guy g, Hayes Alvis b, Sonny Greer d.

"Echoes of Harlem" 4:40 broadcast May 15, 1938. *Duke Ellington at the Cotton Club*. Storyville (2010). Wallace Jones, Cootie Williams tp, Rex Stewart cor, Joe Nanton, Juan Tizol, Lawrence Brown tb, Barney Bigard, Johnny Hodges, Otto Hardwick, Harry Carney reeds; Ellington p, Fred Guy g, Billy Taylor b, Sonny Greer d.

"Echoes of Harlem" (3:32) February 23, 1963, Olympia Theatre, Paris. *The Great Paris Concert*. 2CD. Atlantic (1989). Ray Burrowes, Ray Nance, Cat Anderson, Cootie Williams tp, Lawrence Brown, Buster Cooper, Chuck Connors tb, Johnny Hodges as, Russell Procope cl, as, Jimmy Hamilton cl, Paul Gonsalves ts, Harry Carney bs, DE p, Ernie Shepard b, Sam Woodyard d.

1937   "Harmony in Harlem" 3:12 (Ellington/Hodges/Mills) September 20, 1937. *Original Masters 1932–1939*. Same as "Echoes of Harlem" (1936) except Freddie Jenkins replaces Wallace Jones. Solos: Hodges, Williams.

1938   "The Boys from Harlem" 2:16 (a.k.a. "Cat Rag") December 21, 1938. *Complete 1936–1940 . . . Small Group Sessions* (Mosaic CD). Cootie Williams and His Rug Cutters. Cootie Williams tp, Barney Bigard cl, Johnny Hodges as, Otto Hardwick bass sax, Harry Carney bs, Duke Ellington p, Billy Taylor b, Sonny Greer d (based on *Tiger Rag*). Solos: Williams, Carney/Hardwick, Williams.

1940   "Harlem Air Shaft" 2:57 (originally "Rumpus in Richmond" 1930) July 22, 1940, frequent to 1967. *The Blanton–Webster Band* (RCA). Wallace Jones, Cootie Williams tp, Rex Stewart cor, Joe Nanton, Juan Tizol, Lawrence Brown tb, Barney Bigard, Johnny Hodges, Ben Webster, Otto Hardwick, Lawrence Brown, Juan Tizol tb, Johnny Hodges as, Chauncey Haughton cl, ts, Otto Hardwick as, Ben Webster ts, Harry Carney cl, bs, Duke Ellington p, Fred Guy g, Junior Raglin b, Sonny Greer d. Solos: Nanton, Williams, Bigard, Williams, Bigard.

1943   "Blue Belles of Harlem" 6:03 January 23, 1943, Carnegie Hall, New York. *Carnegie Hall Concerts. January 1943* (Prestige 2CD [1977]). Rex Stewart, Wallace Jones, Harold Baker, Ray Nance tp, Joe Nanton, Lawrence Brown, Juan Tizol tb, Johnny Hodges as, Chauncey Haughton cl, ts, Otto Hardwick as, Ben Webster ts, Harry Carney cl, bs, Duke Ellington p, Fred Guy g, Junior Raglin b, Sonny Greer d.

Composed 1938, and never recorded in the studio by Ellington, though several concert performances survive. Paul Whiteman commissioned Ellington and five other composers (Ferde Grofé, Raymond Scott, Bert Shefter and Walter Gross) to write pieces that use bell tones (according to Leonard Feather 1977, original liner notes).

1951   *A Tone Parallel to Harlem* 13:47 (originally *Harlem Suite*, title often shortened as *Harlem*) December 7, 1951, New York. *Ellington Uptown* (Columbia CD [2004]). Duke Ellington cond, Francis Williams, Shorty Baker, Willie Cook, Clark Terry, Ray Nance tp, Quentin Jackson, Britt Woodman, Juan Tizol tb, Willie Smith as, Russell Procope cl, as, Jimmy Hamilton cl, ts, Paul Gonsalves ts, Harry Carney bs, bcl, Wendell Marshall b, Louie Bellson d.

1963   *A Tone Parallel to Harlem* 14:05 February 2, 1963, Olympia Theatre, Paris. *The Great Paris Concert* (Atlantic 2CD [1989]). Duke Ellington cond; Cootie Williams, Cat Anderson, Ray Burrowes tp, Ray Nance cornet, violin, Lawrence Brown, Buster Cooper, Chuck Connors tb, Johnny Hodges, Russell Procope, Jimmy Hamilton, Paul Gonsalves, Harry Carney reeds, Ernie Shepard b, Sam Woodyard d.

1963   *Harlem* (= *A Tone Parallel to Harlem*, mistitled "Harlem Air Shaft") 14:02 January 31, 1963, Salle Wagram, Paris, France. *The Symphonic Ellington* (originally Reprise Records, Discovery CD [1992]). Duke Ellington Orchestra (as above) with the Paris Symphony Orchestra, cond. Gérard Calvi.

1970   *Harlem* (= *A Tone Parallel to Harlem*) 14:12 May 28, 1970, Cincinnati, Ohio. *Orchestral Works* (originally Decca, MCA Classics CD [1989]). Duke Ellington with the Cincinnati Symphony Orchestra, cond. Erich Kunzel.

Chapter 2

# Forty-Eight Years with the Duke on Trains

> Nobody has yet made more deliberate or effective use . . . of the ongoing, upbeat locomotive onomatopoeia (the chugging and driving pistons, the sometimes signifying, sometimes shouting steam whistles, the always somewhat ambivalent arrival and departure bells). . . . Ellington's use of locomotive onomatopoeia is resonant not only of metaphorical underground railroads but also the metaphysical gospel train.
> —ALBERT MURRAY (1996, 94)

The first half of Edward Kennedy "Duke" Ellington's professional career, from 1923 until about 1948, coincided with the golden age of rail travel in the United States. Long before that, in his youth, he relished the annual train trips that took him every summer from his Washington, DC, home to Asbury Park, New Jersey, with his sainted mother at his side, for summer sojourns at the seaside resort. Those trips lasted into Ellington's teens—his mother still his escort—and affected his life most crucially by giving him his first serious exposure to the "hot" new piano masters on the resort circuit (Tucker 1991, 26–27).

Those summer jaunts at his mother's expense may have clouded his judgment. When he went to New York as a twenty-four-year-old on the promise of a job as a piano player, he traveled in the style that he was accustomed to under his mother's benevolent watch. "He hired a drawing room, ate his way through a couple of the Pennsylvania Railroad's most expensive meals and arrived at Penn Station in New York with little more than a dollar," Barry

Ulanov reported (1946, 31). Fatefully, the job in New York did not materialize. For several months, those few hours on the train looked as if they might be the high points of his career.

After he became the famous—and famously peripatetic—bandleader, Ellington's time on trains grew in miles traveled. Partly it was inescapable. Before the vast web of paved roads and multi-lane highways that became part of the "modernization" after the Second World War in the 1940s, trains were the best way to get from town to town. When the highway network supplanted rail travel with road travel by car and bus, it brought the advantage of setting travelers down at the door of a theater or hotel instead of at a rail depot that was a taxi ride away. Before the commercialization of air travel in the early 1950s, trains remained the best way to cover long distances through the great railway hubs of Chicago and St. Louis and Atlanta, cities whose very magnitude was based in the first place on the convergence of continental rail lines. Air travel brought the advantage of time, cutting the journey from, say, New York City to Los Angeles from three or four days to five or six hours.

For travelers raised on rail movement, the switch to cars and buses and airplanes may have been the "modern way," but they brought with them a whole set of modern anxieties as well—traffic jams and reckless drivers, exhaust fumes and honking horns, inescapable seatmates, white-knuckle take-offs and landings, and—omigod—jet lag.

The toll taken by highway travel was felt by professional musicians, including Ellington's men. Fred Guy quit the band in 1949, after twenty-four years as Ellington's banjo and guitar player, and the reason was not ill health or burnout but the anxiety of hitting the road. "We'd pull in after driving 400 miles, unload, and get a bite to eat," Guy told John McDonough (1969, 12–14). "Then we'd work for four hours. Afterwards, the driver would be up again to help load, and we'd be on our way. I could never be completely comfortable roaring down some turnpike at 65 miles an hour and knowing that the driver had only three hours' sleep." Although Guy's guitar was not an indispensable element in Ellington's orchestral palette—Ellington never hired another guitarist after Guy left[4]—he was perhaps Ellington's closest friend among the bandmembers. His departure took away one more member of Ellington's old Cotton Club coterie.

---

4. Ellington offered the chair to Lawrence Lucie, who had once subbed for Guy for eight days. Unlike Guy, Lucie had mastered single-note lines on the electric guitar, and Ellington had given him solos on "Tiger Rag" and "Sweet Georgia Brown." If he had accepted, he would have brought a new solo voice to the Ellington palette. "But by then my own group was going well and I didn't want to break it up," Lawrence told Stanley Dance (1974, 348–49). So Ellington moved on, guitar-free, for the rest of his days.

Duke Ellington loved trains. As Richard Boyer, the journalist who accompanied him on several train trips, said, "Duke likes trains because, as he says, 'Folks can't rush you until you get off.' He likes them, too, because dining-car waiters know about his love for food and he is apt to get very special attention" (1944, 228). He could move around and fraternize, dine on steak in the brass-and-velour dining car, get trousers pressed and shoes shined overnight, and isolate himself in his coach car for rest or writing—amenities that simply disappeared with the modern alternatives.

## Ellington's Railroad Onomatopoeia

Naturally, the infatuation with rail travel found its way into Duke Ellington's music. He composed twelve pieces that referred directly to train travel, and he recorded three others by other composers—indeed, one of them, "Take the 'A' Train" by his associate composer/arranger Billy Strayhorn, he played almost nightly from 1940 to 1974 as the band's theme song. (See Appendix: The Duke on Trains—The Complete Discography at the end of this chapter, following the Playlist with other recordings referred to in the text in the order of their appearance.)

Ellington's first railway composition came at the dawn of his composing career, in 1924, and the last one in 1972, two years before his death, long after train travel had been supplanted in his daily regimen—though obviously not in his imagination. In making train music over a span of forty-eight years, he invented what Albert Murray (1976, 125) called "railroad onomatopoeia"— "Ellington's unique nuances . . . [for] whistles, steam-driven pistons, bells and echoes." After his first railroad song, he made a point of creating the railroad sounds with musical means, eschewing imported sound effects from whistles and klaxons, and invariably, other composers and bandleaders, his son Mercer among them, could never figure out how to replicate them.

## The First Train Home

Duke Ellington got into the railroad genre at the very start of his composing career. He wrote and recorded "Choo Choo (Gotta Hurry Home)" in 1924, a few months after he arrived in New York City when he was looking for a foothold in the musical big leagues. He was by no means the first composer to take his inspiration from the "iron horse," but he was destined to become a persistent contributor of train songs. Mark Tucker tells us that his "Choo

Choo (Gotta Hurry Home)" in 1924 took its place in a line that already included recordings called "Choo Choo Blues," "Choo Choo Charlie," "Freight Train Blues" (not related to songs with that title by John Lair in 1934 or Bob Dylan in 1962), "Railroad Blues" and "Railroad Man" (Tucker 1991, 141).

If Ellington were climbing aboard a well-traveled line with "Choo Choo (Gotta Hurry Home)," it nevertheless stands as a considerable landmark in his career. Upon arriving in New York with the five-man band called the Washingtonians, Ellington branched out on a business sideline in the selling of songs. While the Washingtonians managed to hustle some playing opportunities by night in various clubs, Ellington made the rounds of music publishing houses by day, hawking his freshly hacked songs in the downtown publishing houses. It was not an easy market to break into. (Years later, he would confess, half-joking, to Ralph Gleason [1975, 220], "I was always a lousy demonstrator. That's the reason I could never get the publishers to take my songs.") "Choo Choo (Gotta Hurry Home)" was the first sale he ever made—a success that is only slightly sullied by the fact that he had to share its composer credits with a pair of agents named Bob Shafer and Dave Ringle, big-city hustlers who would otherwise leave no mark on his story.

By the time Ellington recorded "Choo Choo (Gotta Hurry Home)" with his Washingtonians, it had been recorded by several other bands and "the tune had already become popular" (according to Tucker). The fact that the Washingtonians got to record it at all represented yet a further leap in Ellington's fortunes. The bandmembers, including Ellington, discovered that Elmer Snowden, the banjo player who handled their business affairs, was skimming the profits, meager as they were. Snowden left and, by consensus, Ellington took over the leader's role. Suddenly, he found himself with both a hit song and a band to play it. In November 1924, the young Washingtonians marched into the makeshift recording studio of a small-time label called Blu-Disc, which distributed its wares only in a few theater lobbies.

"Choo Choo (Gotta Hurry Home)" by the Washingtonians is among Ellington's rarest records. (Musicians will relish Mark Tucker's five-page analysis of their performance [1991, 142–46]; the sheet music includes a lyric reprinted by Tucker, but the Washingtonians omit it.)

The piece preserves the first flowering of Ellington's composing. He started writing music for public consumption only about a year before, he says, when a publisher showed an interest in one of his tunes and asked him for a lead sheet. "I had never made a lead sheet before, nor tried to write music of any kind," he says (*MiMM* 70–71). "In spite of ten pianos banging away in ten different booths, I sat down and made a lead sheet. It was satisfactory. . . . I had broken the ice and at the same time gotten hooked on writing music."

The charm of "Choo Choo (Gotta Hurry Home)" comes from the ricky-tick rhythm that underscores the whole arrangement with upfront interludes by George Francis's banjo (the replacement for the displaced Snowden) and a bright solo by Otto Hardwick on C melody saxophone, an instrument seldom heard afterward in Ellington's music. The piece ends with five toots on a train whistle, hooted on who-knows-what forgotten piece of equipment in drummer Sonny Greer's arsenal. It is a carryover of (what Tucker calls) "the good old-fashioned hokum" that pervaded jazz in its earliest days. Beyond a doubt, the Washingtonians are enjoying themselves under their new leader.

The climactic train whistle that caps the Washingtonians' performance of "Choo Choo (Gotta Hurry Home)" introduces a vaudeville effect that is blissfully absent from Duke Ellington's later music. A stage prop for imitating the sound of the train whistle would be tawdry, even embarrassing, in the train music that was to come in the years that lay ahead. This first train song catches the composer/arranger learning his trade and trying to find his role—indeed his personality—in this new situation. What is most important is the fact that Duke Ellington had sold a song in the publishing mill of the big city. He was not exactly young at this moment of his first big-time sale—he was twenty-five—but he was still learning the ways of this new world. He had "broken the ice," as he put it, and he would go on to make music with integrity and grace and dignity, lots of it. Some of it perpetuated his gift for railroad onomatopoeia.

### Full Steam Ahead

His masterpiece in the subgenre was not long in coming. In 1932, he made his return to train songs with "Lightnin'," an affable piece that chugs along at medium tempo; an English reviewer, Vic Bellerby, said, "In 'Lightnin',' we relaxed in the luxury of a Pullman car" (1962, 154). It exhibited a considerable step ahead in the composer's art, but it was overshadowed a few months later by "Daybreak Express."

On first listening, "Daybreak Express" is simply breathtaking with its opening accelerando sweeping seamlessly into a powerhouse rush across the imaginary landscape. Successive listenings bring fresh insights into the ingenious blend of orchestral resources that are integrated in a kind of perfection. The impression of the motion of the train, the clack of the iron wheels on the rails, the hoot of the whistle—no detail is missing, no nuance is overlooked. And yet, for all its spot-on imitation of a vehicle in motion, the composition is completely musical, a complex of musical effects arranged with almost unimaginable precision on an exemplary bedrock of swing rhythm, technical virtuosity, and ensemble precision.

By this time, Ellington's progression had brought exclamations from other composers for his instrumental combinations, especially with "Mood Indigo," which elicited critic R. D. Darrell's encomium in *Phonograph Monthly Review* as "a poignantly restrained and nostalgic piece with glorious melodic endowment and scoring that even Ravel and Strawinski [sic] might envy" (1927–1931, 38). With "Daybreak Express," two years after "Mood Indigo," his skills were equally abundant—some might say, more so. More than forty years later, composers could not replicate them, not even those who had been present at the start. "When Mercer Ellington took over the orchestra after his father's death, he tried in vain to simulate the train whistle effect produced by the reeds in 'Daybreak Express,'" Gary Giddins reported, "ultimately admitting defeat and using a slide whistle" (1991, 105).

The awestruck reaction of generations of listeners—music lovers of all stripes and especially musicians—has withstood the most intense critical scrutiny. Gunther Schuller, the composer/critic/academic, in his review of swing music from 1930 to 1945 (with "over 30,000 listenings to recordings," by his count), praises "Daybreak Express" more comprehensively than any other composition. He calls it "the astonishing, virtuoso tour de force" and provides a meticulous three-page analysis (1989, 61–64), specifying the metronomic tempo of the accelerando as the locomotive attains "express speed" and the role of a growling trumpet and the "high-note wails" of a clarinet. The heart of Ellington's composition is an exquisitely voiced ensemble. Schuller says: "At this point the whole sax section, over the changes of *Tiger Rag*, launches into a virtuoso ensemble chorus that must have represented the ultimate in technical sophistication at the time." Schuller similarly breaks the closing diminuendo into its parts as "the train slows down . . . and comes to rest, exhausted." The final wheeze as the daybreak express reaches the station supplies a fitting denouement for an intense and, uh, transporting listening experience.

## "Traveling Like Kings"

As Duke Ellington's fame grew, he began touring far and wide. In 1927, the band's forays into Boston and other cities due north of their Harlem base led to the declaration by the *New York Tribune* that they had become "New England's favorite dance-orchestra" (Hasse 1993, 94). In 1930, the orchestra crossed the continent to Hollywood to appear in the movie *Check and Double Check,* and they also played engagements in Los Angeles. In 1931, they spent a month away from the Cotton Club while they played in Chicago, Milwaukee, and other Upper Midwest hubs. In 1933, they toured England and France with eye-opening acclaim.

The obvious gap in their itinerary was the American South. "I won't go south," Ellington declared, "I don't care what they offer me" (Ulanov 1946, 152). Following their European success, Ellington made a partial concession to his agent by agreeing to be the first African American band to play in Texas and Missouri. It turned out to be a chastening experience. In St. Louis, Missouri, a white elevator operator refused to take the band to radio studios on the sixteenth floor of an office building for a broadcast date (Hasse 1993, 151). Places that accepted them for dining and accommodations were often hard-scrabble dumps. "In Europe we were royalty," Ellington's mild-mannered saxophone star Harry Carney said, "in Texas we were back in the colored section."

As the clamor for his appearances in southern auditoriums and dance halls grew, so did the financial enticements to get him there. Ellington capitulated, but it took a brainwave to convince him. His manager, Irving Mills, proposed chartering a train and making it the self-contained domain for Ellington and the orchestra. They hired two Pullman cars and a baggage car, emblazoned with "Duke Ellington and His Famous Orchestra" in large letters. Upon reaching the city for their next performance, they pulled the trains onto a siding at the station. They ate, slept, played cards, practiced, and rehearsed on the train.

The excursion took on mythic significance for Ellington and his men. Sonny Greer, Ellington's drummer, exclaimed, "The average one of them crackers down south, they never been inside a Pullman car, never saw it, and them porters used to put in the dog, them cats would put on them beautiful starched uniforms, and the steps to come down, they would lay it down [for us. The locals] would come down out of curiosity. Ofays and everybody would come down. We were traveling like kings" (Cohen 2010, 131). Herb Jeffries, the band singer, said, "We couldn't stay in hotels, we couldn't eat in restaurants, so they had to pull the Pullman up on the sidetrack and we lived in the Pullman. Yet the residents of that town, which of course were basically white, would come backstage and stand, outside in the cold weather, waiting for those men who could not eat or sleep in their hotels, to get their autographs" (Nicholson 1999, 218).

For Ellington, the Pullman venture put him in his natural element. "From 1934 to 1936 we went touring deep into the South . . . and we commanded respect," he told Nat Hentoff (1976, 31). "The natives would come by and they would say, 'What's that?' 'Well,' we'd say, 'That's the way the President travels.'"

Whether presidents or kings (as Sonny Greer had it)—either way, it was a truly emancipated way for Ellington and his men to conquer the Deep South.

Always prolific, Ellington's music proliferated. His sister Ruth told Derek Jewell (1977, 164), "You'd see him in a siding somewhere in Texas, the heat at 110, the sweat pouring off him onto a piece of manuscript paper on his knee, catching up on something he wanted to finish." Geoff Dyer, in his novelistic vignettes on the lives of jazzmen, turned this observation into an anecdote. "In Texas once, a bunch of railroad workers glanced through the window of a train pulled over in a siding and saw him hunched over a manuscript, sweat dripping on the page," wrote Dyer. "He got up smiling and told them what he was working on—'Daybreak Express,' a piece about the guys who built the railroad.... Explaining his music to them, seeing the pride well up in their eyes" (1996, 82).

## The Fastest Way to Get to Harlem—And in the End, the Slowest

Of the three train songs recorded by Ellington but composed by someone else, one is neither a cover nor a revival but in fact quintessential Ellington.[5] It is of course "Take the 'A' Train" composed by Billy Strayhorn at the very beginning of his lifelong tenure as Ellington's associate composer or, more appropriately, in Ellington's words, "my right arm, my left arm, all the eyes in the back of my head, my brain waves in his head and his in mine" (*MiMM* 156). Strayhorn wrote "Take the 'A' Train" in his home city of Pittsburgh in 1939 after auditioning backstage. Ellington said he would hire him and gave him instructions on how to get from Grand Central Station to Harlem— "Take the 'A' train." In his enthusiasm, Strayhorn turned Ellington's directions into a big-band score, and then waited several frustrating months before Ellington actually summoned him to take that subway line. By then, Strayhorn had lost confidence in his score, thinking it did not suit Ellington's style. According to legend, it survived because Mercer Ellington pulled the manuscript out of Strayhorn's wastebasket, flattened it out, and said, "What's wrong with this?" Ellington tried the newly arranged piece at a rehearsal, and a few weeks later, chose it for his radio theme. By the time he recorded it in February 1941, it already had some currency from radio play, and it became, as Hajdu says, "a leitmotif of the swing era" (1996, 84–85).

---

5. The other two train songs Ellington recorded but did not compose (as shown in the appendix) were "9:20 Special," composed by Earl Warren for the Count Basie Orchestra in 1941 (covered by Ellington in 1946) and "Tuxedo Junction," composed by Erskine Hawkins and made a hit by Glenn Miller in 1940 (adapted by Strayhorn or Ellington in 1962).

Apart from its title, "Take the 'A' Train" is not literally a train feature. This train is, after all, a subway train, the only one memorialized in the Ellington canon. And it is formally a jump tune, with no hint of Albert Murray's onomatopoeia of locomotion. The only version in which it is outfitted with the accoutrements of a train sound comes in the opening scene of the movie *Paris Blues*, in which "Take the 'A' Train" plays under the opening credits as the screen shows the arrival of a train carrying a famous jazz musician at Gare St. Lazare (discussed further in chapter 7 on Ellington's Hollywood scores). In the movie, the piece opens uniquely with a sustained, dissonant train whistle simulated by a shrill trumpet and some combination of other instrumental sounds. After six beats, the train whistle segues seamlessly into the familiar opening chorus. If the whistle prelude is composed by Strayhorn rather than Ellington, as circumstantial evidence suggests—Strayhorn recorded this title in Paris before Ellington arrived—it is one more "inimitable" skill that he absorbed from the maestro.

"Take the 'A' Train" immediately appealed to Ellington, and it proved equally infectious to thousands of listeners. Strayhorn's handsome medium tempo never seems rushed, whether it was set by Ellington or, more rarely, by Strayhorn. Listeners find it hummable, invitingly so. Ray Nance's long solo turn became a fixture after the original recording, played first on muted trumpet staying close to the melody, and then, after an emphatic fanfare by the brass, on a bolder turn on the open horn. Nance's solo came to seem like an integral part of the score. It put the spotlight squarely on Nance, and all these years later it is hard to fathom that he was virtually unknown when he was appointed to play it, a thirty-year-old singer/dancer/violinist/trumpeter from Chicago unexpectedly parachuted into Cootie Williams's chair. Indeed, when Nance left the band in 1963, the recently returned Williams took over his role on "Take the 'A' Train."

Listeners had plenty of opportunities to hear Strayhorn's melody. Ellington played it at almost every concert from 1940 on, sometimes just a chorus or two at the end of a set or the end of an evening but often in its entirety. Arrangements changed but not enough to alter its basic character. Most noticeable was an alternate arrangement that inserted Strayhorn's lyric ("Hurry hurry hurry / Take the 'A' train"). One lively performance at a dance in Carrolltown, Pennsylvania, in 1957, entices the dancers onto the floor by juxtaposing both arrangements. Nance takes his star turn on cornet (the instrument he preferred to trumpet in his last decade), and as the applause rises, Ellington brings Nance back for what he calls "his highly animated vocal of our theme." Nance mugs broadly, scats the lyric, and interpolates alien lyrics (from "Yankee Doodle," "I Cover the Waterfront," and others). The delight of the audience is exponential.

Much later, Ray Nance played a completely fresh version of "Take the 'A' Train" under circumstances that quelled his flashy stage persona. Billy Strayhorn died on May 31, 1967, of esophageal cancer, only fifty-one. At his funeral five days later at St. Peter's Lutheran Church, Nance played "Take the 'A' Train" on his violin accompanied by Billy Taylor on piano. They played it as a dirge. The contrast is almost shocking, and in the context heartrending. One of the pallbearers, Don George, said, "When Ray Nance played Billy's 'Take the "A" Train' in slow, New Orleans street-funeral-march tempo, there wasn't a dry eye in the church" (1981, 178).

The church service was not recorded but Nance later recorded his elegiac version on one of his rare recording dates as a leader with Roland Hanna as the pianist. Stanley Dance (1969), in his notes accompanying the record, says, "Full of tender anguish, a fond farewell to a dear friend, 'Take the "A" Train' had never before been heard like this." With the tempo slowed to a walk, each familiar note, usually so kinetic, is brooded over. The melody that for so many years stood as Strayhorn's party favor served majestically in the end as his epitaph.

### The Great Train Robbery

The train composition that rivals "Daybreak Express" as Ellington's consummate achievement in the subgenre has a muddled provenance and a felonious, though not uninteresting, wrinkle in its history. "Happy-Go-Lucky Local" came into being in 1946 as the fourth part of a suite called *The Deep South Suite*. At the time, Ellington was under contract to a new record company called Musicraft and their releases of Ellington's music were rather confused. Ellington was engaged in concert jazz at the time, preparing long pieces and suites for his annual Carnegie Hall concerts. Musicraft issued some parts but not all parts of various suites, with the result that the only sources for the complete *Deep South Suite* and another suite Ellington called *The Beautiful Indians* are live performances, most auspiciously at Chicago's Civic Opera House and Carnegie Hall. Musicraft Records soon found itself struggling financially, and Ellington severed his three-year contract after little more than a year (May 1946 to June 1947).

Out of this fragmented time, one of the heady survivors was the piece called "Happy-Go-Lucky Local," recorded on two sides of a Musicraft 78 rpm record (5:42 altogether, with a pause at 2:55 when you flip the record over). A month and a half later, it was recorded more satisfactorily as a Capitol Transcription, an acetate for radio play that accommodated its full length (5:33) on a single side. (Both are listed in the appendix.) The Musicraft version displays fastidious ensemble precision, especially valued because Ellington's arrangement rewards precision. It suffers technologically from the five-second fade and resumption in the switch-over to what was the second side of the 78 rpm disk.

The definitive studio recording was made eight years later, in the long play (LP) era, at the end of Ellington's contract with Capitol Records (January 1954). The band was rebuilt by then, and the fresh recording features most of the young stars who would carry Ellington's ascension back into the front ranks of American music. There are many good performances of "Happy-Go-Lucky Local," and this definitive Capitol recording has been overlooked because its original album, *Ellington '55*, surrounds it with revisions of big band hits by other people ("Stompin' at the Savoy" by Benny Goodman, "In the Mood" by Glenn Miller, "One O'Clock Jump" by Count Basie, "Flying Home" by Lionel Hampton, and so on). Though these cover versions are played with great spirit by Ellington's rejuvenated aggregation, they are merely promises of the good days to come. Among them, "Happy-Go-Lucky Local" is the indisputable gem.

Duke Ellington honored "Happy-Go-Lucky Local" with one of his elaborate prose poems, an encomium he bestowed on a few of his inspired pieces (*MiMM* 184–85):

> This told the story of a train in the South . . . a little train with an upright engine that was never fast, never on schedule, and never made stops at any place you ever heard about. After grunting, groaning and jerking, it finally settled down to a steady medium tempo. The train had a Negro fireman who loved to pull the string that blew the whistle, and since he seemed to know every house, and to recognize someone watching him go by at every window—in every house and every window on his side of the tracks, that is!—he was forever pulling the string. He played tunes on the whistle, too—blues, spirituals, a little "Shortenin' Bread"—calling somebody as the train rattled along with more than a suggestion of boogie-woogie rhythm. Down in the South, they called the train No. 42, but we just called it the "Happy-Go-Lucky Local."

As with his "narratives" for other compositions, listeners will be hard-pressed to pinpoint specific references in the music to Ellington's narrative—blues in abundance, spirituals perhaps in essence, but no trace of "Shortenin' Bread" or other specifics. What really counts is the feeling, the aura that imbues it.

Ellington's affectionate description suits the Musicraft original (1946) better than the more ebullient Capitol remake (1954). The original version is played slower, as might be expected of "a little train with an upright engine." For all that, it is not exactly chugging along: it settles into a "steady medium tempo," as Ellington says, with the "suggestion of boogie-woogie rhythm."

"Happy-Go-Lucky Local" comprises two distinct themes. The first is a brilliant evocation of the train motif, entirely composed, with the train onomatopoeia projected sonically by interjections from an instrumental mélange: Russell Procope's alto saxophone, Johnny Hodges's alto saxophone, Harry Carney's baritone saxophone, Cat Anderson's trumpet, and the plungered brass choir. It is a concoction that hardly seems conceivable by any other arranger. The one plausible solo slot is a two-chorus blues exchange by Ellington and the bassist, Oscar Pettiford, as the first theme segues into the second. Ellington's masterful piano chorus has been singled out by Dobbins (2017, 133) for his "rapidly descending cascades of whole-tone scales" which are, Dobbins notes, "like bursts of steam, followed by broken chords in left-hand eighth notes as the contented train moves patiently down the tracks."

The composition then moves up an emotional notch into its second theme, the riff-based motif that underpins lively solos and a steamy climax. This theme is known (for reasons that will follow) as the "night train" theme. It actually pays homage to a tune called "That's the Blues Old Man," recorded in 1940 by Johnny Hodges with a septet that included Ellington on piano (in the Playlist). Ellington's arrangement for "Happy-Go-Lucky Local" enriches the bare-bones (but handsome) original as he reorganizes it rhythmically to set it squarely on the railroad tracks. In his original arrangement (on Musicraft and the Capitol Transcription), Ellington brings on the second theme with a stop-time orchestral fanfare that resolves into Jimmy Hamilton's overriding clarinet, and fades into the distance with Cat Anderson's stratospheric trumpet emulating the happy-go-lucky local's whistle.

This second theme, beautifully calculated as the free-swinging release from the highly disciplined first theme, gained special notoriety in the Ellington annals when it was plagiarized by Jimmy Forrest, a tenor saxophone player whom Ellington had tried out in the band for seven months (June 1949 to February 1950). After Forrest left the band, he recorded the second theme as his own composition under the title "Night Train" with a small band in 1952. The plagiarism might have gone unnoticed, but Forrest's pared-down version put the raunchy charm of Ellington's melody into bold relief and, as a result, it received considerable air play. It also had staying power beyond the shelf life of most pop hits when it became the standard theme for bump-and-grind acts in burlesque theaters. Its bawdy nightlife made it a natural fit for yet a third life when it showed up as the raucous showstopper for rhythm & blues acts such as James Brown. Both the raunchy charm and the staying power emanated from Ellington, but Forrest got the credit and the royalties.

Of the numerous jazz versions of the "night train" theme, the most impressive is by Oscar Peterson with his redoubtable trio of Ray Brown on bass and Ed Thigpen on drums. Peterson released that track on an album of the same name, *Night Train*, and it remains Peterson's bestselling record, a noteworthy entry in his voluminous output. The recording was supervised by Norman Granz, Peterson's manager, owner of Verve Records, and annotator of the music. Granz's notes made no mention of the provenance of "Night Train," although Forrest's plagiarism was common knowledge by then. Twenty-five years later, in 1997, when Peterson's *Night Train* album was reissued on CD, Granz was long gone from Verve Records, and the new release made amends by identifying the track as "Happy-Go-Lucky Local (a.k.a. Night Train)" and listed Ellington as the composer; the annotation by pianist/teacher Dick Katz for the CD issue recounts its origin story.

### Ellington's Covert "Night Train" and the Definitive "Happy-Go-Lucky Local"

Ellington continued playing "Happy-Go-Lucky Local" a few times a year for the rest of his days, always with great flair. Naturally, the larceny he had suffered came up frequently in comments by critics and fans, and he turned it into an occasion for one of his more celebrated *bon mots*. "We must be flattered," he said, "and just go write something better." The hurt, we later learned, went much deeper. In 1963, more than ten years after the fact, his composure—the fabled equanimity that Norman Granz so resented—cracked when an interviewer in Calcutta asked him if he was worried that some of his compositions might be turned into "something different . . . under the rock 'n' roll label." Ellington replied, "They did that with *Night Train*. They took *Happy-Go-Lucky Local*. It hurts and it's offensive. You threaten to sue and you postpone until it's too late, and then you get real mad. You do nothing but spoil your disposition" (reprinted by Dance 1970, 22). Years later, Mercer Ellington admitted that they had sued Forrest and accepted a cash settlement (Nicholson 1999, 322).

Ellington finally recorded the "Night Train" theme by itself in 1960 (in the Playlist). He used his own title "Happy-Go-Lucky Local," but what the band played was only its second theme, possibly to avoid attaching his composer credit to someone else's title. It is a new arrangement, not merely a replay of the second half of the original, and it is a rousing rendition.

Ellington's version, more richly orchestrated and more vibrantly played than anyone else's "Night Train," garnered very little attention from reviewers or fans. Its original title appeared to fit right in among a potpourri of mostly older Ellington compositions on an album called *Piano in the Background* (Columbia). Even dedicated Ellington listeners might have surmised that Ellington was tilling familiar soil, but actually the arrangements, several by guests Gerald Wilson and Bill Mathieu, presented an emphatically brassy complexion compared to Ellington and Strayhorn's more subtle textures.

Duke Ellington's spirited remake of the complete "Happy-Go-Lucky Local" for Capitol Records in 1954—eight years after his first studio version and two years after the purloined "Night Train"—was presumably intended by Ellington to put his signature on the melody that was resounding from juke joints and strip clubs by another name. Ellington's remake is played slightly faster and the interjections by the various instrumentalists are noticeably earthier. Jimmy Hamilton, on tenor saxophone, hurls a couple of throaty interjections into it, including a saucy tongue fart, at the very point (3:27) where the night train theme moves into the foreground. This "Happy-Go-Lucky Local" does not fade into the distance but rides Cat Anderson's whistle blasts until he runs out of breath. By then listeners might be out of breath, too. It is an exciting ride.

## Caboose

It is a beguiling tour, accompanying Duke Ellington on all these train trips from 1924 until 1972. His pleasure is palpable in the music he wrote about trains, a visceral feeling that had its origin long before he tried to capture it in music. From his youthful pleasures, riding alongside his mother to their summer respite on the Atlantic seacoast, perhaps as early as when he was two and definitely until he was fourteen, in 1913, when she accompanied him to his summer job washing dishes at the Plaza Hotel in Asbury Park, New Jersey (Tucker 1991, 141)—an underage lad showing his independent streak.

Later, he traveled by trains for short hops to one-nighters and long hops to the movie capital of the world. He moved around Europe on trains, and in his last decade, found himself on diplomatic charters in parts of the Middle East and on bullet trains in Japan. "Ellington always feels that he has found sanctuary when he boards a train," said Richard Boyer (1944, 228). "He says that then peace descends upon him and that the train's metallic rhythm soothes him. He likes to hear the whistles up ahead, particularly at night, when it screeches through the blackness as the train gathers speed." Train rides brought creature comforts and leisure for composing, and the weeks on the Pullmans in the Deep South brought another boon. "It commanded a certain amount of respect," Ellington told an interviewer decades later (quoted by Cohen 2010, 131–32), "and you know we respect everybody else, so there's no reason why they shouldn't respect us."

Respect was a touchstone. As his son Mercer observed, in a slightly different context, "Ellington's composure, wit, and innate dignity 'commanded respect'—to use a phrase he always liked" (1978, 61). Duke Ellington repaid that respect in his own special way with these paeans to train travel, some minor and some monumental, but all of them with a sense of wonder.

## Playlist

(Most of the recordings cited in this chapter are listed in Appendix: The Duke on Trains that follows. Other recordings are listed here.)

Count Basie and His Orchestra, "9:20 Special" 3:07 (Buster Harding comp/arr) Chicago, April 10, 1941. Ed Lewis, Buck Clayton, Harry Edison, Al Killian tp, Dickie Wells, Ed Cuffee, Dan Minor tb, Tab Smith as, Earl Warren as, Lester Young ts, Buddy Tate ts, Coleman Hawkins ts, Jack Washington bs, Basie p, Freddie Green gtr, Walter Page b, Jo Jones d. Solos: Smith, Basie, Edison, Hawkins.

Glenn Miller Orchestra, "Tuxedo Junction" (comp Erskine Hawkins) New York, February 5, 1940. Clyde Hurley, John Best, R. D. McMickle, Leigh Knowles tp, Glenn Miller Tommy Mack, Paul Tanner, Frank D'Annolfo tb, Hal McIntyre, Tex Beneke, Wilbur Schwartz, Jimmy Abato, Al Klink reeds, Chummy MacGregor p, Rowland Bundock b, Richard Fisher gtr, Moe Purtill d.

"Take the 'A' Train" 2:14 (comp Strayhorn) Paris, December 14, 1960. *Paris Blues Soundtrack* (Rykodisc enhanced CD [1997]). Personnel unknown, Strayhorn cond.

"Take the 'A' Train" 4:40 and "Take the 'A' Train" 2:42. (comp Billy Strayhorn) Carrolltown, PA, June 1957. *All Star Road Band,* Vol. II (CBS Signature Special Product [1989]). Harold Baker, Willie Cook, Clark Terry tp, Ray Nance cor, voc, Britt Woodman, Quentin Jackson, John Sanders tb, Russell Procope, Johnny Hodges, Jimmy Hamilton, Paul Gonsalves, Harry Carney reeds, Duke Ellington p, Joe Benjamin b, Sam Woodyard d. Solos: Nance, cor (first), voc, cor (second).

Ray Nance, "Take the 'A' Train" 2:42 (comp Billy Strayhorn) New York, May 1969. *Body and Soul* (Mighty Quinn CD [2006]). Nance vln, Roland Hanna p.

Johnny Hodges, "That's the Blues Old Man" 2:54 (comp Hodges) Chicago, December 2, 1940. *Passion Flower 1940–46* (Bluebird CD [1995]). Cootie Williams tp, Lawrence Brown tb, Johnny Hodges ss, Harry Carney bs, Duke Ellington p, Jimmie Blanton b, Sonny Greer d. Solos: Williams, Hodges (his last soprano saxophone solo on record).

Oscar Peterson Trio, "Happy-Go-Lucky Local (a.k.a. Night Train)" 4:50 Hollywood, December 16, 1962. *Night Train* (Verve CD [1997]). Peterson p, Ray Brown b, Ed Thigpen d.

"Happy-Go-Lucky Local" 5:33 *Ellington '55* (Capitol CD [1999]) Chicago, January 17, 1954. Clark Terry, Cat Anderson, Willie Cook, Ray Nance tp, Quentin Jackson, Britt Woodman, Alfred Cobbs tb, Russell Procope, Rick Henderson, Paul Gonsalves, Jimmy Hamilton, Harry Carney reeds, Duke Ellington p, Wendell Marshall b, Dave Black d.

"Happy-Go-Lucky Local" 3:00 (actually "Night Train" theme) June 30, 1960, Radio Recorders, Los Angeles, CA. *Piano in the Background* (Columbia [CD 2004]). Andres Merenghito (Fats Ford), Willie Cook, Eddie Mullens, Ray Nance tp, Britt Woodman, Booty Wood, Lawrence Brown tb, Johnny Hodges as, Russell Procope as, Jimmy Hamilton cl ts, Paul Gonsalves ts, Harry Carney cl bs, Duke Ellington p, Aaron Bell b, Sam Woodyard d.

## Appendix: The Duke on Trains—The Complete Discography

Here are all the compositions with train motifs recorded by Duke Ellington. Only the first recording of each composition is listed for most entries. Later recordings discussed in the text and recordings by other artists will be found in the Playlist above. Ellington is the composer unless otherwise noted.

1924 "Choo Choo (Gotta Hurry Home)" 3:13 (comp Ellington, R. Shafer, D. Ringle) NY, November 1924. DE *Complete Edition Vol. 1* (*Masters of Jazz* CD, originally Blu-Disc 78 rpm). The Washingtonians. Bubber Miley tp, Charlie Irvis tb, Otto Hardwick Cm-sax, DE p, George Francis banjo, Sonny Greer d.

1932 "Lightnin'" 3:12 New York, September 21, 1932. *Original Masters 1932–1939*. Sony BMG Music (4CD [2008]). Cootie Williams, Arthur Whetsol, Freddie Jenkins tp, Lawrence Brown, Juan Tizol, Joe Nanton tb, Barney Bigard, Johnny Hodges, Otto Hardwick, Harry Carney reeds, DE p, Fred Guy gtr, Wellman Braud b, Sonny Greer d.

1933 "Daybreak Express" 2:54. Chicago, December 4, 1933. *Early Ellington 1927–1934*. (Bluebird CD [1989]). Cootie Williams, Arthur Whetsol, Freddie Jenkins, Louis Bacon tp, Lawrence Brown, Joe Nanton tb, Barney Bigard, Johnny Hodges, Otto Hardwick, Harry Carney reeds, DE p, Fred Guy gtr, Wellman Braud b, Sonny Greer d.

1939 "Way Low" 3:25 June 6, 1939. *Original Masters 1932–1939* (4CD Sony/BMG [2008]). Cootie Williams, Wallace Jones tp, Rex Stewart cor, Joe Nanton, Lawrence Brown, Juan Tizol tb, Barney Bigard, Johnny Hodges, Otto Hardwick, Harry Carney reeds, DE p, Fred Guy gtr, Billy Taylor b, Sonny Greer d. Solos: Carney (main theme), Bigard, Brown, Stewart (muted), Brown.

1940 "Across the Track Blues" 2:58 Chicago, October 28, 1940. *The Blanton–Webster Band* (RCA Victor 3CD [1986]). Cootie Williams, Wallace Jones tp, Rex Stewart cor,

Joe Nanton, Lawrence Brown, Juan Tizol tb, Barney Bigard, Johnny Hodges, Otto Hardwick, Ben Webster, Harry Carney reeds, DE p, Fred Guy gtr, Jimmie Blanton b, Sonny Greer d. Solos: Bigard, Stewart, Brown, Bigard.

1941 "Take the 'A' Train" 2:54 (Billy Strayhorn) Hollywood, February 15, 1941. *The Blanton–Webster Band* (RCA Victor 3CD [1986]). Wallace Jones, Rex Stewart, Ray Nance tp, Joe Nanton, Lawrence Brown, Juan Tizol tb, Barney Bigard, Johnny Hodges, Otto Hardwick, Ben Webster, Harry Carney reeds, DE p, Fred Guy gtr, Jimmie Blanton b, Sonny Greer d.

1946 "9:20 Special" 2:57 (comp Earl Warren for Count Basie 1941) July 16, 1946. (Capitol transcription, Hindsight CD [1987].) Taft Jordan, Shelton Hemphill, Cat Anderson, Francis Williams, Harold Baker, Ray Nance tp, Lawrence Brown, Claude Jones, Wilbur de Paris tb, Russell Procope, Johnny Hodges, Jimmy Hamilton, Al Sears, Harry Carney reeds, DE p, Fred Guy gtr, Oscar Pettiford b, Sonny Greer d. Solos: Ray Nance, Al Sears, Oscar Pettiford.

1946 "Happy-Go-Lucky Local" Pt.1 & 2 5:42 November 25, 1946 (*Sir Duke*, Drive CD [1994] orig Musicraft). Taft Jordan, Shelton Hemphill, Cat Anderson, Francis Williams, Harold Baker, Ray Nance tp, Lawrence Brown, Claude Jones, Wilbur De Paris tb, Russell Procope, Johnny Hodges, Jimmy Hamilton, Al Sears, Harry Carney reeds, DE p, Fred Guy gtr, Oscar Pettiford b, Sonny Greer d.

1947 "Happy-Go-Lucky Local" 6:27 January 7, 1947. Capitol transcription, Hindsight CD (1987). Personnel as above but Wallace Jones tp REPLACES Harold Baker.

1947 "Stomp Look and Listen" 3:21 November 10, 1947. *Complete DE 1947–1952*, Vol 2 (CBS Disques [1989]). Shelton Hemphill, Francis Williams, Harold Baker, Ray Nance, Dud Bascomb tp, Lawrence Brown, Claude Jones, Wilbur de Paris, Tyree Glenn tb, Russell Procope, Johnny Hodges, Jimmy Hamilton, Al Sears, Harry Carney reeds, DE p, Fred Guy gtr, Oscar Pettiford b, Sonny Greer d. Solos: Baker–Nance, Hamilton, Brown, Nance.

1950 "Build That Railroad (Sing That Song)" 2:42 NY, November 20, 1950. *Complete DE 1947–1952*, Vol 3 (CBS Disques [1989]). Cat Anderson, Harold Baker, Nelson Williams, Fats Ford, Ray Nance tp, Lawrence Brown, Quentin Jackson tb, Mercer Ellington Fr h, Johnny Hodges, Russell Procope, Jimmy Hamilton, Paul Gonsalves, Harry Carney reeds, DE p, Wendell Marshall b, Sonny Greer d, Al Hibbler voc.

1958 "Track 360" 2:01 Radio Recorders, LA, February 4, 1958. *Blues in Orbit* (Columbia CD [2004]). Cat Anderson, Clark Terry, Shorty Baker, Ray Nance tp, Quentin Jackson, John Sanders, Britt Woodman tb, Bill Graham, Russell Procope as, Jimmy Hamilton, Paul Gonsalves ts, Harry Carney bs, DE p, Jimmy Woode b, Sam Woodyard d.

1958 "Feet Bone" 3:10 Newport Jazz Festival, RI, July 3, 1958. *Live at Newport 1958.* (Columbia Legacy 2CD [1994].) Cat Anderson, Clark Terry, Shorty Baker, Cootie Williams tp, Quentin Jackson, John Sanders, Britt Woodman tb, Russell Procope as, Johnny Hodges as, Jimmy Hamilton, cl, ts, Paul Gonsalves ts, Harry Carney bs, Duke Ellington p, Jimmy Woode b, Sam Woodyard d.

1962 "Tuxedo Junction" (Erskine Hawkins) 3:27 NY, December 11, 1962. *Will the Big Bands Ever Come Back?* (CD1 *Reprise Studio Recordings* (Mosaic 5CD [1999]) Cootie Williams, Cat Anderson, Roy Burrowes, Eddie Preston tp, Ray Nance cor, Lawrence

Brown, Buster Cooper, Chick Connors tb, Johnny Hodges, Russell Procope as, Jimmy Hamilton, Paul Gonsalves ts, Harry Carney bs, DE p, Ernie Shepard b, Sam Woodyard d. Solos: Cootie Williams (first solo on return after twenty-one years), Hodges.

1966    "The Old Circus Train Turn-Around Blues" July 27, 11:29 CD5, rehearsals July 27 (ca 25:00) CD8. Juan-les-Pins, France. Ella Fitzgerald and Duke Ellington, *Côte D'Azur Concerts* (Verve 8CD 1998). Cat Anderson, Mercer Ellington, Herbie Jones, Cootie Williams tp, Lawrence Brown, Buster Cooper, Chuck Connors b-tb, Johnny Hodges, Russell Procope, Jimmy Hamilton, Paul Gonsalves, Harry Carney reeds, Duke Ellington p replaced by Jimmy Jones after opening choruses, John Lamb b, Sam Woodyard d. Solos: Ellington, Hodges, Hamilton (ts), Cooper, Hamilton, Gonsalves.

"The Old Circus Train Turn-Around Blues" 7:18 July 28, 1966, Juan-les-Pins, France. Ella Fitzgerald and Duke Ellington, *Côte D'Azur Concerts* (Verve CD7 [1998]). Personnel as above but OMIT Cootie Williams and ADD Ray Nance cornet and Ben Webster ts. Solos: Ellington, Hodges, Nance cornet, Webster, Nance/Hodges.

1966    "The Old Circus Train" 7:28 New York, August 18, 1966. *Duke Ellington and His Orchestra 1965–1972*. MusicMasters CD (1991). Cat Anderson, Mercer Ellington, Cootie Williams, Herbie Jones tp, Lawrence Brown, Buster Cooper, Chuck Connors tb, Johnny Hodges, Russell Procope, Paul Gonsalves, Jimmy Hamilton, Harry Carney reeds, Duke Ellington, Jimmy Jones p, John Lamb b, Sam Woodyard d. Solos: Ellington, Williams, Hamilton ts.

1972    "Loco Madi" 5:51 NY, October 5, 1972. *UWIS Suite* on *The Ellington Suites* (OJCCD originally Pablo). Cootie Williams, Mercer Ellington, Money Johnson, Johnny Coles tp, Booty Wood, Vince Prudente, Chuck Connors tb, Russell Procope, Harold Minerve, Norris Turney, Harold Ashby, Russ Andrews, Harry Carney reeds, DE p, Joe Benjamin b, Wulf Freedman e-b, Rufus Jones d.

Interlude 1

# First Impressions of Duke Ellington

## Worlds and Years Apart

I remember probably better than anything the time we were tied up in Shanghai alongside a ship that had come out later, and somebody on it had a record of *Black and Tan Fantasy*—played, as I did not learn at the time, by Duke Ellington. That was a world heard through a porthole, and never to be forgotten.
—OTIS FERGUSON, SEAMAN FIRST CLASS (LATER JOURNALIST), CA. 1928

His music has a truly Shakespearean universality, and as he sounded the gamut, girls wept and young chaps sank to their knees.
—REVIEWER OF ELLINGTON AT THE LONDON PALLADIUM, ENGLAND, 1933

To cure [Fara's] depression, a group of friends . . . took him one evening to the Salle Pleyel where Duke Ellington was presenting a gala program of American Negro music. . . . Stepping out to the front of the stage, Duke Ellington . . . gave the orchestra the down-beat: trumpets, saxophone, clarinet broke into a stampede of wild horses, a mad gallop. . . . After a moment's rest, the jazz began to imitate sounds as grotesque and expressive as the masks of black sculptors.
—OUSMANE SOCÉ, SENEGAL AMBASSADOR TO THE US,
"AN AFRICAN'S VIEW OF ELLINGTON," 1955

# INTERLUDE 1—FIRST IMPRESSIONS OF ELLINGTON: WORLDS AND YEARS APART

> The Ellingtonians played with startling existential freshness, heartfelt profundity, and an interlinked unity of various individual skills. They played for people in love. The performance was a triumph for the band in its high-pressure harmony and hallelujah of groin-grinding surrealistic tension.
> —REVIEWER OF ELLINGTON IN MADRAS, INDIA, 1963

> In 1931 a college roommate of mine, who was something of a pioneer as a jazz critic, was graduating, and he wrote a farewell piece. He recorded the rise and fall—during his four-year stint—of the Red Hot Peppers and the Blue Four and McKinney's Cotton Pickers and Bix and Trumbauer. He ended with the phrase:
> "Bands may come and bands may go, but the Duke goes on forever."
> Ah, how true! We thought it a marvel that Duke had ridden out all fashions for four long years. In fact, his good and lasting music lasted for forty-seven years.
> —ALISTAIR COOKE, REMEMBERING HIS YEARS AT JESUS COLLEGE, CAMBRIDGE, 1927–1931, AT DUKE ELLINGTON'S FUNERAL IN 1974

Chapter 3

# The Piano Player

> When he played the piano, Duke Ellington was real. He never played superficially, and he was always trying to reach somewhere else, constantly searching, looking for new ways, new things to do. That's the truest side of Duke that you'll ever meet, the most sincere side—when he's actually playing the piano.
> —AARON BELL, BASS (AS TOLD TO PATRICIA WILLARD 2004, 7)

At some point during his concerts, Duke Ellington would sidle up to the microphone and announce, in his most unctuous tone, "And now, ladies and gentlemen, it is our pleasure to feature, for your listening and dancing pleasure, the piano player." He would then watch the audience turn to look at the empty piano bench, and he would laugh at them as they laughed at themselves upon realizing that the piano player was Ellington himself.

Duke Ellington the piano player often went unnoticed. He was usually overshadowed by Duke Ellington the composer, arranger, bandleader, songwriter, and master of ceremonies. At the end of a concert or dance, fans who noticed his piano playing at all were most likely to remember him for using the piano like an outsize baton, cueing the band with it and playing filigrees for the singers and rallying his sidemen with a feverish version of "Kinda Dukish" as the preamble to "Rockin' in Rhythm."

And yet Ellington was proud of his piano playing and not reluctant to show it off. Until his genius for composing and arranging blossomed at the Cotton Club in 1927, he must have assumed he would make his career as a piano player. His main ambition as a teenager, he once said, was to master the ambidextrous flourishes of James P. Johnson's "Carolina Shout," and to that end he spent countless hours studying the slowed-down piano roll. "And how I learned it!" he said in *Music is My Mistress* (93). "I nursed it, rehearsed it. Yes, this was the most solid foundation for me.... It became my party piece." His piano playing stood him in good stead in his first years in New York, giving him an entry into rent parties and jam sessions, and accompanying singers.

His teenage strutting morphed into fifty years of professional piano playing. Without consciously trying, in those fifty years, Ellington recapitulated the entire history of jazz piano styles. He made the transition from style to style, apparently instinctively, simply to stay abreast of the currents that were moving his orchestral music and his own restless muse. Jazz historians universally laud Mary Lou Williams as the piano player who stayed ahead of the stylistic curve for her leading role in swing piano and then bebop and then post-bop impressionism. But Ellington's starting point came a style or two before hers, and his finishing point, though seldom mentioned, rivaled stylists born thirty or forty years after him.

### Ellington and Harlem Stride

Not surprisingly, when Ellington arrived in New York in 1923, he made an impression with his well-developed stride style. His earliest recordings were what appear to be odd jobs with singers in the foreground. As his progress as a bandleader caught on, so did his pianistic prowess, albeit comparatively unsung. In 1928, he recorded a pair of piano solos, "Black Beauty" and "Swampy River" (in the Playlist at the end of the chapter). He plays them in the dense Harlem stride style he admired in James P. Johnson, Willie "the Lion" Smith, and Luckey Roberts, the piano patriarchs of the day, and not incidentally, his boosters. The solos are flashy, showing off the genre-defining dexterity in the melodically complex right hand and the bumptious independence of the left hand. There can be little doubt that he would have succeeded in the world of Harlem stride piano if it was his main chance, but the very same recording session that turned out the flashy piano solos also produced a singular orchestral recording, "The Mooche," with Bubber Miley's trumpet growling and Barney Bigard's clarinet soaring in the ersatz uptown jungle. R. D. Darrell immediately declared "The Mooche" an "inimitable masterpiece" in *Phonograph Monthly* (1927–31), a verdict that has held up in all the decades since. The piano solos went largely unnoticed at the time, though "Black Beauty," a lovely melody dedicated to Florence Mills, a singer who had died tragically young the year before, would be played by Ellington throughout his career, especially in the last decades when he began featuring his piano more often.

One recorded piano feature from this relatively quiet period in Ellington's keyboard career is the dazzling "Lots o' Fingers" from 1932. "Lots o' Fingers" occupies the middle part of a medley with orchestral pieces on either side, and it is excerpted on *Solos, Duets and Trios* (in the Playlist). The interpolation of "Lots o' Fingers" between the orchestral features "East St. Louis Toodle-Oo" and "Black and Tan Fantasy," orchestral hits that were then five years old, shows off Ellington's technical prowess in a dazzling display. His two-minute piano solo in the middle of the seven-minute medley represents his crowning achievement as a stride pianist. Ellington never seemed to work on his piano technique, in this period or any other, though he doodled at the keyboard every day of his life, habitually in the hours from midnight to dawn, seeking voicings and harmonies for his arrangements. Apparently, that was enough. His piano technique never faltered.

Already in the 1930s there were portents of change in his approach to the keyboard. As the stride piano style was about to be supplanted by swing, Ellington was already altering his style too, using tenths infrequently in the bass clef and choosing instead richer chords with wider intervals. As Ellington left behind the piano styles that had so beguiled him in his youth, he found a way of making fun—affectionate fun, to be sure—of his youthful dalliance. He would spin a tale about what he claimed to be the first piece of music he ever wrote, something called "Soda Fountain Rag," harking back to his days as a fifteen-year-old soda jerk in Washington. With feigned reluctance, he would embark on a kind of stolid opening and gather enthusiasm as he accelerated, carrying the audience with him—and stop dead after about a minute, claiming that his memory had suddenly failed him. "Soda Fountain Rag" became an entertaining reminder of the changes he had worked through at the keyboard.

## Ellington and Swing

Starting in 1940, Ellington began featuring his piano playing more frequently, but he was spurred not by his own ambitions so much as by his ambitions for the extraordinary young bassist Jimmie Blanton, who joined his orchestra in September 1939. The impression made by this eighteen-year-old was like a lightning flash. It started on a rare evening when Sonny Greer and some of the other musicians were enjoying a night off—"just relaxing with a little taste," as Greer put it—in St. Louis the night before their opening at the Chase Hotel. Greer recalls (Nicholson 1999, 214): "So all right, I see this guy, a nice-looking boy. . . . He come up there and all my life I'd never heard nobody like this guy. Never heard nobody play bass like him. There were some good bass players, but like him, never." Greer ran back to the hotel to get Ellington, and Ellington hired Blanton immediately. Blanton's resonating tone and paradoxically nimble touch gave the walking bass an uncommon presence. All Blanton's successors, knowingly or not, absorbed his style so thoroughly as to make it the hallmark of jazz bass playing.

At the Chase Hotel the next night, Blanton played alongside Ellington's incumbent bassist Billy Taylor. The unusual two-bass configuration did not last long: Taylor, a solid, experienced bass player in his own right, soon moved on, saying, "I'm not going to stay playing up here with that young boy playing all that bass!"

Ellington elevated Blanton into the solo pantheon in the band, allotting him solo choruses alongside the other featured musicians on "Ko-Ko," "Bojangles," and "Sepia Panorama," and showcasing him on the redoubtable "Jack the Bear," one of the first orchestrated features for the string bass (all 1940). As if to make sure no one would miss the point, Ellington also recorded duets with Blanton, thus giving him a prominence previously unknown for bass players. Ellington's fascination with his young bassist inspired him to add a pair of impromptu duets, "Blues" and "Plucked Again," at the end of a recording session in November 1939, a month after he joined the band. Blanton's bass moved into the foreground in these duets, sharing the melodic space as well as maintaining the rhythm in partnership with the piano. Exposing Blanton in this way fortuitously put Ellington's piano in the foreground as well. It may also have sped up Ellington's stylistic move into swing piano, though that move was already discernible. As Mercer Ellington put it, "With such a dominant personality [as Blanton], Ellington had to pay more attention to the bass line. . . . One result of this was that Ellington had to go back to some of his original thinking on the use of the left hand at the piano" (Dance 1970, 35).

Ellington and Blanton recorded four titles on October 1, 1940, that are endlessly interesting and survive hardily with alternate takes. Blanton's most conspicuous strengths are showcased when he plucks the strings, that is, plays pizzicato. On "Mr. J.B. Blues," which Ellington's title dedicates to him, his precocious talent shines as he and Ellington alternate the lead and modulate from major to minor keys with perfect empathy. Brilliant as "Mr. J.B. Blues" is, the treasure of the duets is "Pitter Panther Patter," based on an eight-bar figure that Ellington repeats with variations while Blanton plays countermelodies, apparently improvised, and surges into the lead whenever the piano rests. The nursery cadence of the "pitter patter" in the title expresses not only the syncopated lines of the melody but also the sense of pure joy that imbues this performance in spite of its daunting, uncanny interplay. Although the piece was designed to show off Blanton, it is equally effective at showing off Ellington. His touch, no less than Blanton's, is panther-quick and aggressive, and the patter comes mainly from him in the showy runs into the highest octaves that were elements of his style from the beginning.

Ellington expected that "Pitter Panther Patter" along with "Jack the Bear" and the other orchestral features would launch Blanton into a trendsetting career. Instead, they proved to be his career peaks. Soon after recording these magnificent debut recordings, Blanton was afflicted with coughing fits and waning energy. Thirteen months later, he left the band debilitated by tuberculosis. He had just turned twenty-one when he died in a California sanitarium in 1942.

### Ellington Minimalist and Maximalist

The exposure Ellington accidentally gave himself as pianist in the Blanton duets undoubtedly played a role in the prominence he began giving to his piano from 1940 onward. He composed *New World A-Comin'* as a fourteen-minute showcase for his keyboard versatility and premiered it in a big band arrangement at his second Carnegie Hall concert in December 1943. He had never previously allotted himself the starring role in his orchestral compositions as he had done for Cootie Williams in "Concerto for Cootie," Johnny Hodges in "Jeep's Blues," and his other star soloists. Now, taking the starring role obviously suited him, at least once in a while. He took the title of *New World A-Comin'* from a now-forgotten novel and he invested it with characteristically high-minded optimism. The New World that's coming, he declared in the spoken commentary that prefaces his recording of it with the Cincinnati Symphony Orchestra, is "a place in the future where there will be no war, no greed, no categorization, no non-believers, where love is unconditional, and no pronoun is good enough for God." In its Carnegie Hall premiere, with his piano variations enveloped in big band splendor with Swing Era resonance, the ambitious composition seems destined for the protean existence that it took on.

Ellington adapted *New World A-Comin'* for settings both greater and smaller, from symphony orchestras at one end of the spectrum to piano trios and unaccompanied piano solos at the other. He obviously relished its tempo changes and the moody leaps that are conveyed by the piano and reverberated by the big band or symphony orchestra. The piano parts, on their own, are beguiling, as Ellington's many showcases as a soloist make clear.

At the other end of the spectrum, in the company of a symphony orchestra, perhaps no other recording in Ellington's considerable discography reveals his keyboard mastery as convincingly as does his soloing on *New*

*World A-Comin'* with the Cincinnati Symphony Orchestra in 1970. The symphonic score, prepared by Luther Henderson as a concerto grosso for piano and symphony orchestra, was by that time fifteen years old. It had been premiered at Carnegie Hall in 1955. By the time Ellington recorded it with the Cincinnati Symphony Orchestra, he had played its complex variations on numerous occasions in many different settings. Not that all those repetitions seemed necessary. From his very first rendition in 1943, he played his composition with technical verve. The rich and varied piano interludes seem to fall naturally under his fingers. In his recording with the Cincinnati Symphony, Ellington displays dexterity and discipline worthy of Oscar Levant, Arthur Rubinstein, or the other conservatory pianists in whose company he was never really mentioned. As Benny Green says, "It was his lack of pretension about himself rather than any technical weakness which has caused him to be regarded more as a composer-bandleader who happens to play the piano" (1973, 174). He is, as Green says, "an outstanding technician of unmatched harmonic subtlety." His technical facility and his insouciance are never more obvious than in this turn with the Cincinnati Orchestra.

### Melancholia—A Softer, Gentler Duke

Ellington's style underwent a major change in the comparatively dismal years of 1952 to 1955. Beset by the shrinking big band circuit, he tried in vain to make pop hits in hopes of increasing the cash flow.[6] He was in his fifties, and for perhaps the first and only time in his life, he adjusted awkwardly, maybe even begrudgingly, to the changes taking place around him. Postwar America saw numerous social upheavals, and many of them were making the world a less hospitable place for an itinerant musician— the growth of suburbs, the shuttering of downtown night spots and the decline of dance halls, the need to travel for one-night stands in arenas and gymnasiums miles apart, and the preference for small bands in the diminishing venues that booked jazz.

If it was a fallow period for Ellington, it was a downright disaster for almost every other big band. Most simply folded. Count Basie, Ellington's

---

6. Ironically, the first title recorded at Ellington's first recording session for Capitol (April 6, 1953) was "Satin Doll," a minor hit as an instrumental and one that became Ellington's final contribution to the standard American songbook when it was outfitted with lyrics by Johnny Mercer a few years later. It became a source of welcome royalties when it was recorded by dozens of singers. But "Satin Doll" took a few years to find its niche—Stanley Dance called it "the slowest growing of all Ellington's hits." Had it hit sooner, Ellington might have anticipated high times to come, but the high times were still three years away and on a different record label.

most inventive rival as the Swing Era ebbed, cut down to a septet in 1950. It would have been easy for Ellington to lead a small band, joining the trend that held sway in New York and across the land, or to disband and seek his fortune in composing. Neither choice tempted him. "The only reason we're still in it is mainly artistic interest," he told Nat Hentoff, using the imperial "we." "We're not one of those people who stay in the business so long as the business is good. We stay in it 52 weeks a year" (1976, 33).

Ellington's withdrawal from the daily affairs of his sidemen, who, in any case, came and went with a frequency that was unheard of in all the years before and would indeed never be repeated in the years to come, became part of the regimen. "He'd kid around with us," said a man identified by Nat Hentoff (1976, 34) as "a veteran Ellington sideman," "but if you got too close to him, he'd make a joke or put you on, and edge away."

In the midst of these changes came one stunning consolation. Ellington took solace in his piano playing, and in doing so, produced his masterwork as a piano player. With orchestra sales faltering, he poured his heart into a series of brilliant piano recordings in Los Angeles in April 1953. Microgroove recordings raised the possibility of developing extended themes in a long-play (LP) format. Whether or not Ellington intended these piano pieces as an extended thematic display of his piano playing is unclear. Most of the twelve piano tracks are short enough to be released as 78 rpm singles, and he may have hoped for a hit single with one or another, but instrumental pieces now had diminished prospects with the record-buying public, another postwar change. Instead, he went into a New York studio in December and supplemented his April recordings with three more piano tracks, thus getting enough length to fill a new-look 12" LP under the title *The Duke Plays Ellington,* and later more aptly titled *Piano Reflections.* By design or not, they make a striking collective statement. The somberness of Ellington's mood at the time is reflected in the titles he gives to four new compositions that are the high point, called "Retrospection," "Reflections in D," "Melancholia," and "December Blue."

In this indigo setting, the two most extroverted titles, "Dancers in Love" and "Kinda Dukish," though they have earned their place among Ellington's well-honed compositions for piano, seem intrusive on the same record as "Melancholia" and the other new titles; intrusive in mood, certainly, though as flawlessly played as all the others.

Stylistically, Ellington develops the moods of the new compositions patiently, staying close to the melodies and enveloping them in rich harmonies. Three titles from the band book—"Prelude to a Kiss," "All Too Soon," and Billy Strayhorn's "Passion Flower"—were reinterpreted pianistically. No less than the brand-new "Reflections in D" and "Melancholia," these older titles take on unfamiliar weight and gravity in Ellington's hands.

This is a reformed (re-formed) Ellington at the keyboard, contemplative, moody, if not exactly introverted at least pensive. Gone, or largely gone, are the showy runs and coloristic flourishes. Mark Tucker, annotating the LP (1954), calls "Retrospection" "a sober meditation with harmonies that echo the Victorian parlor songs and hymns of Ellington's youth." If so, it has none of the gaiety of those parlor songs and no hint of the hosannas of the sanctified church. It seems more like a bemused improvisation on familiar harmonies, and that impression is reinforced by the sparse, almost unnoticed bowed accompaniment of bassist Wendell Marshall, which has the feel of an accompanist looking for spaces to fill and not finding many. There is no melody, only a mood—a quiet, brooding mood, far removed from Ellington's characteristic flair. Unlike the other two brooding originals, Ellington never played "Retrospection" again. Maybe it was too spontaneous for recreating, or too genuinely woebegone for the smiling bandleader to recite before an audience.

Unlike "Retrospection," Ellington played "Melancholia" and "Reflections in D" on almost every occasion for the remaining twenty-odd years of his life when he found himself at a piano stool with no orchestra present. Tucker, in his notes, says that "while they draw upon the harmonic vocabulary of jazz, their rhythmic freedom and ethos belong to another world altogether: an idealized realm of memory, nostalgia and spirituality."[7] That other world is impressionism, and its scion is Claude Debussy (1862–1916). Ellington never listened to Debussy, but almost every other serious mid-century piano player did, including his associate composer, Billy Strayhorn. Ellington's impressionism had different roots, more mysterious and more personal. The most unique attribution came from Jimmy Maxwell, the swing trumpeter, who said, "Duke Ellington had a lot of French influence, which he got through Willie "the Lion" Smith, who he said he owed so much to. Willie knew all that stuff" (as told to Gene Lees 2000, 81). Perhaps the Lion was one of the countless subtle sources from whom Ellington tacitly absorbed impressionism, though hardly an obvious one. More likely, Ellington found the recital style that dominated his last decades on his own, as he had developed all the elements of his style as composer/arranger as well as piano player. That recital style with its impressionist tinge was first displayed abundantly on *Piano Reflections*.

---

7. "Reflections in D" was given a rich parallel existence as a "lyrical solo" dance performed by the choreographer Alvin Ailey. Described by his biographer as "one of Alvin's most subtly beautiful works" (Dunning 1996, 172), it remains in the repertoire of the Ailey Dance Company in perpetuity as the showpiece for the featured male dancer.

The shadow cast by Debussy on the generation of pianists younger than Ellington is hardly surprising. Those players had mostly absorbed conservatory influences as youngsters, and Debussy had set precedents that fit the ethos of jazz pianists very comfortably. Alex Ross (2018, 62) pointed out that Debussy "jettisoned rules that had been in place for hundreds of years." He defied his teachers, saying, "There is no theory—you simply have to listen." It is a sentiment that would have drawn the admiration of Ellington had he known about it, and Ross's elaborations on Debussy's methods might equally describe the mellow Ellington of "Melancholia" or any number of the younger contemporaries who came after him. Among several attributes in Debussy's style, Ross notes that "[f]amiliar chords appeared in unfamiliar sequences. Melodies followed the contours of ancient or exotic scales. Forms dissolved into textures and moods." Specifically, on Debussy's use of "exotic scales," Ross notes that "Debussy favored a mode that has become known as the acoustic scale, which mimics the overtone series by raising the fourth degree (F-sharp) and lowering the seventh (B-flat)." Those notes correspond to the blue notes that, as Ross says, "helps to explain Debussy's appeal to jazz musicians" (2018, 63). A century after Debussy's birth, mainstream jazz pianists picked up the torch of impressionism, and it remains the mainstream a century after his death.

Ellington carried that torch a few years before it reached the jazz mainstream. When he recorded *Piano Reflections* in 1953, his slightly younger confreres such as Art Tatum and Teddy Wilson were still displaying their Swing Era verities and doing so with undiminished appeal. The next jazz generation, the likes of Bill Evans, Geri Allen, Jacky Terrasson, and Bill Charlap, were on the horizon, having played Debussy's "Claire de Lune" and "Rêverie" in their student days and having studied Ellington's *Piano Reflections* along the way.

On the reflective pieces in *Piano Reflections*, Ellington's patience in developing and sustaining the somber mood represents a public expression of the private man. Aaron Bell, one of his favorite bassists, said, "I considered all that [stage] talk a sophisticated veneer. But when he played the piano, Duke Ellington was real." With *Piano Reflections*, Ellington's melancholy, so well hidden in his public swagger, seemed closer to the surface than ever before.

Almost twenty years earlier, in 1935, composing "Reminiscing in Tempo" in the gloom that enveloped him after the death of his mother, Ellington had stopped short of revealing the depth of his pain. "Reminiscing in Tempo" presents a studied sorrow. Now, decades later, Ellington's emotion is less guarded, undeniably deeper, more palpable, spelled out in these brilliant pianistic compositions. It makes *Piano Reflections* the most striking of all Ellington's piano records.

### A Rose Petal—"Delicate, Fragile, Gentle, Luminous"

The shadow of impressionism looms over a later piano solo of Ellington's perhaps more squarely than any other of his compositions. The occasion that called it forth was a meeting with Queen Elizabeth II of Britain following a concert at the Leeds Festival in 1958. According to Stanley Dance's press release for that event, "Singled out from the handful of distinguished artists representative of opera, symphony, etc., the cameras concentrated on Ellington while he talked with her" (quoted by Mercer Ellington 1978, 118–19). And Ellington's concentration was clearly on the Queen—transfixed, even. "Beauty—wonder—splendor—and majesty," he wrote. "I think no queen ever carried these with such authority."

He promised the queen that he would write some music for her, and he fulfilled his promise with *The Queen's Suite*, six pastoral compositions recorded in the Columbia studio a few months later (February and April 1959), pressed onto a long-play record, and hand-delivered to Buckingham Palace. Ellington saw the suite as a royal trust and vowed it would never be released commercially in his lifetime. It was in fact the first music that his son released from the copious stockpile of Ellington's music after his death.

*The Queen's Suite* includes one piano piece in its six movements, and its inspiration came to Ellington just days after his encounter with the queen. The tour of England that included the royal reception ended with a dinner party in London hosted by Ellington's friends and patrons, the Diamond family (Lawrence 2001, 348). Ellington, at the grand piano in their drawing room that evening, noticed that one petal had fallen from a bouquet of roses. He began improvising a simple, cascading melody, and the quiet emotion evolved into a composition he called "The Single Petal of a Rose." Whether or not he hearkened back to the poem "Lotus-Eaters" from his schooldays, Tennyson's metaphor provides a fitting analogue:

> There is sweet music here that softer falls
> Than petals from blown roses on the grass.

"So delicate, fragile, gentle, luminous," Ellington wrote of the rose petal. "Only God could make one, and like love, it should be admired but not analyzed." He might equally have meant the music it drew from him.

Ellington's hope that "it should be admired but not analyzed" took an ironic twist. Years later, "The Single Petal of a Rose" became implicated in an academic debate that had nothing to do with the singular grace of the composition itself but reflects in an interesting way on its composer. Travis Jackson, discussing the definition of jazz, notes that the most successful definition for many years was one that maintained there must be a convergence of two defining features, swing and improvisation. The convergence, he points out, serves to rule out ethnic musics that use improvisation but do not swing, on the one hand, and "early rhythm-and-blues," which swings but does not improvise, on the other. He then points out what he sees as the flaw in the definition, saying, "Strict application of that definition, however, might force one to disqualify pieces that are usually described as jazz but neither swing nor prominently feature improvisation, such as Duke Ellington's 'Single Petal of a Rose'" (2002, 85–86). One might quibble with him on the point of swing, because "The Single Petal of a Rose" does swing, always granting, of course, that the definition of "swing" is every bit as problematic as the definition of jazz. ("Swing remains oddly ineffable," says David Schiff [2012, 51]. "Even in the twenty-first century it strangely eludes the grasp of most classically trained musicians. And of the dictionary as well.") But Jackson's point has a salutary resolution. "The Single Petal of a Rose" may or may not be jazz by some Aristotelian definition, but Jackson acknowledges it is recognized as jazz by experienced listeners. It qualifies (he knows) because experienced listeners summon up a family of properties that converge to define the genre. Like most human concepts, jazz requires a definition in terms of prototypes rather than fixed categories.

Needless to say, its composer never gave a thought to the genre any more than Debussy would have. "You merely have to listen," Debussy said, and Ellington put it slightly differently: "If it sounds good, it *is* good." And this much is indisputable: "The Single Petal of a Rose" sounds good. You merely have to listen.

## Tripping into the Post-Bop Jungle

*Piano Reflections* was a landmark, and "The Single Petal of a Rose" a distinguished further reflection. A diametrically different landmark in Ellington's piano legacy came in the controversial *Money Jungle* session with Charles Mingus on bass and Max Roach on drums. This recording was one of three all-star encounters instigated by Ellington in September 1962. His Columbia recording contract had expired and he was about to sign a contract with

Reprise Records. Ellington took advantage of his momentary liberty by organizing two small-group recordings on Impulse! Records with tenor saxophone players as special guests, Coleman Hawkins and John Coltrane, and a third with Mingus and Roach. Hawkins belonged to Ellington's generation, but the others were all about twenty-five years his junior, and at the moment of the recordings, they were as prominent in the jazz world as he was. Presumably, Ellington sought out the relatively youthful Coltrane, Mingus, and Roach to prove that the rapid changes taking place in jazz in the early 1960s had not left him behind. In that regard, *Money Jungle* has to be counted a success.

The recording session featured several sideshows, as befits the yoking together of the lordly maestro with the high-strung Mingus and the volatile Roach. Mingus had committed himself to Bellevue Asylum a few years before and was now making brash, spectacular protest music, and Roach had disrupted a Miles Davis concert at Carnegie Hall by sitting on the proscenium with a large placard reading *Freedom Now!*, the clarion call of civil rights protests that were happening all over the country, and also the title of his most successful LP as a bandleader.

The recording session got off to a rocky start. After a few bars, Mingus abruptly packed up his bass and stomped out of the studio. Accounts differ, depending on who is telling the tale. Some versions say that Mingus was irate because, in his view, Ellington was embarrassing himself by "playing shit." As Ellington remembered it, Roach was the problem. Mingus stomped out declaring, "Man, I can't play with that drummer." That version takes on some credence because it was Ellington who persuaded him to return, either by sauntering up to him at the elevator (Nicholson 1999, 335) or by pursuing him on the street. Producer Alan Douglas says, "I remember leaning out the window, looking up towards Seventh Avenue and seeing Duke Ellington chasing Mingus up the street" (quoted by Levin 2020). Mingus returned, apparently placated by whatever it was that Ellington, his lifelong idol, had said to him.

Some of the music they made that afternoon gives credence to the disruptive beginning because several tunes have a frantic, edgy feeling, especially the title tune "Money Jungle" but also the drum feature called "A Little Max" and a rambunctious version of "Caravan," the old warhorse from Ellington's big band book. On these three tracks, Ellington punches out staccato dissonances against Mingus's repetitive bass drone and Roach's heavy-handed accents. In a metaphor-laden description of the title track, reviewer Matt Levin says that "in the first thirty seconds, [it] is less a collaboration than a tug-of-war, a tangle of thrown gauntlets and cross-purposes." These rambunctious mash-ups on the three tracks are far removed from anything else in Ellington's works, and they aroused some critical ire. "That's ridiculous," Miles Davis complained when Leonard Feather played "Caravan" for him in a blindfold test (1964, 131). "It's a mismatch. They don't complement each other.... Duke can't play with them and they can't play with Duke."

Levin (2020) maintains that "the centerpiece of the album is strife," but that only holds, if it holds at all, for the three rambunctious titles. The other tracks, paradoxically, tend to dispel any hints of rancor in the studio. Four of them—"Very Special," "Wig Wise," a very straight, sensuous rendition of Ellington's old love song "Warm Valley," and the simple atmospheric "Fleurette Africaine"—show a near-perfect balance of contrasts. Indeed, "Fleurette Africaine" is widely lauded. Ellington described how it came about:

> I explained what we were going to do, with no thought as to what they were going to do. I said, "Now we are in the center of the jungle, [where] for two hundred miles in any direction, no man has ever been. And right in the center of this jungle, set in the deep moss, there's a tiny little flower growing, the most fragile thing that's ever grown. It's God-made and untouched." ... I started to play, and we played to the end, and that was it. (Nicholson 1999, 334–35)

"People like Mingus and Roach," Ellington said, "they are so imaginative, and I thought this was the greatest example of it."

Here and elsewhere, the rapport among the three musicians is plainly felt, and strong rapport was surely essential for a single recording session to yield an hour of complete takes, as this one did. Surprisingly, all the compositions are Ellington's, though Mingus was (and is) admired as a composer. Ellington appears in control throughout, as his account of the genesis of "Fleurette Africaine" clearly shows. On the frantic tracks, his amusement at the goings-on is obvious; he sits back like a wry observer and bashes away at the keyboard. On the balanced tracks, he plays inventive, romantic, and ornamented lines, much more in his own métier than Mingus's.

He may have been keeping an eye out for the bassist's famous temper, but the tension in the studio was clearly creative rather than threatening. "Do I think of Charles Mingus as a disciple of my school?" he was once asked at a press conference (quoted by Feather 1970, 259). "Well, that's what *he* says." Ellington's reply is flippant, gently mocking the bear-like Mingus, whose impulsive, often erratic behavior sometimes obscured his gifts as virtuoso bass player and an inventive, original composer. If Ellington had taken the time to listen to, say, Mingus's "Boogie Stop Shuffle," with its fleet ensemble precision shadowed by plunger trombone, or "Hora Decubitus,"[8] with its propulsive string bass and baritone saxophone undercurrent (in the Playlist), he would have recognized his own signature elements transmogrified in a way that goes deeper than mere homage. He might even have exclaimed (as he did on first hearing Thelonious Monk's piano playing), "Sounds like he's stealing some of my stuff." Wry, but not flippant, and a more honest answer to the question.

Mingus was a disciple, certainly, but by no means a fawning disciple. He was as pushy with Ellington as he was with the sidemen in his bands, and that push gave a unique spin to this singular recording session.

A decade later, in 1972, Mingus and several other musicians came together with Ellington at Yale University to receive honorary citations as Duke Ellington Fellows.[9] Mingus took Ellington aside and proposed that they should make a recording. "Duke, why don't you, me, Dizzy and Clark Terry and Thad Jones get together and make an avant-garde record?" he asked (as recounted in the memoir of his wife Sue Graham Mingus, 2002, 106). "Duke's reply was very quick: 'Why should we go back that far? Let's not take music back that far, Mingus. Why not just make a modern record?'" Mingus was impressed. "And so that appeared to me to be very funny," he wrote. "Duke dropped out because he considers what they call avant-garde today old-fashioned music. And it's true. It's old-fashioned because it's played by beginners." In the decade that had passed since *Money Jungle*, Mingus seemed to have lost sight of the fact that they had already made a record, and indeed it was a record that had elements of avant-garde music and is indisputably a "modern record."

The encounter with Mingus and Roach, and for that matter, the encounter with John Coltrane the same year, provide incontrovertible evidence for Benny Green's proclamation (quoted by Stanley Dance 1962), which appeared in print before any of these encounters took place. Green wrote that Duke Ellington's "grasp of harmony and instrumental voicing is more advanced than anybody else's in the entire range of jazz, and the reason why many modern fans [fail to credit] him is not that they are too modern for Duke, but that Duke is too modern for them."

---

8. *Hora Decubitus* is Latin for the "hour of lying down" and pseudo-Latin for the "hour of bedsores." Decubitus ulcers are pressure sores that bedevil bedridden patients.
9. Ellington's honorary Yale doctorate and the fellowships in his name were the brainchild of Willie Ruff, the bass player and French hornist who became a jazz professor at Yale and a benevolent force for the music; on the Ellington Fellows (and much more), see Ruff 368–72.

## Piano Recitals

We now know that Ellington played a piano recital as early as November 16, 1943, when he entertained Royal Canadian Air Force personnel on a base near Ottawa, Canada. The performance pushes back the accepted date of Ellington's debut as a concert pianist by almost twenty years. Before that, all sources claimed that Ellington's first piano concert took place at New York's Museum of Modern Art on January 4, 1962, but journalist Doug Fischer uncovered a note in the *Ottawa Citizen* on "a special solo piano performance Ellington gave for servicemen and their wives at the RCAF station at Uplands air base." At the time, this piano concert appears to be an isolated event in Ellington's itinerary, but it is clearly a sign of his growing involvement with the piano in the wake of his Blanton duets.

An impromptu piano recital took place a few years later, in April 1946, in the aftermath of a homecoming concert at Howard University in Washington, DC. After the concert, Ellington was interviewed at radio station WWDC by Willis Conover for the influential Voice of America (VOA) broadcasts that propagated the image of America in war-torn Europe and incidentally disseminated the sound of jazz behind the Iron Curtain, where jazz had been suppressed. After the interview with Conover, the VOA hosted a reception for Ellington's entourage and local admirers. At some point, the guest of honor, bemused, sat down at the studio piano and spontaneously played an eleven-minute version of *New World A-Comin'*, then a relatively unfamiliar work. Despite the casual setting, it was a beautifully rendered piano solo. When he finished, Conover informed him that he had recorded it, and Ellington asked, "Can I have a recording of that?" On being assured that he can, he then made room for Billy Strayhorn to join him and they amused the guests by playing ten minutes of four-handed piano. The rare document came to light among Conover's effects in the late 1990s, yet another accidental blessing of the piano player's indomitable spirit.

In his long career, Ellington presented only eight known piano recitals counting these two (itemized with access information in the appendix at the end of the chapter). Half of them were accidental. In 1971, a quarter century after the Washington recital, a longer and more organized one was the result of a meteorological trauma, as unexpected for Ellington as it was for his sparse audience. On February 22, 1971, Ellington made his way to Baltimore, Maryland, expecting to play afternoon and evening concerts with his orchestra. A sudden blizzard blanketed the Atlantic region, with the result that most of the bandmembers were grounded en route. That afternoon, Ellington entertained the ticketholders who had braved the storm with a piano recital, joined for some or all of it by his bassist Joe Benjamin and drummer Rufus Jones. By the evening, the snowfall had apparently abated so that both the bandmembers and the audience had arrived, and the big band show went on as advertised.

Another accidental recital came about a few months later, when Ellington was presented with the inaugural honorary D. Mus. at Berklee College of Music, in Boston, on May 22, 1971. After the ceremony, the dignitaries moved to the Charter Room for the reception. There was a piano in the room, naturally, and Ellington needed little coaxing to sit down and play requests for seventeen minutes.

There were, of course, planned recitals as well. The one at the Museum of Modern Art (MoMA) in New York in January 1962, hitherto considered Ellington's first, is more substantial. Ellington played the first half alone and included three compositions from his bountiful *Piano Reflections* album, then nine years old. (Ellington's inclusion of "Melancholia," "Reflections in D," and "Janet" after so many years marked a welcome revival.) In the second half he was joined by Aaron Bell on bass and Sam Woodyard on drums. This trio had recorded an album for Columbia, *Piano in the Foreground* (Columbia), a few weeks before this concert at MoMA. Judging by its timing, one might have assumed that *Piano in the Foreground* was a kind of warm-up for the imminent MoMA recital, but when the repertoire at MoMA came to light, it turned out to be much more conservative in both style and content than the *Foreground* recording. The MoMA recital is transitional in its format, with echoes of the band's performances. Bell and Woodyard are more prominent than accompanists would be in the later recitals, with Bell chiming in with a handsome duet on "Satin Doll" and Woodyard indulging in a six-minute drum outing on "Kinda Dukish." Ellington is more voluble at the microphone than in the later recitals, and he inserts an eight-tune, ten-minute medley in penultimate position.

An unexpected gem among Ellington's recitals, one of a kind, was preserved in July 1970 by French ORTF (*Office de Radiodiffusion-Télévision Française*). The national broadcaster invited Ellington to discuss his concept of jazz and he obliged them in fine style. The producers simply sat him at a grand piano facing the camera, with no audience and no interviewer, and left him to ruminate. As expected, Ellington obfuscates with characteristic eloquence: "jazz is a never-ending discussion," "jazz is a tree," "it goes east west north south," it has "blue-black deep roots." He intersperses his unscripted musings with improvisations on some of his most beautiful melodies. Among the eleven titles are a few uncommon ones for his solo piano excursions ("Warm Valley," "Black Beauty," "Come Sunday," and, with a clever nod to his surroundings, "Paris Blues"). The French producers surely did not expect such a generous outpouring, and Ellington may have even surprised himself. After forty-three minutes of verbal whimsy and pianistic charm, Ellington blurts out a hasty thanks and farewell in French, and with a wave of his hand and a broad, self-conscious grin, sidles into the wings and out of the camera shot. Although at one point (twenty-seven minutes in) Ellington peeks at a note to remind himself of a name, the whole production has a wonderfully spontaneous air—an intimate forty-five minutes with a man of elegance and wit that integrates more than half an hour of his piano playing.

### Crystallizing the Concert Style

The other two recitals crystallize Ellington's final piano style. One might be tempted to call it his *mature* style if it were not for the fact that he had reached maturity, pianistically and in every other way, years before. His final style is leagues removed from the ostentatious Harlem stride that beguiled him in his twenties, and considerably removed from the swing style that he had moved seamlessly into in his thirties and forties. It is, in the peak performances, reflective and romantic. Where the stride style prides itself on moving the hands faster than minds can fathom ("lots o' fingers," as Ellington titled his culmination of the style), his final style, the recital style, moves gracefully through hummable melodies, exalts harmony over rhythm, and gives the impression of a man searching for the perfect next note.

Ellington seemed fully aware of the transformation, though he was never likely to say so directly. In an interview for a TV documentary called *The Duke* for the Canadian Broadcasting Corporation (broadcast March 3, 1965), Ellington had this exchange with the host, Byng Whittaker:

> Q: Where do you get your ideas from?
> Ellington: Ideas? Oh, man, I got a million dreams. That's all I do is dream—all the time.
> Q: I thought you played piano.
> Ellington: No, no, this is not piano. [He improvises a few quiet bars on the piano.] This is dreaming.

Ellington, famously elusive as always in interviews, was not being merely flippant. For the last twenty years of his life, when he played piano for his own purposes rather than for the purpose of meeting orchestral demands or cajoling post-bop collaborators or filling other ulterior designs, he played with a dream-like impressionistic strain. That strain, that contemplative mood, had seemed surprising, almost out of character, when it first came to light in *Piano Reflections* in 1953, but it flowed abundantly in recitals and other moments from then on, whenever Ellington's piano was in the foreground.

*New York Concert* captures a performance at Columbia University in May 1964, with cameo appearances by Billy Strayhorn and Ellington's old backroom tutor, Willie "the Lion" Smith. Ellington had been invited for a piano concert by the New York chapter of the Duke Ellington Society, and it was undoubtedly the prospect of a highly sympathetic audience that encouraged him to accept. He opens with tried-and-true numbers, easy for him and more than satisfactory for this audience ("Take the 'A' Train," "Satin Doll," "Caravan"), but he grows more venturesome. He introduces a new composition, "Skillipoop," from the incidental music he had written a few months earlier for *Timon of Athens* at the Stratford Shakespearean Festival in Canada, and he takes obvious pleasure, as does his audience, in explaining its title: "One of its meanings is trying to make what you're doing look better than what you are really doing." He delights the audience by bringing on Willie "the Lion" Smith to play James P. Johnson's stride anthem "Carolina Shout," and then he brings on Billy Strayhorn to play a four-handed duet with him on their party piece "Tonk."

The real surprise, and the treat, comes in what appears to be the second half when Ellington comes on alone and plays "Melancholia/Reflections in D" from *Piano Reflections* and a newer composition, "Little African Flower" (introduced two years before as "Fleurette Africaine" in the recording with Charles Mingus and Max Roach [in the Playlist]). He then swings into a very old and very rare piece, "Bird of Paradise," a composition he wrote in 1934 and published as sheet music, where it was promoted as "a modern composition for piano." Mysteriously, Ellington did not record the piece at the time, though that would seem to have been an essential adjunct for promoting the sheet music. Unaccountably, he waited almost forty years before he chose to play "Bird of Paradise" in public. This Columbia University recital became its world premiere as a piano piece.[10] He also plays "The Single Petal of a Rose," the piano gem from *The Queen's Suite*.

The other recital released commercially, *Live at the Whitney*, is a priceless memento from the Whitney Museum, Manhattan, in April 1972. It too provides a relatively candid view of the usually guarded Ellington with the spotlight on him alone, both musically and personally. At the Whitney

---

10. The chronology gets all the more befuddling by the fact that it was recorded in a big band arrangement in 1935 not by Ellington but by the Jimmie Lunceford Orchestra (Lambert 1999, 253).

Museum as at Columbia University, eight years earlier, Ellington relies more on intuition than on advance planning, and he buys time between tunes by bantering with the audience, at one point reciting homemade doggerel: "Into each life some jazz must fall / With afterbeat gone kickin' / With jive alive, a ball for all / Let not the beat be chicken." He solicits audience participation ("We'd like to invite you to sing with us—even if you don't know the lyric"), and generally struts like the seasoned stage performer he was.

More important, these two recitals at Columbia University and the Whitney Museum testify to the tremendously resourceful piano player he was. The repertoire is partly predictable ("Satin Doll," "Caravan," "C-Jam Blues," the medley of old favorites) but it is also partly surprising and innovative (for instance, the only extant piano versions of "Le Sucrier Velours" from the *Queen's Suite*, "Amour Amour" and "Soul Soothing Beach" from *Togo Brave Suite*, and the only trio versions anywhere of "John Sanders Blues" and "A Mural from Two Perspectives," as well as Ellington's only performance of "Bird of Paradise").

At the Whitney Museum, where he was appearing as part of a prestigious subscription series called Composers' Showcase, he starts off subdued. "I might as well warn you that you must be prepared for a totally unprepared program," he says, and after rambling for a while, announces, "I'm going to sit down and see if I'm in tune with the piano." He sounds tired, and no wonder. He was about to turn seventy-three, he had just finished a cross-country tour as far afield as California, he had performed the Second Sacred Concert the night before at St. Peter's Lutheran Church, and he was slightly wheezy, probably from the lung cancer that would kill him almost exactly two years later. So he had lots of reasons for coasting through this superfluous Monday date in its upscale setting, and for the first few minutes he seems resigned to doing just that. But something overtakes him as he is noodling away at "Black and Tan Fantasy," the first number in the tried-and-true medley. His interest begins to quicken, and by the time he reaches "Caravan" six minutes later, he is in full swing. The rest of the hour is a brilliant, multi-faceted performance, moving smoothly through shtick ("Dancers in Love"), anecdotal history ("Soda Fountain Rag"), nostalgia ("Mood Indigo," "Satin Doll"), technical adroitness (*New World A-Comin'*), lyricism ("Lotus Blossom"), and piano adaptations of band melodies ("Meditation" and "The Night Shepherd" from the Second Sacred Concert the night before, "Amour Amour" and "Soul Soothing Beach" from *Togo Brava Suite*). The diffident beginning only makes the high points in the rest of the performance seem that much higher. *Live at the Whitney* might be the most comprehensive view of Ellington as a piano player. It is not the most profound or the most ambitious, but apart from the one-man show in the French TV studio, it is the most entertaining.

## A Choice One

If you had to choose *one* piano performance among the dozens that Ellington left us—so many, notwithstanding the slow start—you could hardly do better than a piece that Ellington played at the end of an exhausting recording session. It is "Lotus Blossom," the sumptuous Strayhorn melody. By a stroke of luck, an engineer captured it before shutting down the recording equipment for the day. Ellington and the orchestra had just wrapped up a session in August 1967, playing four Strayhorn compositions for the commemorative album that would celebrate Strayhorn's long, brilliant collaboration with the Ellington orchestra before he died of cancer three months earlier. The album is . . . *And His Mother Called Him Bill* (Bluebird). As the bandmembers were packing up for the day, Ellington sat down at the piano and began picking out "Lotus Blossom." You can hear the musicians chatting in the background and moving around. At one point (thirty seconds in) Ellington stops for a moment—you might imagine him wiping away a tear—and then resumes with greater gusto. His performance cannot be separated from the elegiac occasion that called it forth. It is plainspoken by Ellington's norms. It is heartfelt. It is heartbreaking.

And it did not end there. Two days later in the same studio, after the band had recorded three more Strayhorn compositions for the commemorative album, Ellington asked Harry Carney and Aaron Bell to stay behind. He began playing "Lotus Blossom" again, this time with Bell's sonorous bass bowing its accompaniment. On the second chorus, Carney's rich baritone saxophone is heard for the first time, easing into the foreground playing Strayhorn's melody while one of the greatest piano accompanists of all time nudges him along. There are no tears this time, just a heady mixture of sorrow and gratitude.

The take with Carney and Bell was released twenty years after Ellington's solo version, and of course it does not strictly belong in a consideration of Ellington's piano music. Fair enough. Both takes are stunning in their different ways. The piano version has a depth of feeling that cannot be replicated. It stands alone, though it was the fount of countless other recitations. For the seven years that remained to Ellington after Strayhorn's death, he played a solo version of "Lotus Blossom" in the encore of every concert in homage to his great collaborator. It was always heartfelt, but a mere shadow of that primal studio elegy. The studio elegy stands alone.

## Acknowledgments

John Hornsby gave me the DVD of the CBC-TV documentary *The Duke* with interviewer Byng Whittaker. Jim Northover directed me to the online sources of the recitals at ORTF, Paris, (1970) and Charter Room, Berklee College, Boston (1971). As archivists at TDES, John and Jim have shared these invaluable resources and many more with me over many years.

## Playlist

(Recordings cited in order of appearance in the chapter)

"Black Beauty," "Swampy River." October 1, 1928. Okeh, NYC. *Okeh Ellington*, Columbia (1991). Duke Ellington p.

"The Mooche" same session as "Black Beauty." Bubber Miley, Arthur Whetsol tp, Joe Nanton tb, Barney Bigard, Johnny Hodges, Harry Carney reeds, Ellington p, Fred Guy g, Wellman Braud b, Sonny Greer d.

"Lots o' Fingers" 2:12 New York, February 9, 1932. *Stereo Reflections in Ellington*. Natasha Imports (1993). (A technological marvel, "Lots o' Fingers" is heard as the middle part of a medley in "accidental" stereo as a result of takes recorded on microphones separated by a few feet; the sound was synced by Brad Kay to simulate stereo thirty years before it became the industry standard.)

"Lots o' Fingers" 2:00. New York, February 9, 1932. *Solos, Duets and Trios* (Bluebird CD [1990]). Duke Ellington p.

"Soda Fountain Rag" 1:18. April 10, 1972. *Live at the Whitney* (Impulse!). Duke Ellington p.

"Blues," "Plucked Again." Chicago, November 22, 1939. Duke Ellington p, Jimmie Blanton b.

"Mr. J. B. Blues" 3:02, 3:12, "Pitter Panther Patter" 3:05, 3:01, "Body and Soul" 3:04, 3:10, "Sophisticated Lady" 2:53, 2:46. Chicago, October 1, 1940. *Solos, Duets and Trios* (Bluebird CD [1990]). Duke Ellington p, Jimmie Blanton b.

"Pitter Panther Patter" 3:00. December 5, 1972, Las Vegas, Nevada. *This One's for Blanton*. Pablo 2310–721 (OJC CD [1987]). Ellington p, Ray Brown b.

*New World A-Comin'*. 14:11. December 11, 1943. *Live at Carnegie Hall* (Storyville 2CD [2001]). Ray Nance, Harold Baker, Taft Jordan, Wallace Jones, Rex Stewart tp, Lawrence Brown, Joe Nanton, Juan Tizol tb, Jimmy Hamilton, Johnny Hodges, Otto Hardwick, Skippy Williams, Harry Carney reeds, Ellington p, Fred Guy g, Alvin Raglin b, Sonny Greer d.

*New World A-Comin'* 11:19. April 21, 1946. WWDC radio station, Washington, DC. Ellington p. Privately recorded (see appendix). https://digital.library.unt.edu/ark:/67531/metadc1506210/m1/ (accessed December 2020).

*New World A-Comin'* 11:14. May 28, 1970, Cincinnati, Ohio. *Duke Ellington Orchestral Works* (MCA Classics [1989]). Duke Ellington, piano with Cincinnati Symphony Orchestra conducted by Erich Kunzel.

"Retrospection" 3:53. "Melancholia" 3:17, "Reflections in D" 3:32. Hollywood, CA. April 13 and 14, 1953. *Piano Reflections* (Capitol CD [1992]). Duke Ellington p, Wendell Marshall b.

"Melancholia/Reflections in D" 4:08. Wollman Auditorium, Columbia University. May 20, 1964. *New York Concert* (MusicMasters CD [1995]). Duke Ellington p solo.

"December Blue" 3:32 December 3, 1953, NY. *Piano Reflections* (Capitol CD [1992]). DE p, Wendell Marshall b, Dave Black d.

"The Single Petal of a Rose" 4:03 New York, April 14, 1959. *The Queen's Suite* on *The Ellington Suites* (orig. Pablo Records 1976, OJJCD 1991). Ellington p, Jimmy Woode b.

"Fleurette Africaine" 3:33, "Very Special" 4:23, "Wig Wise" 3:17, "Warm Valley" 3:31. New York, September 17, 1962. *Money Jungle* (United Artists [Blue Note CD]). Duke Ellington p, Charles Mingus b, Max Roach d.

Charles Mingus "Hora Decubitus" 4:40 (a.k.a. "E's Flat, Ah's Flat Too," Mingus comp/arr) New York, September 20, 1963. *Mingus Mingus Mingus Mingus Mingus* (Impulse! CD). Eddie Preston, Richard Williams tp, Britt Woodman tb, Don Butterfield tuba, Jerome Richardson bs, Dick Hafer ts, cl, Booker Ervin ts, Eric Dolphy as, Jaki Byard p, Charles Mingus b, Walter Perkins d.

Charles Mingus "Boogie Stop Shuffle" 4:59 (Mingus comp/arr) New York, May 12, 1959. *Mingus Ah Um* (Columbia CD [1998]). Willie Dennis tb, John Handy as, Booker Ervin ts, Shafi Hadi ts, Horace Parlan p, Charles Mingus b, Dannie Richmond d.

"Bird of Paradise" 4:00 Wolfman Auditorium, Columbia University, May 20, 1964. *New York Concert* (MusicMasters [1995]). Duke Ellington p.

"La Fleurette Africaine" 3:33 New York, September 17, 1962. *Money Jungle*. Blue Note CDP 7 46398 [1987]. Duke Ellington p, Charles Mingus b, Max Roach d.

"Lotus Blossom" 3:54. RCA Studios, NYC, August 30, 1967. . . . *And His Mother Called Him Bill*, Bluebird (CD 1987). Duke Ellington p.

"Lotus Blossom." 4:58. Same studio, same release. September 1, 1967. Harry Carney, bs, Ellington p, Aaron Bell b.

## Appendix: Piano Recitals Annotated

**Ellington's final style, the recital style, moved gracefully through hummable melodies, exalted harmony over rhythm, and gave the impression of a man searching for the perfect next note.**

1943, November 16, Uplands air base, Ottawa, entertained Royal Canadian Air Force personnel. Repertoire unknown.

1946, April 21, WWDC radio station, Washington, DC. After a concert at Howard University, Willis Conover interviewed Ellington for a Voice of America broadcast. Around 2 a.m., Ellington sat at the studio piano and, after warm-up (1:36), plays *New World A-Comin'* (9:08). Conover tells him it is being recorded. Someone asks him to play "one of his new things" (0:34), and he responds by playing "Soda Fountain Rag," his oldest thing (0:58). Billy Strayhorn joins him, they adjust the seat (0:36), and play "Tonk" (2:44), four-handed noodling (0:43), unidentified four-handed piece

(1:19), and four-handed improvisation (4:08). At the end, Ellington is heard saying, "Can I have a copy of that?" (2:05) (Total time 23:52). https://digital.library.unt.edu/ark:/67531/metadc1506210/m1/ (accessed December 2020).

1962, January 4, at Museum of Modern Art, New York. Set 1 Duke Ellington solo: "New York City Blues" (4:43); "Blue Belles of Harlem" (4:14); "The Clothed Woman" (2:44); "Melancholia" (2:13); "Janet" (1:45); "Reflections in D" (2:34); "There Was Nobody Looking" (2:53); *New World A-Comin'* (9:47). Set 2 Ellington with Aaron Bell b, Sam Woodyard d: "Take the 'A' Train" (4:26); "Lotus Blossom" (2:08 piano solo); "Satin Doll" (3:02); "Single Petal of a Rose" (3:25 piano solo); "Kinda Dukish" (8:18); medley (10:15 "Do Nothing Till You Hear From Me" / "Solitude" / "Don't Get Around Much Anymore" / "Mood Indigo" / "Asphalt Jungle Theme" / "I'm Beginning to See the Light" / "Sophisticated Lady"); "Caravan"; "Dancers in Love" (2:45). Available in limited edition at La Maison du Duke. www.maisondueduke.com.

1964, May 20, at Columbia University with cameo performances by Strayhorn and Willie "the Lion" Smith, with Duke Ellington p, Peck Morrison b, Sam Woodyard: "Take the 'A' Train" (3:56); "Satin Doll" (4:01); "Caravan" (2:57); "Skillipoop" (6:04); "Into Each Life Some Rain Must Fall" (poem 0:33); Blues Medley ("Happy-Go-Lucky Local" / "John Sanders Blues" / "C Jam Blues" [5:40]); "Tonk" (duet with Billy Strayhorn 2:08); "Things Ain't What They Used to Be" (2:29); "Melancholia/Reflections in D" (4:08); "Little African Flower" (2:23); "Bird of Paradise" (4:00); "The Single Petal of a Rose" (3:04). Issued on *New York Concert*. MusicMasters 1612–5122 (1995).

1970, July 2, recorded by French ORTF—intimate forty-five minutes of musings in words and music. Duke Ellington, piano, plays "Little African Flower," "Take the 'A' Train" (Strayhorn), "Warm Valley," "Things Ain't What They Used to Be," "Paris Blues," "Come Sunday," "In the Beginning God," "Lotus Blossom" (Strayhorn), "Black Beauty," *New World A-Comin'*, "Satin Doll," and "Dancers in Love." https://jazzon-thetube.com/video/solo-piano/?omhide=true (accessed January 2018).

1971, February 22, in Baltimore, Maryland. A blizzard interrupted the arrival of the musicians, so Ellington played an afternoon concert on piano with Joe Benjamin b and Tony Watkins voc (four songs). Discographies list "Take the 'A' Train," "Lotus Blossom," "Sophisticated Lady," "Satin Doll," "Dancers in Love," "Mood Indigo," "I'm Beginning to See the Light," "Flamingo," "Kinda Dukish," "Jeep's Blues," "Caravan," "East St. Louis Toodle-Oo," "Carolina Shout," "Misty," and two unidentified titles. Unissued.

1971, May 22, at Charter Room, Berklee College of Music, Boston. After receiving an honorary D. Mus., Ellington played requests for seventeen minutes at the reception: "Satin Doll," "Take the 'A' Train," "Baby You Can't Miss" (Ellington voc), "Sophisticated Lady," "Honeysuckle Rose," "Love You Madly" (Nell Brookshire voc), "Come Sunday" (Tony Watkins voc). http://tdwaw.ca (accessed January 2018).

1972, April 10, at Whitney Museum, New York. Duke Ellington p, Joe Benjamin b, Rufus Jones b: Medley ("Black and Tan Fantasy" / "Prelude to a Kiss" / "Do Nothing Till You Hear From Me" / "Caravan" 6:51), "Meditation" (2:39), "A Mural From Two Perspectives" (2:56), "Sophisticated Lady" / "Solitude" (4:44), "Soda Fountain Rag"

(1:18), "New World A-Comin'" (9:02), "Amour Amour" (1:41), "Soul Soothing Beach" (2:51), "Lotus Blossom" (2:35), "Flamingo" (1:35), "Le Sucrier Velours" (1:44), "The Night Shepherd" (2:45), "C Jam Blues" (3:04), "Mood Indigo" (2:06), "I'm Beginning to See the Light" (1:23), "Dancers in Love" (2:13), "Kixx" (1:35), "Satin Doll" (3:07). *Live at the Whitney*. Impulse! IMPD-173 (1995).

Chapter 4

# Wordless Articulation

> One of [Kay Davis's] first experiences in Ellington's band came when he taught her the simple melody to "Creole Love Song" [sic]. Within an hour she was onstage with him performing the song. The year was 1944. The place was Carnegie Hall. "I sang, it got a wonderful ovation and then I got the heck off the stage!" she exclaims.
> —CARRIE MOEA BROWN (2006, 13)

R. D. Darrell, author of the first serious appraisal of Duke Ellington as a composer, made an incisive point about one of Ellington's innovations—his creative use of vocalization in his music. "Ellington writes naturally for instruments alone, unlike the tunesters of Tin Pan Alley who can never divorce themselves from 'words and music,'" Darrell wrote in 1932. "Words may sometimes be added to his pieces.... The human voice is not disdained but in his works it operates only in an instrumental technique, wordlessly, one might say inarticulately if it were not for the definite articulation of its expressiveness.... Ellington has emancipated American popular music from text for the first time since the Colonial days of reels and breakdowns" (1932, 64). Though Darrell plainly states, "The human voice is not disdained," he extols Ellington's natural inclination toward instrumental composition.

All these decades later, Darrell's statement requires considerable qualification. Ellington is now recognized as a major contributor to the Great American Songbook, the composer and occasional lyricist of a long list of standard songs from "Mood Indigo" (1931) to "Satin Doll" (1953). Indeed, Ellington's "music with words" is the subject of the next chapter. In 1932, when Darrell published his article, he may or may not have been aware that

Mitchell Parish had recently added words to Ellington's "Mood Indigo," giving Ellington a hit song destined to become a standard, but he certainly knew the instrumental version that came out the year before because he praised it in *Phonograph Monthly Review* as "a poignantly restrained and nostalgic piece with glorious melodic endowment and scoring" (1927–1931, 38).

Darrell could not possibly have known that ten years earlier, in Ellington's apprentice years, 1923–1925, he scuffled on the fringes of Tin Pan Alley, attempting to sell songs with the singer and lyricist Jo Trent and sometimes succeeding, as with "Choo Choo (Gotta Hurry Home)." Sometime after 1925, Ellington discovered that his métier was composing and arranging for instruments. Indeed, composing for instruments was his métier for his entire career, even though, as we shall see, commercial pressures led him to pay closer attention to the writing of songs.

Darrell's interest in—and his admiration for—Ellington's gift for composing "for instruments alone" was undoubtedly nurtured by his immersion in concert music of all kinds. Darrell was "steeped in European music, both classical and modern," as Mark Tucker, the editor of Darrell's critique, says. Little wonder, then, that in appraising Ellington's first five formative years, Darrell makes passing comparisons with Stravinsky ("Strawinski," as he spelled it), Bruckner, Delius, Mahler, Robeson, Copland, Brahms, Debussy, and others. Darrell understood that musical cognition is quintessentially nonverbal, an axiom that was once taken for granted and is recognized to this day by listeners steeped in symphonic music, string quartets, ballets, and perhaps even Sousa marches. Music with words attached was once reserved for praising the deity or wooing a lover or spinning yarns about heroes and villains. When words are attached to music, they relegate the piece to the mundane world, where we find diary entries, business letters, postcards, shopping lists, and countless other speech acts. Words with music, whether high-flown or folksy, clever or clumsy, are rooted in the consciousness of everyday experience.

Darrell knew the difference. He exalted Ellington's exploitation of the human voice as "it operates only in an instrumental technique, wordlessly." It was no passing fancy. Ellington made use of wordless articulation throughout his career. To the best of my knowledge, notwithstanding Darrell's prescient observation, his use of vocalizations has never received an overview until now.[11]

---

11. A useful adjunct, brought to my attention by Steve Bowie, is Lisa Clark's doctoral thesis (Clark 2017) that provides "a performance guide and research tool" for five of Ellington's compositions with wordless vocalization.

## A Love Call

Darrell's admiration for Ellington's gift for integrating wordless vocalizations in his compositions almost certainly began, as it has begun for countless listeners over the years, with "Creole Love Call," an early treasure that never seems to grow stale. "Creole Love Call" was released in the midst of that heady effusion that coincided roughly with the band's move from the Kentucky Club to their charmed residency at the Cotton Club, a short physical move but a quantum leap in terms of Ellington's growth as a composer. "East St. Louis Toodle-Oo" and "Black and Tan Fantasy" came before "Creole Love Call," and "Black Beauty" and "The Mooche" came soon after it. Those five compositions formed the bedrock of the career that flourished thereafter.

"Creole Love Call" is a twelve-bar blues that features ringing solo choruses by Bubber Miley on open trumpet and Rudy Jackson on clarinet. Miley and Jackson, as it happens, are listed with Ellington as co-composers, which leads one reviewer to suggest that Jackson, who was a guest with Ellington on this recording but a regular player with New Orleans paterfamilias King Oliver, brought the melody he plays in his solo with him from Oliver's band (Lambert 1998, 20). He gives his chorus a fine polish, providing a self-consciously pretty theme that he plays with rich vibrato.

Ellington's opening is breathtaking. A clarinet trio (Jackson, Otto Hardwick, and Harry Carney) lays down a deep harmonic carpet and the silky soprano voice of Adelaide Hall intones a wordless countermelody on top of it. Hall then sits silent while Miley and Jackson play their choruses and again while the clarinet trio returns with a composed chorus. Hall steps back into the foreground to sound out a blues chorus of her own, again wordlessly, but this time with raspy effects, a tougher, more emphatic statement in the context than any of the instrumental solos, inserting occasional nonsense syllables that bear a momentary resemblance to the scat singing that Louis Armstrong introduced to the world the year before (by his own admission, Armstrong 1999, 131–32). Hall's vocalizations convey the "love call" of the title in two contrasting guises: her opening chorus presents come-hither cooing, and her later improvisation raises the temperature with a dash of raunch. Ellington's deft touch shines in his writing for the clarinet ensemble, but his manipulation of Hall's vocal effects steals the show. Darrell anointed it "a veritable masterpiece of its genre!"

In a long career, Adelaide Hall dined out on this hit record she made as a twenty-six-year-old ingenue. As she recalled many years later, it came about as a happy accident. She was a singer and dancer in Broadway chorus lines, including Noble Sissle and Eubie Blake's smash hit *Shuffle Along*. One night, she happened to be working on a theater bill that included Ellington's band. "I was standing in the wings behind the piano when Duke first played it," she told Steve Voce in the 1980s. "I started humming along with the band. Afterwards he came over to me and said, 'That's just what I was looking for. Can you do it again?' I said, 'I can't, because I don't know what I was doing.' He begged me to try. Anyway, I did, and sang this counter melody, and he was delighted and said, 'Addie, you're going to record this with the band.' A couple of days later I did."

"Creole Love Call" amounted to "her most lasting fame," as the *Biographical Encyclopedia of Jazz* puts it. A few years later, domestic life interrupted her career. While touring England in a revue in 1931, she married an English gentleman. Music historians lost track of her when she spent a few quiet but hardly invisible decades in London society. When they caught up to her, she was known as Dame Adelaide Hall. "Creole Love Call" had not been forgotten, and she became, all those years later, a genial revivalist on stages and in conference halls. In 1991, she celebrated her ninetieth birthday at a gala with a famous cast at Queen Elizabeth Hall in London. The progenitor of her fame, the boyish Duke, who had died at seventy-five, would have turned 101 that year. Needless to say, Adelaide Hall was importuned to sing her sinuous love call at Queen Elizabeth Hall as she had been everywhere she went. It never grew old for her, or for generations of music lovers.

## "The Sweet Singing Drummer"

R. D. Darrell might have assumed that Ellington learned to exploit the instrumental hue of the human voice as a result of the happy accident of hearing Adelaide Hall's harmonizing in the wings. In that, he is not alone. "Creole Love Call" occupies a significant niche among Ellington's formative works, and it is his first documented vocalization. But it was not the very first. Adelaide Hall was the beneficiary of an unheralded pioneer who had a great influence on young Ellington. The use of vocalized effects had their origins back in the days before the band left Washington.

The vocalist in the garage band that became the Washingtonians was drummer Sonny Greer. Recorded evidence is sparse because the Washingtonians never made records in pokey old Washington. When they arrived in New York, they had to pay their dues before they got to record their own material. Ellington's first record found Ellington and Greer accompanying Alberta Prime (an alias for Alberta Hunter) on a number called "Parlor Social De Luxe" (November 1924). It was a make-work assignment, very welcome at the time. Greer is heard bantering playfully with the singer at the start of the record, supplying vocal accompaniment when the acoustic technology made him downplay his drums. The Washingtonians got to cut a record of their own, though under the name "Sonny and the Deacons," anointing Greer as leader. The song, "Oh! How I Love My Darling," finds Greer intoning Jo Trent's lovelorn lyric; Eddie Lambert, usually a glass-half-full reviewer, says simply, "vocal, quite excruciating, by Sonny Greer" (1998, 7).

If later critics found his style "excruciating," at the moment of his currency, Greer's singing made an impression. Louis Metcalf, who played trumpet in the Cotton Club orchestra in Ellington's first year, says, "I remember Sonny Greer got so big at the Cotton Club that New York didn't know nobody but Rudy Vallee and Sonny Greer. He used to have a beautiful voice" (Orgel 2021, 8). Ellington agreed. "Sonny Greer was in his element here," Ellington said, "and he was known as The Sweet Singing Drummer in those days" (*MiMM* 72).

Those early successes are long forgotten, and Greer's role as band vocalist goes largely unmentioned. But he deserves recognition for inaugurating the wordless vocalized solo in the tradition that Adelaide Hall brought to fruition. His best turn at it came a few years after hers on a blues called "Sloppy Joe," composed by Ellington and Barney Bigard (in the Playlist). If Greer lacks Hall's grace, he nevertheless brings his own charm to the twelve-bar blues played by a sextet in 1929, when the band was lighting up the Cotton Club. The winsome melody is stated by trumpet, alto saxophone, and clarinet in the opening and closing choruses, with Greer's wordless vocal adding colorations to the sparse ensemble. The solos by Ellington, Bigard, and Cootie Williams are exemplary in the context, and so is the arranged melody in uniquely Ellington timbres. Greer's doleful vibrato riding over that melody embellishes it and lends an exotic touch. It is the crowning memento of Greer's vocal career, easily the best surviving evidence.

This outing provides a taste of the camaraderie that the Washingtonians strove for in their heyday when dapper Sonny Greer twirled a drumstick in his right hand and intoned his wordless vocalizations through the megaphone in his left. Lambert says, "This kind of vocal by Greer was featured at the band's theater and dance engagements a good deal at this time, Sonny using a megaphone to project his voice" (1998, 35). It provides the best clue to the origins of the wordless vocals in Ellington's devices, the humble beginnings—and the inspiration—for Adelaide Hall's masterstroke.

Sonny Greer was the drummer in Ellington's orchestras for over thirty years, until 1951. Ellington sums up his talents by saying, "He was the world's best percussionist reactor. . . . When he heard a ping, he responded with a most apropos pong" (*MiMM* 53). When he quit the band in 1951, his departure was not lamented by the inner circle. Ellington's son Mercer, in his memoir, said, "By this time, Sonny was beginning to lose his legs. He was in trouble with tempos . . . and Pop had to revert to more comfortable tempos for him to be effective" (1978, 105–6). Ellington, ever loyal, kept him on salary for the rest of his days.

Sonny Greer lost his will to sing many years before he lost his velocity as a drummer. He was expected to sing "Three Little Words" in the 1930 film *Check and Double Check* when, according to Ellington, "he got mike fright, light fright, Hollywood fright . . . and he said, 'Man, I can't sing, I'm not a singer, I'm a drummer,' and he was just scared to death." So the film's producers went to the posh Cocoanut Grove and recruited the Rhythm Boys, a trio of young singers named Bing Crosby, Harry Barris, and Al Rinker. "The Rhythm Boys made the track," said Ellington, "and they photographed it [in the film] as if our three trumpet players were singing" (Cullen 1962, 339). Greer's old bandmate Louis Metcalf explains his "mike fright" in plainer terms. "He used to have a beautiful voice, but he just drank his self away," he says. "He drank so much, and I don't know why, because he certainly was successful and people loved him" (Orgel).

### Enter the Coloratura

Ellington added a female singer to the orchestra in 1931, when Ivie Anderson came into the band (as discussed in the next chapter, "Ellington's Music with Words"). Thereafter, the band always had a female singer. In the 1940s, inexplicably, Ellington had three at the same time. Kay Davis, Joya Sherrill, and Marie Ellington all joined the band in the fall of 1944. Why Ellington felt the need for three women's voices has never really been explained, and in the end, it probably comes down to one of those circumstances in which he made a commitment to a musician and then elected to live with it rather than rectify it with a hurtful decision. Whatever the circumstances, the three coexisted for a year. Marie Ellington left the band in September 1945. Duke Ellington makes her departure into a fairy tale (*MiMM* 220): "Nat 'King' Cole took one look at her, scooped her up, carried her off to the preacher, married her, and took her to his beautiful Beverly Hills love nest, where she listened to his love songs the rest of her life." Joya Sherrill first sang with the band as a teenager in 1942, but Ellington had to wait until she graduated from high school in September 1944 before her mother would let her join the band; she stayed only a year and a half, until early 1946. Like Marie Ellington, she left when she settled into married life, but she was on call for special assignments for many years (as we shall see in the next chapter).

Kay Davis had a longer tenure with the orchestra, more than six years, starting in the good times in September 1944. She was featured in four of the annual Carnegie Hall concerts that were Ellington's showcases in these peak years, and she stayed with the band until July 1950, the difficult postwar years when dance dates and theater engagements were out of fashion and big bands were fading.

Kay Davis occupies a special niche in the Ellington annals as the designated wordless vocalizer, the only one the band ever had apart from Adelaide Hall, who was just a guest for one recording date. Ellington seems to have known from the start that he could exploit the special gifts of his new coloratura soprano for the "wordless articulation" that he relished. Within weeks of her joining the band, he stood her front and center at Carnegie Hall as she intoned Adelaide Hall's colorations on "Creole Love Call." The orchestra had recorded "Creole Love Call" several times since its original recording in 1927 but always without the vocal colorations—and always, for those who knew the original, it seemed bland without them. At Carnegie Hall, with Kay Davis new to the band, he revived it in all its glory in an extended concert version, albeit with an incongruous ill-tempered plunger chorus by trombonist Tricky Sam Nanton (that goes unmentioned by Ellington in his accolades at the end) and sweeter turns by Ray Nance on trumpet and Harry Carney on clarinet (both acknowledged by Ellington). But it is Kay Davis's soprano turn at start and end that supplies the spice. Though Kay Davis could sing words to music—Ellington's words and the words of others, as we shall see in the next chapter when she delivers the world premiere performance of Billy Strayhorn's "Lush Life"—her singular achievement comes from her wordless vocals. The first salvo was her renewal of "Creole Love Call" at Carnegie Hall in 1944.

Kay Davis was only twenty-four when she joined the orchestra in 1944, but she had already completed a degree in music, majoring in voice and piano, at Northwestern University in her hometown, Evanston, Illinois. From there, she had gone on to present recitals and perform in operas in nearby Chicago, where she also worked as a voice coach. "She had perfect pitch, could sight-read, and had all the gifts," said Ellington (*MiMM* 219). Her 'audition' seemed like make-believe. She and a friend had attended a concert by Ellington in Chicago and "on a whim" decided to go backstage. When Ellington found out she was a singer, he asked for a song, and she obliged. "When she saw that Ellington seemed to enjoy it—and feeling even braver—she invited him to an upcoming performance," she later recalled (Brown 2006). To her amazement and the delight of her small audience, he showed up with his entourage. At the end of her recital, she pushed through the crowd that had gathered around him. When she got to the front, he smiled broadly and said, "Can you be in Baltimore next week?" "I went home and packed my little trunk, and that was the beginning of my career," she said.

The time was ripe. Ellington had embarked upon a career phase that involved considerable exposure in relatively formal concert venues, and he knew he would find numerous opportunities for Davis's trained soprano voice. He had already played the first two of his near-annual Carnegie Hall concerts before she joined him, and with the third one imminent, he immediately pressed her into service on "Creole Love Call" (December 19, 1944). It was the first of many performances of "Creole Love Call" for her. Ellington had never invited any other vocalist to reprise Hall's vocalization, and after Davis left, no other vocalist would sing it. Only Davis, in his view, could be trusted with that legacy.

## A Spotlight on Concert Jazz

The concert venues brought broader audiences, front-page newspaper notices and expansive programming. Carnegie Hall, as the emporium of 'serious music' in the United States, carried prestige at the time, and performing there had considerable cachet across the nation. There was a trickle-down effect that took Ellington into Symphony Hall (Boston), Civic Auditorium (Cleveland), Syria Mosque (Pittsburgh), Cornell University, Metropolitan Opera House (New York), Civic Opera House (Chicago), and other high-toned venues. The impetus toward "concert jazz" had had an influential precedent in the decade before via Paul Whiteman, who had commissioned works from Ellington and others for his own concerts at Carnegie and elsewhere. Ellington inherited his mantle and became the leading proponent of concert jazz, both in quantity and quality (see Howland 144–67). Ellington's concerts carried the patina of authenticity, where Whiteman's had often seemed fabricated, and they gained plaudits and proved profitable. In the immediate fallout of Ellington's first Carnegie Hall concert (January 23, 1943), the repeated program at Symphony Hall in Boston five days later (January 28) had the impact of a command performance. "Despite the year's worst blizzard," Hasse says (1993, 270), "[it brought] a capacity audience of 3,000 ... and 1,200 were turned away."

Davis made an impact in one of Ellington's singular accomplishments. President Franklin D. Roosevelt died in office in April 1945. The funeral fell on the following Saturday, a day that coincided with Ellington's regular

Treasury Show radio broadcast, sponsored by the United States Treasury Department. The nation was in mourning, and Ellington prepared a program of exquisite solemnity. He opened and closed with Mercer Ellington's "Moon Mist" in an arrangement featuring Ray Nance's mournful violin and moved smoothly from one melody to the next through the thirty-minute broadcast (see *FDR Memorial Broadcast* in the Playlist). Kay Davis sang a hymn-like song called "Poor Pilgrim of Sorrow (A City Called Heaven)," credited to Ellington and never played afterward, and a grieving "Creole Love Call." On the hymn, Davis's formal diction suits the context, intoning Ellington's simple sentiments—"I heard of a city called Heaven / I've started to make it my home"—with appropriate respect. Davis's wordless vocal on "Creole Love Call" left a grieving nation in tears.

The praise for Ellington's commemoration was universal. The show-business journal *Variety* proclaimed, "No other dance band could have filled this spot without rousing criticism," apparently unaware that Ellington was by now much more than a "dance band." *DownBeat* noted that Ellington "provided a more moving tribute than any of the symphony works of the old masters that pervaded the networks." Rob Bamberger (2000), citing these sources, points out that those old masters "bore no particular cultural relevance to the times in which Roosevelt lived. . . . Ellington's program . . . does not convey a simple, reflexive grief, but something more complex and layered with expectation."[12]

Another highlight for Kay Davis came up after she had been in the band for four years. Ellington, anxious to renew acquaintances with his rabid British fan base now that the privations following the Second World War were finally abating, faced a quandary. British union rules at the time prohibited foreign musicians in the country except in exchanges with British musicians, but they made an exception for singers and dancers, along with their accompanists. Ellington accepted a booking for a six-week tour in June and July 1948, but he had to conjure up a "cabaret act" in order to qualify. He chose Kay Davis along with Ray Nance, in his capacity as singer and dancer (and incidentally trumpeter and violinist). The three of them would play with British bassists and drummers as one act among many at the London Palladium and other venues. Davis's "wordless vocals reminded a lot of our older fans of the early records we made with Adelaide Hall," Ellington wrote

---

12. His achievement was sadly forgotten twenty-one years later, when Ellington's Middle East tour for the US State Department was suspended because of the assassination of President John F. Kennedy. Ellington offered to play a memorial concert at his scheduled Cairo engagement but instead the concert was canceled. "They thought jazz concerts might be in bad taste," he told the *New York Post*, and he added, "I'm always fighting against the shady associations people have given it" (quoted by Cohen 440).

(*MiMM* 220). But the real fans were hoping for more than cabaret. Unlike the triumphal tour of England and France in 1933, this austere return in 1948 brought little joy to the locals, who were still clearing bombsites and scuffling for rationed foodstuffs. (The union ban was lifted in 1958; Ellington toured England with the orchestra that year, and from then on it became a regular stop on his globetrotting itinerary.)

### Blue Fogs and Turquoise Clouds

It was Davis's gifts as a well-schooled coloratura that gave her a special place in Ellington's ensemble. He celebrated those gifts affectionately (*MiMM* 219):

> I shall never forget her first [*sic*: second] Carnegie Hall appearance in January 1946. Subtitled "A Blue Fog You Can Almost See Through," "Transblucency" was a last-minute kind of composition, and the two featured musicians (Jimmy Hamilton on clarinet and Lawrence Brown on trombone) had to have music stands at the mike, because it had been completed too late for them to memorize. So we put Kay's part on a music stand at the mike, just like those of the musicians, and the performance was a smash.

The complexities of the performance went somewhat beyond the lack of rehearsal time. "Transblucency" on its own is a complex melodic excursion, requiring Davis's vocalized part to intermingle with melodic lines played by trombone and clarinet. Added to that is a logistical complication that almost scuttled the Carnegie Hall performance. Ellington conceived the composition as a link between the two parts of his 1937 work "Diminuendo in Blue" and "Crescendo in Blue." Ellington's title, "Transblucency," at first glance an awkward pun on "translucency," cleverly implies the link—too cleverly, perhaps—as a portmanteau of the first syllable of TRANSition yoked to the BLUe of the Diminuendo" and "Crescendo." It was premiered—cold, as Ellington admits—at the Carnegie Hall performance.

"Transblucency" is played and sung as the linking movement in an eleven-minute big band extravaganza. The intention was to play the three disparate parts as an entity at the concert without breaks in between. The music is complex, and the onstage logistics introduce an element of makeshift choreography. Its Carnegie Hall premiere includes a few near-stops while the musicians scramble back and forth, with smatterings of excuse-me applause from the audience while Hamilton, Brown, and Davis make their way from the orchestra section to their music stands. Ellington twice fills the pauses at the piano, supplying impromptu continuity. "Diminuendo," the first movement, is played mellower than usual, presumably in anticipation of the ethereal "Transblucency" to come, but "Crescendo," which follows, roars into its climactic shout, no doubt reflecting the band's relief that the end is in sight. Despite the turmoil, or perhaps because of it, the performance was received, as Ellington said, as "a smash."

As a transition between the swinging diminuendo and rollicking crescendo, the legato "Transblucency" was a miscalculation. A few years later, Ellington tried to insert Mercer Ellington's mournful "Moon Mist" as the transition. As suitable as it was as a dirge for the late president, as a transition between romping big band numbers, it was, if anything, more incongruous.[13]

After Ellington gave up on it as a transition, "Transblucency" came to occupy a niche all its own. Standing alone, it has an eerie delicacy. It has "a particularly warm and rich vertical sonority," as the vocalist/analyst Lisa Clark puts it (2017, 58), from the harmonic mating of the voice on top, trombone in the middle, and clarinet on bottom. Ellington's fanciful subtitle catches its spirit—"A Blue Fog You Can Almost See Through." Six months after its Carnegie Hall debut, it was recorded in Hollywood. By this time, it was well rehearsed. Kay Davis sings long harmonized lines to Lawrence Brown's sweet trombone (Brown is co-composer with Ellington) and to Jimmy Hamilton's plaintive clarinet. The piece exudes calm, but just as its blue fogginess threatens to become glacial, Ellington rings in sharply placed piano interjections to roil the texture, and when the wordless vocal returns, it is intertwined with the cool instrumental lines, giving it the grace of a *pas de deux*.

That glacial texture is always a threat in the basic elements of "Transblucency" and of its companion piece, "On a Turquoise Cloud," which came soon after. The slickness of the vocal acrobatics over the mellow trombone threatens to become cloying. Indeed, that precarious balance overwhelms another composition built around the same elements called "The Beautiful Indians—Minnehaha." Like "Transblucency" and "On a Turquoise Cloud," "Minnehaha" pairs Davis's wordless vocal with Lawrence Brown's mellow trombone, but Davis's vocalization has a kind of stridency that she elsewhere manages to avoid. The stridency is presumably intended as a melodramatic analogue for Hiawatha's doomed lover who succumbs to the cruel elements and the uncaring deities in a once-revered poem (1855) by

---

13. Ellington famously found the consummate transition in 1956, when he had tenor saxophonist Paul Gonsalves play a gyrating spaced-out barroom wail that incited dancing in the aisles at the Newport Jazz Festival (Morton 2008).

Henry Wadsworth Longfellow that Ellington undoubtedly studied in his school years. Intended or not, the effect is grating.

"Minnehaha," with its excesses, exposes the fragility of incorporating coloratura effects in jazz. It makes Ellington's successful use of those effects the next year at Carnegie Hall seem all the more impressive. The concert introduced another specialty for Kay Davis, called "On a Turquoise Cloud," and as its title suggests it emits a slightly different hue from the blue fog of "Transblucency." It, too, is a collaboration by Ellington and trombonist Brown, and very much a reflection from the same prism. As if to guard against onstage pratfalls at its Carnegie Hall premiere, it had been brought to a fine sheen in the Columbia recording studio five full days before the concert. Davis's soprano glides along with Jimmy Hamilton's clarinet and Brown's trombone, muted and softly melodic. The instrumental textures are denser than "Transblucency." The final statement of the melody pairs Davis with Hamilton again, and then, in thickly layered harmonies, with a trio of Brown and Harry Carney on bass clarinet and Ray Nance's plucked violin. The unusual timbres of this exotic ensemble place the music in a unique realm. "Beyond category," in Ellington's favorite catchphrase, and a far cry from "jungle music." The reception by the Carnegie Hall audience in December 1947 was long and loud.

Hearing "On a Turquoise Cloud" alongside "Transblucency" perhaps dulls the originality of both. "On a Turquoise Cloud" is darker in mood and richer in texture, but the elements that formed the two pieces are identical. Spacing them out a year apart for the Carnegie audience provides a real-world measure of the artistry that could summon such ovations in the august setting.

### Creole Love Call: The Finale

Both compositions obviously bore Kay Davis's signature, and Ellington never played them again after she left the band.[14] His reverence was similar to the reverence he had shown for "Creole Love Call," never performing it with the vocalized solo when Adelaide Hall was not there to sing it—never, that is, until Kay Davis came along. After Davis sang "Creole Love Call" at her 1944 debut at Carnegie Hall, she sang it countless times thereafter, propitiously the

---

14. "On a Turquoise Cloud" made a semi-serious appearance in a kind of cabaret setting Ellington devised for a television appearance (July 18, 1950). It was sung by a vocal trio—Marion Cox, June Norton, and Chubby Kemp—in a context that included tap dancers Bunny Briggs, Honi Cole, and Georgie Prince, and a mixed musical repertoire.

next year at the wake for the dead president and daily on her European tour with Duke Ellington's cabaret act in the summer of 1948. She was given the opportunity to record it at her final studio recording session with the band, which took place soon after returning from a grueling European tour. Her recording is perhaps its consummate performance (at the considerable risk of raising the hackles of Adelaide Hall's advocates). By September 1949, she was thoroughly attuned to it. She sings the first chorus perfectly faithful to Adelaide Hall's original, and then Ellington lets Ray Nance loose with a bold chorus on his plunger-muted trumpet, which provides an incentive, or so it seems, for Kay Davis to unleash her jazz soul in her final choruses. She does so in her own way, first playing modestly with the familiar obbligato, and then giving it a small personal touch, and in the end allowing herself to show off the upper reaches of her magnificent range. It is a sophisticated adieu, very much in character.

And then she leaves the studio and her bandmates in the Ellington orchestra. "After a four-week tour of Europe, I was tired," she says. "I got home and said, 'That's it.'" Ellington's ultimate compliment came years later: "I always say that we are primitive artists, we only employ the materials at hand," Ellington told broadcaster Jack Cullen in 1962. "And when someone comes in—just like when Kay Davis came in, she was a soprano, so we employed her in her natural character." The terms he uses are akin to his praise for Bubber Miley and Johnny Hodges and Cootie Williams and his other great instrumentalists—but only Kay Davis and, years later, Alice Babs, of the dozens of vocalists who came into the band, were accorded a place in that pantheon.

### Occasional Masterpieces

After Kay Davis's departure, Duke Ellington never again carried a designated vocalization specialist with the band. His use of wordless vocalization became less frequent. A major factor was the sharp turn the music business took in the direction of "words and music" (that is, toward songs). That change of emphasis did not mean that he had lost interest in the musical power of wordless vocalizations. Rather, he now turned to them as occasions arose, or perhaps more accurately (from his perspective), as occasions demanded. In the end, at least two wordless vocalizations resulted in masterful performances that rewarded his careerlong inspiration for instrumental vocal roles. The performances came into being in each of his remaining decades—in 1956 and 1968 (and persisting until 1974).

## The Bluest Rose

Duke Ellington's final term with Columbia Records, from 1956 to 1962, began auspiciously with *Ellington at Newport*. It was a smashing start to these Columbia years. Marketing lore might have called for a cover project, something that might cash in on the Newport excitement. Instead, the second release came as a considerable departure. It was called *Blue Rose*, and the billing on the label shared the credit between Rosemary Clooney and Duke Ellington and His Orchestra. During an extended engagement in Café Society in New York, Irving Townsend, Ellington's Columbia producer, worked out details with Ellington and Billy Strayhorn for an album that would feature vocalist Rosemary Clooney singing Ellington/Strayhorn songs backed by the orchestra. "This unusual album," he wrote (1956), capitalized on Clooney's "long experience as a band singer, her admiration for Ellington and his music, and the special sort of supercharged satin in her voice."

What *really* made it unusual were the geographic hurdles. The recording was made—assembled, really—while Ellington and his orchestra were in New York and Clooney was a continent away in Los Angeles. She was confined there for health reasons while pregnant with what would be her fourth daughter. Nevertheless, it was a project that the Columbia brass wanted. Townsend has a point, at least arguably, in saying that Clooney was "qualified more than any other singer" to sing Ellington's songs with his band. She had first been noticed, as were most of her slightly older age-mates (she was born in 1928) singing with a dance band of Tony Pastor's. She emerged as a name act in her own right, as had so many band singers, but in the dumbing-down of the pop music industry in the early 1950s, her talents diminished even though her income blossomed with the hit songs "Come On-a My House," "Botch-A-Me," "Mambo Italiano," and "This Ole House," forgettable ditties that she delivered with great clarity in her expressive contralto. She also showed considerable poise acting (and singing) in popular movies such as *Here Come the Girls* (1953 with Bob Hope) and especially *White Christmas* (1954 with Bing Crosby). Her hit songs were bonanzas for Columbia Records, and in mating their pop singing star with their newly signed big band master, they saw an opportunity to show off Clooney's musical substance and gain a crossover audience for Ellington.

Strayhorn and Ellington worked out the repertoire, and Strayhorn crafted the arrangements with the singer over a long distance. Will Friedwald, in notes accompanying the digital release of *Blue Rose* (1999), tells us that Strayhorn crossed the continent three times, once to settle the song list and twice to supervise Clooney's overdub of the lyrics. The orchestra recorded the charts in New York in January 1956, and Clooney, though her health was precarious, added her vocals in February. Against long odds, the collaboration worked. "What makes *Blue Rose* great has nothing to do with either money or machinery," Friedwald writes. "There is such a thing as an Ellington mood, what might be called a thinly 'muted' approach to emotion, and Clooney latches on to it no less perfectly than any of the [instrumental] soloists."

One of the songs on the album is "Blue Rose," the title piece, composed by Ellington especially for the record. It is a blues in a medium tempo, and Strayhorn's arrangement of Ellington's melody allots it first to the richly harmonized reeds with brass comments, all with an easy swing. After the first choruses, Strayhorn brings on Clooney with a one-bar fanfare, and she takes over the melody in a wordless vocal while the reeds seem to embellish her melodic line. Clooney's vocalizations are made up mainly of scat syllables ("boo," "baa," "bee"), but she is in perfect sync with Strayhorn's arrangement. As Friedwald says, "Clooney . . . displays a rare talent scarcely exhibited before or since as she turns in earthly sensual nonverbal vocalizations on 'Blue Rose.'"

Clooney obviously warmed to the task of reclaiming her musical chops after years of coasting. The album includes several small treasures, but perhaps chief among them is this unexpected link to Ellington's penchant for wordless vocals on "Blue Rose." If the novel melody and the wordless vocal of "Blue Rose" posed challenges for her, it never shows. Gratifying as it undoubtedly was for Ellington and Strayhorn in closing the continent-wide gap so smoothly, for Clooney, inspired by the arrangement and the melody, it was resuscitating. (The composition stands on its own as well; Ellington later recorded "Blue Rose" in an instrumental version with a small group from the band, as shown in the Playlist.) Clooney's inspiration resulted in a performance that can take its own honorable place in a distinguished line of Ellington vocalizations.

Because of the vagaries of pop stardom, her excursion with Ellington boded well for her long-term destiny. By the 1970s, she was singing exclusively jazz-oriented material on Concord Records, an enterprising California label, and taking a featured role in nightclubs and jazz festivals on both coasts. The fads and fancies of pop music had shifted, as they must to keep the pot boiling. "Botch-A-Me" and her other bubblegum hits were mercifully left behind.

### "A Composer's Dream"

If there is a singer whom Ellington revered more than Kay Davis it is Alice Babs, the Swedish soprano. "Alice Babs is a composer's dream," he wrote (*MiMM* 288), "for with her [the composer] can forget all the limitations and just write his heart out." They met in 1963, when Ellington was preparing for a televised concert in Stockholm and the producer asked him to listen to an album she had made. Ellington was immediately captivated by her soprano voice, seemingly effortless in all reaches of her great range. She joined his band for the television show and sang "Come Sunday" and "Take the 'A' Train." She was thirty-nine and a celebrity in Scandinavia. "By that time Alice had become the idol of a nation through radio, records and films," Frank Hedman (1987) says. "In the '40s she personified the swing era." To Ellington, in 1963, she was a revelation. "She sings lieder, she sings opera, she sings what we call jazz and blues, she sings like an instrument, she even yodels," he wrote. "No matter how hard the intervals, when you hand her the music, she sight-reads and sings it as though she had rehearsed it a month." In 1973, as her reputation spread abroad, she was invited to sing at the Newport Jazz Festival in the United States, and she agreed on the condition that she could perform with Ellington. "Baby, you're making me famous," he said.

Musically, their extraordinary rapport seemed preordained. Ellington loved Sweden and Swedish musicians from the moment he landed there. His first visit was April 1939, and he was greeted by bands everywhere he traveled, most unforgettably by a band on the sidewalk outside his hotel in Stockholm that woke him from his slumber on April 29, serenading him with "Happy Birthday." The entire nation, it seemed, congratulated him on turning forty. He repaid the compliment by rearranging an old composition called "Moody" and renaming it "Serenade to Sweden." Twenty-five years later, when he 'discovered' Babs, he hustled her off to Paris for a two-day recording session and made "Serenade to Sweden" a feature for her coloratura vocalization along with eight other tracks (and six more with words). He conferred on her the uncommon courtesy of releasing the album (on Reprise) as an "Alice Babs & Duke Ellington collaboration." Ellington's sumptuous melody on "Serenade for Sweden" exploits Babs's extraordinary range in one of the most striking wordless vocals in his canon.[15] Their final studio recording of it came about in New York following their 1973 Newport performance. It seems especially nuanced, despite (or perhaps because of) Ellington's fatigue from the health problems that were taking a toll on him at the time. On this occasion, Ellington plays his piano introduction and

---

15. My current research charts Ellington's adaptations of older minor compositions into brilliant showcases for special occasions called "Ellington's metamorphs." See <http://torontodukeellingtonsociety.com/wpcontent/uploads/2017/05/Jack-Chambers-2024_merge.pdf>. The metamorphosis of "Moody" into "Serenade for Sweden" is an example; two others, "The Star-Crossed Lovers" and "Isfahan" come up in chapter 6 ("The Lotus Eaters") and another, "Riba," comes up in chapter 10 ("A Final Masterpiece.") Some critics have viewed Ellington's reparation of older works as a kind of opportunism, but his ability in grooming them so impeccably for higher purposes is a unique, though unsung, gift.

embellishes her vocalization with a kind of deliberation that makes no secret of their mutual esteem.

By then, their musical alliance was well established. In 1968, Ellington conscripted her for his *Second Sacred Concert*. "There were a couple of things in that concert which required real musicianship, which had to be read and executed just as they were planned, and she was the one I had complete confidence in to do that," he said. The Sacred Concerts were augmented by two or three choirs, a tap dancer, additional brass and percussion in the orchestra, and four or five singers in addition to Babs, but the roles she was assigned still stood out from the assembled throng. Reviewer John S. Wilson wrote, "Her voice has the warm translucence of Johnny Hodges's saxophone, it shares the dark blues feeling of Russell Procope's clarinet, it is dazzling in a virtuosic duet with Ellington's electric piano and it is the stirring lead horn in the concert's concluding ensemble" (quoted by Hedman 1987).

One of the pieces that Ellington composed for her was the song "Heaven," which starts out hymnlike, with Babs accompanied by Ellington's piano in a litany of simple sentiments ("Heaven my dream / Heaven divine / Heaven supreme / Heaven combines / Every sweet and pretty thing"). Johnny Hodges takes over with two choruses accompanied by quiet sustained orchestral chords. Surprisingly, in this ecclesiastical setting, Ellington doubles the tempo and brings in Babs repeating the litany in a celebratory mood over a Latin vamp, and then closes with vocalization into the highest reaches of her incomparable range. The performance proved to be a show-stopper every time Babs sang it in the great cathedrals of Europe and the United States.

Most auspiciously, Babs's voice in the five-minute recording of "Heaven" from the Second Sacred Concert resounded throughout the Cathedral Church of St. John the Divine in New York on May 28, 1974, as Ellington's coffin was carried out with ten thousand mourners in its wake. "For the recessional," Stanley Dance reported, "very few of those present were left dry-eyed as Alice Babs and Johnny Hodges sang 'Heaven'" (1974a).

Her most striking performance at the Sacred Concerts is the wordless vocal on a composition called "T.T.G.T." Ellington offered a rationale for that odd title in the program notes. "'T.T.G.T.' means 'Too Good to Title,'" he wrote, "because it violates conformity in the same way, we like to think, that Jesus Christ did." And then he proceeds to explain how it "violates conformity" in purely musical terms, not theological. "The phrases never end on the note you think they will," he says. "It is a piece even instrumentalists have trouble with, but Alice Babs read it at sight."

"T.T.G.T" is Ellington's final excursion into wordless vocalization, and, as he implies, it is hard to imagine any other singer negotiating its vocal turns with such facility and grace. She is accompanied austerely by Ellington on electric piano; so austerely, in fact, that you might wonder if he is providing any cues for the startling octave leaps that take Babs into what must be close to the top of her range. She is also asked to sidle down the scale, and she does so with flawless control and apparent, but surely deceptive, ease. In her "performance guide" for "T.T.G.T.," Clark (2017, 78) notes, "The thin textured accompaniment does little to provide a sense of tonal security, [and] therefore, the performer should possess a strong sense of the unusually tuned intervals and phrase resolutions." Babs's recitation lasts two and a half minutes and, as Ellington promised in his program note, he leaves her very much to her own devices. Her vocal virtuosity is impeccable, but her technical mastery is never a distraction, here or elsewhere; it does not draw attention to itself. Instead, she harnesses it in the expression of longing, the spiritual striving, that is Ellington's purpose, and notwithstanding the vocal calisthenics, she conveys it with a gentle swing, a completely natural, unhurried rhythm.

Duke Ellington's nonpareil use of vocalization made its auspicious professional debut with Adelaide Hall's colorful line on "Creole Love Call." With "T.G.T.T," Ellington may have saved his consummation—what forty years earlier R. D. Darrell had called "the human voice in an instrumental technique"—for the last.

## Acknowledgment

Thanks to Steve Bowie for directing me to Lisa M. Clark's "performance guide to Duke Ellington's wordless melodies for soprano" (2017).

## Playlist

(Recordings cited in order of appearance in the chapter)

"Creole Love Call" 3:10 (comp Ellington/ Miley/ Jackson) "Blues I Love to Sing" 3:07
(Ellington/Miley) NY, October 26, 1927. *Early Ellington 1927–1934* (Brunswick CD [1989]) Bubber Miley, Louis Metcalf tp, Joe 'Tricky Sam' Nanton tb, Otto Hardwick, Rudy Jackson cl, Harry Carney reeds, DE p, Fred Guy banjo, Wellman Braud b, Sonny Greer d, Adelaide Hall voc. Solos: Hall, Miley, Jackson cl, Hall.

Alberta Prime, "Parlor Social De Luxe" 3:09 NYC, November 1924. *Mrs Clinkscales to the Cotton Club* (JSP Records, UK4CD [2005]). Duke Ellington p, Sonny Greer perc, voc, Alberta Hunter a.k.a. Alberta Prime voc.

"Oh, How I Love My Darling" 2:52 (Ellington, Jo Trent) New York, November 1924. Sonny and the Deacons *Duke Ellington Vol. 1 1924-1926 (Masters of Jazz* CD [1991] Fr.). Otto Hardwick Cm-sax, Duke Ellington p, George Francis bjo, Sonny Greer d, voc.

"Sloppy Joe" (Ellington, Bigard) 3:11 New York, January 16, 1929. *Jubilee Stomp* (Bluebird CD [1992]). Cootie Williams tp, Barney Bigard, cl, Otto Hardwick as, Duke Ellington p, Freddie Guy bjo, Wellman Braud b, Sonny Greer d, voc. Solos: Ellington, Greer (vocalese), Bigard, Williams.

"Creole Love Call" 5:42 Carnegie Hall, December 19, 1944. *The Carnegie Hall Concerts, December 1944* (Prestige 2CD [1991]). Taft Jordan, Cat Anderson, Shelton Hemphill, Francis Williams tp, Lawrence Brown, Claude Jones, Wilbur De Paris tb, Johnny Hodges, Otto Hardwick, Jimmy Hamilton, Al Sears, Harry Carney reeds, DE p, Fred Guy gtr, Junior Raglin b, Hillard Brown d. Kay Davis vocalese.

*FDR Memorial Broadcast.* New York, 400 Restaurant, April 14, 1945. Duke Ellington, *The Treasury Shows*, Vol. 1. Denmark: D.E.T.S. (2CD 2000).

"Diminuendo in Blue/Transblucency" 7:28 "Crescendo in Blue" 3:40 Carnegie Hall, January 4, 1946. *The Carnegie Hall Concerts, January 1946* (Prestige 2CD [1991]). Taft Jordan, Cat Anderson, Shelton Hemphill, Francis Williams tp, Lawrence Brown, Claude Jones, Wilbur De Paris tb, Johnny Hodges, Otto Hardwick, Jimmy Hamilton, Al Sears, Harry Carney reeds, DE p, Al Lucas gtr, Oscar Pettiford b, Sonny Greer d, Kay Davis voc on "Transblucency."

"Transblucency (A Blue Fog That You Can Almost See Through)" 2:58 (Duke Ellington, Lawrence Brown) Los Angeles, July 9, 1946. *Complete RCA Victor Mid-Forties Recordings* (RCA Victor 3CD [1999]). Shelton Hemphill, Taft Jordan, Francis Williams, Cat Anderson, Harold Baker, Ray Nance tp, Joe Nanton, Lawrence Brown, Claude Jones, Wilbur De Paris tb, Jimmy Hamilton, Russell Procope, Johnny Hodges, Al Sears, Harry Carney reeds, Duke Ellington p, Fred Guy gtr, Oscar Pettiford b, Sonny Greer d, Kay Davis voc. Solos: Brown, Hamilton, Davis.

"The Beautiful Indians—Minnehaha" 2:55 New York, December 5, 1946. *Sir Duke* (MCA Music Media CD [1994]). Shelton Hemphill, Taft Jordan, Cat Anderson, Harold Baker, Ray Nance tp, Claude Jones, Wilbur DeParis, Lawrence Brown tb, Jimmy Hamilton cl, ts, Russell Procope as, cl, Johnny Hodges as, Al Sears ts, Harry Carney bs, cl, bcl, Duke Ellington p, Oscar Pettiford b, Sonny Greer d. Solos: Kay Davis voc, Lawrence Brown.

"On A Turquoise Cloud" 3:22 (Ellington/Brown) NYC, December 22, 1947. *Complete Duke Ellington 1947-1952, Vol. 2* (CBS Fr CD [1989]). Ray Nance violin, Lawrence Brown, Tyree Glenn tb, Johnny Hodges as, Russell Procope, Jimmy Hamilton cl, Al Sears ts, Harry Carney bs, Duke Ellington p, Oscar Pettiford, Junior Raglin b, Sonny Greer d, Kay Davis voc. Solos: Davis, Hamilton, Brown.

"Creole Love Call" 2:56 September 1, 1949. *Complete Duke Ellington 1947-1952, Vol. 3* (CBS Fr CD [1989]). Harold Baker, Al Killian, Nelson Williams, Dave Burns, Ray Nance tp, Lawrence Brown, Quentin Jackson, Tyree Glenn tb, Johnny Hodges, Russell Procope, Jimmy Hamilton, Charlie Rouse, Jimmy Forrest, Harry Carney reeds, Duke Ellington p, Wendell Marshall b, Sonny Greer d. Kay Davis voc. Solos: Davis, Nance.

"Blue Rose" 2:21 NY, January 27, 1956 (band), February 23 or 27, 1956 (vocal). Rosemary Clooney and the Duke Ellington Orchestra, *Blue Rose* (Columbia CD [1999]). Willie Cook, Ray Nance, Clark Terry, Cat Anderson tp, Quentin Jackson, Britt Woodman, John Sanders tb, Johnny Hodges, Russell Procope, Jimmy Hamilton, Paul Gonsalves, Harry Carney reeds, Duke Ellington p, Jimmy Woode b, Sam Woodyard d, Rosemary Clooney voc, Ellington comp, Billy Strayhorn arr, dir. Solo: Rosemary Clooney.

"Blue Rose" 2:48 April 17, 1963. Duke Ellington, *Private Collection Vol. 4* (SABA CD 1987). Ray Nance cornet, Johnny Hodges as, Russell Procope as, Jimmy Hamilton cl, ts, Paul Gonsalves ts, Harry Carney bs, Duke Ellington p, Ernie Shepard b, Sam Woodyard d. Solos: Hodges, Nance.

"Serenade to Sweden" 3:10 Paris, France, March 1, 1963. Alice Babs & Duke Ellington, *Serenade to Sweden* (Reprise Records [Real Gone Music CD 2016]). Unknown four frh, unknown cl, Duke Ellington p, Gilbert Rovere b, Christian Garros d.

"Serenade to Sweden" 3:06 Alice Babs with Duke Ellington and His Orchestra. New York, July 3, 1973. *Faraway Star* (Bluebell CD [1987]). Money Johnson, Johnny Coles, Barry Lee Hall, Willie Cook, Mercer Ellington tp, Vince Prudente, Chuck Connors, Art Baron tb, Harold Minerve, Russell Procope, Harold Ashby, Percy Marion, Harry Carney reeds, Duke Ellington p, Joe Benjamin b, Quentin White Jr. d. Alice Babs voc.

"Heaven" 4:55, "T.T.G.T." 2:25 New York, Fine Studio, January 22, 1968. *Second Sacred Concert* (Prestige 1974, Fantasy CD [1990]). Large ensemble incl Ellington orchestra. Solos: "Heaven" Duke Ellington p, Alice Babs voc, Johnny Hodges as. "T.T.G.T." Duke Ellington el-p, Alice Babs voc.

Chapter 5

# Ellington's Music with Words

> When I joined his band I was just an ordinary singer of popular songs. Duke suggested I find a "character" and maintain it. What's more, [he] believes in taking a lot of time and trouble to find the right background for his singer. He always supplied me with the ideal accompaniment, the one which suited the "character" which I adopted.
> —IVIE ANDERSON (PAUL EDUARD MILLER 1942, 459)

Though Ellington is generally allotted space in serious discussions of American songwriting, it is probably safe to say that he has been undervalued for his contributions to the Great American Songbook. Alec Wilder, whose book *American Popular Song: The Great Innovators 1900–1950* defined the canon more than any other single publication, gives him short shrift. Wilder points out, correctly of course, that most of his songs "were composed as instrumental pieces to which words have been added and for which simplified releases have often been substituted" (1972, 412). He then spends four pages discussing a few of Ellington's songs in a grab-bag chapter at the end of the book in which Ellington appears alongside the likes of Fred Ahlert and Rube Bloom. A more judicious assessment came from Will Friedwald a few decades later. "It's one thing to place Ellington in the pantheon of jazz composers such as Jelly Roll Morton and Thelonious Monk; quite another (and just as right) to see him in the company of Jerome Kern, Irving Berlin, Cole Porter, George Gershwin, Richard Rodgers and Harold Arlen: the 'Big Six' theater-based writers whose work forms the cornerstone of 'The Great American Songbook'. . . . [Ellington] was the only major jazz composer who likewise was seen as a major pop songwriter" (2014, 230).

More than a maker of melody and sometimes (not always happily) a scrivener of lyrics, Ellington was also obviously a bandleader, a stage presence, and occasionally, a presenter of spectacles. The last two entries in this chapter discuss a Strayhorn song and an Ellington song (words and music) that are minimalist in accompaniment but perfect in pitch and execution. One has proved to be historically important and the other is one of the most exquisite presentations of a song in recorded history. It is not only the songs that shine, finely wrought though they are, but also the presentations, both stage-managed by Ellington, that make them a consummation of words and music. In discussing songs, their presentation sometimes intrudes. Music with words, on rare occasions, exists in the intersection of music and drama. Yeats's conundrum about the dancer and the dance works as well for the singer and the song—

> O body swayed to music, O brightening glance,
> How can we know the dancer from the dance?

Ellington became a songwriter out of necessity. A decade or so after he had his first successes as an arranger and composer of music, he came face-to-face with a culture change that by the middle of the twentieth century had virtually reduced music to "music with words," that is, to song. The omnipresence of song probably started with the great achievements of musical theater. In opera and operetta, words are necessarily attached to music when they are required to advance plot lines and develop characters. Musical comedy, a twentieth-century outgrowth of opera and operetta with less exalted settings and (usually) more earthy characters, gave rise to vernacular singing styles. The allure of "Broadway songs" gave rise to the popularity of Broadway singers, and then to movie star heroes who burst into song at odd moments. Dance bands began hiring singers, male and female, known in the Swing Era press as "crooners" and "thrushes." No teenagers hung a lithograph of Caruso on their bedroom walls, but a generation or two later, teenagers hung photos of Bing Crosby, Billy Eckstine, Sarah Vaughan, Julie London, and Frank Sinatra there. Singers became a growth industry, and with them, songs. Ellington had to go along with it, at least to some extent, and in the end, as we shall see, he proved to be very good at it.

The culture shift did not end there. As a result of the worldwide baby boom, adolescents became the global majority in the 1950s and '60s for the first time in history—some 40 percent in the developed nations—and there was a rush led mainly by American entrepreneurs to supply these free-spending, easygoing youngsters with the most accessible entertainments/

amusements/ diversions imaginable. Hence rock 'n' roll and its descendants. If anyone expected the kids to look for deeper thrills when they got older, few did, and probably even fewer as the generations passed by. It takes curiosity and maybe education to get kids to move on from kid stuff.

### "They Don't Hear Us. They Just Hear the Words."

The culture shift from music as a nonverbal art form to predominantly music-with-words was once much closer to consciousness than it is now. In 1950, a very popular movie, *Young Man with a Horn*, based on the bestselling novel by Dorothy Baker, used it as a plot point. The movie dramatizes the decline of a brilliant jazz trumpet player (Kirk Douglas, whose trumpet playing is dubbed by Harry James) as he finds his gifts wasted on the indifference of younger audiences. The trumpet player, Rick, is baffled and falls into dissolution helped along, in a well-established jazz movie motif, by *femmes fatales* and booze. At one point, his wise old piano player, Smoke (played by Hoagy Carmichael, an accomplished character actor as well as one of the finest songwriters of the twentieth century) sits Rick down in an attempt to straighten him out (the script is by Carl Foreman):

> **Rick:** Hey, Smoke. Hey, you know what we ought to do? We ought to make our own records. Make them the way we want. Boy, we could make records that'd really split them wide open. Make them sit up....
> **Smoke:** They won't buy them.
> **Rick:** Who won't?
> **Smoke:** People. You know who buys records? High school girls. You know why? To learn the words. They only buy the new songs to learn the words.
> **Rick:** I never thought of it that way.
> **Smoke:** Nobody knows what we're doing except us, the guys that do it. They don't hear us. They just hear the words. We could drop dead tomorrow, and nobody would know the difference.

The dialogue is prescient, coming at the moment in time when former big band singers like Doris Day, Peggy Lee, Ella Fitzgerald, and Frank Sinatra, along with small band singer Nat "King" Cole, had ascended as headliners in clubs and on records. The band singers, once allotted thirty or forty seconds on a three-minute big band recording, the same amount of time as the star trumpeter or saxophone player, had knocked their bosses—Les Brown,

Benny Goodman, Chick Webb, Tommy Dorsey, and the others—off their pedestals and grabbed the spotlight.

These lines from *Young Man with a Horn* were met with nods from millions of moviegoers. They had lived through the shift. In 1950, they might have thought it was a fad. They could not know that the "crooners and thrushes" were about to be knocked off their perch with three-chord harmonies and rudimentary rhythms tooled for their younger siblings—*sha-boom, sha-boom*—and that the rock 'n' rollers would be supplanted by the British Invasion—*luv-me-doos*—and so on in a continuous history of lavishly marketed, widely disseminated youth-oriented songs.[16]

Ellington, obviously, was well aware of the shift. When he arrived in England on his "cabaret" tour in 1948, he told a reporter, "I wanted to get back to Europe for a while. It's good for the morale. . . . Over there [in the US] you get too used to the Hit Parade. You know it means nothing, and yet after a while, you start paying attention. That's bad for your music" (Cohen 2010, 247). Unlike the fictional Smoke and his beleaguered protégé Rick, Ellington was not going to give in easily.

### Ivie Anderson Anoints a Generation

Hiring a singer was not Ellington's decision. On his first venture into the Midwest, he was booked to play a Chicago theater, trusting the band's New York success at the Cotton Club, and on his radio remotes, would attract audiences further afield. As Ellington remembered it, "The producer thought it would enhance our show if we were to add a girl singer" (*MiMM* 122; the term "girl singer" for female vocalists of all ages, now recognized as demeaning, was in everyday use by fans and musicians, singers included, for several decades). When the promoter chose Anderson over a more experienced competitor, Ellington was surprised, but he was also practical. "They were paying," he said, shrugging.

Sonny Greer remembered it differently. When the band arrived in Chicago, Anderson was working in Earl Hines's Grand Terrace Revue. Before that, she had worked as a dancer and singer at the Cotton Club when Ellington was leading the Washingtonians at the Kentucky Club. She toured with the musical revue *Shuffle Along*, a similar career path to Adelaide Hall. In Sonny Greer's recollection, he discovered her on his night out. "We were living in a

---

16. Rap is the most verbal pop music in history, words set not to melody but to rhythm. That is why it works as dialogue for Lin-Manuel Miranda's musical tragicomedy *Hamilton*, its greatest hit, and probably its most lasting.

hotel right next door to the Grand Terrace in Chicago, so I'm a cabaret man and I went next door and she was in a show there," Greer said (Nicholson 1999, 113–14). "I saw this girl, a cute brown-skinned girl. Really something, so the Duke say[s], 'What do you think of her?' I say, 'Man, that's the girl.'"

Ellington treated her at first as a work in progress. She was inclined toward multicolored gowns and Ellington told her she should wear only white onstage. His instinct was sound: she made a striking figure, erect and elegant, and numerous commentators remarked on the way she glowed in the spotlight. He waited almost seven months before recording her with the band. What convinced him about her talent was a kind of coup that grew out of a Cotton Club review. For eight weeks, his orchestra accompanied Ethel Waters, the biggest star of all African American singers and actors. Waters stopped the show night after night with her singing of "Stormy Weather," a melancholy love song written especially for her by Harold Arlen and Ted Koehler, in a stately arrangement by Ellington.

The show was the talk of the town, but the musicians were not exactly starstruck. One of the dancers, Cleo Hayes, said, "She was a very evil woman, Miss Waters. I was scared to death of her. Everybody stayed as far away from her as they could" (Gavin 2009, 119). Sonny Greer said, "Ethel Waters was very hard to get along with. . . . She didn't take no back-talk off nobody . . . You had to know how to handle her and stay a little ahead of her" (Nicholson 128). Ellington said nothing, of course but, soon after the show closed, Ellington and the orchestra made a nine-minute film for Paramount called *Bundle of Blues* and he gave prominent space to Ivie Anderson singing "Stormy Weather," using the arrangement he had crafted for Waters. Anderson's performance received enthusiastic notices. Greer, delighted, said, "I don't know who sang it the best, her or Ivie. Ivie picked it up and sang it beautiful."

Immediately after, the orchestra embarked for England on what turned out to be a triumphant inaugural tour in 1933. Anderson's performance of "Stormy Weather" at the London Palladium stopped the show every night. Ellington was exultant. "All the audience and management brass broke down crying and applauding," he says. "Tears streaming down her cheeks, Ivie did the most believable performance ever." And he added a subtle barb: "This was topping our eight weeks of playing 'Stormy Weather' at the Cotton Club for Ethel Waters" (*MiMM* 124).

Curiously, despite Anderson's star turn in *Bundle of Blues* and her showstopping performances all over England and France, Ellington left her out when he recorded "Stormy Weather." He played it as an instrumental, giving full value to his elaborate orchestration, with Lawrence Brown's lyrical trombone reciting the handsome ballad melody as Anderson's surrogate (in the Playlist). Stately though the instrumental version is, it seems uncharacteristically shortsighted of Ellington not to capitalize on Anderson's singing the dramatic lyric in a commercial recording. Anderson finally got her turn on "Stormy Weather" in Columbia Studios in Chicago in 1940, some six years after she put her imprint on the song. By then, she had made her intention clear about leaving the band, though it would actually be almost two more years before she would make the break. There were some consolations. The orchestra in 1940 was a formidable aggregation. Anderson's voice was hardy enough, despite the asthmatic condition that would force her into retirement in California, her home state. The recording session for "Stormy Weather" also gave her the opportunity to record, for the only time, two of Ellington's finest songs, "Solitude" and "Mood Indigo." Like "Stormy Weather," she had often sung them in concerts but had been denied the more permanent mementos of the recording studio. Strangely, the records she made in her years with Ellington are heavily weighted toward ephemeral pop material—"Happy as the Day Is Long," "Get Yourself a New Broom," "Raising the Rent," "Five O'Clock Whistle"—novelty songs, perhaps showing 1930s' charm, but none of them contenders for the Great American Songbook. The Chicago recording session belatedly makes it up to her with three songs—"Stormy Weather" by Arlen and Koehler, Ellington's "Solitude," and "Mood Indigo"—all firmly embedded in the Great American Songbook. It was a fitting valedictory for Ivie Anderson and an overdue one.

By the time Anderson took the spotlight in *Bundle of Blues*, she had already shown her mettle by scoring a hit with the Ellington orchestra one year earlier. After waiting seven months before she got a chance to make a record, it was an auspicious debut, perhaps worth waiting for, for it came on "It Don't Mean a Thing (If It Ain't Got That Swing)," a tune destined to be a perennial in Ellington's repertoire and standard fare for numerous bands, then and now. This classic jump tune is replete with hot instrumental moments, and Anderson's assertive vocal fits seamlessly among them. She opens the piece with a few syllables of vocalese ("Wot-dat-doo") over thumping bass, and then stands aside while Tricky Sam Nanton states an ebullient variation on the melody on his muted trombone. Ellington's lyric is made up largely of repetitions of the title (a personal mantra of Bubber Miley's, according to legend). Anderson's vocal is effectively punctuated by wah-wah brass, and the release provides her with a few more words to sing ("It makes no difference if it's sweet or hot / Give that rhythm everything you've got") before the title comes back again. Anderson's vocal turn lasts thirty-five seconds; the other two and a half minutes are given over to instrumental contributions over a rousing full-band orchestration. And in case anyone missed the point, the record ends with Anderson's final shout of the title.

That title was about to take on global resonance. By a stroke of luck, Anderson found herself conveying in words the sentiment that is expressed so articulately in the notes played by her bandmates. As Friedwald (2014, 234) puts it, "This song of 1932 christened an entire era of popular music: Swing."

Ivie Anderson was a band singer—a member of the band, a sound wave in the ensemble, a voice that Duke Ellington could bring to the fore for a chorus or two as he did with his instrumental voices. She filled the space he gave her with high spirits and, when the material was commensurate, a measure of dignity.

### Ivie Passes the Torch

Joya Sherrill was not Ivie Anderson's immediate successor as the band singer—that was Betty Roche, who was in the band from October 1942 until December 1943. Due to an odd convergence, Sherrill made a surprise debut with the band before Roche arrived, while Ivie Anderson was still the incumbent. At a Detroit concert, Ellington and Billy Strayhorn had agreed to audition a nineteen-year-old high-school girl backstage at the Paradise Theater in 1941. It was Joya Sherrill. With her mother at her side, she sang a pop song while Strayhorn accompanied her on the upright piano. The men were duly impressed, but then they were informed that her mother would not consider a singing career for her until she finished high school.

She made a second appearance as a schoolgirl the next year when Ellington persuaded her mother to let her join the band for the summer holidays after school ended. Anderson had announced that she would retire at the end of 1942 and settle in California, where she would spend her active retirement as proprietor of Ivie's Chicken Shack. So Sherrill, with her mother again at her side, joined the band in July at the Sherman Hotel in Chicago. "Ivie Anderson, I shall never forget, was still with the band," Sherrill said, recalling her harrowing debut: "[Ellington] called me to sing 'Mood Indigo' (it was Ivie's song), and she pulled me back before I walked out to sing, and said, 'Sing it *good*, or I'll come behind you and sing it too!' I was terrified" (*MiMM* 218).

By the time Sherrill graduated from high school in 1944 and joined the band full-time, Anderson was gone. Like Anderson, Sherrill struck it lucky with her very first recording. Although Marie Ellington and Kay Davis were also in the band, Ellington assigned the vocal of his newest song, "I'm

Beginning to See the Light," to Sherrill. It proved a perfect matchup of singer and song. The loose bouncy melody originated in a few bars that Johnny Hodges played in warm-ups. Together with the lyricist Don George and Ellington, the three of them developed those bars into a song. As it happened, RCA Victor, Ellington's label, was locked in a dispute with the American Federation of Musicians, the union that had imposed a recording ban. Ellington dispatched George to California in hopes of selling the song, and after some frustrating rejections (George 1981, 55–57), he scored with Harry James, who, in George's view, "led the top band in the country." (As a result, the credit line added another name—Ellington/Hodges/James and George.) James's record got noticed, and the song became the top hit in the country when it was recorded by Ella Fitzgerald and the Ink Spots.

By the time Ellington recorded it in 1945, the song was a year old and well known. Happily, it caught a second wave that kept it in the top ten songs for several months. It got that boost, George believes, from current events. "Near the end of the war, it became popular just as the blackout was lifted," he says. "The song was interpreted in many ways, including that in dreams or at the end of the road, there is sunlight and the brightness of the future."

Ellington's arrangement opens with the melody stated by a pair of saxophones, legato, almost sweet, before the band breaks into the easy dance tempo—the lyricist aptly calls it "walking tempo." After the infectious melody gets aired for a minute and a half, Sherrill chimes in with George's radiant imagery—

> I never cared much for moonlit skies
> I never wink back at fireflies
> But now that the stars are in your eyes
> I'm beginning to see the light

Ellington's biographer, Hasse (1993, 298), says, "Ellington, for a change, got lucky with lyrics." Sherrill profited the most. The picturesque imagery and the comfortable tempo brought out all her charms.

In the year and a half that she traveled with the band, Joya Sherrill was heard prominently on records and on Ellington's weekly Treasury radio broadcasts. Ellington entrusted the anthem called "The Blues" from *Black, Brown and Beige* to her when he got around to recording it in the studio (December 12, 1944), belatedly, after its well-publicized debut at Carnegie Hall (January 1943; at Carnegie Hall, it had been sung by Betty Roche). Because Sherrill's time with the band coincided with a songwriting binge by Ellington, she got to sing Ellington's melodies with the words supplied by a bewildering number of lyricists including Bob Russell, Don George (twice more), Harry Nemo, and Eddie DeLange, all of whom Ellington hired at one time or another. "He was lyrically promiscuous and noncommittal," Friedwald notes (2014, 243), "not wanting to settle down with any one songwriting partner." Friedwald's explanation for Ellington's curious recycling of lyricists is as convincing as any that has been offered: "One gets the feeling (sadly enough) that Ellington wanted to assert sole authorship over his catalogue, and therefore took preventative measures so that no partner could lay claim to any significant part of his songwriting canon."

After she left the band, Sherrill remained on Ellington's first-call list. In August 1963, when he assembled a stage troupe for *My People*, a two-hour commemoration as part of the "Century of Negro Progress" exhibition in Chicago marking the centennial of the Emancipation Proclamation, he recruited Sherrill as the principal vocalist. (Duke Ellington's score for *My People*, including Sherrill's vocals, is available on a Storyville CD.)

In 1965, Mercer Ellington produced a tribute album called *Joya Sherrill Sings Duke* that put the singer among some of her old colleagues and some new ones. One of the "new" ones is Cootie Williams, who was never in the band with Sherrill but was now back in it after a twenty-two-year absence. The highlight of the album, among many, is "Mood Indigo," in which Williams plays a very active muted trumpet all the way through, when Sherrill is singing and when she is not. As we have seen, this standard song, perhaps Ellington's best known, was the one Ellington chose for Sherrill when she auditioned as a teenager while Ivie Anderson glared at her from the wings. Ironically, Ellington recorded "Mood Indigo" frequently as an instrumental but seldom in its vocal version, and Sherrill never got to record it until this tribute album, twenty-odd years later.

"Mood Indigo" carries special resonance among Ellington's songs. Two years before Sherrill's recording of it, the reviewer of Ellington's 1963 concert in Madras, India, rhapsodized, "The all-time favorite 'Mood Indigo' was the mood of the century, purging the emotions in the classical manner through pitiful sounds, exalting its composer as the poet of the jazz world" (quoted in *MiMM* 316). Decades after her schoolgirl audition, Joya Sherrill sings the song in the richer contralto of her mature years. On other pieces on this tribute album, she occasionally ornaments the lyrics, but on "Mood Indigo" she sensibly leaves the ornamentation to Cootie Williams. It is an exquisite performance of Ellington's first hit song.

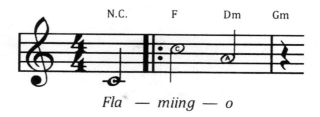

The Flamingo call (lyric by Ed Anderson, music by Ted Grouya).

### The Call of the Flamingo

Ellington had a pop hit in 1940 with Herb Jeffries's vocal interpretation of a strange song called "Flamingo" by little-known Ted Grouya. The handsome young Jeffries had already made some movies playing a singing cowboy known as the Bronze Buckaroo. "Flamingo" came into being at a moment when the Ellington orchestra was in top form, and Billy Strayhorn, who was beginning his second year as Ellington's associate composer/arranger, had settled comfortably into the multifaceted role he would fill for the rest of his days. These two convergences—the stellar musical aggregation and the fresh confidence of young Strayhorn—were not enough, on their own, to make "Flamingo" the flaming hit it became. The other factor, a more ineffable one, was the sophisticated taste of a generation of music lovers who had been reared on big band swing. Nothing else can explain the adulation for "Flamingo," a song with a cringeworthy vocal that was salvaged—nay, immortalized—by Strayhorn's stunning arrangement.

"Flamingo" opens with eerie iterations of the "flamingo call" (*flami-i-i-i-i-ingo*) sounded by Lawrence Brown on trombone, leading into a big band fanfare that brings on vocalist Jeffries with an entry worthy of Superman. The flamingo-call motif returns in many guises, including a vocalized variant by Jeffries ("aaah-ah-aaaah Flamingoooo"), an Ellington trademark cleverly integrated by Strayhorn.

The melody is then taken up by Lawrence Brown, muted, playing variants on the first *AA* parts, and Johnny Hodges on the bridge (*B*) before Jeffries returns and sings the final *A* chorus: "Flami-i-i-i-ingo / When the sun meets the sea / Say hello to my lover/ and hasten to me."

Walter van de Leur, in the preamble to his six-page analysis of the arrangement (2002, 38–43), says, "Setting out with this material, Strayhorn composed an arrangement that is a triumph of form and orchestration." John Lewis, distinguished composer/arranger for the Modern Jazz Quartet, first heard the record as a twenty-year-old music student at the University of New Mexico. "It sounded as if Stravinsky were a jazz musician," he said.

Herb Jeffries left the band in California in 1942, but the glow of his hit record never left him. For the rest of his days, he told fans that he was "delivered by a flamingo" instead of the proverbial stork. For a while, he ran a nightclub in Florida called the Flamingo Club. He reminisced endlessly about selling "a million records for Duke," but when he was interviewed by Dempsey Travis in 1994, he openly wondered why he had not been invited to Duke Ellington conferences and alumni reunions. Travis titled his interview "Ellington's Forgotten Flamingo," but Jeffries was not exactly forgotten as long as there were couples who had courted to the stately strains of his greatest hit. When Travis met him, he was a featured performer on a jazz cruise, where he belted out "Flamingo" at age eighty three, with a pickup band led by Mercer Ellington.

The success of "Flamingo" had two long-term consequences. First, Strayhorn's striking arrangement determined one aspect of his life's work with Ellington. "After that," Strayhorn said, "I inherited all the writing for vocalists, though not for those vocalese things he [Ellington] wrote for Kay Davis" (Coss 1962, 500). Second, Ellington took Jeffries's style as a template and all his successors in the band came with the same conservatory equipment he had brought with him: baritone solemnity, semiformal enunciation, strict breath control, sustaining notes on vowels only, and straight, impersonal interpretation. The style was a throwback to the first half of the twentieth century, contrary to the more intimate, modulated vernacular style that supplanted it. Year by year, Ellington's male singers came to sound more fussy and oldschool, not because they changed, but because they didn't.

### Ellington's Own Indigo Mood

Like his contemporaries among songwriters, Duke Ellington was not inclined to write songs that were in any sense confessional, at least not openly.[17] Ellington was expert at conveying emotions in music—ebullience in "Rockin'

---

17. It befell a much later generation to make confessional music such as "We Are Never Ever Getting Back Together" (2012: "I hate you," sings Taylor Swift), "Emotionless" (2018: Drake reveals paternity), and "Don't Hurt Yourself" (2016: Beyoncé's opening line to Jay-Z, "Who the fuck do you think you are?"). One obvious problem: only the songwriter can rightly sing the song—or maybe that's a blessing.

in Rhythm," charm in "Dancers in Love," melancholy in "Blue Light," and so on, all unmistakable in feeling. When words were attached, usually but not always by a second party (as in all his songs discussed so far except "It Don't Mean a Thing" and the songs in *My People*), the feelings became less distinct or more general, perhaps impersonal.

One composition by Ellington that always seemed to have its origins as a personal lament is "Solitude," which has the feel of a late-night *cri de coeur*. Ellington's hours of solitude took place between about 3 a.m. and 10 a.m., when the afterglow of the night's performance had dissipated and the last of the hangers-on finally left. These were his composing hours, and if dark moods invaded the music he was making, they were never seen, though they might be heard. Occasionally, he let his guard down. "Ellington has, like most entertainers, a stage self and a real self," said Richard Boyer in 1941 (217). "His usual manner is one of ambassadorial urbanity, but it is occasionally punctuated by deep despair. In explaining his moods, he says, '[I] can be too low to speak one minute and laughing fit to kill the next, and mean both.'" That melancholy strain was sometimes sensed by his intimate acquaintances. Rex Stewart, who traveled with the band for eleven years, wrote, "At various times I have been his barber, chef, valet, third trumpet man . . . and his poker opponent," but he had to admit, "From where I sit, Ellington fits the description of an iceberg: there's much more beneath the surface than above" (1972, 93). More provocatively, beautiful young Lena Horne said, "You could never get to know Duke Ellington. He was only about music," and then she added, "Well, you could get to know him carnally" (Gavin 2009, 95). Mercer Ellington recognized that his father's music was the barometer. "I know he spent many despondent hours," he said. "The only time he was off guard was in his music. . . . The way to name his various moods, or to tell how he felt from time to time, was to analyze the feeling exhibited in what he wrote at that particular time" (1978, 184). Generally, no one was around when the indigo moods engulfed him and the man disappeared into the solitude where the music came from.

His melancholy side became noticeably public in 1953, when his solos on *Piano Reflections* laid it bare. At the time, it came as a surprise to fans after more than twenty years of watching the genial man in the spotlight. Suddenly, unexpectedly, in *Piano Reflections* we were presented with spare, brooding meditations called "Retrospection," "Melancholia," and "Reflections in D."

His song "Solitude," composed in 1934, at a time when his mother's health was ebbing, is an early harbinger of those dark moods. It was not a state of mind that Ellington could easily reconcile. Boyer (1941, 234) cited Ellington's blatantly self-deceptive account of the song's origins:

> Someone asked him about "Solitude" and he said, "I wrote it in Chicago in twenty minutes while waiting for a recording date. The other band, the one ahead of us, was late coming out and I wrote it holding a sheet of music paper against a glass wall. When we went in, it was the first thing we made."

This mundane origin story hides the sorrow that listeners have empathized with in this song more than any other. Ellington was well aware of its evocative power. He goes on to recount its impact on the people in the studio that day:

> The sound engineer was half crying. It filled everybody up. To make people cry, that's music at its highest. My songs had a tendency in those days to be laments. There was always that melancholy in them. You look at the same melancholy again and again from a different perspective.

The emotive power of the music puts the lie to Ellington's story about its casual source. His tales about his songs are usually innocent fantasies, but this one seems offensive. Ellington's "Solitude" obviously springs from a darker animus, not from some momentary impulse in a studio hallway. The melancholy in "Solitude" became an atmospheric evocation in a poem by the Senegalese poet/statesman Léopold Sédar Senghor (quoted by Woideck 2017, 242):

> The impatient fit leaves me. Oh! the dull beat of rain on the leaves!
> Just play me your "Solitude," Duke, till I cry myself to sleep.

Ellington met Senghor on his only visit to Senegal in 1966, and their bond was immediate. As for Senghor, he had recognized the kindred feeling years earlier, in 1945, when he wrote the poem that saw his own anguish sublimated in Ellington's "Solitude."

Ellington recorded "Solitude" twice as an instrumental in 1934, and years later, as a piano solo (1941). Though the ornate colorings of that piano recitation would have fit uncomfortably among the later, less adorned and more revealing works on *Piano Reflections*, the melancholy is patent, and his improvised chorus deepens the feeling.

The melody is straightforward. The rise in the first two bars ("In my solitude") is reversed in the next two ("you haunt me"), conveying the letdown, plaintive and yearning. Though the melody was composed before the lyric, Ellington's opening bars perfectly reflect the words "In my *sol*itude," with the high note sustained on the stressed syllable. The lyric is written by Eddie De Lange, but Ellington's title and the perfect fit on its opening bars came first; De Lange was handed them as his starting point, and undoubtedly, other phrases as well. (Ellington was not a reluctant lyricist.) The conceit of the lyric is a kind of dreamscape with the singer bemused by despair over the departed lover; the singer is not bemoaning the loss but brooding on it. De Lange's lyric at the bridge gets downright prosaic, reportorial even, dominated by monosyllables, but it is saved from banality by the lovely lilt of the melody: "I sit in my chair / Filled with despair / No one could be so sad / With gloom everywhere / I sit and I stare / I know that I'll soon go mad."

Singers have found it inviting. Louis Armstrong recorded it first (1935), though for most of his career, he radiated a personality that seemed a stranger to solitude in any guise. Appel (2002, 126) notes that young "Armstrong would occasionally record a slow number in a clear lovely tenor voice (e.g., Ellington's 'Solitude')." Years later, Armstrong and Ellington recorded "Solitude" the only time they were in a studio (1961), and they ignored its melancholy altogether. Celebratory solitude, so to speak. It has been a staple on most of the Ellington songbook compilations—Ella Fitzgerald, Nina Simone, Sathima Bea Benjamin, and Sarah Vaughan all included it. None of them captures the late-night despair that hangs over the instrumental version.

Will Friedwald provides an antidote in his discussion of Ellington as "the accidental songwriter." Discussing "Solitude," he writes:

> To me, it will always be a signature of Billie Holiday, who recorded it at least three times (not counting live versions), most definitively in 1947. She makes it even more haunting by concluding on the sixth degree of the scale, rather than the third, as written by Ellington. More than anyone else, she conveys the blue feeling of abject loneliness—as if it were not 32 bars but a hundred years of "Solitude." (2014, 236)

Holiday's singing always carried the impression of one who has taken knocks and gotten back up. In her final years, when her range narrowed and her notes sometimes grew creaky, that impression of toughing it out could sell her songs pretty much on its own. Before that, she both conveyed the melancholy and held the pitch. Holiday's critic/biographer Robert O'Meally notes that her recording of "Solitude" came in the second great period of her career, ushered in by "Strange Fruit," the gritty lament about the macabre lynchings of African Americans in the Deep South. The period is marked by "declamatory songs in which Holiday the dramatist and poet comes boldly forward working roots and magic" (O'Meally 1991, 141–42). "Solitude" is hardly declamatory, but it certainly offers scope for the dramatist and poet and the opportunity to work magic. The band included pianist Bobby Tucker, perhaps the singer's favorite accompanist, and a roster of skilled veterans. It was a setting calculated to give Holiday complete freedom for evoking the feeling in Ellington's melody. "She was a thoroughly seasoned artist," O'Meally says (152), "very much in control of her powers and possibilities."

Early and late in her career, she felt the meaning of the words she was singing with a kind of authenticity that her more florid contemporaries missed. Singing "Solitude," Holiday gives more than full value to the words "haunt" and "taunt" in the first verse, stretching the vowels to the point where you fear she might not make the next note. She does it again in the final verse, sustaining "my" in "*my* solitude," making it acutely personal, and then refusing to let the despair drift away. She ends the song (as Friedwald says) on a note that suggests it is not over.

Holiday's performance gives full value to Ellington's moody music. In her delivery and more tellingly in her intonation, she sees through De Lange's words and sings the song the music conveys.

### Two Luminous Performances—One Spotlit, One Unlit

As living memories of Duke Ellington fade, we have his music in unimaginable abundance, but his role as a showcaser of great talents is seldom celebrated. He had an instinct for devising contexts that could set off a performance like a gemstone on velvet. Thankfully, some of those performances have been preserved. Two of them are vocal performances. Difficult though it may be to know the singer from the song, one of them showcases a brilliant song, and the other showcases brilliant singing.

### Premiere of a Masterpiece

When twenty-three-year-old Billy Strayhorn auditioned for Duke Ellington backstage in Pittsburgh, he played several pieces on the piano, and then, at Ellington's urging, sang a couple of his own songs. One of the songs was "Something to Live For," and Strayhorn earned something close to instant gratification from it. Ellington recorded it in March 1939, soon after Strayhorn took the "A" train to Harlem and became a permanent member of his entourage. Strayhorn sang another song at the audition as well. "I asked him the name of a tune he'd played for me, and he just laughed," Ellington said. "I caught that laugh. It was the laugh that first got me" (Hajdu 1996, 51). The laugh was presumably an embarrassed giggle because Strayhorn had not yet gotten around to naming his song, even though he had been working on it, he said, since his high school days. Was it the laugh that Ellington found endearing rather than the song? It was "something visceral," Strayhorn's biographer, David Hajdu, says, and it helped to keep young Strayhorn in Ellington's mind as he went about his busy schedule. In the fullness of time, almost a year after that meeting, he phoned Strayhorn and told him to make his way to Harlem for what turned into a lifelong commitment as Ellington's associate composer/arranger.

What Ellington thought of the second song is not clear. Unlike "Something to Live For," the untitled song never became part of Ellington's repertoire. It was played only twice at Ellington's performances in Strayhorn's lifetime, as far as we know, and never in a recording studio. The reason for Ellington's relative neglect is hard to fathom. The song was eventually titled "Lush Life," and it is Strayhorn's most celebrated song. It is a perennial favorite of singers and a notable entry in what is known as the Great American Songbook.

For many years, Strayhorn must have assumed that "Lush Life" had no future at all—that it would be found some day among the stash of unrecorded materials—in the "hundreds of handwritten scores that are safely stored in various music collections" (as Walter van de Leur noted, in his annotation for a collection of posthumous arrangements in 1996). Indeed, one of those handwritten scores was an instrumental version of "Lush Life" called "Lonely Again"; it was retrieved and recorded by the Dutch Jazz Orchestra in 1997 (in the Playlist). Van de Leur writes, "This is one of two arrangements that Strayhorn wrote the very day after he first met Duke Ellington, December 1938," and he adds, "Strayhorn arranged the work at Ellington's request, who was deeply impressed with the song and its lyrics." The hard evidence belies van de Leur's claim that Ellington was impressed. Ellington never played that arrangement, or any other. On the two occasions that he admitted "Lush Life" into the nightly repertoire, years later and years apart, it was sung with piano accompaniment—that is, in a minimal arrangement. The second came about in a New York nightclub, Basin Street East, in 1964, when Ellington unexpectedly cleared the stage and asked Strayhorn, in a gay, late-night mood, to accompany himself on his most famous song. But the first of those performances was the kind of spectacle that illuminated Ellington's flair for the dramatic and guaranteed that "Lush Life" would find the audience it deserved.

"Lush Life" became justly celebrated in Strayhorn's lifetime and remains to this day a much lauded and widely recorded song. Its premier performance was framed by Ellington in an illustrious setting and a dramatic tableau.

From that beginning, the song found its own way, as Ellington surely knew it would. He gave it its start and left its ascendancy to others. Perhaps he thought it too personal for a regular place in his nightly repertoire. "Lush Life" is the pained outcry of an abject romantic with a broken heart who seeks solace in "jazz and cocktails." As a product of Strayhorn's adolescence, it seems incongruously precocious, though no one has ever disputed it. "Friends recall him singing parts of it *a cappella* as early as 1933, when the composer would have been 17 or perhaps had just turned 18," according to Gioia (2012, 272). Its maturity shows not only in its Debussy-like harmonies and creative manipulation of the song form, but even more so in its lyrical allusions to "jazz and cocktails" and "weeks in Paris," literal reflections of the life Strayhorn led *after* leaving behind the steel mills of Pittsburgh.

If Ellington's decade-long wait before giving it its debut seemed in retrospect overlong, the outcome could hardly have been more propitious. The setting was Carnegie Hall, and the occasion was the sixth (and last) of the near-annual concerts by Duke Ellington and His Orchestra in the concert hall that was, in those years, the citadel of serious music in the United States. (Its stature was celebrated in the hoary old musicians' joke—*Tourist*: How do you get to Carnegie Hall? *Musician*: Practice, man, practice.) Ellington's Carnegie concerts from 1943 to 1948 were black-tie affairs attended by governors, mayors, sophisticates in evening gowns and tuxedos, musicians, music lovers, and music journalists from the major dailies and several weeklies. As Ellington said, "Our series there had helped to establish a music that was new in both its extended forms and its social significance" (*MiMM* 190).

At the 1948 concert, Ellington opened the second half with an extended version of Billy Strayhorn's "Take the 'A' Train," and then, as the applause subsided, the lights went down and a pencil-thin spotlight isolated the grand piano, recently vacated by Ellington. The sense of occasion was heightened by Ellington's minute-long introduction:

> And now I'd like to introduce the—our writing and arranging companion, who we've been so much indebted to for quite a period for contributing so much of the high—so many of the high spots of our performances, particularly in the writing. I'd like to at this time present Billy Strayhorn. [Applause] And now—have a seat there, Billy. Of course you know Billy Strayhorn wrote our radio theme "Take the 'A' Train." And now the purpose of course of him appearing on tonight's program, which is an extra little added thought—I should say—is that I'd like for him to play for Kay Davis to introduce a new tune of his called "Lush Life." [A pause, and he announces] Kay Davis!!

"A new tune" it is not, of course, at least not to Strayhorn or Ellington, though it is to everyone else.[18] Strayhorn vamps and brings on Kay Davis in a red satin gown to a microphone placed in the crook of the grand piano. Erect and dignified, she sings the seven-part lyric in her precise diction, while Strayhorn complements the sentiments. He actively embellishes the first two eight-bar verses ("I used to visit all the very gay places . . .") but in the final verses, as the mood darkens ("Life is lonely again"), he leaves telling spaces. Davis's bell-clear diction gives full value to Strayhorn's lyric. After a rhapsodic sixteen-bar piano interval, Davis sings the final two verses, the first seemingly relieving the anguish ("A week in Paris will ease the bite of it"), but the second retreating into bleak prospects ("I'll live a lush life in some small dive").

It is a highly dramatic reading, delivered with great clarity by Davis and sympathetically modulated by the piano player. It met with tumultuous applause and with Ellington calling the soloists to take a bow: "Kay Davis! Billy Strayhorn!" and repeating their names ten seconds later for another bow.

Nat "King" Cole was in the audience that night with his wife, Ellington's former singer and Kay Davis's former colleague, Marie Ellington. Four months after the Carnegie premiere, in March 1949, Cole recorded "Lush Life" for Capitol Records. Either he or more likely his producer had failed to grasp that its minimalism was one of the essential strengths of the Carnegie Hall performance. Cole's version had a busy orchestration by Pete Rugolo, Capitol's jazz producer and, tellingly, former chief arranger for Stan Kenton's brassy big band. Cole's version never found a niche among his signature tunes, but his record received enough air play to bring the song to the attention of other musicians and singers. "Lush Life" has since been sung thousands of times.

It received a radiant start when Kay Davis stood tall in the spotlight with the proud composer guiding her through an incomparably articulate reading. The public debut took place before a discerning audience at a concert that received national coverage. Its time had come.

### Blinding Light in a Dark Studio

In 1958, Duke Ellington recorded an album called *Black, Brown and Beige*. That title was already famous in the Ellington annals from his forty-five-minute suite that premiered with great publicity at Carnegie Hall in 1943, his inaugural performance at that fabled site. The 1958 recording with the

---

18. Legalistically, it was indeed a "new tune." Notwithstanding the song's ten- or fifteen-year prehistory, it is ©1949 by Ellington's Tempo publishing company.

same name was a mere shadow of the original, taking two of its many themes and making arrangements tailored to the musicians then in the band—one of Ellington's greatest bands though only three musicians remained from the Carnegie Hall crew fifteen years earlier. (In 1958, when this record was released, not everyone knew that it was not really the whole suite because the 1943 Carnegie Hall performance had not yet been issued publicly.)

The reason Ellington chose that venerable title for the pared-down revival was because the new version made prominent use of his gospel-influenced song "Come Sunday," which had its origins in the *Black* movement of *Black, Brown and Beige*. For Ellington, "Come Sunday" was an inevitable choice. The great gospel diva Mahalia Jackson consented to make a record with Ellington, and Ellington was well aware that Jackson refused to sing secular music. "Come Sunday," obviously, would be acceptable to her. Ellington's Sacred Concerts would eventually provide other music that she might have found acceptable, but they were still to come; indeed, they took their impetus from this recording, when the rectors of Grace Cathedral in San Francisco invited Ellington to prepare a concert of sacred music modeled on his recording with Jackson. The Sacred Concerts had their beginning in 1965, but in 1958, "Come Sunday" was all he could offer.

Mahalia Jackson (1911–1972) was born in New Orleans and raised there until age eleven, when her family moved to Chicago. Her father worked as a dock laborer by day, a barber by night, and a Baptist preacher on Sundays. Though secular music was strictly forbidden in her household, Jackson confessed in her autobiography that she heard plenty of it growing up in New Orleans. "I heard all the marching brass bands, the showboat music on the Mississippi, the great jazz orchestras of King Oliver, Louis Armstrong, and Jelly Roll Morton, and learned to love their powerful beat," she said. "But I loved to sing all the more in the choir of our hard-shell Baptist church" (1969). Her familiarity with jazz and blues comes as no surprise to those who know her music. Jackson's singing voice is widely recognized as one of the most magnificent instruments of all time for its great range, perfect pitch, and heartfelt ardor, but it also excels in its easy swing and dramatic sense, elements that cross over impeccably into the forbidden jazz range. Willie "the Lion" Smith recalls a very direct influence on Jackson from the blues diva, Bessie Smith. "As much as she [Bessie Smith] roared, drank and dissipated, she was always considered to be a devout religious woman—truly one of God's children," he says, and then he delivers the punchline. "Our great gospel singer of today, Mahalia Jackson, stood outside a New Orleans theater to listen to Bessie and derived a great deal of her inspiration from what she heard" (1964, 29). Unlikely as it seems, Jackson's delivery, though pitch-perfect and more disciplined than Bessie Smith's, carries similar punch and, on occasion, grit.

Despite her refusal to sing secular music, she enthralled musicians in every genre, especially singers. Her talent, Jackson said, was God-given. Many listeners conceded that it was miraculous. The singer Carol Sloane recalled a mythical night at the Newport Jazz Festival: "I was there the night Mahalia Jackson sang 'Didn't It Rain.' We'd been sitting there for hours waiting for her to come on. We all had umbrellas. She came out and sang, 'Didn't it rain, children,' and it stopped raining. We couldn't believe it" (Enstice 2004, 311). At the March on Washington in August 1963, when Dr. Martin Luther King enthralled 250,000 civil rights advocates and a global television audience with his sermon "I Have a Dream," King himself credited Mahalia Jackson, who had sung two hymns before he took the microphone. In a letter he sent her in 1964, he said, "When I got up to speak, I was already happy. I couldn't help preaching. Millions of people all over this country said it was my greatest hour . . . but if it was, you, more than any single person, made it so" (Chang 2021).

Jackson's lifelong prohibition on jazz somehow overlooked Duke Ellington. Long before they were collaborators in the Columbia studio, they were drawn together by their mutual attraction to the Old Testament. When a Columbia executive took Ellington aside to boast about a sensational singer they had just signed, Ellington replied, "Oh yeah, she's a good cook," and then he explained, "I had been to her house several times before she signed with Columbia, and she always had fine soul food out there" (*MiMM* 255–56). Mercer Ellington (1978, 184) says that Jackson, "knowing [Ellington's] feeling for sacred music," asked Duke if he would produce her records. He turned her down, but in the most salubrious terms; he said he couldn't "because he thought it wrong to profit from the church," and her admiration for him soared.

When they became label-mates, the Columbia executives saw a chance of merging their talents in hopes of a crossover, as they had done a few years earlier with Rosemary Clooney. Ellington was eager, of course, but he knew that he had to tread lightly if it was to come to fruition. He would prepare "Come Sunday" for her, and when he thought about filling out the slate, he reckoned she could hardly object to an arrangement of the 23rd Psalm ("The Lord is my shepherd / I shall not want"). The rest of the album would be instrumental. For that, he revived the most memorable melody from *Black, Brown and Beige*, "Work Song," and arranged it for the orchestra, along with an orchestral version of "Come Sunday" featuring Ray Nance on violin. For the remaining seven minutes of the thirty-six-minute LP, he made the strange choice of melding the themes of "Work Song" and "Come Sunday" into an instrumental feature. The resulting album is melodically frugal (three melodies in six tracks identified not by their titles, which would make the frugality plain, but abstrusely as Parts I–VI). It is also instrumentally narrow, with features for a violin, a trumpet, and one incomparable voice. When this austere *Black, Brown and Beige* was released, critical reaction was polite. Coming between the Shakespeare suite (*Such Sweet Thunder*) and the soundtrack/suite *Anatomy of a Murder* in a period of peak creativity, it was a bit of a letdown.

Its greatest moment took forty-one years to surface, in 1999, when the complete studio sessions with alternate takes were released along with the original tracks. Attentive fans had known for years that Ellington had treated Jackson with utmost reverence. His Columbia producer, Irving Townsend, in a journal article published in England in 1960, talked about his work for Ellington in this peak period, and in the paragraph on *Black, Brown and Beige,* he wrote, "Records made in one take are rare . . . and rarer for Ellington. One I remember particularly is the *Come Sunday* section of *Black, Brown and Beige,* sung by Mahalia Jackson. Duke treated this first performance like a kind of divine revelation and would not let Mahalia repeat it until the next day." With the release of the complete record session in 1999, we now know that the master take, the one Townsend refers to, was actually the second take. It had been preceded by an incomplete take when Jackson coughed partway through it. We also know that Ellington's insistence on having her wait a day to record it again was an elaborate ruse. He already had the complete take on the first day, the first full performance, and he knew that it was a master take. It was released on the original LP, and listening to it, as generations have now done, it is known to be flawless: cleanly played, the musicians reverential in the background, Mahalia in resplendent voice in the foreground, including a nonverbal final chorus that intensifies the feeling. As Townsend says in the original liner notes, "[S]he hums an extra chorus as if she were aware of the power of her performance and wanted it to linger a moment more" (1958, 11).

With the master take in the can, Ellington still had Mahalia Jackson booked for another day in the studio. It was not an opportunity he was going to waste. Townsend, in his 1960 reminiscence, reveals what happened the next day: "He asked her to sing it not for records but for him. She sang the never used Take 2 of *Come Sunday* the following afternoon without a light in the studio and without a sound from the band." Jackson's magnificent performance on that second day, finally made public in 1999, captures her singing "Come Sunday" *a cappella* except for occasional prompts from Ellington's piano. On the CD, this alternate take is preceded by a short (seven-second) exclamation that captures Jackson's reaction when Ellington asks her to sing "Come Sunday" *a cappella*. That was challenging enough, but after she grudgingly assents, Ellington turns out the studio lights. "Ooh!" she bellows, "you fix the lights too!" and then she mutters, almost inaudibly, "Cheezus!"

Any qualms she might have had about undertaking an *a cappella* recital in the blue glow of the ON AIR sign obviously dissipated before she sang the first note. Ellington plays a four-bar introduction to lead her in and then leaves her on her own. "Lordy Lord of love / God almighty," she sings, sounding this opening invocation with full voice, and then more tenderly, "Please look down and see my people through." She invests every phrase, every word, with piety, conscious that she is delivering a message of great consolation. When she finishes the first complete cycle (*AABA*), Ellington returns on piano and coaxes her gently into the next verses: "Lilies of the valley / They neither toil nor spin / And flowers bloom in spring / And birdies sing." After she completes the verse, she hums a wordless chorus in quiet ecstasy, as if easing herself and her rapt listeners back down to earth.

It is a stunning performance. Is it a hymn? Though both Jackson and Ellington shared a kind of fundamental Protestantism, the song is a paean to no one's god unless "Lord, dear Lord of love" comes to be venerated by a new schism. Is it gospel music? Not canonically, though its image of the "lilies of the field" is an allusion to the Gospel of Matthew (6:28). Is it a pop song? Not really, though it uses the prototypical *AABA* structure of Broadway and pop songs. Is it an aria? Hmm, not really, though the control of vibrato and the flawless range would ennoble any opera, and the depth of passion and longing it expresses would surely evoke bravos at La Scala. Is it jazz? Probably not, though it is a spontaneous creation, unscripted, and discovered note by note from start to finish.

It is, to borrow Duke Ellington's favorite maxim, beyond category. Undeniably, some kind of divine rapport came into play. Mahalia Jackson later said, "He didn't rehearse me nothin'. He said, 'Just open the Bible and sing!'"

## From the Top

It is worthwhile to hearken back to where we started—to R. D. Darrell's prescient critique of Ellington's music in 1935, decades before the magic moment with Mahalia Jackson took place or most of the other gems involving wordless vocalizations and sung lyrics. "To me again there is absolutely nothing in popular music, all too little in any music, that touches the uncannily twisted beauty, the acrid pungence of nostalgia which Ellington in his great moments achieves," Darrell wrote. "He has given us and I am confident will give us again more than a few moments of the purest, the most sensitive and ineluctable revelation of feeling in music today."

A few of the "great moments" that Darrell anticipated came when singers were involved, as we have seen, and among these surely "the purest, the most sensitive and ineluctable revelation of feeling" came on this "private" take of "Come Sunday" with Mahalia Jackson. *Primus inter pares*, it is the culmination among many other high points by the likes of Adelaide Hall, Ivie Anderson, Kay Davis, Joya Sherill, Rosemary Clooney, Alice Babs, and others. On rare occasions, Ellington must have known, and even Darrell would perhaps have conceded, when all the elements come together in a kind of perfection, the human voice singing ordinary words can plumb the deepest roots of our esthetic faculties.

## Playlist

(Recordings cited in order of appearance in the chapter)

"Stormy Weather" 3:02 (instrumental) New York, May 16, 1933. *Classics 1933* CD (1992). Cootie Williams, Arthur Whetsol, Freddie Jenkins tp, Lawrence Brown, Juan Tizol Joe Nanton tb, Barney Bigard cl, ts, Johnny Hodges as, Otto Hardwick as, Harry Carney bs, Duke Ellington p, Fred Guy gtr, Wellman Braud b, Sonny Greer d. Solo: Lawrence Brown.

"Stormy Weather" 2:30, "Solitude" 2:55, "Mood Indigo" 2:40. New York, February 13, 1940. Ivie Anderson, *With the Duke and Beyond* (Jasmine CD [1999]). Wallace Jones, Ray Nance, Rex Stewart tp, Lawrence Brown, Juan Tizol, Joe Nanton tb, Barney Bigard, Johnny Hodges, Otto Hardwick, Ben Webster, Harry Carney reeds, Duke Ellington p, Fred Guy gtr, Jimmie Blanton b, Sonny Greer d, Ivie Anderson voc. Solo: Ivie Anderson voc.

"It Don't Mean a Thing (If It Ain't Got That Swing)" 3:14 February 2, 1932. *Duke Ellington, Original Masters (1932–1939)*. (Sony/BMG 4CD [2008]). Cootie Williams, Freddie Jenkins, Arthur Whetsol tp, Lawrence Brown, Juan Tizol, Joe Nanton tb, Barney Bigard, Johnny Hodges, Harry Carney reeds, Duke Ellington p, Fred Guy gtr, Wellman Braud b, Sonny Greer d, Ivie Anderson voc. Solos: Nanton, Anderson voc, Carney bs, Bigard cl, Hodges, Anderson.

"I'm Beginning to See the Light" 3:09 (Don George/Duke Ellington/Harry James/Johnny Hodges) December 1, 1944. *Complete RCA Victor Mid-Forties Recordings* (RCA Victor 3CD [1999]). Shelton Hemphill, Taft Jordan, Cat Anderson, Ray Nance tp, Joe Nanton, Lawrence Brown, Claude Jones tb, Jimmy Hamilton, Otto Hardwick, Johnny Hodges, Al Sears, Harry Carney reeds, Duke Ellington p, Fred Guy gtr, Alvin "Junior" Raglin b, Sonny Greer d, Joya Sherrill voc.

"The Blues Ain't" 5:50, "What Color Is Virtue" 2:50 Chicago, August 20–21, 1963. *My People: The Complete Show* (Storyville 1018430 CD [2012]). Large orchestra. Solos: "The Blues Ain't" Harold Ashby ts, Joya Sherrill voc. "What Color Is Virtue" Joya Sherrill, the Irving Bunton Singers.

"Mood Indigo" 2:17 (Ellington/Bigard/Mitchell Parish) Chicago, January 12, 1965. *Joya Sherrill Sings Duke* (Verve CD [1999]) Cootie Williams tp, Johnny Hodges as, Ernie Harper p, John Lamb b, Sam Woodyard d, Joya Sherrill voc. Mercer Ellington producer.

"Flamingo" 3:22 (Grouya/Anderson) Chicago, December 28, 1940. *The Blanton–Webster Band* (RCA 3CD [1986]). Wallace Jones, Rex Stewart, Ray Nance tp, Joe Nanton, Lawrence Brown, Juan Tizol tb, Barney Bigard cl, Johnny Hodges as, Otto Hardwick as, Ben Webster ts, Harry Carney bs, Ellington p, Fred Guy g, Jimmie Blanton b, Sonny Greer d, Herb Jeffries voc. Billy Strayhorn arr.

"Solitude" (instrumental) Chicago, January 10, 1934. Cootie Williams, Freddie Jenkins, Arthur Whetsol tp, Lawrence Brown, Joe Nanton tb, Barney Bigard, Johnny Hodges, Harry Carney reeds, Duke Ellington p, Fred Guy gtr, Wellman Braud b, Sonny Greer d.

"Solitude" (instrumental) September 12, 1934. Same as above but add Juan Tizol tb.

"Solitude" (piano solo) New York, May 14, 1941. Duke Ellington p.

Billie Holiday "Solitude" 3:12 (Ellington/De Lange) February 13, 1947. Billie Holiday, *The Complete Decca Recordings* (Decca 2CD [1991]). Billy Butterfield tp, Bill Stegmeyer cl, as, Toots Mondello, Al Klink as, Hank Ross, Art Drellinger ts, Bobby Tucker p, Dan Perry gtr, Bob Haggart b, Norris Shawker d, Billie Holiday voc, Bob Haggart arr,

Dutch Jazz Orchestra, "Lonely Again" 4:23 (a.k.a "Lush Life," Strayhorn comp/arr 1938) Hiversum, The Netherlands, October 13–17 , 1997. *So This Is Love: More Newly Discovered Works of Billy Strayhorn*. (Challenge Records [2002].) Jerry van Rooyen cond, Walter van de Leur researcher. Solos: John Ruocco cl, Jan Oosthof tp.

"Lush Life" 3:31 (Strayhorn) Basin Street East, New York City, January 14, 1964. Strayhorn piano and vocal. Billy Strayhorn, *Lush Life* (Red Baron CD [1992]).

"Lush Life" 6.33 (1:03 spoken introduction by Ellington) *Carnegie Hall, November 13, 1948*. (Vintage Jazz Classics [1991]). Reeds (Johnny Hodges, Ben Webster, Al Sears, Jimmy Hamilton, Harry Carney, [probably Russell Procope]), and rhythm (Strayhorn p, Fred Guy gtr, Wendell Marshall b, Sonny Greer d) are heard on last chorus. Solos: Kay Davis voc, Strayhorn p.

"Come Sunday" 3:46. New York, February 11, 1958. *Black, Brown and Beige* (Columbia CD [1999]). Cat Anderson, Harold Baker, Clark Terry tp, Ray Nance tp, vln, Britt Woodman, John Sanders, Quentin Jackson tb, Jimmy Hamilton cl, Bill Graham as, Russell Procope cl, as, Paul Gonsalves ts, Harry Carney bs, Duke Ellington p, Jimmy Woode b, Sam Woodyard d. Mahalia Jackson voc.

"Come Sunday" (*a cappella*) 5:47. New York, February 12, 1958. *Black, Brown and Beige* (Columbia CD [1999]). Mahalia Jackson voc, Duke Ellington p.

Interlude 2

# Musicians' Impressions of Duke Ellington

## Years and Genres Apart

The three greatest composers in the history of music are J. S. Bach, Frederick Delius and Duke Ellington.
—PERCY GRAINGER (1882–1961), TO HIS COMPOSITION CLASS AT COLUMBIA UNIVERSITY, 1932

Only in Harlem could I find the music that I craved. Duke Ellington and Fletcher Henderson were playing in the Don Redman style, but the Duke especially was going much further. His arrangements had a color that no one else approached and he was doing jazz a real service in transforming the ugly picture that some people had of it into beautiful fantasies.
—HOAGY CARMICHAEL (1899–1981) SONGWRITER, PIANO PLAYER, AND ACTOR, REMEMBERING THE COTTON CLUB, 1930

The best records of Duke Ellington . . . can be listened to again and again because they are not just decorations of a familiar shape but a new arrangement of shapes. Ellington, in fact, is a real composer, the first jazz composer of distinction.
—CONSTANT LAMBERT (1905–1951), ENGLISH COMPOSER, 1934

Stan Kenton can stand in front of a thousand fiddles and a thousand brass and make a dramatic gesture, and every studio arranger can nod his head and say, "Oh, yes, that's done like this." But Duke merely lifts a finger, three horns make a sound, and I don't know what it is!
—ANDRE PREVIN (1929-2019), PIANIST, COMPOSER, AND CONDUCTOR, 1950

I think all the musicians in jazz should get together on a certain day and get down and their knees to thank Duke.
—MILES DAVIS (1926-1991), TRUMPETER AND BANDLEADER, EULOGY FOR ELLINGTON, 1974

If I dare to include Ellington in the pantheon of musical greats—the Beethovens, the Monteverdis, the Schoenbergs, the prime movers, the inspired innovators—it is precisely because Ellington had in common with them not only musical genius and talent, but an unquenchable thirst, an unrequitable vision for translating the raw materials of musical sounds into his own splendid visions.
—GUNTHER SCHULLER (1926-2015), COMPOSER/TEACHER, 1974

The great thing about Duke Ellington is that he is always affirming his basic propositions. When you hear his music throughout his entire career, he's never running from himself.
—WYNTON MARSALIS (1961-), TRUMPETER AND BANDLEADER, 1999

Chapter 6

# The Lotus Eaters

> Ellington sought a sensuality in the way his music was expressed.
> ... He was always very conscious of the need to make the listener
> feel experiences with the sound, almost as though he were creating
> apparitions within the music.
> —MERCER ELLINGTON (1978)

In 1956, on a rare night off for the Ellington band, nine of the virtuoso sidemen recorded a romantic ballad with the beguiling title "Ballade for Very Tired and Very Sad Lotus Eaters." Its composer, Billy Strayhorn, played piano in Ellington's stead, and Johnny Hodges, Ellington's star saxophonist, was the nominal leader of the band. The album it appeared on was called *Duke's in Bed*, as if they were making music while the boss wasn't looking. Ellington's shadow, however, hovered over the record session: three of the tunes they played were written by him, and another was "Take the 'A' Train," written by Strayhorn but indelibly associated with Ellington as his orchestra's theme song. The other tunes on the album consisted of an old pop song and two riff-based jump tunes by Hodges, called "Confab with Rab" (because "Rabbit" is Hodges's nickname) and "A-Oodie-Oobie," tossed off for this record and destined never to be played again.

Billy Strayhorn's "Ballade for Very Tired and Very Sad Lotus Eaters" was also destined never to be played again. Though no one was likely to rue the short shelf life of "A-Oodie-Oobie," there is good reason to rue it for the "Ballade." It is a hitherto unheard impressionistic dream sequence in which Hodges's incomparably sensuous alto saxophone glides over Strayhorn's incomparably lush harmonies in a kind of late-night absinthe haze. Its title makes an oblique reference to "Lotus Blossom," another beautiful ballad in the unique Strayhorn/Hodges genre. Other titles in the genre similarly reflect Strayhorn's floral predilection, including "Passion Flower," "Ultra Violet," "Violet Blue," and "A Flower Is a Lovesome Thing." Like those compositions, "Ballade for Very Tired and Very Sad Lotus Eaters" is a showpiece, albeit a minor one, for the Strayhorn/Hodges alliance.

## Lotus Eaters, Genus and Species

Listening to the lotus-eating, dreamlike music Johnny Hodges and Billy Strayhorn made together for thirty years, there can be no doubt that they were soul mates. They shared a romantic strain that at its core evokes the French impressionists and, like the impressionists, verges at its edges on sentimentality. The lotus eaters of Homer's *Odyssey* make an apt metaphor for their music, as Strayhorn's title acknowledges. In the *Odyssey*, a fierce storm blows Ulysses' ship onto an island as he and his fatigued warriors are making their way back to Ithaca after the decade-long siege of Troy. Two of the men are dispatched to find food, and they come upon a tribe of benign, laconic souls lounging in the shade. The only food on the island, the men are told, is the fruit of the lotus tree. When they eat it, they too become benign, laconic souls, like the natives, with no cares or ambitions. Tennyson (1832) evokes the spell cast by the mystic lotus fruit:

> They sat them down upon the yellow sand,
> Between the sun and moon upon the shore;
> And sweet it was to dream of Fatherland,
> Of child, and wife, and slave; but evermore
> Most weary seem'd the sea, weary the oar,
> Weary the wandering fields of barren foam.
> Then someone said, "We will return no more";
> And all at once they sang, "Our island home
> Is far beyond the waves; we will no longer roam."

Ulysses finds his men and takes them bodily back to the ship, where they reluctantly resume their onerous trek back to the "Fatherland of child, and wife, and slave."

The collaborations of Strayhorn and Hodges have a lotus-eater calm. They move with grace across lovely soundscapes. Beneath the calm, there is often a lingering sorrow, keenly felt though never spoken, the shadow of a dream abandoned or forsaken. The music resonates with unity of feeling and shared compassion and easy soulfulness that is rare in music or any other art.

And it is contradicted by everything else we know. In the faces that the two men showed to the world, there seemed to be nothing kindred, no hint of empathy or compassion or fellow-feeling.

Billy Strayhorn (1915–1967) was small, dapper, and outwardly cheery. His nickname in the band was "Swee' Pea," after the cartoon baby in the Popeye comic strip, and the nickname was bestowed on him as much for his sweet temper as for his diminutive stature. As a schoolboy, Strayhorn dazzled his teachers and classmates with his musical talents at Westinghouse High School in Pittsburgh. At his graduation, he played his own *Concerto for Piano and Percussion* and received a standing ovation. "Well, Strayhorn—he was just like, you'd say, a genius," one of his classmates told his biographer David Hajdu (1996, 17), and all the other classmates nodded in agreement. But after he left high school, Strayhorn's worldly ambitions faltered and he seemed content to rest on his high school laurels. He was gay and openly so, a rarity at the time, and his openness about it was not for declamatory purposes but because it was not in his temperament to pretend otherwise. He was attentive and observant and good company. He was a lifelong chain-smoker and in his final decades, a benign and witty alcoholic.

In 1938, when he was twenty-three and looked younger, some well-placed friends arranged a backstage audition for him with Duke Ellington after a Pittsburgh concert, and Ellington did him the courtesy of listening as he played some of Ellington's compositions and then sang some of his own songs. Ellington was immediately impressed by Strayhorn's ability as a lyricist and told him he might be able to use him. Strayhorn was flattered, of course, but after hearing no more as weeks and months went by, he had pretty much put the moment behind him. Then months later, in 1939, Ellington called and arranged for Strayhorn to go to New York. He was put up at first in a YMCA in Harlem, but Ellington's son Mercer, just four years younger than him, invited him to move into the Harlem apartment of Ellington's sister Ruth, the same age as Strayhorn, where Mercer also lived.

While Ellington was on tour with the orchestra, Mercer and Strayhorn busied themselves studying some of Ellington's band scores and working out the elements of his composing and arranging style. They proved apt pupils. Both Strayhorn and Mercer Ellington would contribute original music to the orchestra within the year. Eventually, Strayhorn would augment the Ellingtonian elements with classical devices from his teenage studies. His first major success, however, showed none of that. He composed "Take the

'A' Train," named for the Manhattan subway line that had carried him to the Harlem apartment where his destiny lay. "Take the 'A' Train" is an exercise in big band swing, rhythmically hot, eminently hummable and, in the spirit of the day, inviting for agile dancers. Ellington immediately recognized that Strayhorn had more to offer than lyrics and gave him assignments as a composer and arranger. From then on, his salary would be boosted with royalties on his composer credits from Ellington's publishing wing, Tempo Music, which was administered by Ruth Ellington.

Within a few years, the relationship between Ellington and Strayhorn grew from a loose master-apprentice arrangement to one of mutual dependency. Their bond proved durable, in fact indissoluble, though their orbits seldom intersected. While Ellington spent his days and nights in hotels and on stages all over the world, Strayhorn found his niche with the New York cabaret crowd, developing musical ideas for the orchestra at Ellington's beck and call by day while leading a vibrant life among the smart set by night. The antithetical work habits suited both men perfectly, and their bond was constant, whatever the distance between them. Their partnership lasted twenty-eight years, ending only with Strayhorn's untimely death from cancer at fifty-one. In his memoir, Ellington wrote, "Billy Strayhorn was my right arm, my left arm, all the eyes in the back of my head, my brainwaves in his head, and his in mine" (*MiMM* 156).

Johnny Hodges (1907–1970), nine years older than Strayhorn, viewed the world through shifty eyes. He quit school at fourteen and scuffled in the hard-knocks music world, joining the Ellington orchestra in 1928, when he was twenty-two. On the bandstand, he fixed his gaze on his music stand or on the floor. When he soloed, he stood stock still, sometimes flicking a glance to the left or right but otherwise frozen in place. Bob Udkoff, a well-heeled tagalong in Ellington's entourage, said of him, "He had little or no personality. . . . Beautiful player, very soulful, but you couldn't have a conversation with him" (1999, 326). His bandmate, Al Sears, said, "We sat beside one another for seven or eight years. We laughed about things, but it was always a chuckle. He didn't smile too much" (Chapman 2019, 151). Barry Ulanov, Ellington's first biographer, thanks "the oldest members of the band . . . who freely put their memories and their scrapbooks at my disposal"; Johnny Hodges is conspicuously absent.

Though Hodges spent thirty-eight years in Ellington's orchestra (from 1928 to 1951, and then from 1955 to his death in 1970), he had a thorny relationship with his boss. In November 1940, he quit playing the soprano saxophone forever to spite Ellington, according to rumor, because Ellington refused Hodges's demand to pay him extra for playing soprano as well as alto saxophone. In his last years, he insisted on being paid nightly in cash because, he declared, "When I was pickin' cotton I used to get paid at the end of every day," leaving it to listeners to figure out where the cotton fields sat in relation to Cambridge and Boston, Massachusetts, where he was born and raised. Ellington, always one to avoid a dispute, went along with it, forcing Mercer Ellington, his road manager in those years, to carry a briefcase full of cash on road trips. It was all the more onerous because Hodges earned the highest salary in the band. Trumpeter Rolf Ericson, who played in the band from 1963 to 1964 and was one of the lowest paid, may have discovered his real motive for the cash payments. "Johnny Hodges had a habit of walking around in front of us counting rolls of hundred dollar bills," Ericson said. "He wanted to make us feel envious and he enjoyed it" (Westin 2018, 11). Hodges titled one of his riff tunes "sweet as bear meat," and the gamy irony of that title seemed an apt epithet for the image he projected.

Mercifully, the impression most people had of Johnny Hodges came from the music he made, and from that, they were likely to envision a poetic figure, a spinner of melody, sometimes overly sensitive when the tempo was down but lyrical at all tempos. It was an impression very much at odds with the sullen figure they saw on the bandstand. The shifty-eyed stone face seemed like an impostor, and maybe he was. Edith Cue Hodges, his wife, said, "Everybody said Johnny was gruff. They thought he was cold. He was just afraid" (Hajdu 178). At least that view reconciled the gap between the man and his music. What did it really matter, this gap between the man and his music? To his bandmates, it meant nothing. "Nobody knows what Johnny Hodges feels inside when he walks out to the mike," trumpeter Shorty Baker told Stanley Dance (1970, 89). "He may look as though he's on his last walk to the gallows, but . . . he thanks the audience with a million dollars worth of melody!"

We search in vain for the common ground that made Billy Strayhorn and Johnny Hodges such otherworldly, spectral collaborators. Maybe Wild Bill Davis, the organist and arranger who knew Hodges as well as anybody, said it best. "Neither one of them guys was really who they seemed," he opined. "Johnny was just as mushy inside as Strayhorn was froufrouy." Whatever that means, Ellington obviously understood it from the start. He recognized the potential for an alliance where many others would have simply looked away, and he orchestrated the alliance with all the ingenuity he showed in his musical compositions. It does not seem too far-fetched to say that the alliance between Strayhorn and Hodges was one of Ellington's most exhilarating creations.

## Penetrating Warm Valleys

The first step leading to the alliance came with Ellington's ballad "Warm Valley" in 1940. The title is a double entendre intended to evoke female physiology as well as geographic topography, and that neatly captures the mood of intimacy and quiet passion evoked by the sinuous, undulating melody. (Side B of the original 78 rpm release was "The Flaming Sword," sustaining the sexual imagery in its masculine side.) The quiet sensuality of "Warm Valley" has its roots in the dance hall convention of ending the evening with a quiet number that encourages the dancing couples to press closely together and slowly make their way around the floor. It was a venerable tradition, of course, much older than "Warm Valley." Previously, Ellington had ended his dance dates with a quiet blues such as "Mood Indigo." "Warm Valley" is patently sexier, specifically designed for stimulating intimacy as the couples prepare to disappear into the night. It exploits Hodges's gift for sinuous melody, as do all the dream-like collaborations with Strayhorn that would follow. Indeed, at Fargo, North Dakota, in 1940, the most famous dance date ever recorded, Ellington calls "Warm Valley" twice, once leading up to the first intermission and again, at the end of the long evening, immediately before sending the dancers home for the night with "God Bless America."

Billy Strayhorn remembered the process of composing and arranging "Warm Valley" in considerable detail a couple of decades later even though, by then, his work with Ellington had evolved into a much closer, reciprocal collaboration. In 1940, in his first months with the band, Strayhorn was still absorbing lessons in jazz orchestration from his new boss. What made "Warm Valley" especially memorable for Strayhorn was the rare deliberation and close contact as it unfolded. Strayhorn told Bill Coss, "You remember 'Warm Valley'? It was less than three minutes long. But we wrote reams and reams of music on that, and he [Ellington] threw it all out except what you hear. He didn't use any of mine. Now that's arranging. The tune was written, but we had to find the right way to present it" (1962, 501).

Strayhorn's schoolboy experience in Pittsburgh, however dazzling it may have seemed to his schoolmates, was more than just a subway ride from the place he would occupy as Ellington's collaborator. Some of the leaps he had to make are neatly conceptualized by Ethan Iverson, the pianist and educator. "Strayhorn needed to learn a lot about aesthetics from Ellington," Iverson (2017) points out. "Strayhorn wrote a corny piano concerto in high school; he knew more about musicals than jazz; in the first decade of writing for Duke he had a lot of meaningless decoration that Duke had to pare down in order to give it the right feel."

In the "reams of music" by Strayhorn that Ellington threw out in the making of "Warm Valley," it is not hard to imagine that much of it involved the paring down of what Iverson calls "meaningless decoration." Strayhorn's comment about finding "the right way to present it" is what Iverson calls giving it "the right feel." Strayhorn had similar experiences working beside Ellington on numerous other arrangements in these apprentice years, but none of the others stuck with him with the immediacy of this one. With "Warm Valley," Ellington seems to be nurturing Strayhorn's flair for what became a kind of subgenre for the orchestra. As he worked with the younger man at getting "the right feel" in "Warm Valley," there was something larger at stake. Ellington was fostering what would become a new dimension for exploiting the strengths of his orchestra. Ellington would keep his hand in it for another year or two, and after that, he would sit back and watch as Billy Strayhorn and Johnny Hodges brought it to a bright polish.

### Dreaming Day and Night

Strayhorn did not need a second invitation. In the next year, a busy one in which he took on all kinds of unfamiliar tasks for his boss, he composed two new compositions that came to stand as badges of the lotus eaters' union. "Day Dream" was recorded in November 1940, just two months after "Warm Valley," and "Passion Flower" was recorded eight months after that, in July 1941. The very titles spin a story about the music—somnambulant, otherworldly, florid, exotic. Both "Day Dream" and "Passion Flower" were first recorded by small combos made up of the cream of the orchestra and marketed under the name "Johnny Hodges and His Orchestra." They were part of a spin-off enterprise in which Ellington's star players fronted small bands on the cut-rate Bluebird subsidiary as a supplement to the big band offerings on parent RCA Victor. One of the many duties Ellington assigned to Strayhorn was organizing the music and personnel for these dates. Presumably, Strayhorn arranged "Day Dream" and "Passion Flower" for the full orchestra and then pared them down for the septet because Ellington immediately started playing both numbers with the big band at concerts, broadcasts, and dances.

"Day Dream" credits Ellington as co-composer, indicating that it went through an editing process like the one for "Warm Valley," in which Ellington again deleted some Strayhorn decorations. Strayhorn's beautiful melody hardly needs decoration, and the background of deep chordal harmonies is impeccably calculated to simultaneously enhance Hodges's recital of the melody and keep out of his way. The recording found an audience, and when

Ellington announced it at his first Carnegie Hall concert more than two years later (January 1943), he could introduce it with some flair, saying, "And now comes All-American number one saxophonist Johnny Hodges with another Strayhorn arrangement." Hodges plays the complete *AABA* melody once, and then repeats only the bridge and last chorus (*BA*) adding some grace notes including a dramatic glide at the bridge but otherwise respecting Strayhorn's winsome melody all the way.

"Day Dream" remained a favorite of Johnny Hodges long after several other memorable pieces in the same subgenre contended with it. It stayed in the orchestra's repertoire as long as Hodges was there to play it. As familiar as it was in the original small-band recording and in numerous concert recordings, it was several years later when "Day Dream" finally received its definitive big band rendition. The occasion was an unexpected recording session made for Verve Records with Ellington nominally absent. The session came near the end of Ellington's recording contract with Columbia in December 1961. At the time, Ellington was unhappy with Columbia for denying him the budget to record an album of his symphonic works, among other grievances, and this surreptitious Verve session appears to have come about as a show of defiance. Hodges is credited as leader of the Ellington orchestra for the recording, with Ellington's normal roles filled by Jimmy Jones on piano and Strayhorn conducting as well as arranging all the numbers. The album, called *Johnny Hodges with Billy Strayhorn and the Orchestra* (Verve), otherwise includes the full Ellington orchestra intact. Beyond a doubt, Ellington is overseeing the whole affair.

The music glows, perhaps reflecting the furtive occasion that called it forth. Strayhorn's arrangement of "Day Dream," extended and updated, sacrifices a touch of its serenity by raising the tempo slightly and giving the orchestra more notes (extending the arrangement to four minutes instead of the characteristic three of previous versions). But the orchestral nuances are sumptuous and they are richly preserved in Rudy Van Gelder's famous recording studio in Englewood Cliffs, New Jersey. There is a kind of collective exhilaration that imbues every note. The musicians play as if they are intent on making a masterpiece. In its numerous surviving performances, "Day Dream" was never less than delightful, but this performance, twenty years after the original airing, is its consummation.

The other absinthe ballad in the afterglow of "Warm Valley," "Passion Flower," recorded in July 1941 by the seven-piece spin-off known as Johnny Hodges and His Orchestra, gives composer credit solely to Strayhorn, tacit recognition that Ellington now believed Strayhorn could be trusted to edit himself. It is tempting to view this fourteen-month sequence from "Warm Valley" to "Day Dream" to "Passion Flower" as a report card charting Strayhorn's progress, with Ellington rejecting all his embellishments on "Warm Valley," and then tweaking his arrangement of "Day Dream" as co-composer, and finally accepting "Passion Flower" pretty much as Strayhorn presented it.

"Passion Flower" is darker, more somber. Hodges opens with sixteen bars (two eight-bar *AA* sequences) in a gradual descending scale. The bridge presents a contrast as a sustained ascension up the scale before descending again to the final iteration of the melancholy *A* melody. The long rise in the bridge, contrasted with the slow descent of the quiet *A* melody, gives the impression of a mournful sigh. The characteristically spare background here includes a prominent bass line by Jimmie Blanton (characteristic of numerous arrangements by Ellington in this period and clearly co-opted by Strayhorn here). One of the highlights is a stunning glissando when Hodges seemingly glides up the scale in a continuous run; the continuity is legerdemain, of course, as each note is made on a separate key on the alto saxophone and Hodges moves masterfully from one to the next in one sustained breath.

Though the records found their audience, the novelty of the keening alto over resonant impressionist chords represents a refinement of sensibility that was uncommon in the Swing Era. The delicacy was not appreciated by some fans, who liked their music hotter. In 1943, a young English critic wrote scornfully, "Mr. Strayhorn is an example of today's youth in jazz. He throws tradition overboard. He will have originality at the expense of beauty.... [He has] an obsession for tone colour and voicing which excludes everything else that matters" (quoted by Hajdu 1996, 197–98). The English critic was Stanley Dance, who moved to the United States soon after publishing this cavil and ironically "slipped into Ellington's inner circle" (as Hajdu puts it), where, among many other benisons, he produced the record session that included the "Ballade for Very Tired and Very Sad Lotus Eaters." Dance obviously managed to reconcile his antipathy for Strayhorn's "originality at the expense of beauty" or at least to keep it hidden. John Hammond, the influential talent scout, expressed a similar gripe. Of the Carnegie Hall concert in 1943, he opined that "Billy Strayhorn's three tunes had little to contribute except unconventional harmonies" (1943, 173). Strayhorn's ally, Johnny Hodges, was also taken to task for mellowing his tone in the absinthe ballads. Charles Fox bemoaned Hodges's playing in the small-band configurations because "quite a few featured Hodges playing in the lachrymose, rhapsodic style he started using around this time" (1959, 126). Those sentiments aligned the authors with the jazz reactionaries who longed for the imagined innocence of the jungle.

The reactionaries would soon be swamped by a generation of musicians and critics who saw that Ellington, though the purveyor of unforgettable harmonies labeled "jungle music," was equally adept at unforgettable harmonies evoking warm valleys. Strayhorn was seen as the torch bearer. Walter van de Leur (2002, 182) sums up what he calls the "Strayhorn Effect": "Strayhorn provided Ellington with new compositional concepts that led to a different musical world.... Many other composer-orchestrators (knowingly or unknowingly) based their work on Strayhorn's music." Gerry Mulligan, twelve years younger than Strayhorn and a leading composer and arranger in the 1950s, told Hajdu (1996, 86–87), "When Strayhorn came on the scene, he just blew us away, because he was doing very complicated, sophisticated things, and they didn't sound complicated to the ear at all—they sounded completely natural and very emotional." Dan Morgenstern, a passionate reviewer of the music in all its forms, recognized "the creative scope and emotional range of Strayhorn," whose music "dares the grand gesture, and with all its sophistication, it wears its heart on its sleeve" (2004, 128–29).

Like "Day Dream," "Passion Flower" got its consummate orchestral performance several years later, also in a revamped and extended arrangement and also under unusual circumstances. In 1956, Ellington and Strayhorn undertook a long-distance project with the singer Rosemary Clooney (as discussed in "Wordless Articulation"). Strayhorn prepared arrangements of a selection of their songs and the orchestra recorded the instrumental parts in New York. Strayhorn then took the tapes to Hollywood and worked with Clooney in the studio, dubbing in her vocal parts. One of the further oddities of the album *Blue Rose* (and one of its treasures) is the inclusion of "Passion Flower," an oddity because Clooney does not sing on it. Probably Strayhorn and Ellington intended Clooney to add a wordless vocal to it, but if so, it must have proved unsatisfactory. Or they may have meant it to stand alone from the start, because it constitutes a tacit celebration of the return of Johnny Hodges, who had rejoined the orchestra two months earlier after a five-year absence. "Passion Flower" on *Blue Rose* marks Hodges's first recorded solo with the orchestra after his return, and it is a glorious one, as might be expected, a grand reunion with Hodges's incisive tone framed sumptuously in Strayhorn's elaborated harmonies for the full orchestra.

## A Lovesome Lull before the Lotus Blossoms

After "Passion Flower" in 1941, Strayhorn and Hodges, left to their own devices by Ellington, appear to have momentarily exhausted their inspiration. Though they kept trying, their next attempts at absinthe ballads failed to find the integrity that made "Day Dream" and "Passion Flower" such paradigms.

Perhaps they mistook the success of those tunes for their superficial sentimentality. An element of sentimentality was undeniably part of the genre, but it was not the crucial element. What was crucial was the underlying sense of loss and longing that colored Strayhorn's music and Hodges's performance of it. It was the heartfelt depth of the blues, not the hangdog frown, that gave them their power. Strayhorn and Hodges would recover that depth in their last decade together in three remarkable compositions that stand as masterpieces of their unique genre. Until then, however, "Day Dream" and "Passion Flower" would hold their places as perennial gems in Ellington's repertoire. The new attempts, and there were several, had their moments, but they lacked staying power.

First came "A Flower Is a Lovesome Thing," as blatantly sentimental as its lugubrious title suggests. The tune is pretty and danceable but somehow wispy. Ellington tried it on radio audiences on his regularly scheduled Treasury Show broadcasts starting in June 1946, and then a month later, recorded it noncommercially on a Capitol Transcription, a studio recording made for radio use only, always with Strayhorn replacing him at the piano (as well as receiving sole credit as composer). A small band with Hodges as nominal leader recorded it the next year, 1947, for a label called Sunrise Records that Ellington owned. Ellington dropped it from the band's repertoire that year.

Another Strayhorn–Hodges collaboration from the same time had a similar history. It was called, in keeping with Strayhorn's florid muse, "Violet Blue," invoking a slightly mellower shade than Ellington's celebrated "indigo" mood of 1930. "Violet Blue" also received its debut recording in a small-band session under Hodges's name for the short-lived Sunrise label. It is a little livelier in tempo than the other ballads, and it has an undulating vamp that might make for intimate dancing. Ellington dealt with it as he had "A Flower is a Lovesome Thing," introducing it first on radio broadcasts starting in 1945 (under the title "Ultra Violet") and recording it noncommercially as a Capitol Transcription in 1947 (as "Violet Blue"). After that, it was left to Strayhorn and he recorded it on both of his dates as a leader, as a piano feature in Paris in 1961, and as a vocal feature for Ozzie Bailey in New York in 1965, under yet another title, "Multi-Colored Blue," its third hue and a less distinctive one at that.

The third Strayhorn–Hodges collaboration from this period was more successful but its success did not come in the late-night ballad tradition. It was first heard in a brilliant small-band debut in 1947 under the title "Charlotte Russe," named not for a flower but for a French dessert (literally, a Russian *charlotte*), a cream-filled sponge cake with a cherry on top. Strayhorn's minor key melody has a haunting noir feeling, perfectly realized in the original recording in Hodges's sinuous tone and made all the more haunting in Strayhorn's arrangement by Taft Jordan's muted trumpet fills. Here, surely, is a worthy new entry into the Strayhorn–Hodges canon of absinthe ballads. The recording caught the attention of other musicians, and Strayhorn immediately renamed it "Lotus Blossom," reverting to his floral theme. (The new title became the inspiration for the "lotus eater" epithet in his 1956 *Ballade*.)

"Lotus Blossom" is one of Strayhorn's most beautiful melodies (among many), but strangely Ellington never admitted it into his orchestral repertoire. He largely ignored it until 1961, when he recorded it as a piano feature with Aaron Bell on bass and Sam Woodyard on drums on *Piano in the Foreground* in a studio take that went unreleased for over forty years (in the Playlist). Ignored though it was by Ellington's record company, it loomed large for him. He played it frequently as a piano feature, sometimes accompanied by bass and drums but more often by bass only and sometimes as an unaccompanied piano solo. In 1967, he recorded a moving solo performance of it at the recording session that was the memorial for Billy Strayhorn, who had died that year, and from October 1971 until his last performance in March 1974, Ellington played "Lotus Blossom" at every concert, usually as the encore, in a perpetual tribute to Strayhorn.

Strayhorn and Hodges had found their métier early with "Day Dream" and "Passion Flower." The attempts that followed gained momentary currency but never rivaled the first two, which held their places tenaciously in Ellington's repertoire. Strayhorn was, in a sense, competing with himself, and he had set a very high standard. Unhappily, the alliance of Strayhorn and Hodges was interrupted decisively when Hodges quit the band for almost five years to pursue his misadventure as leader. When he returned to the fold in 1955, the alliance formed anew, beginning with the unexpected definitive recording of "Passion Flower" inserted into Rosemary Clooney's vocal album, and from that moment on, it grew stronger than ever.

### Back to His Natural Habitat

They were obviously happy to see each other, Strayhorn and Hodges. Not that they had been complete strangers. In the five years that Hodges had been gone, he recorded prolifically as a leader of small bands, thanks to the generosity of the impresario Norman Granz. Strayhorn was often among the cadre of Ellingtonians hired for the day to make records with him. The tunes were mainly simple riffs and easy blues by Hodges, devoid of sweat, as they were on *Duke's in Bed*, which they recorded the year after Hodges's return. The records Hodges made for Granz were pleasant, sometimes delightful, but no audience lined up to hear them, and fewer than half were issued in Hodges's lifetime.

After a few years without the cover of the Ellington orchestra where he had sat for twenty-three years, Johnny Hodges was scuffling. By 1955, Whitney Balliett wrote in the *New Yorker* (1962, 124), "Hodges had become an out-of-fashion bandleader of a small semi-rock-and-roll group." Discouraged but diffident as always, Hodges persuaded his wife, Cue, to make the phone call. "His wife called up and asked if I wanted an alto player," Ellington recalled. "I said, 'Oh yeah!'" (Nicholson 301–2).

It was not exactly a homecoming. In the four and a half years that Hodges was adrift, Ellington had pretty much rebuilt the band. Hodges found himself sitting among seven players who had not been there when he left—half the band, as it were, and formidable presences they proved to be. The new men (and the year they joined): Paul Gonsalves (1950), Willie Cook, Clark Terry, and Britt Woodman (all 1951), John Sanders (1954), and Jimmy Woode and Sam Woodyard (both 1955). It had taken a few years, but Ellington assembled a band to rival the Blanton–Webster years. Hodges's return was the tipping point.

If Hodges felt blessed by the opportunity of rejoining Ellington in October 1955, he did not betray his elation. On stage and off, he maintained what Ellington's biographer Don George eloquently called "his old kiss-my-ass attitude" (1981, 40). It was his playing, as always, that gave him away. Perhaps he felt the need to assert himself for the newcomers. His brilliant sound on the alto saxophone was now more assertive, more dramatic, freer than ever. If others took it for granted, Hodges did not. In October 1958, arriving in England on tour with the orchestra, a reporter for *Melody Maker* asked him why he had returned to Ellington. "I had my own band and I had to scuffle, and when you scuffle you can't play what you like," Hodges explained, "but when you are famous and popular you can." His answer, a long one by his standards, is also more revealing than most. In Ellington's orchestra, Hodges followed Ellington's agenda, traveled Ellington's itinerary, and played Ellington's music. To some onlookers, including Norman Granz, who cajoled him into leaving in the first place, it appeared that, far from playing what he liked, as he said, he was really in bondage to the Duke. That was nonsense, of course, and now Hodges knew it. He truly was playing what he liked, and the boss's agenda, itinerary, and music were the annoyances he had to put up with to do it. Ellington's saxophone section, where Hodges would sit for fifteen more years until his death in 1970, was his natural habitat.

Hodges's first display of his musical rejuvenation was the definitive recording of "Passion Flower," though it went almost unnoticed as the lone instrumental on the recording of Rosemary Clooney vocals. Instead, his rejuvenation was very boldly proclaimed six months later at the Newport Jazz Festival on July 7, 1956, the concert that made headlines with dancing in the aisles and curfew-breaking high spirits. Though most of the musical discussion of that concert has centered on "Diminuendo in Blue" and "Crescendo in Blue" with Paul Gonsalves's rollicking twenty-seven-chorus interval, the consummate musical moment actually belongs to Hodges with his keening, magisterial rendition of "Jeep's Blues," his wail riding the crest of the band in full shout and the roar of the crowd rising in waves around them. Ellington and Hodges had played "Jeep's Blues" dozens of times since its debut in 1938 and they would play it dozens more, but this Newport performance has no rival.

Hodges had been a master of his instrument long before his unhappy hiatus. On his return, he brought a heightened dramatic sense to that mastery, a tolerance—perhaps even a receptiveness—for the occasion. It is surely no accident that the definitive performances of Billy Strayhorn's "Day Dream" and "Passion Flower," brilliant though they were in the 1940s when they were composed, came years later, in 1956 and 1961, when Hodges was temperamentally disposed to rise to the occasion. There would be more occasions: the pinnacles of the alliance were still to come.

### Masterpieces with the Bard, the Basmala, and the Biopsy

After their reunion, the lotus-eaters resumed their alliance with obvious relish. Among their absinthe-soaked romances were three masterpieces that will take their place in any reckoning of Duke Ellington's finest moments. All three were written for specific contexts so that they were buoyed conceptually by stimuli more concrete than "lovesome" flowers and cherry-topped *charlottes russe*. The new masterpieces show that the allies were prepared to make music that could inspire higher impulses than close dancing at the end of the night—though they could inspire that too, if the need arose.

**The Bard**, William Shakespeare, provided the context for the first of the masterpieces. In 1956, in the heady glow of the Newport Festival triumph, Ellington and Strayhorn launched an ambitious project for a suite that would be "a tone parallel" to some of Shakespeare's memorable characters (discussed in "Diamonds in a Glittering Heap" below). Among the characters chosen after Ellington and Strayhorn's fastidious review of the plays were two of Shakespeare's fabled romantic couples, either of which might have provided opportunities for Strayhorn and Hodges. The plays *Antony and Cleopatra* and *Romeo and Juliet* probe intense love affairs that go tragically awry—ideal fodder for lotus-eaters. In the end, it was *Romeo and Juliet* that received their masterful treatment. By contrast, *Antony and Cleopatra* is represented by a winsome piece called "Half the Fun"; though written by Strayhorn[19] and featuring Hodges, its mood is one of charming frivolity, a far remove from the scent of lotus blossoms.

"The Star-Crossed Lovers," the lament for the doomed teenage lovers from feuding families, is a triumph for the lotus-eaters' alliance, arguably its apogee. It is credited to Strayhorn alone as composer, but its final form was partly worked out in the recording studio, as can be heard in a nine-minute rehearsal take released under the working title "Pretty Girl" that was recorded five months before the final version. Strayhorn's astute commentator, Walter van de Leur (2002, 150), documented the many changes from Strayhorn's original score to the definitive recorded version, including the omission of what he calls the "original majestic modulation and coda," replaced by a straightforward reiteration of the theme by the trombones. This stripping of ornament suggests the hand of Ellington. Another change, a modulation from D♭ to D, may have come about at Hodges's insistence, as it would have been, van de Leur says, "definitely uncomfortable for the alto." If so, it provides an example of the kind of change Strayhorn said he regularly made to accommodate Hodges: "If [Hodges] says, 'This is awkward here. This is an awkward position of notes,' then you say, 'Is it really? Is it impossible?' If he keeps trying it, and it is impossible, you say, 'Well, all right, I'll change it'" (quoted by van de Leur). The changes from Strayhorn's original score to the definitive recording, however they came about, resulted in "the right feel" (as Ethan Iverson put it)—the right *everything*, one is tempted to say.

Even his bandmates, who were used to playing Strayhorn's melodies, agreed. At the recording session for "The Star-Crossed Lovers," clarinetist Jimmy Hamilton told Strayhorn, "Nobody going to forget this, man. This is the most beautiful thing you ever wrote" (quoted by Hajdu 1996, 180). Hamilton was remembering the tune from its earliest incarnation, two years earlier, when Strayhorn brought a sketch called "Pretty Little Girl" to a small-band session under Hodges's leadership. In that early version, the

---

19. Composer credits for *Such Sweet Thunder* are confusing because Billy Strayhorn had recently lodged a complaint about his lack of credit. Ellington had been oblivious, and, with characteristic nonchalance, credited ten of the twelve movements jointly "(Ellington, Strayhorn)" with one to Strayhorn alone ("The Star-Crossed Lovers") and one to Ellington alone ("Half the Fun"). These credits are patently incorrect. Inspecting the MSS, Walter van de Leur (134–35) determined that Strayhorn was mainly responsible for both "The Star-Crossed Lovers" and "Half the Fun" and also "Up and Down, Up and Down." Van de Leur says, "Other than scoring a small section for Ellington's forceful opener of *Such Sweet Thunder*, Strayhorn apparently had little to do with the other nine movements."

tempo is slightly brighter, the arrangement, for an octet, is rudimentary (little more than half the length of "The Star-Crossed Lovers"), and Hodges shares the solo duties with Strayhorn, who plays a concerto-like piano interval. The original is a mere shadow of what it would become under its Shakespearean mantle, but the gorgeous melody is intact from the start, as Hamilton noticed. Hearing the small-band sketch alongside the definitive big-band version on *Such Sweet Thunder* provides an otherwise ineffable measure of the inspiration Shakespeare could bring to the music, for Ellington as well as Strayhorn. Subtle though the changes were, they turned a sketch into a masterpiece.

The melody of "The Star-Crossed Lovers" is unconventional, organized in a melodic sequences *AA'BC*, in which *B* appears where the bridge normally occurs but then is superseded as the new *C* melody ascends from it as a dramatic *cri de coeur*, ramping up the drama from the mellow flow of the ballad that has gone before. That melodic sequence (*AA*), Strayhorn's "most beautiful thing" (in Hamilton's phrase), captures the forbidden passion of teenaged Romeo and Juliet. The climactic *C* melody represents the portent of woe that would befall them. In Strayhorn's ingenious arrangement, Hodges carries the composition with subtle orchestral shadings, and the melody (*AA*) is then repeated by the orchestra in low-key dissonances, leaving the dramatic *BC* statements for Hodges's controlled anguish in a resounding finale.

Admirers of the lotus eaters, reveling in "The Star-Crossed Lovers," might have quietly wondered if the subgenre had reached its zenith. Perhaps it had, but amazingly, there would be other legitimate contenders still to come.

**The basmala**, the ornate symbol of Islam, transfixed Duke Ellington in the autumn of 1963, when the State Department of the United States government sponsored him on a tour of the Middle East. From September until November, the orchestra played for large, appreciative audiences in twelve cities. (The musical sway on Ellington is discussed at length in chapter 8, "Ellington in the Global Village.")

Though Ellington was by this time a seasoned traveler, he found the sights and sounds of the Mideast, with a relatively relaxed itinerary (by his hectic standards), endlessly fascinating. Always an interested and involved tourist, Ellington breathed in the new surroundings as never before. He published a detailed diary of the tour in *Music is My Mistress* (301–30), celebrating "the smells of spices and garlic and exotic perfumes, . . . marvelous brocades , oriental rugs, glass and copper trays, inlaid and engraved . . . [and] swarming masses of people everywhere."

His most direct reaction gave birth to the *Far East Suite*, a sparkling forty-five-minute potpourri. The gem among its movements, though there were many, is the ballad "Isfahan," played with sinuous brilliance by Johnny Hodges. Named for the city in central Iran that was the capital of Persia in the eleventh century, Ellington remembered it in his diary (325) as "a city of poetic beauty, where they give you poems instead of flowers." The composition had its origin in an earlier piece by Strayhorn called "Elf" that was played in a rehearsal session (in the Playlist). It was, as annotator Stanley Dance (1987) says, "somewhat tentative" on its original airing, but he is quick to point out that it was "later to be made famous when remodeled and beautifully restyled." Dance was witness to its "remodeling" under the new title. He reported (1967), "There were only two [complete] versions of the exquisite *Isfahan*, but they were born after much earnest discussion between Ellington and Johnny Hodges, particularly concerning those pauses during the performance that add so much significance to the picture of a city 'where everything is poetry.'"

The "pauses" refer to the stunning compositional device whereby Hodges starts every melodic phrase *a cappella* and then carries the downward glide through what van de Leur calls the "unfolding major seventh chord in the alto" (2002, 170), as the orchestra sidles in behind him with a subtle grace that is felt rather than heard. Van de Leur calls it "a cunning composition." Though Strayhorn alone receives composer credit, the restyling, as Dance calls it, owes its existence to the collective muse that Ellington fostered. "Isfahan" became an immediate favorite among jazz saxophone players and a staple in the repertoire, but the performance by Johnny Hodges in the *Far East Suite* provided the benchmark for all who followed.

On the occasion of its recording, the performance may have gained emotional depth because Strayhorn was conspicuously absent from the session. Early in 1966, he had been diagnosed with cancer of the esophagus, and at the time that the band recorded "Isfahan" in December, he was undergoing radiation therapy, as everyone in the band knew too well. Amazingly, "Isfahan" was not the last of his absinthe ballads. He would float one more to the world on the wings, so to speak, of his biopsy.

**The biopsy** was a death sentence, but Strayhorn was determined to make his demise a creative one. Around the time that his esophagus was removed and Strayhorn was sustaining himself on a liquid diet ingested through a tube directly into his stomach (which included, to no one's surprise, dry martinis), he wrote a score at first called "Freakish Lights" and then "Blue Cloud" but later renamed "Blood Count." When Strayhorn completed it, Ellington and the orchestra were in the middle of a crowded European tour (January 24 to March 19, 1967). On receiving it, Ellington called a rehearsal in Milan, Italy, an uncommon occurrence when the band was occupied with nightly concerts. They polished Strayhorn's arrangement, and they then played it nightly for the remaining three weeks of the tour. Live performances are preserved in Stuttgart (where it is identified as "Freakish Lights") and a few other cities. The hallmarks of the lotus-eater genre are all in place in these performances—the alto saxophone of Hodges soaring over sepulchral muted horns. Obviously, it would take an extra-special performance before it could be mentioned alongside "Star-Crossed Lovers" and "Isfahan." And it would get it.

Billy Strayhorn died on May 31, 1967. Three months later, Ellington and the band, still distraught, gathered in the RCA Victor Studio in New York to record fourteen compositions by Strayhorn for an album that would be called . . . *And His Mother Called Him Bill*. (Ellington's elegiac piano performance of "Lotus Blossom" from this recording is discussed in chapter 3, "The Piano Player.")

"Blood Count" was one of the fourteen compositions. It was not an obvious choice, having been introduced in European concerts just six months before and never recorded. It was, however, Strayhorn's final composition, and its title carried a reminder to all of his bandmates of his fate. Chapman (2019, 87) says, "'Blood Count' is a dark piece, with forebodings of death, but free—in the words of one of Strayhorn's 'Four Freedoms'—from self-pity."

"Blood Count" is Billy Strayhorn's *memento mori*. The power of the performance was described by Robert Palmer (1968) in his notes for the album that convey its inspiration as well as could be expressed by anyone: "*Blood Count* has an immediate and devastating impact, speaking simultaneously of fear, longing, resignation, pride, doubt, faith and many more apparently conflicting emotions, all balanced on the knife's edge of a man's life, all vividly brought to life whenever the music is heard." The core of the performance, its heart, as Palmer also notes, belongs to Strayhorn's longtime ally. Palmer writes

> This is one of Johnny Hodges's greatest performances. He is still *angry* that Strayhorn has been taken, and for once the familiar adjectives—serene, unruffled—cannot be applied to his playing. He sings, from deep inside, the certain knowledge that any moment can be a man's last moment, and his playing cuts right to the heart.

The aura surrounding Hodges with the airy, richly harmonized backgrounds is reverential but somehow, for the other fourteen musicians as for Hodges, there is also a kind of defiance shining through. It is a glittering monument to mark the final chord in the alliance of the lotus-eaters.

## Last Gasp of the Lotus Eater

In 1951, when Johnny Hodges was eking out a living playing second-rate music on his own, he was asked why he had quit the Ellington orchestra. He grumbled, "We didn't like the tone poems too much" (Jewell 1977, 115). A few years later, in a much better mood after he had returned to the band and reclaimed his rightful place in Ellington's cosmos, he recanted, so to speak, in a conversation with Stanley Dance (1970, 89). "*Warm Valley* is one of my favorite records. I like playing that kind of number—if it has the right backgrounds," he said. "*Day Dream* too. When I'm playing that, it's supposed to be very, very soft, and you're supposed to close your eyes and dream a while." It is reassuring to think that at least this one time, when he was for the moment not trying to bait his boss, Johnny Hodges was willing to acknowledge the summit to which his boss had led him.

Billy Strayhorn, of course, needed no second chances to express his gratification for the alliance. He knew, as Johnny Hodges surely did if only he would admit it, that Duke Ellington had made their dreams come true—had provided many kinds of settings for putting their singular gifts on display. Those settings included many musical forms from prom jive ("Clementine") to jump blues ("The Intimacy of the Blues") to svelte ornaments ("Half the Fun"), but best of all, they included their late-night absinthe reveries. That handful of sensuous nocturnes is unique in all music, at once one-of-a-kind and a genre unto themselves, momentary but somehow momentous.

If Strayhorn's and Hodges's entire expansive careers with Ellington were *charlottes russe* (to dip into Strayhorn's sucrose imagery), then their spectral alliance on those "tone poems" was the cherry on top.

## Playlist

(Recordings cited in order of appearance in the chapter)

"Ballade for Very Tired and Very Sad Lotus Eaters" 3:19 September 1, 1956. *Duke's in Bed* on CD1 of *Johnny Hodges and the Ellington Men 1956–1957*. 2CD. Fresh Sound (2010). Clark Terry flg, Ray Nance tp, Quentin Jackson tb, Hodges as, Jimmy Hamilton cl, Harry Carney bs, Billy Strayhorn p, comp, arr, Jimmy Woode b, Sam Woodyard d.

"Warm Valley" 3:33 (CD1), "Warm Valley" 0:51 (CD2), *The Duke at Fargo 1940*. Crystal Ballroom, Fargo, North Dakota, November 7, 1940. Storyville Special 60th Anniversary Edition 2CD (2000). Personnel as for studio recording of "Warm Valley" below except Ray Nance replaces Cootie Williams.

"Warm Valley" 3:20 October 17, 1940. *Blanton–Webster Band*. RCA Victor CD2 [1986]. Cootie Williams, Wallace Jones, Rex Stewart, tp, Joe Nanton, Lawrence Brown, Juan Tizol tb, Barney Bigard cl, Johnny Hodges as, Otto Hardwick as, Ben Webster ts, Harry Carney bs, Ellington p, comp, arr, Fred Guy g, Jimmie Blanton b, Sonny Greer d. Solos: Ellington, Hodges, Rex Stewart (muted obbligato), Hodges again.

"Day Dream" 2:56 November 2, 1940. Hodges, *Passion Flower*. Bluebird CD (1995). Cootie Williams tp, Lawrence Brown tb, Hodges, Harry Carney bs, Duke Ellington p, Jimmie Blanton b, Sonny Greer d.

"Day Dream" 3:56 December 12, 1961. *Johnny Hodges with Billy Strayhorn and the Orchestra*. Verve CD (1999). Cat Anderson, Shorty Baker, Bill Berry, Ed Mullens tp, Lawrence Brown, Quentin Jackson, Chuck Connors tb, Russell Procope, Jimmy Hamilton, Paul Gonsalves, Hodges, Harry Carney reeds, Jimmy Jones p, Aaron Bell b, Sam Woodyard d, Strayhorn arr, cond.

"Passion Flower" 3:05 July 3, 1941. Hodges, *Passion Flower*. Bluebird CD [1995]. Ray Nance tp, Lawrence Brown tb, Hodges, Harry Carney bs, Duke Ellington p, Jimmie Blanton b, Sonny Greer d.

"Passion Flower" 4:33 January 23, 1956. Rosemary Clooney and Duke Ellington, *Blue Rose*. Columbia CD (1999). Cat Anderson, Willie Cook, Ray Nance, Clark Terry tp, Quentin Jackson, John Sanders, Britt Woodman tb, Johnny Hodges, Russell Procope, Jimmy Hamilton, Paul Gonsalves, Harry Carney reeds, Ellington p, Jimmy Woode b, Sam Woodyard d. (Clooney absent on this track.)

"A Flower is a Lovesome Thing" 3:22 Capitol Transcription, Hollywood, CA. July 17, 1946. *Jazz Legends Vol. 12*, Naxos (2006). Taft Jordan, Shelton Hemphill, Cat Anderson, Francis Williams, Shorty Baker, Ray Nance tp, Lawrence Brown, Claude Jones, Wilbur De Paris, Tricky Sam Nanton tb, Jimmy Hamilton, Johnny Hodges, Russell Procope, Al Sears, Harry Carney reeds, Billy Strayhorn p, Fred Guy g, Oscar Pettiford b, Sonny Greer d. Solo: Hodges.

"A Flower is A Lovesome Thing" 2:44 New York. Autumn 1947. *The Johnny Hodges All Stars*. . . . Prestige CD (1992). Taft Jordan tp, Lawrence Brown tb, Johnny Hodges as, Al Sears ts, Billy Strayhorn p, Oscar Pettiford b, Wilbur De Paris d. Solo: Hodges.

"A Flower is a Lovesome Thing" 3:12 Hollywood, CA. July14, 1960. *At the Bal Masque*. Orig Columbia LP, reissued Essential Jazz Classics CD (2006). Ray Nance tp, Lawrence Brown tb, Johnny Hodges as, Harry Carney bs, Duke Ellington p, Aaron Bell b, Sam Woodyard d. Solo: Carney.

"Violet Blue" 2:57 New York, June 1947. *The Johnny Hodges All Stars*. . . . Prestige CD (1992). Shorty Baker tp, Johnny Hodges, Al Sears ts, Harry Carney bs, Strayhorn p, Oscar Pettiford b, Sonny Greer d.

"Charlotte Russe" (a.k.a. "Lotus Blossom") 3:02 Autumn 1947, New York. Personnel, date and CD issue same as "A Flower Is a Lovesome Thing" above.

"Passion Flower" 3:16 New York, March 2, 1961. *Piano in the Foreground* (Columbia CD [2004, track first released in France 1984, globally on this CD in 2004]). Duke Ellington p, Aaron Bell b, Sam Woodyard d.

"Half the Fun" 4:19, "Pretty Girl" 8:54 (a.k.a. "Star-Crossed Lovers" rehearsal) and "The Star-Crossed Lovers" 4:00. New York, August 7, 1956, December 6, 1956, and May 3,

1957. *Such Sweet Thunder*. Columbia CD (1999). Cat Anderson, Willie Cook, Ray Nance, Clark Terry tp, Quentin Jackson, John Sanders, Britt Woodman tb, Harry Carney, Paul Gonsalves, Jimmy Hamilton, Johnny Hodges, Russell Procope reeds, Ellington p, Jimmy Woode b, Sam Woodyard d.

"Pretty Little Girl" (= "Star-Crossed Lovers") 2:26 New York. September 8, 1955. Johnny Hodges, *Creamy* (originally Verve Records), CD2 on *Four Classic Albums*, Avid (2010). Clark Terry tp, Lawrence Brown tb, Jimmy Hamilton ts, cl, Johnny Hodges as, Harry Carney bs, Billy Strayhorn p, Jimmy Woode b, Sonny Greer d.

"Elf" (= "Isfahan") 3:19 New York, 1July 18, 1963. *Private Collection*, Vol. 4. WEA International CD (1987). Cat Anderson, Cootie Williams, Rolf Ericson, Eddie Preston tp, Ray Nance cor, Lawrence Brown, Chuck Connors, Buster Cooper tb, Jimmy Hamilton cl, Russell Procope cl, as, Johnny Hodges as, Paul Gonsalves ts, Harry Carney cl, bs, Duke Ellington p, Ernie Shepard b, Sam Woodyard d.

"Isfahan" 4:02 and "Isfahan" (alternate take) 4:11 New York. December 20, 1966. *The Far East Suite: Special Mix*. Bluebird CD (1995). Cat Anderson, Cootie Williams, Mercer Ellington, Herbie Jones tp, Lawrence Brown, Buster Cooper, Chuck Connors tb, Harry Carney, Paul Gonsalves, Jimmy Hamilton, Johnny Hodges, Russell Procope reeds, Ellington p, John Lamb b, Rufus Jones d.

"Freakish Lights" 4:15 (= "Blood Count") Liederhalle, Stuttgart, Germany. March 6, 1967. *Big Bands Live*. Jazz Haus CD (Austria 2011). Personnel as for "Isfahan" above.

"Blood Count" 4:17 Victor Studios, New York. August 28, 1967. *And His Mother Called Him Bill*. (Bluebird CD [1987]). Cat Anderson, Mercer Ellington, Herbie Jones, Cootie Williams tp, Lawrence Brown, Buster Cooper, Chuck Connors, tb, Jimmy Hamilton, Russell Procope, Johnny Hodges, Paul Gonsalves, Harry Carney reeds, Ellington p, Aaron Bell b, Steve Little d.

Chapter 7

# Accidental Suites

## Duke Ellington's Hollywood Scores

> It was a great experience. It's a wonderful education. You know, I learned a lot of things, a lot of things. Music in pictures should say something without being obviously music, you know, and this was all new to me.
> —DUKE ELLINGTON (AS TOLD TO RALPH J. GLEASON 1975, 185–86)

### American Jazz and American Movies

Duke Ellington composed soundtrack music for four Hollywood movies. That number might seem surprisingly few for a celebrated American composer whose career in one indigenous American art form paralleled the growth and efflorescence of another essentially American art form. The music called jazz, which was the genre practiced by Ellington at the beginning and the one he is identified with (whether he calls it that or not), originated around the turn of the twentieth century, found a national audience in the 1920s and an international audience by the 1930s, and attained creative peaks from 1935 to 1945 and 1955 to 1965, with high points in a continuous history to this day. Ellington spans the formative years of the music as a main force in growing its audience at the start and one who flourished as the music flourished in *both* its peak periods, as did no other individual musician.

Cinema history follows a similar twentieth-century trajectory, although its dependence on technological progress gave it a ponderous start: multi-reel motion pictures developed out of staccato-motion vignettes in the 1920s, and motion was mated with sound in the 1930s; color came soon after but became standard only in the 1950s. Jazz music was natively American from the start, but it took a decade or more before cinema took on a dominant American identity. That happened in the 1920s when powerful studios, centered in Hollywood, California, seized control of production and distribution, promoting star directors and star actors with ironclad contracts, surpassing foreign competition quantitatively and soon rivaling it qualitatively.

When talkies took over, Hollywood studios hired screenwriters, obviously, and also staff composers, conductors, and musicians, and kept monopolistic control over them as they had for directors and actors. For an outsider like Duke Ellington, getting an opportunity to compose a soundtrack meant short-circuiting the studio system and effectively being given a commission, something that could only be pulled off through the advocacy of a star director or a star actor, someone with enough clout to buck the system. Even after the Hollywood contract system was declared illegal by antitrust laws in 1948, the hierarchical structure remained almost impenetrable for a few more decades.

## A Prewar Fling with the Movies

Though my focus here is on the music that resulted from Ellington's four soundtracks that came along when he was in his sixties, he had an auspicious youthful fling in the movie business years earlier. Ellington appeared in an eighteen-minute short, *Black and Tan*, filmed in Astoria, New York, in 1927, before the Hollywood monopoly had a firm grip. He played the part of a hardworking composer (named "Duke"). As critic Krin Gabbard (1996, 166) points out, Ellington is presented as a "sophisticated artist of the Harlem Renaissance," a significant upgrade from the "minstrel stereotypes" that surrounded him in the film. Ellington's role in *Black and Tan* was the only speaking part he had in a film until decades later, when he made a cameo appearance in *Anatomy of a Murder*. Though silenced elsewhere, he made several appearances, starting with *Check and Double Check* (seventy-five minutes, Hollywood, 1930), *Bundle of Blues* (nine minutes, 1933), *Symphony in Black* (nine minutes, 1935), and cameo roles with his orchestra in feature films *Murder at the Vanities* (1934), *Belle of the Nineties* (with Mae West, 1934), *Hit Parade* (1937), and *Cabin in the Sky* (with Lena Horne, 1942). He was also featured in several soundies, three-minute films that played on nickelodeons in drugstores and restaurants like an audio-visual jukebox. Ellington's involvement in these early films is documented thoroughly by Stratemann (1992), and its significance, especially its racial implications, is discussed by Gabbard (160–84).

By the time Ellington was invited to prepare soundtracks for Hollywood feature films, two more decades had passed. There had been rumors from time to time before that; Billy Wilder, the great director/screenwriter, proposed a racially mixed musical, *Camille*, starring Lena Horne, Tyrone Power, and Paul Robeson, with a score by Ellington (reported by Zolotow in 1977), but it was too bold an undertaking for Hollywood. By the time Ellington got his chance, his advocates from his early days in film—among them, Orson Welles, Mae West, directors Dudley Murphy and Vincente Minnelli—were either blacklisted in the Communist witch hunts or fettered by the studio moguls. He would find new advocates, as we shall see, and under the studio dictates, the results were mixed, though never dull.

## A Smattering of Jazz Gems

Ellington's four Hollywood commissions actually represent a fair boon. Few of his contemporaries in jazz or classical music received as many commissions unless they were under contract to studios, as were, for instance, Andre Previn and Michel Legrand. Jazz scores had a brief vogue in France, beyond the grip of the Hollywood bosses, for Miles Davis (*Ascenseur pour l'Échafaud*, in English *Lift to the Scaffold*, dir. Louis Malle, 1957), John Lewis (*Sait-On Jamais*, in English *No Sun in Venice*, dir. Roger Vadim, 1957), and Thelonious Monk (*Les Liaisons Dangereuses*, dir. Roger Vadim, 1959). These works received near-unanimous praise as jazz scores, whatever their merits as movie soundtracks.[20] The distinction between scores and soundtracks is crucial. In this chapter, I am interested in the music that was elicited under the stimulus of a particular motion picture, that is, the music as *music* and not in the way it was matched to the plot of the motion picture, i.e., as sounds that track the dramatic action. The difference is considerable. The soundtrack version is almost always matched to the onscreen drama by someone other than the composer and is cut up and spliced in ways that are intended to have dramatic integrity with little regard for musical integrity. The main purpose of the soundtrack is to enhance the on-screen action. Played back sequentially as *music* devoid of the accompanying visual focal point, soundtracks are mostly a mishmash.

Failing to recognize the distinction between film scores as compositions and film scores as soundtracks has led to some muddled critiques; for instance, Max Harrison, in his review of Ellington's film score for *Anatomy*

---

20. Monk's pre-recordings (= score) for *Les Liaisons Dangereuses* were only discovered in 2017 and so the praise was belated.

*of a Murder*, seems keenly aware of its strengths in portraying characters and conveying situations, but he nevertheless concludes, "He should have been more concerned with enhancing the dramatic and visual specifics of Preminger's film." As if that was Ellington's task! Beyond a doubt, matching music to dramatic action is a craft that requires considerable training. It is hardly relevant to the appreciation of the music in its own right.

The four commissions Ellington received for Hollywood movie scores were concentrated (if that is the right word) in one decade as follows:

1959 *Anatomy of a Murder*
1961 *Paris Blues*
1966 *Assault on a Queen*
1969 *Change of Mind*

As films, the merits are in reverse order to the chronology. Not coincidentally, in terms of the music that resulted, the same reverse chronology applies. The first two films, *Anatomy of a Murder* and *Paris Blues*, were successful movies, and their musical scores resulted in more interesting compositions. Soundtrack recordings were normally released only for films that were box-office hits in hopes that the hit movie would rub off on record sales and vice versa, making a marketing spiral. The success of the film—not the quality of the music—determined the release of the recording. The latter two films that Ellington scored were not enthusiastically reviewed at the moment of their release—through no fault of his, obviously. By contrast, the first two were well received as movies, and Ellington's scores were nominated for Academy Awards, the annual honors bestowed by the American Academy of Motion Pictures, and for GRAMMY Awards, bestowed by the National Academy of Recording Arts and Sciences. His scores for *Assault on a Queen* and *Change of Mind* might have deserved the same recognition, but without commercial releases, they went unheard except as fragmented soundtracks in a darkened movie theater. In the discussions that follow, I consider the scores for *Change of Mind* and *Assault on a Queen* briefly. The main discussion considers Ellington's masterly scores for *Paris Blues* and *Anatomy of a Murder*.

## Change of Mind (1969)

Duke Ellington was enticed to write the score for *Change of Mind* because of its race-sensitive script, the kind of edge that he had expected in *Paris Blues* seven years earlier but had been foiled by studio censors. And he no doubt hoped that his experience with the meddlesome hierarchy on *Assault on a Queen* three years earlier would not arise with the smaller enterprise that was intended to bring *Change of Mind* to the screen (Sagittarius Productions, dir. Robert Stevens). The screenplay, by Seelig Lester and Richard Whiston, is set in the Deep South and revolves around the dilemma of a Black man who has undergone a brain transplant operation in which the brain of a white liberal District Attorney is transplanted into his cranium. From that bizarre premise, both social and professional conflicts abound. The recipient of the transplant, David Rowe (played by Raymond St. Jacques), is rejected by both his own wife and the donor's wife. When he prosecutes a case against a white sheriff accused of an interracial murder (Leslie Nielsen), he finds himself distrusted by both sides. His life a shambles, he leaves town in hopes of making a new start elsewhere. (For full details, see Stratemann 1992, 587–91.)

Ellington's pre-recordings were preserved, with some anomalies, in his stockpile of self-financed studio recordings. One of them survives obliquely as a piano trio called "Edward the First." In the movie, the melody comes up in the form of a song called "What Good Am I Without You," sung by an unidentified female vocalist. Ellington originally recorded this song almost three decades earlier, in November 1930, with words and music by Milton Ager. The vocal version heard in the movie has not come to light. Curiously, the other numbers are also revisited from the 1930s. "Wanderlust" is a simple atmospheric blues recorded by Johnny Hodges in 1938 and credited to him as composer. Ellington resuscitated it in 1962 for a small-band session featuring Coleman Hawkins, with Hodges in the band and Ellington now listed as co-composer. For the movie version, with Ellington listed as sole composer, he cues the band by announcing, "We are now approaching Soulville!" whereupon Cootie Williams, true to form, plays a soulful solo on muted trumpet over the somber ensemble. Another piece, "Black Butterfly," is an updated version of the beautiful ballad that Ellington wrote and recorded in 1936. Dance (1959) says, "*Black Butterfly* . . . might well be said to improve on the original if only because of Johnny Hodges's beautiful solo." (On the original, the principal soloist was trombonist Lawrence Brown.) The theme music for *Change of Mind* is called "Neo-Creole," and it gets appropriate exposure in the film by playing under the title at the start, under the credits at the end, and at intervals throughout. As the title slyly implies, it, too, is an updated theme. It is the half-sister of *Creole Rhapsody*, a landmark composition from 1931, originally recorded just two months after the feckless "What Good Am I without You?" that got an unlikely revival in this same movie.

Was Duke Ellington reliving his Cotton Club days? The movie obviously points toward ultramodern times with its sci-fi medical miracle and civil rights theme. Divorced from the movie that called it forth, Ellington's score might someday inspire a theoretical study of what it was that Ellington retained and what he ignored when he undertook the task of reinventing his source music of the 1930s for a motion picture of the late 1960s.

### *Assault on a Queen* (1966), and on a Duke

Some of Ellington's hard lessons about the Hollywood studio hierarchy came from working on *Assault on a Queen*. The lessons must have been all the more bitter because, at its outset, it appeared to be a golden opportunity. Frank Sinatra, coproducer of the movie and the lead actor, insisted on Ellington for the score, and Norman Granz made it a lucrative commission. The script was written by Rod Serling, the first scriptwriting superstar of the upstart television industry. The plot was suitably simpleminded: Sinatra and his gang (Richard Conte, Verna Lisi, and Anthony Franciosa) restore a sunken German submarine and hijack the ocean liner *Queen Mary* in hopes of ransacking her safe. They are foiled when they are discovered by a Coast Guard cutter (captained by Reginald Denny). All but three of the pirates end up dead.

On Ellington's two studio days in Hollywood, the studio orchestra augmented by seven men from the band recorded nine titles (listed by Stratemann 1992, 528) that amounted to about thirty-two minutes of music. Ellington then left for engagements with his band, and in his absence, his music underwent revisions, first by a studio orchestra assembled under the direction of Nathan Van Cleave, a Paramount staffer, and then by an orchestra conducted by Irving Talbot that recorded numerous short takes with strings for a set of "sweeteners," intended to be overdubbed on pre-recorded pieces. Preoccupied as he was with his nightly rounds, it took Ellington a while to realize what had been done to his score. In the meantime, he did his duty in publicizing the movie at his concerts by playing two of the titles he had written for it. The movie was released late in 1966, and Ellington played "Beautiful Woman Walks Well" in live performances at least eighteen times from December 1966 to February 1967 and "Blessings of the Night" at least three times in January 1967, each time telling audiences about the Frank Sinatra movie it had been his pleasure to work on. By February, the movie had disappeared from theaters and the soundtrack recording was canceled. Ellington dropped both titles from his concert repertoire and never played them again.

Fifty years later, a facsimile of the soundtrack recording of *Assault on a Queen* was released in a limited edition (1,000 copies). The annotation that accompanies the CD, by Jon Burlingame, points out, "This premier release of the music from *Assault on a Queen* satisfies, at least, a long-missing entry in the Duke Ellington discography." True enough, and the sound is good considering the challenges posed by the source material. The long-awaited release has some worthy additions to Ellington's output, but it also bears witness to the dilution of his score. Ellington is credited as composer of the entire score, nineteen titles, but his soundprint is clearly identifiable on only five of them (in the Playlist). Among the more gratifying titles are a *faux* Jamaican lilt in two guises: "Mama Bahama," a simple riff played by plunger-muted trumpets, and "Mama Bahama Islander," a simple flute solo by Bud Shank accompanied by harp, with both pieces amounting to about two minutes of music. One of the two compositions that Ellington played in concerts, "Blessings on the Night," provides the underscore for the love scenes between Sinatra and Lisi. The soundtrack version unfortunately fades after a few minutes. The gem in the soundtrack is "She Walks Well," which Ellington called "Beautiful Woman Walks Well." It captures Ellington's impression of Verna Lisi's graceful motion as she moves across the big screen, with Johnny Hodges's solo chorus as lissome as the movie star herself. Verna Lisa (1936–2014) was a Hollywood phenomenon when she starred in *Assault on a Queen*. Born in Ancona, Italy, she was "discovered" as a scene-stealing beauty in minor films in her native country and conscripted to Hollywood, where she made several movies in the 1960s. In retrospect, perhaps the pinnacle of her Hollywood career is "Beautiful Woman Walks Well," Duke Ellingson's tone parallel, so to speak, for her elegant deportment in a bar scene.

If Ellington was disillusioned by the postproduction meddling, Frank Sinatra just shrugged. He was a commanding presence in the movie business almost as long as he had been in the music business, and he understood the difference between them as did few others. "Once you're on that record singing, it's you and you alone," he told a biographer in 1962. "If it's bad and you get criticized, it's you who's to blame—no one else. If it's good, it's also you. With a film, it's never like that; there are producers and scriptwriters, and hundreds of men in offices, and the thing is taken right out of your hands" (quoted by Talese 1966, 125). Sinatra's capitulation, enlightened though it undoubtedly is, makes an ironic comment on Ellington's praise for him in his memoir. "He's an individualist, and he never trails the herd," Ellington wrote. "Nobody tells him what to do or say" (*MiMM* 239). Except, apparently, the Hollywood bosses.

### *Paris Blues* and the Accidental *Paris Blues Suite*

Though it was more pleasurable overall, *Paris Blues* went through its share of the vagaries that seemed to be built into the culture for Hollywood studio productions. Ellington signed on to compose the score for the film early in 1960 and spent some days in Hollywood in May and June on pre-recordings. The movie is about two expatriate Americans pursuing their jazz ambitions in Paris, and Ellington's pre-recordings partly entailed ghosting trombone parts for lead actor Paul Newman, whose trombone is played by Murray McEachern, and tenor saxophone parts for Sidney Poitier, played by Ellington's ace Paul Gonsalves. As Ellington put it, "This film was about musicians. Paul Newman and Sidney Poitier were musicians in a band, so we had to have a track for them to use that wouldn't be kidding the musicians and kidding the audience" (Nicholson 1999, 324).

Script changes required more pre-recording. Inconvenient though the changes were, Ellington gave it a positive spin by attributing them partly as a reaction to his music: "They get ideas for dramatic things after they hear the music for the first time," he told Ralph Gleason (1975, 194). In October, five months after his Hollywood sojourn, the producers told Ellington he had to go to Paris, where the film was being shot on location. Ellington, tied up by his concert schedule, sent Billy Strayhorn to "sort things out" (Stratemann 432). Strayhorn recorded a version of his own "Take the 'A' Train" in Barclay Studios in Paris in November. It would be used as the underscore of the opening credits, which focuses on the arrival of a train at Paris's Gare St. Lazare. Ellington arrived in Paris in December and directed further recordings in Barclay Studios, including the music for scenes featuring Louis Armstrong in a cameo role. Back in New York in May 1961, Ellington presided over post-production recordings for three days, with McEachern and three drummers (Philly Joe Jones, Max Roach, and old stalwart Sonny Greer) added to the Ellington orchestra.

With all this recording activity, even Klaus Stratemann, the indefatigable chronicler of every appearance Ellington ever made on film, wrestles with the provenance of the music that survived in the soundtrack, though true to form, in the eight tabloid-size pages he devotes to *Paris Blues* (429–37), he provides the best guesses we will ever have. Whatever the provenance, the soundtrack album that resulted presents a rich variety for listeners, from the rah-rah excitement of jam sessions featuring Louis Armstrong to romantic blues themes for the handsome couples that fill the central roles. The movie itself touches on social issues involving bonds of loyalty, race relations, and the conflict between artistic integrity and earthly delights, but the movie is mainly an entertaining stroll through the City of Light in the company of attractive characters.

Because the main characters are jazz musicians, Ellington's score gave him opportunities to write music for the foregrounded nightclub scenes as well as the background music for the romantic turns. Expatriate trombonist Ram Bowen (Paul Newman) and tenor saxophonist Eddie Cook (Sidney Poitier) play at the jazz bistro Marie's Cave by night and compose by day. At the opening, they join the mob at Gare St. Lazare that has gathered to greet jazz star Wild Man Moore (Louis Armstrong) on his arrival in Paris, and they run into holidaying American schoolteachers Lillian Cornell (Joanne Woodward) and Connie Lampson (Diahann Carroll). They have a romantic fling and the women try to persuade them to return to the United States with them. When a jazz concerto that Ram has labored over, "Paris Blues," is rejected by a concert promoter, he is disconsolate. At first, he agrees to return home, but then, instead, chooses to stay and pursue his artistic goals. The women embark for home brokenhearted.

The original script focused on the love affair of the expatriate American trombone player, who is white, and the holidaying American schoolteacher, who is Black, as in the novel by Harold Flender, on which the movie is based. It was only when Ellington arrived in Paris that he discovered that United Artists, the distributors, had ordered a script change, so that the expatriate musicians, one white and one Black, maintain racial lines when they pair off with the white and Black schoolteachers.

Ellington was disheartened by the change. "The theme was one he upheld: the romantic story of a white boy and a black girl," his son, Mercer, said (1978, 183). "When he arrived in Paris and discovered the switchover, he was very disappointed and firm in his belief that they should have stuck to the original version." Indeed, racial mixing was a plot turn on which Ellington had once invested considerable time and energy. In 1946, he had written a Broadway musical, *Beggar's Holiday* (with lyricist John La Touche), based on John Gay's Restoration drama *Beggar's Opera*, in which his white gangster hero (played by the redoubtable tenor Alfred Drake) has a Black lover (played by Bernice Parks). The cast and crew were biracial. Ellington says, "It enjoyed a tremendous *succès d'estime*, but the public was not ready for it" (*MiMM* 186). The biracial Broadway production attracted pickets in apartheid America in the 1940s, and the show closed after fourteen weeks, to Ellington's bitter disappointment. He harbored the hope that it would be revived someday, when "the public will be ready." Fifteen years later, he was disappointed anew by *Paris Blues*, upon learning that the public was still not deemed ready.

The script change, incidentally, meant that the gifted young actress Diahann Carroll, who plays Connie, ended up with supporting billing, while her peers Paul Newman, Sidney Poitier, and Joanne Woodward were named in big print—"above the title," in movie parlance. Presumably, in the original conception, Carroll would have been Newman's love interest and would have received top billing with him. In the revised version, where she is Poitier's love interest, her role is hardly lesser, but on the poster, her name appears in small print, after Louis Armstrong's, who is on camera for about ten minutes, most of the time with his trumpet at his lips. Carroll is on camera, of course, in most of the film, and as the character who voices the social issues most winningly and with considerable presence, her role is no less seminal than are the "stars."

Happily, the score at least partly drowns out the production blips. The foregrounded music—that is, the music that plays a role in the plot—is appropriately flashy. Armstrong's character makes a grand entry with the jubilant greeting at Gare St. Lazare, arriving in a sea of French fans with an oom-pah band supplying a fanfare. Ellington's music for the scene, titled "Wild Man Moore," posed a unique challenge for Ellington. "There was one new experience—writing for a 'squeezaphone,'" Ellington said.[21] "The band that meets Louis's train in the picture included an accordion, baritone [saxophone], clarinet, trumpet, bass and drums, and it was to play in the French or European serenade style of those exuberant little bands that meet you at stations" (Stratemann 432). Ellington made the music appropriately exuberant, and even the accordion—the 'squeezaphone'—almost swings.

More congruously, the plot provides a setting for a no-holds-barred jam session. Wild Man Moore and his band burst into Marie's Cave, the jazz cellar where Newman and Poitier's band plays nightly, and engage in a raucous battle of the bands between Moore's hoary entourage coming through the door and Newman's youngbloods on the stage. The music is "Battle Royal," a piece Ellington revived the following year for his extravaganza when his band and Count Basie's played together in the Columbia studios (*Duke Ellington Meets Count Basie*, 1962). In the crowded cellar, with trombone slides bobbing, clarinets shrieking to the ceiling, and fans jumping around in ecstasy, it is impossible to tell who might be playing at any time, but the visual impact carries the momentary thrill of a roller coaster. Some jazz reviewers may have missed the dramatic point. "Armstrong's still potent playing is almost entirely wasted in one of those unfortunate Hollywood 'jam sessions' born in fantasy

---

21. Ellington apparently forgot that thirty years earlier, he recorded a tune called "Accordion Joe" with accordionist Joe Cornell (a.k.a. Cornell Smelser) in the band (April 22, 1930, two takes on *Early Ellington*, Decca-GRP 3CD [1994]).

and dying in bedlam," said John Tynan in *DownBeat*. By contrast, the movie reviewer for the *New York Times*, Bosley Crowther, got the point and may even have oversold it. "Best number in its presentation and for its musical ostentation too is a thing called 'Battle Royal'. . . . The kick of it comes in the musical vying of old Satchmo's trumpet and the juicy, hot trombone." Crowther's point is well taken. For movie fans with no concern about venerating Louis Armstrong of the Hot Fives, "Battle Royal" makes a striking impression. The hurly-burly of the music complements the visual riot perfectly.

No reviewer, whether of jazz or movies, could rightly disapprove of the rendition of "Mood Indigo," in which Paul Newman's character intones Ellington's romantic ballad from the late-night bandstand at Marie's Cave with such sensuality that Joanne Woodward's character falls head over heels in love with him. Ellington frames Murray McEachern's trombone solo in soft background tones with guitar accompaniment (thought to be Barney Kessel), an uncommon pairing in Ellington's arranging but perfect in this setting. Strayhorn is heard (but not seen) complementing the guitar with sparse piano fills. The dulcet arrangement serves a crucial plot point by softening Newman's character, revealing a tenderness that is not obvious in this man who presents himself as a single-minded, obsessive composer. At one point, he says to Woodward's character, "Honey, I *live* music—everything else is just icing on the cake. I have no time, no serious time, for anything else." On the darkened stage, in close-up, his eyes closed and completely absorbed in the beautiful melody he is playing, we get a glimpse of a softer character, one perhaps capable of affection and more to the point of the plot, one capable of arousing the passion of a sophisticated schoolmarm on vacation.

Ellington's stage-managing of McEachern's solo won him a stunning accolade. Thirty years later, trombonist Milt Bernhart, a veteran of Stan Kenton's big band and others, now McEachern's section-mate in the star-studded Hollywood studio orchestras, reminisced about his days with Ellington in Hollywood. "Duke wrote a solo for Murray. I've long forgotten the name of the picture, but it was a beautiful solo," Bernhart recalled (1996). "Just before the recording light came on, Duke leaned toward Murray and said, 'Break their hearts.' I understood at that moment why playing with Duke made all the difference." Needless to say, MacEachern obliged.

As fetching as the foregrounded music is, it is Ellington's score underlying the dramatic action that has special resonance. The movie's title, *Paris Blues*, is the name of the jazz concerto that Newman is composing in hopes of making a breakthrough into big-time music. Ellington's stately melody for "Paris Blues" recurs throughout the film in several guises (though, strangely, not under the opening titles, which are underscored by Strayhorn's "Take the 'A' Train"). The "Paris Blues" melody is noodled on piano by Woodward's character in Newman's apartment, and later by Aaron Bridgers, an expatriate American who plays the part of the piano player in Newman's band at Marie's Cave. Near the end, Newman idly plays its main strain as he broods over his decision to stay in Paris and follow his dream. In another scene, Newman plays a recorded version of "Paris Blues" on his phonograph to appease the curious Woodward. The fullest version, and the one that is included on the soundtrack recording, accompanies the final farewell at Gare St. Lazare, as the schoolteachers, unlucky in love, take their solitary leave from Paris. This final orchestration is a kind of crescendo, starting wistfully with Jimmy Hamilton's clarinet and brought to the fore by the trombone in a swirl of elaborate orchestration, and then breaking into a train motif as it swells for the climactic finale.

Ellington's simple melody, familiar in the film from its many iterations, is hummable even by viewers who might not have been paying special attention to the music, but this final orchestration, the only version of "Paris Blues" on the soundtrack release, gives it glancing notice in the densely textured drama of the finale. As a result, one of the highlights of Ellington's score is underplayed on the soundtrack recording. Fortunately, there are several orchestral versions apart from the soundtrack recording that give better value to the melody. The definitive recording—though removed from the dramatic context of the movie—came a year later, when Ellington prepared an album called *Midnight in Paris*, inspired by his sojourn there for the making of the movie. On the album, "Paris Blues" is surrounded by fairly uninspired French *chansons* and shines all the brighter in that context. It opens with a richly harmonized statement of the melody by the saxophones, and then maintains the orchestral textures in support of solos by Lawrence Brown on trombone, Paul Gonsalves on tenor saxophone, and Johnny Hodges on alto saxophone—a majestic recitation of Ellington's handsome melody that might easily be overlooked on an otherwise minor Columbia album (in the Playlist).

Two of Ellington's atmospheric melodies that provide the undertone for the romantic pairings of the plot show off that melody in different contexts. "Autumnal Suite" ambles along at a pace that makes perfect accompaniment for infatuated young couples in no hurry to end their afternoon together. Ellington opens with the keening sound of the oboe (played by New York symphony musician Harry Smiles), and the orchestra nudges into the foreground, always sustaining its easy mood. When it releases into a defined melody, it turns out to be the familiar twelve bars of "Paris Blues," carried first, almost subliminally, by McEachern's trombone and moving seamlessly from one instrumental voice to another.

Another track, "Nite," opens with the strains of "Paris Blues," again played by the oboe, and then seemingly finding a new groove, upping the tempo for the night scene, and allowing instrumental voices (McEachern, Hodges) to penetrate the atmosphere, if only momentarily.

The score for *Paris Blues* thus contains movements, so to speak, that echo reiterated melodies, variations on a theme. Ellington composed many suites among his works, and critics occasionally raised objections to them because they were generally comprised of episodic impressions rather than thematically unified movements. His impressions—"tone parallels," as he called them—of, say, Liberia, the Far East, Latin America, New Orleans, Shakespeare's characters, and so many other places and people, consist formally of self-contained vignettes often evoked by real-world subjects rather than musical variations on a developing theme. In *Paris Blues*, Ellington realized this alternative conception of a suite, that is, thematic elaborations that recur in various movements. The melody called "Paris Blues" reverberates through the ninety-eight minutes of the film as it arises in at least four individual scenes, and on each reverberation, Ellington manipulates and modulates and contextualizes it with seemingly limitless imagination.

If Ellington had chosen—if he had taken the time instead of moving onward to the next project– he might easily have crafted a stand-alone *Paris Blues Suite*. With a little imagination, we can see how the parts might fit, in fact, by juxtaposing the big band arrangement of "Paris Blues" from *Midnight in Paris* and coupling it with "Autumnal Suite" and "Nite" and the climactic "Paris Blues" from the *Paris Blues* soundtrack. Obviously, these parts lack the transitions that would make the suite cohesive, but Duke Ellington, if he had been so inclined, could have supplied that. The cohesion is there in the sustained and ingenious variations on the "Paris Blues" melody as it reverberates through the extended score.

The idea of an accidental suite (in this sense) seems even more persuasive in his score for the movie *Anatomy of a Murder*.

## "A Vernacular American Symphony"

Duke Ellington's first Hollywood commission was for the movie *Anatomy of a Murder*, based on a bestselling "nonfiction novel" (Truman Capote's term) by Michigan Supreme Court Justice John D. Voelker writing under the pseudonym Robert Traver. The novel, a courtroom drama, is riveting, and the movie, with a screenplay by Wendell Mayes, meets the challenge of bringing to life the vivid characters on the movie screen. The plot revolves around a small-town lawyer in Michigan's Upper Peninsula, Paul Biegler (James Stewart), who agrees to defend an Army officer on a murder charge. Lt. Frederick Manion (Ben Gazzara) shot a tavern owner because his wife Laura (Lee Remick) claims he beat and raped her. Laura is flirtatious and her husband possessive, and there is a strong suspicion that she might have received her bruises from her husband when he discovered the affair. Biegler enters a plea of temporary insanity, but all appears lost when bigwig lawyer Claude Dancer (George C. Scott) is brought in by the District Attorney to prosecute the murder charge. Biegler is charmingly feckless, and Dancer is incisive and sharp. In the end, Biegler persuades the murdered man's daughter Mary Pilant (Kathryn Grant) to take the stand and support the defense plea. Manion is found not guilty, and when Biegler makes the trek to the Army post to offer congratulations and, incidentally, collect his professional fee, he finds that Manion and his wife have packed up and run off to parts unknown.

No plot summary can do justice to the rich cast of characters. The *femme fatale* (Remick) is coy and kittenish, and she seems genuinely mystified when the paternalistic Biegler chastises her for late-night partying while her husband is in jail. Biegler's legal researcher is an old washed-up alcoholic (Arthur O'Connell), once his mentor in the law profession. And then there is Pie Eye (Duke Ellington), leader of a bar band called the P. I. Five (Ray Nance, Jimmy Hamilton, Jimmy Woode, and Jimmy Johnson), at a bar frequented by Biegler, who sits beside Pie Eye at the piano and plays four-handed with him in one scene.

Ellington was given the soundtrack commission (and presumably the supporting role, which was not in the novel) by director Otto Preminger. He was a Hollywood maverick, as Gabbard points out (1996, 190), directing films that failed to get the seal of approval of the Producers Guild (*The Moon is Blue* [1953] used the word "virgin" and *The Man with the Golden Arm* [1955] dramatized heroin addiction). He had no qualms about rankling the powers-that-be, making an all-Black version of Bizet's *Carmen* (called *Carmen Jones* [1954]) and naming the blacklisted Dalton Trumbo as screenwriter in the credits for *Exodus* (1960). Hiring Duke Ellington and putting him on screen was only slightly audacious by Preminger's standards.

As the unnamed reviewer in *Variety* said, "Duke Ellington's score ... is a probing exercise in moods and colors" (Stratemann 407). Predictably, a few reviewers—John Tynan in *DownBeat* and Krin Gabbard (1996, 190), for instance—found the soundtrack obtrusive. Mercer Ellington saw the discrepancy and suggested that its source lay not in the music but in the ears of the beholders. The score, Mercer said (1978, 140), "was unusual, a success, and it won awards, but it is still criticized by ... reviewers who don't know the language of jazz and don't understand what is being said," and then he got personal. "Of course, they have been conditioned by the sound of symphony orchestras swelling out of gopher holes on the prairies, the patter of bongos to indicate tension, and stealthy bass lines to denote the approach of criminals, the clichés in other words, of Hollywood hacks." Most moviegoers would surely line up with *Variety* and Mercer Ellington, judging by the lasting appeal of the movie. The soundtrack works, and the score is exceptional.

Ellington, true to form, deflected the praise, or at least appeared to, when asked about it. "Even though the reports from screenings and from the studio were excellent," said Ralph J. Gleason, the San Francisco jazz critic, "Duke kept repeating, 'The next one will be better. I'll try another one and then I'll show them. I'm young. Give me a chance!'" (1975, 194). Ellington's tone is coy, as so often, as if he is telling Gleason what he expects to hear whether he believes it or not. He was not so young, at sixty, and by no means unhappy with his score. When he said this, the score had been nominated for an Academy Award and won three Grammy Awards including Best Motion Picture Soundtrack of the Year. In another interview, in a slightly more serious vein, he said, "*Anatomy of a Murder* was my first movie score as such. I never thought it would earn an Academy Award because it really hadn't an outstanding melody to hang on to. . . . What I mean is it wasn't done with the intention of trying to get a tune out of it, or a movie theme that would get an award. I was trying to do background music fittingly. And that, of course, I think is important!" (Nicholson 1999, 320). And then he added, in case you thought he was taking himself too seriously, that the score had come about as a kind of afterthought. "When we did the Preminger picture, we get to Hollywood and the guy gives me a beautiful seven-room apartment, and what I used to do for three weeks was to walk around the patio . . . and people would come out and we'd have drinks and I'd show them all over the place, and so one day he calls up and says, 'Hey, Duke, you know we're recording the day after tomorrow!' and so you have to get things together, quick!" That account is self-deprecating blarney, of course, inconceivable in the first place, picturing Ellington sitting idle for three solid weeks.

Ironically, when Ellington says, "[I]t wasn't done with the intention of trying to get a tune out of it," in fact a tune did come out of it and actually made its way onto the pop charts. Ellington's bopping main theme, identified below as the *Anatomy Theme*, was fitted out with equally bopping lyrics by the swing diva Peggy Lee and turned into a song called "I'm Gonna Go Fishin'" (in the Playlist). Lee's ingenuity, when it came to Ellington's attention, seemed to soften his public view. "The picture people have been very kind," he admitted to Ralph Gleason (1975, 186). "They feel the music is great and they like the songs. Peggy Lee is doing words to 'Flirtibird,' for instance [*sic*, actually to 'Main Theme,' a.k.a 'Anatomy of a Murder']." Lee's 45 rpm Capitol record with a big band arrangement by Bill Holman made a dent in the pop charts at a time when they were dominated by rock 'n' roll. Ellington made an instrumental arrangement with her title that leaned heavily on Ray Nance's cornet, both muted and open, foregrounded over the infectious *Anatomy* rhythm, perhaps thinking vaguely of the prospects of some radio airplay. If so, he abandoned hope. He recorded it privately (May 25, 1962, released posthumously in 1988) and never played it publicly.

"Satin Doll" is usually credited as Ellington's last hit song (1953), but that distinction really belongs to "I'm Gonna Go Fishin'" seven years later, though Ellington contributed the melody inadvertently and it was Lee who heard its potential and made it singable.

The movie score is widely acknowledged as an Ellington masterpiece. Hasse (1993, 364) says, "The twelve pieces that make up *Anatomy*'s suite of mostly related themes are brilliantly composed and orchestrated, well rehearsed, impeccably played, and make an effective soundtrack." Wynton Marsalis, writing the liner notes for the sonically upgraded 1999 CD release, says, "This is the album with the most mature sound of the band" and "*Anatomy of a Murder* is music made when Duke and the band were very mature.... This makes for very interesting voicings... very advanced harmonic conceptions." Stanley Crouch, in the program notes for a concert by Marsalis's Lincoln Center Jazz Orchestra that included selections from *Anatomy of a Murder* (1988, 442), called it "one of Ellington's grandest accomplishments," and in his characteristic combative style, Crouch added, "In a period when one jazz composer after another was floundering around trying to fuse jazz and European concert music, Ellington and his musicians went right on using blues, swing, idiomatic polyphony, plungers, dance rhythms, and a grasp of the majestic that was as old as the Negro spiritual."

Ellington's achievement in *Anatomy of a Murder* is succinctly captured by Tom Piazza's description of it as "a vernacular American symphony" (1988, 58), and he elaborates on that description (60):

> At first it appears to be another suite, consisting of short, apparently self-contained mood pieces. But the pieces are subtly and ingeniously braided together—a theme stated early on in a chalumeau clarinet solo shows up later as a muted introduction for brass choir, a main theme reappears completely reharmonized, or reorchestrated, or at a different tempo. Ellington uses the theme-and-variations technique to brilliant advantage here, adding layer upon layer of meaning to

Bass ostinato in the *Anatomy Theme*, music by Duke Ellington (transcribed by Michael Perkins).

the thematic material. Rhythmically and melodically, the two main themes of the piece—the first a bluesy, rueful melody; the second a ballad—are closely related, almost mirror images of each other.

These structural nuances are realized masterfully by the orchestra's control of them—what Marsalis recognizes as "the most mature sound of the band." As Piazza puts it, "By the time of *Anatomy of a Murder*, Ellington could make muted trumpets sound like afternoon sunlight on the side of a brick building."

The two main themes identified by Piazza were called the *Flirtibird Theme* and the *Polly Theme* by Ellington. A third theme, the *Anatomy Theme*, emerged when the complete recording sessions were collated in the 1999 digital reissue on the centenary of Ellington's birth. Ellington himself identifies those three themes in a ten-minute interview that came to light when reissue producer Phil Schaap tacked it onto the end of the CD as "The Grand Finale." This extraordinary document was originally made for distribution to radio presenters ("disc jockeys," as they were known in 1959) so they could pretend to interview Duke Ellington with his pre-recorded answers to a set of scripted questions (in References, see Ellington 1959, "Open-End Interview").

The *Anatomy Theme* is aptly referred to by Ellington as "the bass theme." In all its iterations, the dominant motif is a bass ostinato. It is a tricky beat, with quarter notes and sixteenth notes (ba-*bump* ba-ba ba-*bump* baa, the rhythm to which Peggy Lee fitted the words "I'm gonna go fishin'").

The bass motif shows up emphatically in the track called "Main Title and Anatomy of a Murder," with resounding brass punctuation and a soaring clarinet solo by Jimmy Hamilton. Ellington characterized the *Anatomy Theme* as "real colloquial, homespun, folksy and I should say gutbucket." The "homespun, folksy" aspect is what Peggy Lee fastened onto in her "fishin'" lyric. The theme is dramatically enhanced on "Main Title" while the opening credits roll by. Two versions show up on the record as "Anatomy of a Murder," one mono and the other stereo. "Main Title" is a more histrionic arrangement, with two solos by Ray Nance, one on open trumpet and the other muted, and a solo by Paul Gonsalves in between. In all its iterations, bassist Jimmy Woode sustains the signature bass vamp from start to finish.

The *Polly Theme* commemorates James Stewart's character. Ellington and his orchestra spent time in small-town Ishpeming, Michigan, where the film was shot, and got to know Chief Justice Voelker, the prototype for Stewart's character, who lives in the town. Ellington admired the real-life judge, and it shows in the music that characterizes Polly. "There's a theme that I use, well, it's rather serious, it's a deep emotional theme," he says in the publicity material (1959, 32). "Well, I don't really know how to describe it actually because to me it represents sort of a smoldering and a sophistication—a thing that is in the interior of this man. Here's a man who is a Supreme Court Judge and in his home town the guys like waiters and bartenders, policemen, oh, maybe garbagemen—people who are, you know, just people, and they call him by his first name and that's it. That to me is great."

In the film the young lawyer comes off as uncomplicated, likeable, and unpretentious. The verdict he wins, on the contrary, comes about through plotting and guile, but the country lawyer cleverly submerges that side of his personality. The *Polly Theme* captures his lack of pretension as a lilting ballad. It recurs in numerous musical sequences. The purest statement is in the piece called "Haupe," where Johnny Hodges states the melody with appropriate sophistication. But there are numerous interesting statements of it: "Polly," with Hodges and Ray Nance, on violin; "Hero to Zero," with Paul Gonsalves stating the theme; "Low Key Lightly," with Ray Nance (again on violin); and, more obliquely, "Midnight Indigo," with Harry Carney on baritone saxophone and a surprising duet with Billy Strayhorn on piano and Ellington on celeste. The *Polly Theme* comes in many colors.

The *Flirtibird Theme* also comes in many colors. Ellington calls it "my Number 1 theme." It represents Laura, played by Lee Remick, "the girl who has the incident that brings about all the trouble," as Ellington puts it. "The flirtibird is the girl in the story who's always flirting but nothing ever happens" (1959, 30–31). Its definitive version is easier to isolate than the other themes. "Flirtibird" is played with great sensuality by Johnny Hodges in a straightforward two-minute statement with the band providing subtle nudges that do not distract him or us. It is sinuous, it is sultry. Ellington explains, "It was the [theme] that sort of presented itself, sort of flew into me, sort of knocked me down and sort of wrote itself. . . . I saw the rushes the first Sunday in Ishpeming and the minute I saw [Laura] there leaning against that car I knew that I was on the right track . . . because she was the picture—I mean it was a thing with her eyes and she absolutely appeared to be, you know, sort of flirting all the time, which could easily be mistaken by someone—and was." Here Ellington obliquely refers to the crucial plot point when the bartender interprets Laura's flirting too literally and ends up assaulting her.

As full of character as Hodges's "Flirtibird," is, it is not without rival in the soundtrack. Shorty Baker provides a worthy contender on the same theme with his pitch-perfect trumpet on "Almost Cried." The theme comes to the fore in other contexts as well, memorably in a forthright clarinet solo by Russell Procope in the second half of the piece called "Way Early Subtone" (from 1:30 to 2:50). Ellington captured Remick's voluptuous portrayal of Laura incisively, and he knew it. "Ahhh, Lee Remick," he sighed. "She came in and listened to me play the thing and I said, 'This is you,' and she listened and she said, 'Oh yeh, that's me, yeh.' Just like that."

The *Flirtibird Theme* enhanced Remick's movements and conveyed her provocative charms, a scintillating matchup of sound and sense. The film scholar Gabbard (1996, 189), seems to have come down on the side of the few for whom Remick's kittenish pose "could easily be mistaken by someone" (as Ellington put it); Gabbard avers that "Hodges's typically lush solo for 'Flirtibird' is reduced to . . . the signification of 'sleaze.'" Wynton Marsalis more aptly stated the critical and popular consensus when he said that Ellington "was able to evoke feelings you've never heard in a movie. . . . One was the sound of sex—it's a sensual sound." Lee Remick's character is indeed, as Ellington said, "the girl who brings about all the trouble," but that does not mean the composer—or the audience—dislikes her.

In *Anatomy of a Murder*, the *Flirtibird Theme* has an equal presence with the *Anatomy Theme*, perhaps greater. It insinuates its way into many contexts, hence Ellington's rubric for it as "my Number 1 theme." In "Upper and Outest," the *Anatomy Theme* occupies the first minute and then it modulates smoothly into the *Flirtibird Theme* for the remaining minute. In "Way Early Subtone," "Flirtibird" is heard for eight bars near the beginning (played by Hodges) and then the music meanders into a beautifully relaxed blues with finger-snapping intervals and sudden silences, unlike anything else in Ellington's oeuvre. It is delightful music quite apart from the thematic organization.

If an arranger sought to construct a suite based on Ellington's score for *Anatomy of a Murder*, some parts seem ready-made. The dramatic, even melodramatic, "Main Title and Anatomy of a Murder" seems like the inevitable opening movement with its attention-grabbing brass shouts. After a further iteration of the *Anatomy Theme* in any of its guises, "Upper and Outest" makes a natural transition from the *Anatomy Theme* to the *Flirtibird Theme*. Apart from these pieces, the challenge is selecting from many possibilities when there is such a wealth of music to choose from.

As with the great promise for the unrealized *Paris Blues Suite*, we wish in vain that Duke Ellington had taken the time away from his restless itinerary to put together the suite embedded in the *Anatomy of a Murder* score for concert presentations. Its inevitable title, *Suite Anatomy*, sounds like an

Ellington title. The pieces are all there, parti-colored tiles awaiting the artist's caress to set them into a dazzling mosaic.

## Accidental Suites and Purposeful Portraits

Ellington's movie scores, like so much of his music, repay listeners on many levels. For all that, they have not been given much attention. Perhaps that is not surprising when the occasions that called them into existence were in the service of another medium. Thankfully, the films are less distracting when we give our attention to the pre-recordings and other studio performances that are the sources of the soundtracks. The fragments and splices that make the movie soundtrack are derived from pieces of music that, if we are lucky, have a beginning, middle, and end. At their best, they are accidental suites.

It should not be surprising that Ellington was adept at movie scores. His muse was always piqued by the real world—by the sounds and sights and characters that surrounded him in his daily rounds. He was a masterful portraitist. He composed portraits starting with the ill-starred Florence Mills, the inspiration for "Black Beauty" (1928), ending with Martin Luther King (1974), along the way with Bojangles (1940), Hamlet (1957), Mahalia Jackson (1961, 1970), Louis Armstrong (1970), and dozens of others.

In the movies, the sensory encounters were contrived for him by screenwriters and directors and actors, but he reacted to them with characteristic wit. In any gallery of Ellington's portraits, there will be a place of honor for James Stewart's Polly ("Haupe"), Lee Remick's Laura ("Flirtibird"), Diahann Carroll and Sidney Poitier cruising down the Seine ("Autumnal Suite"), and Raymond St. Jacques's befuddled district attorney ("Wanderlust"). If the opportunity arises, we will happily watch Verna Lisi step down from her barstool and we might sigh, as Duke Ellington did before us, "Beautiful woman walks well." Beyond a doubt, the movies could have exploited his gifts to greater advantage, but he took what they gave him and created some indisputable gems.

## Acknowledgment

I am beholden to Ted Ohno, music and film collector *par excellence*, for my DVD copy of *Change of Mind*. Michael Perkins transcribed the bass ostinato for the *Anatomy Theme*.

## Playlist

### (Recordings cited in order of appearance in the chapter)

"Edward the First" 3:20 New York, April 25 (Dance) or May 26 (Stratemann) 1969. *The Intimate Ellington* (Pablo [OJC CD 1992]). Duke Ellington p, Paul Kondziela b, Rufus Jones d.

"Wanderlust" 6:26 New York, April 25, 1969. *Up in Duke's Workshop* (Pablo [OJC CD 1979]). Cootie Williams, Willie Cook tp, Benny Green, Benny Powell tb, Russell Procope, Paul Gonsalves, Harold Ashby, Harry Carney reeds, Duke Ellington p, Paul Kondziela b, Rufus Jones d. Solos: Williams, Ashby.

"Black Butterfly" 3:40, "Neo-Creole" 3:52 New York, June 20, 1969. *Up in Duke's Workshop* (Pablo [OJC CD 1979]). Cootie Williams, Willie Cook, Mercer Ellington, Money Johnson tp, Lawrence Brown, Benny Green, Chuck Connors tb, Johnny Hodges, Russell Procope, Norris Turney, Paul Gonsalves, Harold Ashby, Harry Carney reeds, Duke Ellington p, Victor Gaskin, Paul Kondziela b, Rufus Jones d. Solos "Black Butterfly": Hodges as, Turney cl, "Neo-Creole": Ashby ts, Turney as.

*Assault on a Queen* Hollywood, January 19 and 20, 1966. Dragon's Domain Records (CD 2016). Cat Anderson, Cootie Williams, Conte Candoli, Al Porcino, Ray Triscari tp, Milt Bernhart, Murray McEachern, Ken Shroyer tb, Jimmy Hamilton, Johnny Hodges, Paul Gonsalves, Bud Shank, Buddy Colette, Harry Carney reeds, Duke Ellington p, John Lamb b, Louie Bellson d, Catherine Gotthoffer harp. Timings and soloists of tracks that bear Ellington's sound (numbered as in CD reissue):

7. "The First Dive (Raising the Sub)" 8:04 Paul Gonsalves, perhaps Duke Ellington p
2. "Mama Bahama" 1:05 Cootie Williams/Johnny Hodges, Duke Ellington
11. "Mama Bahama Islander" 1:13 Bud Shank flt, Catherine Gotthoffer harp
12. "Blessings on the Night (The Kiss)" 2:41 Murray McEachern, Bud Shank flt
3. "She Walks Well" 3:36 Duke Ellington, Johnny Hodges, Murray McEachern
19. "The Big Heist (Album Version)" 5:49 Paul Gonsalves, Bud Shank flt, Jimmy Hamilton

"Wild Man Moore" 1:49, "Battle Royal" 4:31, "Mood Indigo" 3:15, "Paris Blues" 3:22, "Autumnal Suite" 3:15, "Nite" 3:32 (first two titles) Paris, December 14, 1960, (3rd and 4th titles probably) Hollywood, May or June 1960, (last two titles) New York, May 2–3, 1961. *Paris Blues Soundtrack* (Rykodisc enhanced CD [1997]). Personnel varies. Louis Armstrong tp (1, 2), Bill Byers tb (on "Battle Royal"), Murray McEachern tb (all others).

"Paris Blues" 4:21 New York, January 30, 1962. *All American in Jazz + Midnight in Paris* (originally Columbia, Essential Jazz Classics EU [CD 2013]) Cat Anderson, Bill Berry, Harold "Shorty" Baker, Ray Nance tp, Lawrence Brown, Chuck Connors, Leon Cox tb, Jimmy Hamilton cl, Russell Procope as, Johnny Hodges as, Paul Gonsalves ts, Harry Carney bs, Duke Ellington p, Aaron Bell b, Sam Woodyard d. Solos: Jimmy Hamilton, Paul Gonsalves, Johnny Hodges.

Peggy Lee "I'm Gonna Go Fishin'" 2:07 (D. Ellington—P. Lee) Hollywood, July 26, 1960. Originally Capitol 45 rpm, Peggy Lee, *The Capitol Years* (Capitol CD [1997]). Bill Holman Orchestra.

"I'm Gonna Go Fishin'" 3:52 (comp Ellington) Bell Studios, New York, May 25, 1962. *The Feeling of Jazz* (Black Lion CD [1988]). Cat Anderson, Roy Burrowes, Bill Berry tp, Ray Nance cnt, Lawrence Brown, Leon Cox, Chuck Connors tb, Jimmy Hamilton, Johnny Hodges, Russell Procope, Paul Gonsalves, Harry Caney reeds, Duke Ellington p, Aaron Bell b, Sam Woodyard d. Solo: Ray Nance.

*Anatomy of a Murder*, Hollywood, May 29 and June 1 and 2, 1959. Columbia CD (1999). Cat Anderson, Clark Terry, Shorty Baker, Gerald Wilson tp, Ray Nance tp, vln, Quentin Jackson, John Sanders, Britt Woodman tb, Johnny Hodges as, Russell Procope as, Jimmy Hamilton cl, ts, Paul Gonsalves ts, Harry Carney bs, Duke Ellington p, Jimmy Woode b, Jimmy Johnson d. Timings and soloists of tracks cited in text (numbered as in CD reissue):

1. "Main Title and Anatomy of a Murder" 3:56 Jimmy Hamilton cl, Ray Nance tp, Paul Gonsalves ts, Duke Ellington p
2. "Flirtibird" 2:12 Johnny Hodges
3. "Way Early Subtone" 3:56 Russell Procope cl
4. "Hero to Zero" 2:10 Paul Gonsalves
5. "Low Key Lightly" 3:37 Duke Ellington p, Ray Nance vln
7. "Midnight Indigo" 2:43 Harry Carney, Billy Strayhorn p, Duke Ellington celeste
8. "Almost Cried" 2:24 Harold "Shorty" Baker tp
12. "Haupe" 2:38 Johnny Hodges
13. "Upper and Outest" 2:19 Ray Nance, Cat Anderson
14. "Anatomy of a Murder" (stereo single) 2:43 Jimmy Woode, Ray Nance tp, Paul Gonsalves, Nance muted tp, Ellington p fade
18. "Polly" 3:36 Johnny Hodges, Ray Nance vln
24. "Anatomy of a Murder" (mono single) 2:43 Jimmy Woode, Ray Nance tp, Paul Gonsalves, Nance muted tp, Ellington p fade
25. "The Grande Finale" 10:47 Ellington interview with musical illustrations

Chapter 8

# Ellington in the Global Village

> In Damascus, Duke had woken up to an earthquake roar of cars, as if all the rush-hour traffic of the world had become snarled up in this one city.... The light in Bombay, the sky drifting over the Arabian Sea, a filth storm in Ceylon ... wherever he was, however tired, he'd note it down, confident he'd find its musical potential later.
> —GEOFF DYER (1996, 59–60)

In his sixties, after traveling thousands of miles from Harlem to Hollywood and visiting every port in Europe, Ellington's crowded itinerary suddenly exposed him to what he called "the other side of the world." It started with a ten-week tour of the Near and Middle East sponsored by the US State Department in the autumn of 1963. The tour took him to Amman (Jordan), Kabul (Afghanistan), New Delhi (India), Colombo (Ceylon, now Sri Lanka), Tehran (Iran), Madras (now Chennai, India), Bombay (now Mumbai, India), Baghdad (Iraq), and Ankara (Turkey). (Concerts in five more cities were canceled when the orchestra was abruptly flown home after the assassination of President John F. Kennedy in Dallas, Texas.) Ellington's state-sponsored tour, like the state-sponsored tours of Louis Armstrong and other jazz musicians in the early 1960s, was a blatant attempt by the US government to counteract Soviet propaganda about the American persecution of their African American citizens.

Political issues inevitably reared up. "At the press conferences ... I always told them that the Negro has a tremendous investment in *our* country," Ellington wrote in "Orientations" (1964, 17–18), his journal of the trip. "We have helped to build it, and we have invested blood in every war the country has fought." Without denying that there was an issue, he dismissed its propaganda value. "It must be remembered," he told the foreign press, "that this is not an international issue but a national one."

Ellington, characteristically, blinked at the political overtones and luxuriated in the first-class treatment of his musicians, the regimen of playing three or four concerts a week instead of seven or eight, and the lavish hospitality in the embassies, in theaters great and small, and on the streets. "The tour was a great adventure for us," Ellington wrote on his return. "Sometimes I felt it was this world upside down. The look of the natural country is so unlike ours and the very contours of the earth seem to be different. The smell, the vastness, the birds, and the exotic beauty of all these countries make a great impression" ("Orientations," 14). Ellington's sensations naturally found their way into his music, starting with the *Far East Suite* (1966) and persisting as an Afro-Eurasian thematic thread in his music from then on.

## Seeping Impressions of the East

Inspiring as the indigenous music was for him, Ellington had no interest in imitating what he heard in the Middle East or importing its musical devices. "The minute you become academic about it you are going to fall into the trap of copying many other people who have tried to give a reflection of the music," he said. It was the same esthetic instinct he had followed all his life, when the musical currents that surrounded him were less exotic than the ones he was now encountering. His artistic impulse led him to making music that he once incisively called "a genuine original synthetic hybrid." That phrase popped up when the band played a dance date at Travis Air Force Base in March 1958, and he took the microphone to announce, "We have a request for some real genuine authentic Latin-American music. Now this will not be a mambo, a cha cha, or a rhumba, or a merenguita." And then, the punchline: "This will be a genuine original synthetic hybrid." On the spur of the moment, an unforgettable generic category.

The sounds he heard in his Middle East travels he would conceptualize in his own terms based on the self-reliance that he had always counted on. About the exotic rhythms and scales, he said, "It's more valuable to have absorbed them while there. You let it roll around, undergo a chemical change, and then seep out on paper in the form that will suit the musicians who are going to play it." The gestation period for Ellington and Billy Strayhorn took more than three years as they tried out some pieces in concerts, until December 1966, when they recorded the music of the *Far East Suite* in nine movements.

The second movement, "Bluebird of Delhi (Mynah)," makes a simple illustration of the way they transmuted their Eastern experience. The trumpeter Rolf Ericson said, "Ellington and Strayhorn were very observant with what was going on around them. I remember once when we were sitting at a café in Hyderabad in India and a bird was twittering in a bush. Strayhorn said to Duke, 'Hey, you hear that?' The bird was twittering something and they pulled out a piece of paper and wrote it down. That became the idea to *The Far East Suite*" (Westin 2018, 11).

"Bluebird of Delhi (Mynah)" is built around a two-bar trill played on clarinet by Jimmy Hamilton. Out of context, this short melodic figure seems a bit effete—a staccato run up and down the scale. The trill, Ellington tells us, imitates "the pretty lick" sung by the mynah bird. Tellingly, not *any* mynah bird but a particular mynah bird. "He sang [the pretty lick] all the time Billy Strayhorn was in his room," Ellington says, and in fact it "was the only answer the bird ever made to Strayhorn's repeated efforts at conversation throughout his stay" (Dance 1967). From this germ of melody, a modest starting point by any standard, the mynah's repeated call becomes the decorative foreground for the busy, bustling orchestration that surrounds it and gives it substance. Like the teeming city that was the elegant mynah bird's habitat, the orchestration is dense but somehow supple, weighty but sprightly, indeed toe-tapping. The pretty lick from the bird makes a playful contrast to the swirling urban landscape.

Another movement, the unpronounceable (and unexplained[22]) "Depk" brings the busy, bustling background of "Bluebird of Delhi" into the foreground. Its inspiration was more oblique. It originated, Ellington said, in "a wonderful dance by six boys and six girls" that entertained the band at one of the stops along the way. Not that the music imitates the dance. By the time he got around to writing it, Ellington says, "All I could remember afterwards was the kick on the sixth beat" (Dance 1967). That kick on the sixth beat is what Ellington "absorbed" of the dance, and "Depk" is the tune that seeped out onto Ellington's manuscript paper. Notwithstanding its putative origin as a dance, "Depk" would pose a challenge for any choreographer. It proves well suited, however, as a platform for solos by Jimmy Hamilton on clarinet and Harry Carney on baritone saxophone. The East inspired it, but it is the East filtered through Ellington and his men.

---

22. According to the Free Dictionary, DEPK stands for "Department of Environment and Pollution Kumamoto." https://acronyms.thefreedictionary.com/DEPK, but it is irrelevant geographically and thematically to Ellington's composition.

## The Global Village

As Ellington's travels became global, he grew acutely conscious of the shrinking of the planet. People in exotic places like Senegal, when he got to meet them face-to-face at the Negro Arts Festival in 1966, melded into a common humanity. It was the same in the Near East, the Middle East, the Far East, the Balkans, the Iron Curtain countries, Austronesia, Oceania, South America—everywhere he traveled. The places may have looked exotic, but the people were the same. They responded to his music with roars of approval and tears of joy. Not because it was about mynah birds or didgeridoos or little African flowers but because it was an "authentic synthetic hybrid" as only Duke Ellington could make it.

Ellington's encounters with the shrinking planet coincided perfectly with the thinking of a fashionable professor of English literature, Marshall McLuhan, whose musings on mass media and telecommunications in *Understanding Media* (1964) and other books were a revelation at the time. McLuhan had an epigrammatic bent, spinning out maxims such as "the medium is the message" and "art is anything you can get away with" and "there are no passengers on planet earth, we are all crew." The maxims were mostly inscrutable but in their moment of currency, they traveled very well. In the hip 1960s, they resonated as smartly anarchic. (With guile worthy of Ellington himself, McLuhan habitually told interviewers, "I don't necessarily agree with everything I say.") McLuhan presented a conception of the world as a "global village," and that was a concept that resonated with the globetrotting Duke Ellington.

McLuhan inspired the title of Ellington's *Afro-Eurasian Eclipse*, a 1971 suite in eight movements. It opens with a long composition called "Chinoiserie," a perfect title for Ellington's slant on the Orient. The French word *chinoiserie*, literally "Chinese-like" or perhaps better "China-ish," came into being as the name for Westernized impressions of Chinese decoration, and Ellington's conception, as the word implies, is predictably as much Ellington as Orient. Ellington concocted a wry spoken introduction to the suite that took up a minute and a half at performances. In his most studious tone, he explained the inspiration for the title:

> This is really the chinoiserie. Last year about this time we premiered a new suite titled *Afro-Eurasian Eclipse*. And of course the title was inspired by a statement made by Mr. Marshall McLuhan of the University of Toronto. Mr. McLuhan says that the whole world is going Oriental, and that no one will be able to retain his or her identity, not

even the Orientals. And of course we travel around the world a lot, and in the last five or six years we, too, have noticed this thing to be true. So as a result, we have done a sort of thing, a parallel or something, and we'd like to play a little piece of it for you. . . . Harold Ashby has been inducted into the responsibility and the obligation of possibly scraping a tiny bit of the charisma off the chinoiserie, immediately after our piano player has completed his rikki-tikki.

As promised, Ellington's piano opens the piece in a style well described by his phrase "rikki-tikki" for less than a minute (0:45, from 1:39 to 2:24 following the spoken introduction). His piano gives way to a ravishing alto saxophone duet played by Russell Procope and Johnny Hodges, a thirty-second masterpiece (2:24 to 2:54) that is one of those sonic marvels that only Ellington could write; listeners will wish it were much longer. Then comes the orchestra, dense and brooding, and then the promised soloist (at 3:24 for four and a half minutes), tenor saxophonist Harold Ashby, "scraping a bit of the charisma off the chinoiserie," as Ellington puts it, as Ashby wails at estimable length. "Chinoiserie" provides a rousing opening for the suite.

In the five years between the *Far East Suite* and *Afro-Eurasian Eclipse*, Ellington and the orchestra had completed a Pacific tour of Japan, Taiwan, the Philippines, Hong Kong, Thailand, Myanmar (then known as Burma), Malaysia, Indonesia, Singapore, New Zealand, Australia, and Hawaii; in Hong Kong, he was intrigued at seeing the junks were "motor-powered," which, he says, "confirms the views of Marshall McLuhan."

### An African Stamp of Approval

Ellington's Afro-Eurasian impulse was further quickened in 1967, when he was honored with a postage stamp by the Togolese Republic, the small West African state sandwiched between Ghana and Benin. Ellington's stamp was one of four that commemorated composers, and he found himself in good company alongside Bach, Beethoven, and Debussy. Soon after, he began performing new compositions that he introduced as parts of what he called the *Togo Brava Suite*. He told his audiences, "Our humble suite is just a token of gratitude and appreciation." In concerts, he performed the suite in four parts, but posthumous releases contain three additional movements making seven in all (released in 2001 by Storyville Records). The confusion surrounding *Togo Brava Suite* is a symptom of Ellington's hyperactive schedule in these last years. Self-imposed as it was, the hectic schedule meant that several projects were left in varying states of completion. They were ambitious and often masterful, though the absence of recorded works meant that they seldom received full attention from the composer and certainly less notice from listeners and critics than they deserved.

When the seven parts of *Togo Brava Suite* were finally collated, listeners discovered that Ellington had imbued the suite with a kind of serenity that was distinctly different from his more energetic, typically restless, bottom-heavy approaches to his other Afro-Eurasian dedications. He never visited Togo, and his impressions of it were formed by hearsay and undoubtedly from travel writers.

The serenity of the suite had a straightforward interpretation in the opening movement, which is called "Soul Soothing Beach," a reference to what tourist guidebooks such as *The Lonely Planet* call "palm-fringed beaches along the Atlantic coastline," one of Togo's main attractions. Ellington's "Soul Soothing Beach" does indeed soothe the soul, notably by assigning harmonic prominence to the mellow trombone section. Over the lush blend of the three trombones, Ellington solos on piano with unhurried flourishes and then turns over the foreground to Norris Turney on flute. Until this moment, the sound of the flute was unfamiliar in Ellington's music. Suddenly, we discover it elevated as the principal solo instrument in *Togo Brava Suite*.

Norris Turney joined the orchestra primarily as an alto saxophone player. He was versatile, and in addition to alto saxophone, he also showed mastery on clarinet, tenor saxophone, and, for the first time in Ellington's sound scheme, flute. The delicacy of the flute imbues the suite. It is impossible to know which came first: was it Ellington's newly discovered affection for Norris Turney's deft intonation on the transverse horn that inspired the delicacy of so many of the movements or was it the serene mood Ellington chose to honor Togo's generous gesture that gave the flute its ascendant role? Either way, Ellington conjoins the flute and the mood adroitly.

### Menacing to Soothing in One Theme

That delicacy rings clear in a movement of the *Togo Brava Suite* known as "Toto." As it happens, "Toto" recycles the theme of the composition called "Afrique" from the *Afro-Eurasian Eclipse*. Listening to these two thematically related compositions in succession highlights the contrasting moods of these two suites with stunning directness. "Afrique" is a complex, roiling big band shout. The orchestration is wafted along from start to finish by Rufus Jones's hyperkinetic drum work. When Jones replaced drummer Sam Woodyard in 1966, he brought a different sensibility to the band. His nickname was "Speedy," and Ellington discovered that he excelled in "African, jungle, and oriental pieces" (as Stanley Dance put it). "Afrique" exploits those aspects of Jones's drumming. It opens with a rapid propulsive paradiddle that will sustain the entire composition (five minutes in the studio version but longer in concert performances; Dance [1995] says, "the other musicians like [drum solos] because they can leave the stage for a smoke or a taste while the drummer gets his exercise"). Over this steady beat, the instrumentalists play individual lines that are long and sustained, like chants or incantations. They provide a diversion from the insistent roll of the drums—indefatigable, as it goes on, though undeniably dynamic and definitely "speedy."

Admittedly, almost any other performance would sound quiescent after the drum-heavy "Afrique." The value in considering "Toto (Afrique)" from *Togo Brava Suite* alongside "Afrique" from *Afro-Eurasian Eclipse* is not to expose "Toto" as a pallid reflection of "Afrique" but to demonstrate how Ellington can manipulate the same melodic content to create an entirely different mood. "Toto," like "Soul Soothing Beach," is relatively relaxed. Though still exotic, its movement is undulating rather than driving. The orchestral textures are spare, dance-like verging on trance-like. Instead of the drums providing the rock-steady undertow as they do in "Afrique," Jones's drums assume the more familiar accompanying role, supporting Ellington's piano, Joe Benjamin's bass, and once again, Norris Turney's flute.

Eddie Lambert, the most comprehensive reviewer of Ellington's music, sees his latter-day Afro-Eurasian impulse as a kind of throwback to his beginnings. Ellington, he says, is "re-asserting an aspect of his musical character which had been dormant for much of the time he worked with Strayhorn. The music of . . . *The Afro-Eurasian Eclipse* relates to the menacing music of Ellington's first period such as *Black and Tan Fantasy* and *The Mooche*." "Had Ellington been a time traveler," says Lambert, "*Afrique* would have been a wholly acceptable substitute for *Jungle Nights in Harlem* as a background for a Cotton Club dance routine" (1998, 298–99).

Lambert would undoubtedly have revised that opinion if he had heard "Toto," the twin sister of the song "Afrique," or other pieces from the *Togo Brava Suite*. Perhaps some of Ellington's Afro-Eurasian music hearkens back to the jungle music of the Cotton Club, as Lambert says, but much more of it does not. Afro-Eurasian Ellington exists on a spectrum from "menacing" (Lambert's term) to "soul soothing" (Ellington's term).

## Soul Flute—An Intimate Interlude

Norris Turney joined Duke Ellington's orchestra in May 1969, when he was forty-eight, as a temporary replacement for Johnny Hodges who was having health problems. Before that, Turney had shuttled back and forth between his native Ohio and New York City, an itinerant musician finding work with various bands. He was versatile on all the reeds, so that when Hodges returned, Ellington kept him in the band. Under ordinary circumstances, that would have overloaded the alto saxophone contingent with the veterans Russell Procope and Hodges already there, but Turney's mastery of other reed instruments curtailed that problem. Indeed, Turney's versatility led to a real oddity in the annals of the Ellington orchestra (or any other): after he became the extra man in the band, the trombone player, Booty Wood, injured his hand, and so Ellington moved Turney into the trombone section where he played trombone parts on his tenor saxophone. And it didn't end there. "I played a lot of roles, all around the sections," he told Mike Lewis (2009). "I've handled just about every part in this band, except for Harry Carney's baritone part. To begin with, we were to leave for Europe in '69, and one of our trombone players wasn't able to make it. So I went back into the trombone section to fill the sound out there. And I read trumpet parts; I played Willie Cook's [trumpet] part on clarinet. On the Japanese tour, I had to take care of Paul Gonsalves's tenor part. I'm like a policeman—troubleshooting here and there." His versatility kept him in the band, and he was proud of it.

When Johnny Hodges died unexpectedly in May 1970, Turney naturally moved into the saxophone section and took over his alto saxophone parts. His role included occasional ensemble turns on clarinet, but with Turney, there were other possibilities. For the first time, Ellington had three tenor saxophone players. At almost every concert, he asked Turney to pick up his tenor saxophone, warm up the reed, and step onto the proscenium to form a trio alongside Paul Gonsalves and Harold Ashby. The music they made was energetic rather than artful, but the sight of the three big horns strutting their stuff on a simple blues made a visual spectacle that audiences responded to.

Before Turney came along, the only flute parts in any music ever written by Ellington were some solos he tailored for Bud Shank, a great jazz musician now a studio player in the Hollywood orchestra that played his score for the movie *Assault on a Queen*. Ellington was so impressed by Shank, a virtuoso player on alto saxophone as well as flute, that he offered him a place in the orchestra (Jack 2004, 202). At the time, it seemed that Ellington's ardor was for Shank rather than for the flute in general. Jimmy Hamilton, perhaps inspired by Ellington's regard for Shank's flute when he sat beside him in the studio orchestra, took up the flute around this time. "He practised flute assiduously and became very proficient on it during his last years with Ellington," Stanley Dance reported (1970, 139), "but the leader never elected to make use of this new skill." Two years after Hamilton retired, Turney reawakened Ellington's feeling for the timbre of the flute.

Ellington's infatuation with Turney's flute from 1970 onward represented a considerable turnaround. As Dance observed in his notes on the Third Sacred Concert, "Ellington, with his strong likes and dislikes where tone color was concerned, long resisted the use of the flute in his orchestra." His conversion was not unlike his enthusiasm for the tenor saxophone in 1940 after resisting it for so many years. His exploitation of the flute in the *Togo Brava Suite* in 1971 might be explained as an adjunct to his Afro-Eurasian zeal; Ellington might have regarded the flute as the conservatory descendant of all kinds of Afro-Eurasian pipes and whistles and ocarinas. But if so, Ellington soon found himself exploiting it in contexts beyond the Afro-Eurasian theme.

Among the flute specialties that came to light posthumously (as did the full *Togo Brava Suite*) in this period of relatively rare studio recordings are a few minor delights. "Soul Flute" was a showcase for Turney that was played regularly in live performances. At a concert in Bristol, England (not coincidentally, a concert that featured four parts of the nascent *Togo Brava Suite* as well), Ellington entrusted six solo choruses to Turney on "Soul Flute," the kind of showing that he occasionally might have reserved for such stalwarts as Johnny Hodges and Paul Gonsalves but unusual even for them. The composition itself is a simple blues with a rock rhythm, and Ellington gives Turney plenty of freedom to show off his prowess.

Ellington's growing feeling for the flute also shows in a studio recording in which he reduced the band to a quintet in order to highlight the magnificently contrasting timbres of Turney's soaring flute and Harry Carney's bass clarinet. The minimalist arrangement, called "Intimate Interlude," is an unhurried lope characteristic of the music Ellington liked to play when winding down at the end of recording sessions. It may have originated as a kind of trial run so that Ellington could gauge the mettle of the man with the unfamiliar instrument that he was then integrating into his musical palette. Like "Soul Flute," "Intimate Interlude" shows Ellington finding a space for Turney's flute above and beyond the copious use he made of its "exotic" sound in his Afro-Eurasian excursions. "Soul Flute" was played frequently at concerts for the next two years, but "Intimate Interlude" was never played afterward; it remains one of dozens of Ellington's buried treasures.

Sad to say, this late-career kinship between the Maestro and his flutist ended on a sour note. As his son, Mercer, noticed, "As he became older, he became much less restrained.... He didn't placate anyone anymore" (1978, 155). Turney felt the brunt of it. He went to Ellington sometime in 1972, when he had been in the band for three years, and told him he thought Ellington was setting the tempo too fast on one of his features. Ellington returned a blank stare. Turney, obviously unknowingly, had crossed a line. In Ellington's view, he was, as Ellington's son says, "defying his authority" (161). From that day on, Ellington increased the tempo every time he called the number. Turney simply put up with it for a while, but after several months, in the middle of the feature at the Persian Room in the Marco Polo Hotel in Miami Beach on February 1, 1973, Turney quietly packed up his horns and walked off the bandstand for good.

For Turney, the aftermath turned out well enough. He found himself in some demand after he left, playing regularly in good company and making his first recordings as a leader. (He died in 2001 at seventy-nine.) After laboring in relative obscurity for more than two decades, he had blossomed in his four years with Ellington. The unique sound he brought to Ellington's palette put him in the spotlight night after night. Blessedly, its afterglow carried him through the rest of his days. It is, in the scheme of things, Norris Turney's legacy, and Turney knew it. "I'm part of the family—an Ellingtonian," he told Mike Lewis (2009) years later.

### "These Blue-Blooded Black Roots"

These years of Ellington's "unending world safari" (as Derek Jewell [1972] called it) brought another excursion that thrilled Ellington. He was invited to perform at the First International Festival of Negro Arts in Dakar, Senegal, in January 1966. In his memoir, Ellington celebrated it in a diary entry, saying, "After writing African music for thirty-five years, here I am at last in Africa! I can only hope and wish that our performance of 'La Plus Belle Africaine,' which I have written in anticipation of the occasion, will mean something to the people gathered here" (*MiMM* 337).

He had good reason to fret about its reception, of course, because he knew very well that the music he had written for the occasion was not really "African music" any more than his "Bluebird of Delhi" was Indian music. Both compositions were Ellington music, with a nod in the direction of whatever he might have absorbed or imagined as ethnically congruous. Indeed, in his original remarks on the occasion, in a newspaper interview, he referred to his compositions more appropriately as "pseudo-African music."

And he admitted, "Now I'll be happy to know a lot more about what the music sounds like over here" (quoted by Woideck 2017, 244).

At the performance in Dakar, his fretting about the reception of "La Plus Belle Africaine" was dispelled by the most salutary reception imaginable. "When the time for our concert comes, it is a wonderful success," he wrote (*MiMM* 337–38). "We get the usual diplomatic applause from the diplomatic corps down front, but the cats in the bleachers really dig it. You can see them rocking back there while we play. When we are finished, they shout approval and dash for backstage, where they hug and embrace us, some of them with tears in their eyes. It is acceptance at the highest level, and it gives us a once-in-a-lifetime feeling of having truly broken through to our brothers."

His experience in Senegal gave even greater depth to his Afro-Eurasian sensibility. He expressed it in a virtuoso display of words and music in an impromptu recital for French ORTF television (July 2, 1970). Though the Senegal excursion was then four and a half eventful years in the past, Ellington recounted its impact with such spontaneous lyricism as to make it into a kind of found poem (as in my transcription below). He began, "When I was in Africa, in Senegal, I met Papa Ibra Tall, a great Senegalese artist, and I was giving him a theme on jazz because it's a constant question, 'What is jazz?' And I was busy adlibbing this extravagant picture of jazz, and I said—

> Jazz is a tree.
> It has many branches that reach out to many directions.
> At the end of each branch is a twig,
>     and at the end of each twig there are many different-shaped leaves
>     and many vary-colored flowers.
>     . . . it goes into the far east and picks up an exotic blossom.
> It goes east, west, north, south and everywhere,
>     and everywhere it goes it picks up a certain influence. . . .
> And as it goes down into the deep roots
>     that go way down into the earth
> then you'll find that these blue-blooded black roots
> are deep in the soil of Black Africa
>     which of course is the foundation of everything that is in the beat—
> the beat that, today, is the most listened to in the world.

The beat he refers to, of course, archetypically four beats to the bar, propels jazz, but has been a hallmark of the many musical genres that originated in the United States from field chants to gospel and the Charleston and Broadway songs and the hucklebuck and rock 'n' roll. And it is the beat that now propels Brazilian bossa nova, West Indian reggae, Korean K-pop, and virtually every other form of pop music in the world.

The composition Ellington wrote for the festival, "La Plus Belle Africaine," immediately occupied a highly personal space for him, Afro-Eurasian or not. It is the piece he played most frequently. On his return from Senegal, he immediately put it on display in his concerts, and he played it nightly with few exceptions for the remaining eight years until March 1974, his last concert. Like so much of the music of these peripatetic years, the only studio recording was made privately (March 29, 1966, unissued but in the Playlist; Harry Carney, a key voice in the arrangement, was unaccountably absent for this recording, which may explain why it has never been released). In a studio recording, we might expect its shouting brass and insistent percussion to be perfectly balanced and the exciting, headstrong charms of the piece to be reined in slightly so that they could glow all the more brightly. We await the studio version, but in the meantime, we have abundant live performances and they boast a spontaneity, the spirit of abandon, though far from reckless abandon, that would be hard to replicate without the stimulus of a bobbing, engaged audience—the "cats rocking in the bleachers," as Ellington put it after its first public performance.

Among the numerous concert performances to choose from, Eddie Lambert preferred the fourteen-minute turn at Juan-les-Pins, France, just six months after the Dakar premiere, as "full of fire and inspiration" (1998, 269). A worthy contender is the eight-minute rendition at a concert in Warsaw, Poland, almost six years later, with the band in superb form. Another nominee is the performance in Birmingham, England, in 1971, "of which the performance here," in the words of the annotator Derek Jewell (1972), "is "the best I've ever heard." (All are in the Playlist.)

One of the testaments to Ellington's feeling for "La Plus Belle Africaine" is that he kept it in the active repertoire even after two of the original soloists left the band: Jimmy Hamilton, clarinet, and John Lamb, bass, soloed along with mainstays Harry Carney, baritone saxophone, and Ellington himself, but by 1969 they were gone. Instead of retiring the piece, as he often did under similar circumstances, Ellington reassigned their solos to Russell Procope and Joe Benjamin, respectively, and carried on playing it. Perhaps more crucial was the loss of drummer Sam Woodyard. Though the bass player takes on the most fundamental rhythmic role, the drummer complements him in propelling the piece; Woodyard was replaced in 1966 by Rufus Jones, who has a much heavier touch. The differences in the performances before and after 1969 are hardly glaring, but they are audible, though the composition, both before and after, never failed to earn a rousing reception.

The bass ostinato in "La Plus Belle Africaine" (transcription by Michael Perkins).

In the absence of a studio version and with so many live performances that might vie for the definitive version, the most likely candidate—unequalled, surely, among the rest—emerged belatedly. At a scintillating concert in Coventry Cathedral on February 21, 1966 (not released until 2018), Ellington surprised the audience, and perhaps the orchestra, by calling for "La Plus Belle Africaine" as an encore. It was unexpected because the concert was made up mainly of sacred music ("Come Sunday," "Come Easter," "Tell Me It's the Truth," "In the Beginning God" with choir, and a contemplative piano solo, *New World A-Comin'*). These pieces, many of them carried over from his inaugural Sacred Concert at Grace Cathedral in San Francisco just five months before, are perfectly calibrated for the august setting in Coventry, one of the most awesome houses of worship in the world.

Ellington, perhaps impishly, raises the tempo in the encores. "We would like to do another encore, if you don't mind," he says in a quiet voice. "La Plus Belle Africaine" does not exactly disturb the solemnity of the occasion. It has its own dignity, though it is a dignity that encourages toe-tapping and might arouse thoughts of finger-snapping at the pauses on the second and fourth bars. (Ellington actually led the audience in finger-snapping in the last chorus when he played it in Birmingham, England, in October 1971.) In Coventry, a few weeks after its Senegal premiere, the band plays it with easy familiarity and cool discipline. The original soloists, including Woodyard, are all present. The studio recording, if it is finally issued, will be hard-pressed to improve on the Coventry version.

"La Plus Belle Africaine" is densely rhythmic. It is propelled throughout by an eight-bar ostinato, shown in the illustration. The ostinato is carried principally by the bass player, and then covered by the piano player when the bassist solos, and it is parroted rhythmically by the drummer all through.

The clarinet plays a simple melody over the ostinato and is abruptly interrupted by the cascading brass in a twelve-bar shout that recurs as if demarcating movements. The ostinato is then taken up by the piano while the bassist solos with the bow. After the brass shout marks the end of the bassist's outing, there is a ruminative orchestral interval that momentarily interrupts the ostinato, with trombones and other harmonic elements adding coloration to the rhythmic undercurrent. (For analysis of the two modalities, see Woideck 2017, 241–42.) Carney then brings his sonorous horn into play, and the clarinet returns and makes a gentle diminuendo. The piece fades away over the ebbing bass ostinato.

The composition flows more directly from the rhythm trio than perhaps any other orchestral work by Ellington, embodying what he calls its "blue-blooded black roots." He composed many pieces that were essentially (or basically) rhythmic—"Rockin' in Rhythm," "Daybreak Express," "The Mooche," "Harlem Air Shaft," and "Dance No. 2" in *Liberian Suite*, among others—but in them, the rhythmic pulse was carried by the whole orchestra. Here, the clarinet, arco bass, and baritone saxophone caress the beat instead of punctuating it, seemingly floating on it. The heartbeat of the piece is down low, in the piano, bass, and drums. Ellington's "African music," or more aptly his "pseudo-African music," makes an idiosyncratic mix of grit and grace.

### Afro-Eurasian Ellington Is Still Ellington

Afro-Eurasian Ellington represented a fresh offshoot after forty-odd years of music-making. The epitome of Afro-Eurasian Ellington, for me at least, is his composition "Blue Pepper (Far East of the Blues)." Though it is placed near the middle of *The Far East Suite*, it is hardly unobtrusive. The pushy rhythms and brassy repetitious riffs in "Blue Pepper" could accompany belly dancers in Beirut or saber jugglers in Senegal or any number of mind-boggling rites in some exotic setting. And then, when the orchestra softens momentarily and Johnny Hodges takes center stage with a glimmering alto saxophone solo, it suddenly becomes clear that what we are hearing is the blues. For all its rhythmic trappings, "Blue Pepper (Far East of the Blues)" is a blues, and as such, it is a kindred spirit to all the blues we have heard before. As for those pushy rhythms and brassy riffs, they are not so exotic after all. They could equally accompany a kickline at the Cotton Club or a pole dancer in Atlantic City or, with a small stretch, a tap dancer in St. Patrick's Cathedral. Those too, come to think of it, are also exotic settings.

"Blue Pepper (Far East of the Blues)" may be prototypically Afro-Eurasian Ellington, but it is still Ellington. "The audiences that come to see us want to hear us, so they don't expect anything but us, and they don't get anything but us," Ellington told a critic at a press conference in Calcutta (1964, 19). Mozart might have said something similar two hundred years earlier when he faced his critics in the farthest reaches of the world *he* lived in, that is, London to the west and Prague to the east.

Duke Ellington saw more of the world in the last decade of his life than he could have imagined. The greatest social changes when he was growing up manifested themselves in mobility—social and occupational mobility, and above all, geographical mobility. Born into a world where steam engines were a source of wonderment, gawked at by the lucky few at state fairs, and telephones, radios, motorcars, and airplanes were still science fiction, the chances of an ordinary American visiting Rome or Athens or Stockholm in one's lifetime were slim. Europe was remote, and India, China, and Japan were beyond imagining. In the 1960s, which were also Ellington's sixties, he visited them all. He became an annual fixture in London, Paris, Stockholm, Rome, Tokyo, and other great cities. He traveled to Singapore, Sydney, Auckland, Dakar, Monaco, Zurich, Vienna, Venice, Warsaw, Ljubljana, and points between.

As a tourist, Ellington was most of all a sensualist. He left no recollections about museums or palaces or battlegrounds. Instead, he talked about the sounds and smells and sights wherever he went. About the birds and the snake charmers and the bustle in the bazaars. His reaction to Damascus in 1963 was assimilated by him in the same way as his reaction to Harlem in 1923. Both piqued his creative juices. Where Harlem had raised him into the ranks of the most interesting composers of his time, the Levantine cities rejuvenated those instincts for a spirited flourish.

What he made of those sensations, the inner urge, unique and personal, was a mystery even to him. In Harlem, he learned from his elders, but he never borrowed from them. In faraway lands, he heard the rhythms and the harmonies, but he never replicated them. He had no interest in becoming a master of generic stride piano or of world music. He settled for the role of master of what he identified as "genuine original synthetic hybrids." The real value of going places, as he said, is soaking in the rhythms and the harmonies along with the sights and smells. Nobody said it better: "You let it roll around, undergo a chemical change, and then seep out on paper in the form that will suit the musicians who are going to play it." A whole esthetic theory in fewer than thirty words.

Ralph Gleason, jazz critic for the *San Francisco Chronicle* from 1952 to 1975 and an unabashed Ellington booster, gave an interesting twist to it. "If Marshall McLuhan's prediction of the end of identity ever comes about, it will be a world that is without the kind of genius Ellington personifies," he wrote. "And that will be a sad world indeed." He needn't have worried, at least where Ellington was concerned. Afro-Eurasian Ellington is still Ellington.

## Playlist

### (In order of appearance in the chapter)

"Bluebird of Delhi (Mynah)" 3:18. (Ellington/Strayhorn) *The Far East Suite* (Bluebird CD [1995]). December 21, 1966, RCA Victor Studio, New York. Cootie Williams, Cat Anderson, Mercer Ellington, Herbie Jones tp, Lawrence Brown, Buster Cooper, Chuck Connors tb, Russell Procope as, cl, Jimmy Hamilton cl, Johnny Hodges as, Paul Gonsalves ts, Harry Carney bs, John Lamb b, Rufus Jones d. Duke Ellington conducts; there is no piano.

"Depk" 2:38. Same as "Bluebird of Delhi" but add Duke Ellington p.

"Chinoiserie" (Ellington) 8:13. *The Afro-Eurasian Eclipse* (Fantasy 1975, OJCCD 1991). New York, February 17, 1971. Cootie Williams, Money Johnson, Mercer Ellington, Eddie Preston tp, Booty Wood, Malcolm Taylor, Chuck Connors tb, Russell Procope as, cl, Norris Turney as, cl, Paul Gonsalves, Harold Ashby ts, Harry Carney bs, Ellington p, Joe Benjamin b, Rufus Jones d. Solos: Ellington spoken introduction (to 1:35), Ellington piano (1:39–2:24), alto saxophone duet (to 2:54), Harold Ashby enters at 3:24 over dense orchestration (to 8:09).

"Soul Soothing Beach" ("Mkis") 3:34. *Togo Brava Suite* (Storyville CD [2001]). New York, June 28, 1971. Cootie Williams, Money Johnson, Mercer Ellington, Richard Williams tp, Booty Wood, Malcolm Taylor, Chuck Connors tb, Russell Procope as, cl, Buddy Pearson, Norris Turney fl, Paul Gonsalves, Harold Ashby ts, Harry Carney bs, Ellington p, Joe Benjamin b, Rufus Jones d. Solos: Ellington, Turney.

"Afrique" 5:23 New York, February 17, 1971. *The Afro-Eurasian Eclipse*. Fantasy Records (Original Jazz Classics CD [1991]). Cootie Williams, Mercer Ellington, Money Johnson, Eddie Preston tp, Malcolm Taylor, Booty Wood, Chuck Connors, tb, Russell Procope, Norris Turney, Harold Ashby, Paul Gonsalves, Harry Carney reeds, Duke Ellington p, Joe Benjamin b, Rufus Jones d. Solo: Rufus Jones.

"Toto (Afrique)" 2:58 (same as "Soul Soothing Beach" except June 29, 1971). Solos: Ellington, Benjamin, Turney.

"Soul Flute" 3:05 *Togo Brava Suite* (Blue Note CD [1994]) Odeon Theatre, Bristol, England October 22, 1971. Cootie Williams, Johnny Coles, Mercer Ellington, Eddie Preston, Harold Johnson tp, Chuck Connors, Malcolm Taylor, Booty Wood tb, Russell Procope, Harold Minerve, Norris Turney, Paul Gonsalves, Harold Ashby, Harry Carney reeds, Duke Ellington p, Joe Benjamin b, Rufus Jones d. Solo: Turney fl plays six choruses.

"Intimate Interlude" 5:01 *The Intimate Ellington* (Pablo 1977 [CD 1992]) New York, February 2, 1971. Norris Turney fl, Harry Carney bass cl, Ellington p, Joe Benjamin b, Rufus Jones d.

"La Plus Belle Africaine" New York, RCA Studios, March 29, 1966. *Unissued*. Personnel as at Juan-les-Pins below except Jerome Richardson replaces Harry Carney.

"La Plus Belle Africaine" 13:49 Juan-les-Pins, France, July 27, 1966. *Soul Call* (Verve CD [1999]). Cat Anderson, Cootie Williams, Mercer Ellington, Herbie Jones tp, Lawrence Brown, Buster Cooper, Chuck Connors tb, Johnny Hodges, Russell Procope, Jimmy

Hamilton, Paul Gonsalves, Harry Carney reeds, Duke Ellington p, John Lamb b, Sam Woodyard d. Solos: Hamilton, Lamb, Carney.

"La Plus Belle Africaine" 8:12 Congress Hall, Warsaw, Poland, October 30, 1971. *Live in Warsaw* (Gambit Records [2009]). Cootie Williams, Mercer Ellington, Johnny Coles, Eddie Preston, Harold "Money" Johnson tp, Malcolm Taylor, Booty Wood, Chuck Connors tb, Russell Procope, Harold "Geezil" Minerve, Norris Turney, Harold Ashby, Paul Gonsalves, Harry Carney reeds, Duke Ellington p, Joe Benjamin b, Rufus Jones d. Solos: Procope (cl), Benjamin, Carney.

"La Plus Belle Africaine" 8:37 Birmingham Theatre, Birmingham, England, October 24, 1971. *The English Concert*, BGO Records (CD 1999). Personnel as above.

"La Plus Belle Africaine" 12:03 Coventry Cathedral, Coventry, England, February 21, 1966. *Duke Ellington in Coventry* (Storyville [2018]). (Same personnel as at Juans-les-Pins above.)

"Blue Pepper (Far East of the Blues)" 3:00 *The Far East Suite*. Date, place, and personnel same as "Bluebird of Delhi (Mynah)." Solos: Johnny Hodges, Cat Anderson.

Interlude 3

# Poets' Impressions of Duke Ellington

## Ages and Styles Apart

Such music is not only a new art form but a new reason for living.
—BLAISE CENDRARS, SWISS SURREALIST POET, 1933

There are only two things: love, all sorts of love, with pretty girls, and the music of . . . Duke Ellington. Everything else ought to go, because everything else is ugly.
—BORIS VIAN, FRENCH NOVELIST/ POET/ TRUMPET PLAYER, 1947

On Sunday, October 5, for the first time since George V was on the throne and Ramsay MacDonald at Downing Street, London will hear Duke Ellington and his orchestra.
For thirty years this remarkable man has coaxed from successive teams of musicians that unique blend of composition and improvisation, flamboyance and restraint, programme music and down-to-earth jazz utterance for which his name is famous.
—PHILIP LARKIN, ENGLISH POET, LIBRARIAN, AND JAZZ REVIEWER, 1958

INTERLUDE 3—POETS' IMPRESSIONS OF ELLINGTON: AGES AND STYLES APART

None of us will be the same if we hear the things his music says, that loving is the gift of life and making music was his way of love.
—JUDY COLLINS, AMERICAN FOLKSINGER, ON ELLINGTON'S PASSING 1975

The immeasurable gift of Duke Ellington, his musical genius and his personal elegance, lift us high beyond the reach of those who would pull us back to the cruel, mean earth.
—MAYA ANGELOU, AMERICAN POET, 1998

Chapter 9

# Diamonds in a Glittering Heap

> The man that hath no music in himself,
> Nor is not mov'd with concord on sweet sounds,
> Is fit for treasons, stratagems and spoils . . .
> Let no such man be trusted.
> —*THE MERCHANT OF VENICE*, V, I

Of all Duke Ellington's music, his Shakespeare suite, which he called *Such Sweet Thunder*, has been for me the most abiding. I first heard it in 1957, when it was brand new. It was not my first taste of Ellington's music, but it was the one that stayed on my phonograph most frequently, traveled with me to halls of residence and other temporary quarters, and has kept its place ever since. As a teenager intent on searching out a music with more depth than the pop banalities of the day, I recognized its twelve movements as genuinely inspired, rich in their diversity, and full of feeling. It took a few more years, probably in my undergraduate years as a literature major, to realize how deftly Ellington's suite, which he called "a tone parallel to the works of William Shakespeare," matched Shakespeare as a sprawling outpouring of human creativity, somehow capturing in its own modality the Shakespearean attributes as entertaining and beguiling and seductive and foreboding.

Later, when I took a critical view of jazz music and started writing about it, I realized that an Ellington masterpiece was almost foreordained at the time. In 1957, his orchestra, which he had assembled one man at a time in the first half of the 1950s, was finally replete with talent and character, a combination capable of executing these intricate pieces so flawlessly. Ellington himself was riding a crest. He conceived the Shakespeare suite in 1956, while reveling in a three-night stay at the Stratford Shakespearean Festival, an upstart corn-country institution that treated Shakespeare as a celebrity and Ellington likewise. His concerts there were on the eighteenth and twentieth of June, a Wednesday and Friday. Eleven days earlier, his orchestra made international headlines with a curfew-busting, dancing-in-the-aisles, near-riot at the Newport Jazz Festival in Newport, Rhode Island. Their performance would result in his bestselling Columbia album, *Ellington at Newport*, along with a cover story in *Time* magazine (Harman 1956) and a generous record contract, lauded in the *Time* story as one that will give him "time to write more big works, both instrumental and dramatic" (1956, 64). The first of those "big works," as Ellington told his audiences at the Stratford Festival and everywhere else he traveled, would be his tone parallel to the works of William Shakespeare.

I have written elsewhere about the extraordinarily fruitful relationship Ellington had with the Stratford Festival and about the Shakespeare suite (2005, 2019) and talked about it publicly many times. Here, my purpose is simpler. I want to point out the structure and content of the twelve movements of the suite, each one a gemstone, and then show how Ellington left them woefully—perhaps tragically—incomplete.

## "This Curious Mixture"

The twelve movements of the Shakespeare suite are strikingly diverse both in mood and in structure. Eight of them are conceived around Shakespeare's characters in their dramatic settings. Ellington explained the challenges and how he met them most articulately in a radio interview a few years later. "You have to adjust your perspective as to just what you're going to do and what you're to say and what you're going to say it about and how much of it you're supposed to be covering," he said (Smith 1962). "Actually in one album you're not going to parallel anything of Shakespeare. What do you need? A thousand writers and a thousand years to do it, you know, to cover Shakespeare. So we said we'll just devote one number to one Shakespearean word or one Shakespearean phrase." Instead of "word" or "phrase," he might have said one Shakespearean character in one particular situation, but either way, the rationale underlying the suite becomes clear.

That rationale came about from meticulous preparation. Ellington's personal style was to downplay or even deny deliberation of any kind, but in a few interviews, he admitted that he and Billy Strayhorn had "consultations with two or three Shakespearean actors and authorities.... We'd sit down and discuss for hours, you know, so forth and so on." Even that admission was modest. Strayhorn was more forthcoming when Stanley Dance quizzed him about it (1970, 28). "We read all of Shakespeare! We had to interpret what he said.... We had all these books we used to carry around, and all these people all over the US we used to see and talk to."

For Ellington, Shakespeare was not a passing fancy. He had taken a shine to his plays and his sonnets in Miss Boston's English class at Garrison Junior High School from 1913 to 1914 in Washington, DC. His biographer and occasional lyricist, Don George, pointed out that his personal library included "everything by Shakespeare, in many different versions" and "in all of his copies of the Shakespearean plays he had underlined parts that appealed to him" (1981, 136). Billy Strayhorn was equally enthralled. He "took it on excitedly, glowing to his friends about having an Ellington project geared especially to him" (Hajdu 1996, 155). He composed two of his themes soon after ("Half the Fun" in August 1956 and the piece that would evolve into "The Star-Crossed Lovers" in December) whereas Ellington, characteristically, left his to the deadline date the following summer. For both Ellington and Strayhorn, the exposure, old and new, was fruitful. At the grand premiere of the Shakespeare suite in Stratford, Tom Patterson, founder of the festival, said, "We were literally with the top Shakespeare scholars in the world, and Strayhorn didn't have a thing to apologize for. His knowledge was very deep" (Hajdu 1996, 183).

Facts like these were not well known at the time of the public release of the suite. There was in fact a noticeable sniff of disdain by some reviewers and even by Ellington's producer at Columbia, Irving Townsend. In a memoir a few years after the fact, Townsend (1960, 320–21) dismissed the Shakespeare suite with lofty Ivy League disdain. He recalled, "We all searched later for the final titles, and I found 'Such Sweet Thunder' in Bartlett's Quotations." So the Shakespeare project, according to Townsend's recollections three years after recording it, was accidental (a compilation), superficial (the result of a cram course), arbitrary (titled after the fact), and ersatz (Bartlett as a scholarly shortcut).

Ellington faced disdain early in a radio interview with Harry Rasky at Birdland (1957), where the band was polishing the movements at night and recording them by day. "How do you think Shakespeare purists or even jazz purists will take to this curious mixture of the Bard and jazz?" asked Rasky. Presumably, it was Rasky's tone that led Ellington to make a serious defense of his aims and, incidentally, reveal how carefully he had worked them out. "We sometimes lean a little bit toward caricature, but other people have gone about the business of actually changing Shakespeare, which I think is a much more hazardous thing than what we've done. All we did is just little thumbnail sketches, you know, of very short periods, never at any time trying to parallel an entire play or an entire act or an entire character throughout, but just some little short space of time during a character's performance."

And in that, Ellington succeeded brilliantly. "Jazz purists" can revel in the music for its own sake, and they have for generations. And it surely increases the enjoyment if they are also "Shakespeare purists," or at least Shakespeare adepts, and can appreciate the perspicacity of Ellington's musical portraits.

## Scenes and Sonnets

Ellington's twelve movements are divided into what might be called scenes and sonnets. Musically, the eight scenes in the Shakespeare suite are built around the standard structures used in jazz and most other forms of American music—the thirty-two-bar songbook form with eight-bar *AABA* sequences, and the twelve-bar blues form. The four sonnets are musical adaptations of the highly formal Shakespearean sonnet in fourteen lines made up of three quatrains and a rhyming couplet. Ellington's metamorphosis of the sonnet form into musical structure is scrupulously precise and unique in any musical genre.

The breadth of coverage in Ellington's suite, like so many other aspects, is comprehensive. Shakespeare's plays are conventionally categorized as Comedy, Tragedy, History, and Romance (originally "Romantic Drama" by G. B. Harrison [1939], who standardized the names). Ellington's "thumbnail sketches," as he called them, the scenes, include representatives from each category, and so do the four sonnets.

Two of the movements function naturally as the opener and the closer of the suite, and thus stand at the beginning and at the end (as they do in the original LP version).

**"Such Sweet Thunder,"** the opener, takes its title from Queen Hippolyta in *A Midsummer Night's Dream* (IV, 1): "I never heard / So musical a discord, such sweet thunder." It is well suited as the title of the movement, but much less appropriate as the title of the suite itself (and for that reason it is often called "the Shakespeare suite" instead). The music of "Such Sweet Thunder" is indeed thunderous, a twelve-bar blues carried rhythmically by a cracking drum accent on the strong beats and a primitive vamp by the low horns. It makes an explosive opening for the suite, akin as it is to a burlesque bump-and-grind but richly textured in its harmonies, and in that way a deft proclamation of the riches to come. (For a perspicacious analysis, politically and musically, see Schiff 2017, 190–92.)

**"Circle of Fourths,"** the closer, is a wailing vehicle for tenor saxophonist Paul Gonsalves, the hero of Newport. It has no discernible relation to the themes of the suite (and its title is Ellington's, not Shakespeare's). The annotator of the record claims, "It is inspired by Shakespeare himself and the four major parts of his artistic contribution: tragedy, comedy, history, and the sonnets" (Townsend 1957). The "fourths" of the title literally refers to the composition's cycling through the twelve tones of the chromatic scale ascending by fourths. "There is no beginning or ending," says trumpeter Bill Berry (1999, 16). As such, the piece provides an exclamatory finale for the riches that precede it.

The rest of Ellington's scenes visit all four of Shakespeare's categories, though not symmetrically. We consider, in turn, History ("Half the Fun"), Comedy ("The Telecasters," "Up and Down, Up and Down"), Romance ("The Star-Crossed Lovers"), and Tragedy ("Lady Mac," "Madness in Great Ones").

**"Half the Fun,"** notwithstanding its flippant title (perhaps Strayhorn's, who composed it, but clearly Ellington's style), celebrates Cleopatra's smoldering charms with a sly grin. The title suits the mood, and the mood inspired one of Ellington's fanciful verbal flights: "Imagine this great golden barge floating down the Nile, with beautiful dancing girls, mounds of food and drink, elephants, ostrich feather fans, a hundred slaves rowing the barge and Cleopatra lying on a satin bed" (Berry 1999, 16). Shakespeare has Cleopatra say, "Give me some music—music, moody food / Of us that trade in love" (II, 5). Strayhorn obliges her with this bawdy meander.

**"The Telecasters"** has an excruciating anachronism as its title, which was rationalized (feebly) by Ellington: "It seems that the three witches [from *Macbeth*], and Iago [from *Othello*] . . . all had something to say, so we call them the Telecasters" (Townsend 1957). The music, thankfully, never invokes the three toothless witches or the scheming psychopath. Instead, it is a sonorous feature for the low horns—the trombone choir (Britt Woodman, John Sanders, and Quentin Jackson) and baritone saxophone (Harry Carney). The music, notwithstanding its title, is lilting and engaging, more akin to the innocent nonsense of *All's Well That Ends Well*.

**"Up and Down, Up and Down (I Will Lead Them Up and Down)"** is an incisive portrait of the hobgoblin Puck in *A Midsummer Night's Dream,* as he goes about making fools of the coupling aristocrats in the idyllic Forest. His taunt in the title (III, 2) matches the lilt of the music. The humans are represented in Ellington's score by a nursery-like theme for unison violin and clarinet (Ray Nance and Jimmy Hamilton), while the impish Puck, played with wonderful animation by Clark Terry on flugelhorn, bobs and weaves around them. Ellington and Strayhorn create an indelible sonic portrait of one of Shakespeare's well-loved characters.

**"The Star-Crossed Lovers"** (titled from the Prologue to *Romeo and Juliet*) is Juliet's lament for the suicide of her young lover. It is conveyed with abject despair in Billy Strayhorn's exquisite melody as rendered by alto saxophonist Johnny Hodges. The performance is one of the triumphs of the spectral alliance between this composer and soloist, and a brilliant evocation of doomed love.

**"Lady Mac,"** with its jaunty title and Clark Terry's extraverted flugelhorn portrait, might have seemed incongruous to playgoers whose image of Lady Macbeth is the woman who goaded her husband to murder a king and as a consequence went mad with guilt, but Ellington fully intended the paradox. "We portrayed some of her by using a jazz waltz," he told Rasky (1957), "and in so doing we say she was a lady of noble birth but we suspect that she had a little ragtime in her soul." Ellington's Lady Macbeth is the coy schemer in the first two-thirds of the play rather than the pathetic guilt-ridden somnambulist at the end—the image that most people take away with them when the curtain falls. As Townsend said (1960, 321), "Duke likes Lady Macbeth whether you're supposed to like her or not, and he treats her right." In case anyone thinks Ellington missed the point, he ends "Lady Mac" with a hefty, ominous chord that leaves no doubt about her awful fate. With that shuddering note, he completes the striking portrait.

**"Madness in Great Ones"** takes its title from the words of Prince Hamlet's malevolent uncle Claudius, who murdered his father and married his mother, usurping both the throne of Denmark and its queen. "Madness in great ones must not unwatch'd go," says Claudius (III, 1). Ellington's portrait lays down an underscore of melodious swing by the reed section, representing the hypocrisy of the royal court, and then ravages its easy surface with blaring brass exclamations that dramatize Hamlet's jangled psyche. It is a discordant composition, brilliantly orchestrated. The composition makes an unforgettable analogue for Shakespeare's verse (though spoken by Richard II [V, 5], not Hamlet): "How sour sweet music is / When time is broke and no proportion kept! / So is it in the music of men's lives." Ellington brings it to a climax with a cadenza by his high-note trumpet specialist, Cat Anderson, sounding like he is trying to blow his brains out.

Ellington's scenes are chosen astutely from Shakespeare's vast gallery, singling out many of his best-loved characters with incisive, sharp musical sketches. Well-versed listeners are likely to see those characters ever after through Ellington's prism. And the moods swing sharply through the Shakespearean gamut of history, comedy, romance, and tragedy.

### Music in Iambic Pentameter

The other four movements—the sonnets—occupy a completely different sonic space. They are through-composed and last exactly twenty-eight bars, representing the iambic beats (strong, weak) of fourteen lines in a literary sonnet. In each one, the melodic line is recited by one instrumentalist. The recitations are somewhat stiff, like technical exercises, but they are also expressive. Every even-numbered bar ends with a tied note, representing the line-end in a literary sonnet, and the last eight bars are played over stop-time rhythm and sustained chords by the ensemble, representing the rhyming couplet. They are musical transliterations of the Shakespearean sonnet, unique in any musical genre.

Ellington's four sonnets, as formally strict as Shakespeare's 154 sonnets, are individuated by their subject matter—as are Shakespeare's—but also by the personal sound of the soloists, a defining characteristic of all major jazz instrumentalists, and by the distinctive orchestral settings that Ellington crafts as their underscores. The melodic lines of the sonnets last a little more than a minute but the performances vary from 1:24 to 3:00 due to the orchestral settings. They do not swing, and they are so distinctively individuated that they add their own forceful impression in the context of the suite.

Ellington's meticulous adaptation of the sonnet form in musical composition, though seldom noted in jazz literature, is shining evidence of his immersion in the subject matter of the Shakespeare suite. His metamorphosis of the literary form crystalized in the very first recording session for the suite, exclusively devoted to three of the sonnets. As innovative as Ellington was when it came to manipulating blues and song structure, he fastidiously cleaved to the formal restrictions of the sonnet form. So, of course, did Shakespeare; though he had no qualms about taking liberties with formal conventions in his other poems and in his plays, his sonnets are note-perfect.

As a consequence, any one of Shakespeare's 154 sonnets can be sung to any one of Ellington's four sonnets.

The sonnets, like the scenes, run the Shakespearean gamut of History ("Sonnet for Hank Cinq"), Comedy ("Sonnet for Sister Kate"), Romance ("Sonnet in Search of a Moor"), and Tragedy ("Sonnet for Caesar").

**"Sonnet for Hank Cinq,"** Ellington's glib nod to Henry V, the warrior-king who led the British against the French in the Hundred Years' War, features trombonist Britt Woodman in a virtuoso performance that requires octave leaps. "The changes of tempo," Ellington says, "have to do with the changes of pace and the map as a result of wars" (Townsend 1957). Woodman's virtuosity arouses a sense of wonder in astute listeners, especially other trombone players.

**"Sonnet for Sister Kate"** is a comic portrait of Katharina, the shrew of *The Taming of the Shrew* (nicknamed "Kate" by Shakespeare [II, 1, 185–93] as well as Ellington, and, for that matter, by Cole Porter in his musical-comedy *Kiss Me Kate*). The solo voice is Quentin Jackson on plunger-muted trombone. If Woodman's performance on open trombone in "Sonnet for Hank Cinq" proved challenging, consider Jackson's challenge in mastering the cadences of the sonnet form while manipulating the slide with his right hand and the plunger mute with his left. Jackson slips in some grace notes between beats, probably out of habit, but they only enhance the lighthearted mood.

**"Sonnet in Search of a Moor"** features Jimmy Woode's bass in the foreground as he recites the sonnet in sharp contrast to the background trills from piano and three clarinets (Jimmy Hamilton, Russell Procope, and Harry Carney in mellifluous harmony). The title, as spelled out by Ellington (Smith 1962), is a three-way pun, construable as Othello ("the Moor of Venice"), the witches' "blasted heath," the moor in *Macbeth* (I, 3), or a pun on love (*amour*). The plodding bass of the first quatrain increases its range in the second and third quatrains, subtly ramping up the mood.

**"Sonnet for Caesar"** features clarinetist Jimmy Hamilton in a solemn, dirge-like line that might be the analogue for a marble bust of the Roman emperor whom it commemorates. Hamilton's decorous line symbolizes Caesar's naivete as it glides above ominous drumbeats (drummer Sam Woodyard's open hand) and equally ominous chords, symbolizing the political turmoil that leads to his assassination.

## The Glittering Heap

With such dazzling variety and ingenious casting of instrumentalists in their Shakespearean roles, Ellington has met the challenge of the tone parallel to the works of William Shakespeare as promised. So successful is it, in fact, that it is easy to overlook the fact that it is incomplete. At least that is how I rationalize my own failure to notice it for some fifty years. It was only when I put together a presentation on the Shakespeare suite for a roomful of knowledgeable Ellington advocates that it struck me. The problem is best expressed by the high praise conferred on artworks when the whole is greater than the sum of its parts.

When the twelve movements are viewed from a critical perspective, perhaps a literary perspective, they fall comfortably into thematic patterns that are nowhere evident in the suite as it has come down to us. The glorious variety celebrates Shakespeare's disparate, sprawling creative effusion, but in random order, they are like diamonds in a heap, awaiting the lapidarist to craft them into a resplendent tiara. The whole is simply the sum of its parts—no less, but no more.

The scenes run the gamut of History, Comedy, Romance and Tragedy. So do the sonnets, and there are exactly four sonnets, one for each of Shakespeare's subgenres. The sonnets, moreover, are formally prefatory—they are brief and static, like interludes. Though fascinating in their own right, they might have been used to shape the suite into a cohesive unit. In other words, they might have been placed as prefaces, as in the Thematic Order outlined below, to the scenes that elaborate the kindred themes.

If Ellington intended them to be used as interludes for setting in motion the compositions that celebrate the four subgenres, he obviously lost sight of that master plan. Throughout his career, especially in his last decades, he habitually hurried on to the next project—often simply to the next gig. Ellington played the Shakespeare suite in its entirety—that is, as a suite—only three times: first, at a Town Hall Concert in Manhattan on April 28, 1957, when the movements were being composed and recorded; second, in the Columbia studio that produced the original LP recording on April 15 and 24 and May 3, 1957; and third, a few months later, on September 5, 1957, at the grand premiere at the Stratford Shakespeare Festival.[23] The Columbia recording places "Such

---

23. The order of the movements at Town Hall in New York on April 28, 1957, a day before Ellington's fifty-eighth birthday (and, incidentally, five days after Shakespeare's 393rd birthday, both born under the sign of Taurus), was discovered by Lewis Porter (2023). The closer, "Circle of Fourths," was not yet written, and Ellington filled in with "Cop Out," a similar but more rocky romp for Paul Gonsalves on tenor saxophone written a few weeks earlier (March 13, 1957).

| Thematic order | order at Town Hall | Columbia LP | Stratford |
|---|---|---|---|
| **OPENER** | | | |
| 1  Such Sweet Thunder | 6 | 1 | 7 |
| **HISTORY** | | | |
| 2  Sonnet for Hank Cinq | 2 | 3 | 2 |
| 3  Half the Fun | 11 | 11 | unlisted |
| **COMEDY** | | | |
| 4  Sonnet for Sister Kate | 7 | 8 | 8 |
| 5  The Telecasters | 3 | 6 | 3 |
| 6  Up and Down Up and Down | 8 | 7 | 9 |
| **ROMANCE** | | | |
| 7  Sonnet in Search of a Moor | 5 | 5 | 6 |
| 8  The Star-Crossed Lovers | 9 | 9 | 10 |
| **TRAGEDY** | | | |
| 9  Sonnet for Caesar | 1 | 2 | 1 |
| 10  Lady Mac | 4 | 4 | 4 |
| 11  Madness in Great Ones | 10 | 10 | 11 |
| **CLOSER** | | | |
| 12  Circle of Fourths | ["Cop Out"] | 12 | 5 |

In the Thematic Order, the four sonnets serve as interludes, demarking the scenes that match their subgenres.

Sweet Thunder" as the opener and "Circle of Fourths" as the closer, perhaps due to Irving Townsend, whose notes (1957) indicate he is well aware of their motivic roles in those positions. Otherwise, the order on the record and at the live performances might have been determined by flipping coins (as shown in the columns below). At Stratford, with Ellington in charge, "Such Sweet Thunder" was played seventh and "Circle of Fourths" fifth. Particularly galling is the placement of the sonnets, whose intriguing eccentricities are somewhat dulled by placing them together. Separating them as prefaces to the scenes that match their subgenres, as in the Thematic Order above, gives cohesion and allows the scenes themselves to be ordered climactically.

If it is merely accidental that Ellington's four sonnets reflect the four subgenres of Shakespeare's plays, a categorization that every authority he consulted would have taken for granted, then it is a happy accident. Judiciously placed, as in the Thematic Order, they provide dramatic demarcations for the scenes. In the sixteen productive years after completing the suite, Ellington occasionally inserted a few of the pieces into concerts, but he never played more than two or three, and never as movements. He never played them as a suite—not even, inexplicably, when he returned for concerts at the Stratford Festival in 1963, 1966, and 1968.

His neglect of the Shakespeare suite was not an isolated incident. All the suites were abandoned as soon as the parts were recorded except for occasional individual selections injected into the nightly repertoire. Failure to finish projects became so chronic for Ellington that he invented an elaborate rationalization for it. "As long as something is unfinished," he told John Wilson in the *New York Times* (1963), "there's always that little feeling of insecurity, and a feeling of insecurity is absolutely necessary unless you're so rich it doesn't matter." Whatever that really means, if it means anything, Ellington apparently presents it as a kind of charming foible. With hindsight, it appears to go much deeper than that. In the final analysis, as we shall see, he appears to have robbed himself of the rousing curtain call he had earned.

## Acknowledgments

Sjef Hoefsmit, co-curator of the Duke Ellington Music Society (DEMS), gave me cassettes of the radio interviews by Harry Rasky and Bob Smith in which Duke Ellington talks about his preparations for the Shakespeare suite. He later reprinted my article, "Bardland: Shakespeare in Ellington's World," in DEMS Bulletin 05/1 (April/July 2005). I count myself lucky to have met Tom Patterson (1920–2005), founder of the Stratford Shakespeare Festival, at the Toronto Duke Ellington conference in 1996, for a brief but revealing interview, some of which found its way into my writings and presentations on the suite.

## Playlist

(In chronological order by recording date)

All twelve masters are issued with alternate takes on *Such Sweet Thunder* (Columbia Legacy CD [1999]) Recorded in New York, Columbia 30th Street Studios with the personnel shown here and on the dates shown below.

Cat Anderson, Willie Cook, Clark Terry tp, Ray Nance tp, vln, Britt Woodman, Quentin Jackson, John Sanders tb, Jimmy Hamilton cl, ts, Paul Gonsalves ts, Johnny Hodges as, Russell Procope cl, as, Harry Carney cl, bs, Duke Ellington p, Jimmy Woode b, Sam Woodyard d. Composer credits are due to Walter van de Leur (2002, 134–35), based on the handwriting in the MSS in the Smithsonian archives.

"Half the Fun" 4:19 (Strayhorn). August 7, 1956. Solo: Johnny Hodges.
"Sonnet in Search of a Moor" 2:22 (Ellington) April 15, 1957. Solo: Jimmy Woode.
"Sonnet for Caesar" 3:00 (Ellington) April 15, 1957. Solo: Jimmy Hamilton.
"Sonnet for Sister Kate" 2:24 (Ellington) April 15, 1957. Solo: Quentin Jackson.
"Such Sweet Thunder" 3:22 (Ellington) April 24, 1957. Solo: Ray Nance tp.
"Up and Down, Up and Down (I Will Lead Them Up and Down)" 3:09 (Ellington/Strayhorn). April 24, 1957. Solos: Clark Terry, Jimmy Hamilton cl/Ray Nance vln.
"Lady Mac" 3:41 (Ellington) April 24, 1957. Solos: Duke Ellington, Russell Procope as, Clark Terry.
"The Telecasters" 3:05 (Ellington/Strayhorn). May 3, 1957. Solos: Harry Carney, and trombone section.
"The Star-Crossed Lovers" 4:00 (Strayhorn). May 3, 1957. Solo: Johnny Hodges.
"Madness in Great Ones" 3:26 (Ellington). May 3, 1957. Solo: Cat Anderson
"Sonnet for Hank Cinq" 1:24 (Ellington). May 3, 1957. Solo: Britt Woodman.
"Circle of Fourths" 1:45 (Ellington). May 3, 1957. Solo: Paul Gonsalves.

Chapter 10

# A Final Masterpiece, Reluctantly

> What I really want to do is bring to audiences the profundity of this man's contribution—to illustrate not only his music, but his philosophy of life. The public knows him only by his pop pieces. Black composers have a way of disappearing and we want very much for this man to take his rightful place in American and international music history.
> —ALVIN AILEY, *AILEY CELEBRATES ELLINGTON 1976* (QUOTED BY DUNNING 1996, 310)

In 1970, a few weeks before he would turn seventy-one, Duke Ellington accepted a commission from Lucia Chase, director of the American Ballet Theatre, to provide the music for a ballet that would be part of the festivities celebrating their thirtieth anniversary. Chase conceived the commission as an all-star package, signing up Alvin Ailey to provide the choreography for Ellington's score. Ailey, a tall, athletic African American dancer, had risen out of what he called "a rambling, rural" childhood in Texas to Broadway chorus lines, where seemingly, without trying, he stood out from the ensemble. Like Ellington, he had presence, and in 1958 when he was twenty-seven years old, he founded the Alvin Ailey American Dance Theater. The agile grace of his productions became touchstones of modern dance, broadening the audience and influencing classical dance companies. Ailey's crowning achievement, *Revelations*, came early, in 1960, a celebration of gospel music and down-home spirituality conveyed with bright colors, supple motion, and striking elegance. Although Ellington was thirty-two years older than Ailey, Lucia Chase sensed that bringing together these icons of American music and American dance held great promise for an innovative meeting of the minds.

Ellington's itinerary had always been active, but now, in his final four years, he seemed perpetually on the move, as if aware that his time was rationed. Halfway through this period, early in 1972, Ellington was diagnosed with the lung cancer that would kill him exactly two years later. Even before the fatal diagnosis, Ellington sustained a manic globe-trotting regimen, remarkable even by his nomadic standards, covering more miles and performing (usually, repeating) concerts almost daily. Ellington had overcome his aviophobia, acute fear of flying, beginning with a short trial flight in 1958 (according to Dan Morgenstern 2014, 154), a sheer act of will by a man who realized that the only way to maximize the audiences he craved was to cover more miles, and, it followed, the only way to cover more miles was by air.

He accomplished a great deal in these years, and he did it by accepting every commission and every invitation that came his way. Ironically, his hectic pace did not include time set aside for recollecting and recording the fruits of his labors. In the last three years, 1972 to 1974, Ellington probably spent fewer hours in recording studios than at any time since the days of the Washingtonians in the 1920s. Recording sessions for established labels became rare and, surprisingly, so did the informal private studio excursions. His concerts were frequently recorded, often unofficially, but the innovative music he was still producing got short shrift. In a performing art that makes use of improvisation and a compositional rationale that exploits spontaneity, the absence of polished mementos makes a significant gap. The music kept coming, though it was perhaps harder to discover.

Amazingly, the legacy of these hectic years included, amidst so much more, three versions of the ballet suite for the American Ballet Theatre, called *The River*, in three different musical configurations with three distinctive sonic palettes and three overlapping but distinct reimaginings. Not so amazingly, all three versions of *The River* are incomplete, reflecting the frantic pace of these years. More than that, they are all incomplete in different ways, reflecting Ellington's fragmented attention as he seemed intent on spending his waning resources in too many directions.

### "A Kind of Religious Allegory"

Alvin Ailey had worked with Ellington seven years earlier on the production of Ellington's *My People*, the revue Ellington composed as a celebration of African American achievement for the Century of Negro Progress

Exposition in Chicago in 1963. Ailey's role was minor, but he came away mightily impressed. "Duke Ellington *really* is a genius—what an incredible man!" he wrote to a friend in New York (Dunning 1996, 175). "He never seems to sleep & new music pours out of him like a tap—not only was he constantly rewriting the show music but other things for the band to record here—and the most gracious, tactful, charming human being I've ever met." Ailey, needless to say, eagerly accepted the commission from the American Ballet Theatre.[24]

*The River*, Mercer Ellington points out, was a concept that had been mooted for some time by Ellington's inner circle—

> The idea for The River had been kicking around for several years, ever since Stanley Dance had suggested an extended work depicting the natural course of a river. He had the Mississippi in mind . . . and he wrote out a description of it from source to sea. Billy Strayhorn liked it and there was often talk of doing it, but it was not until the American Ballet Theater [sic] accepted the proposal that Pop went to work on it. (1978, 172–73)

The ballet commission not only revived it in Ellington's mind but inspired an ambitious reconception—*overly* ambitious, as we shall see. Stanley Dance, Ellington's "aide-de-camp" (as Whitney Balliett called him [2002, 521]), described his original idea. "I had no thought of a symphonic treatment," he said, "but suggested it as an idea for an LP theme, thinking in terms of the band and a climactic affair like Ravel's *Bolero*" (Slome n.d.). With the ballet commission in hand, Ellington reconceived it as a gargantuan, eleven-movement ballet score that would enact, in music and dance, the river's ambit from the trickle of "The Spring" through waterfalls and lakes and whirlpools to its mouth where it flows into "Her Majesty the Sea."

Ellington conceived the twelfth movement as a reprise of the first movement, "The Spring." As he says in his narrative, "The river . . . romps into the mother—her majesty the sea—and of course is no longer a river. But this is the climax," he wrote, "the heavenly anticipation of rebirth, for the sea will

---

24. Ailey's encomium follows his astute comment on *My People*: "Mr. E. couldn't make up his mind if the show was for Broadway or the Apollo. I had Broadway in mind of course and had asked for lots of effects . . . so the first part of the show has an air of production but the last half descends spectacularly to the level of vaudeville—tasteful—but vaudeville" (quoted by Dunning 1996, 175). Ailey's comment may provide the best insight into Ellington's failure to mount a Broadway hit not only with *My People* but a half dozen other attempts.

be drawn up into the sky for rain and down into wells and into springs and become the river again." Mercer Ellington explained Ellington's motive in plain terms: "By 1970 Ellington's mind was much more on spiritual values, so he turned the whole thing into a kind of religious allegory that dealt with the cycle of birth and rebirth." The "spiritual values" that preoccupied him showed themselves most blatantly in Ellington's Sacred Concerts, the Bible-themed productions that he presented first at Grace Cathedral in San Francisco (September 1965) and last at Westminster Abbey in London (October 1973) and at many other auspicious venues in between. Although *The River* is secular in its theme and theatrical in the occasion that called it forth, it undoubtedly gains its power and spirituality from the plainspoken faith that Ellington professed so openly in these final years. It is no stretch, it seems to me, to hear in the two rhapsodic movements of *The River*, "The Lake" and "Village of the Virgins," a more profound musical expression of Ellington's spirituality than anything in the Sacred Concerts, for all their pleasantries.

## Conception and Realization

No performance of the ballet or its score has ever reprised "The Spring" as the cyclical start and end point. Notwithstanding Ellington's lofty intentions, it was probably not esthetically justifiable. For one thing, "The Spring" is a legato movement; it serves well at the beginning as a kind of awakening, but it would be an anticlimactic note to end on. We are better off, perhaps, with what we ended up with than with Ellington's conceptualization of it.

Paradoxically, that seems to be true of *The River* in all its details. Between the conception and its realization, there is a considerable abyss. As it has come down to us, *The River* has six movements (later seven), not the eleven that Ellington conceived. Performance time is around thirty minutes, about half the length that Ellington envisioned. The movements are scored and arranged for the symphony orchestra not by Ellington but by Ron Collier, the Canadian composer hired by Ellington for that purpose. Collier, as we shall see, constructed the symphonic movements from themes Ellington first picked out in hotel rooms on his portable Wurlitzer keyboard and then from arrangements he wrote for his jazz band as he traveled the world on his endless concert round.

Ellington was "an absentee composer," in Luther Henderson's terms. Henderson had orchestrated Ellington's earlier symphonic works but not under these circumstances. "He was on the road with his band," Henderson said. "He would never leave his band to work on a show"—or a ballet or symphony or anything else. "The band always came first." He added, "I've worked on many musicals... but I've never worked with an absentee composer" (Singer 2000). Luckily for Ellington, Collier had no such qualms. While Ellington was playing in Toronto, Collier's hometown, Collier said, "I'd go up there almost every night and he'd have a couple of sheets of music sketched out and I'd take them home. There was never any indication of what he wanted. He would give me little bits of music" (Collier 1996). But eventually, Ellington had to go on the road, and when his own commitments permitted, Collier joined him. "So this went on, and I chased the band across the United States and various little towns and cities working on this piece."

As remote as Ellington was from the actual workshopping of the ballet, his imprint is on the work. His conception, though pared down, is intact. His harmonies echo in Collier's transliteration of the sketches. And it is because of Ellington's physical distance from the place where *The River* was being developed that we have the three versions of the music. First, chronologically, came the piano sketches, played by Ellington in a recording studio and delivered to orchestrator Collier and choreographer Ailey in hopes that they could develop the orchestral score and fashion the choreography from them. When Ailey found the piano sketches too sparse to serve as guides for his choreography, Ellington worked out band arrangements and took his orchestra into local studios to record them. The third version was Collier's symphonic adaptation of Ellington's sketches.

As mentioned, all three of the versions are incomplete. The piano sketches, recorded on May 11, 1970, include six of the eleven projected movements. The big band sketches, recorded at various dates in May and June 1970, are the most complete, with all eleven available, but as the deadline for converting them into ballet productions grew critical, they became sketchier; the looming time frame probably outweighed their brevity in determining what could be staged. Finally, the symphonic score ended up as seven movements—six at the premiere, with the seventh added in later performances. (In the Playlist, all recorded performances are listed in turn for the movements.)

## "The Band Was His Stradivarius"

Ellington's hyperactive schedule along with his disdain for hard deadlines resulted in a creative frenzy that drove his would-be collaborators to near madness. Collier got around to reminiscing about his experience only after twenty-six years had passed, and by then he could say, with considerable aplomb, "I had to orchestrate from the band charts. For most of the pieces he [Ellington] would write them out because the choreographer needed pieces of music so that he could work with the dancers; and instead of Duke writing out a piano piece, he would write out a chart for the band, send [the recording] on to Alvin Ailey and that's what they would use to work with." One can only guess at the challenges Collier faced in transforming the sketches, whether by piano or jazz band, into full symphonic scores with the composer largely incommunicado.

Ailey was not so benign. The recording dates of the big band recordings shows why there was panic in the rehearsal hall. Ellington recorded piano sketches of six of the eleven movements on May 11, about six weeks before the June 25 premiere. When Ailey required fuller sketches, the magnitude of Ellington's task, writing big band scores and herding the orchestra into studios while maintaining his round of travel and nightly performances, brought inevitable delays. Ellington's big band sketches of the first five movements were recorded a month before they were due to be performed by a full orchestra and *corps de ballet* at Lincoln Center. Even if they were delivered by courier a day or two after the recording date (in the pre-internet era), that comes perilously close to the limit for orchestration, choreography, and rehearsal time. After that, it gets really tense. Four other movements were recorded with three weeks to spare, and another, "The Falls," five days after that. They were presumably delivered to Collier and Ailey about two weeks before the performance. The projected final movement, "Her Majesty the Sea," recorded ten days before its scheduled performance, was never orchestrated or choreographed. That timeline explains how Ellington's master plan was reduced by almost half.

Getting any music at all from Ellington required pursuing him on his seemingly endless rounds. After Lucia Chase had the two icons under contract for her project, she sent Ailey to Vancouver, where Ellington and his orchestra were playing in a hotel ballroom for several nights, so that Ailey and Ellington could work out preliminary details of their collaboration. Ailey discovered that Ellington's workdays had a fixed, idiosyncratic shape. "My workday begins the minute I wake up, and ends the minute my head hits the pillow—only God knows what time that is," Ellington told a reporter for *Jet* magazine. Ailey found out that Ellington really meant it. In Vancouver, the band finished playing at 1:30 a.m. Ellington received visitors backstage and then more visitors in his hotel room after the show. When the room finally cleared, Ailey got his moment. "I told him that I wanted to do a kind of rhapsodic ballet," Ailey said, "but Duke had another idea." Ellington talked about his conception for *The River* and illustrated the movements on the electric piano at the foot of his bed. Ailey (1995, 114–16) recalled: "At five o'clock in the morning I was sitting in Duke Ellington's apartment bathed in beautiful music. I said, 'Let's do it. Let's do *The River*.'" They shook hands, and Ellington left the next day for Los Angeles for his next performance. Ailey was mesmerized, though he came away from their meeting with no music in hand.

"After we agreed to a collaboration, he was gone all of the time," Ailey said.

Weeks later, Ailey caught up with the band in a Toronto jazz club. Ellington's routine now had a familiar ring. "At eight his room would be full of sixty-year-old ladies, probably Canadian, whom he called girls," Ailey said. "They just adored him. The shows were at nine and eleven, and during the interval between shows he would party with the ladies." Finally alone together in the wee hours of the morning, Ellington proudly showed Ailey a collection of water themes he had acquired in his travels—recordings of Handel's *Water Music*, Debussy's "La Mer," and other classics. He told Ailey, "I've been listening to this to see what other people have done with water music." The water classics are not discernible in the music that Ellington eventually composed, but Ailey was willing to believe that Ellington's interest in them, amidst all his distractions, meant that the music for *The River* was palpably in progress. "He liked to work from 4:30 until 7 o'clock in the morning," Ailey said. "Then he would go to bed and sleep until 3 or 4 in the afternoon." Ailey recounts answering the phone in his hotel room at 4 a.m. It was Ellington. "'Did I wake you, Alvin?' I'd say, 'No, Duke,' and he'd say, laughing, 'Come on over, I've got something for you to hear.'"

Ailey, exhausted, returned to New York with a few scraps of music. "The music was just beautiful, but it was driving me out of my mind," Ailey said. "I talked to people who worked with him. They said, 'Well, that's the way he works. You're just going to have to learn how to work with him like that. He'll take sixteen bars into a studio, eight bars of this and two bars of that, and come out four hours later with eight fantastic pieces. That's just the nature of the way he works.' He wrote with the orchestra—the orchestra was his instrument. He composed in the recording studio; his band was his Stradivarius" (reported by Henken 2007).

Jennifer Dunning, Ailey's biographer, says, "The rest of the score ... arrived in pieces, sometimes brought to the sixth floor studios at City Center by Ellington himself to the delight of the dancers and a nervously watchful Chase, who was growing worried that *The River* would never be completed. 'Ah, we have a few more bars here,' Alvin would slyly announce to the dancers after such a visit. 'Let's go on'" (Dunning 1996, 257).

Finally, with the performances only days away, Ailey reached his breaking point. Don George, Ellington's spirited biographer, describes the climactic events (1981, 195–96):

Three days before the rehearsals were to start, Ailey still hadn't received the written music. He had occasionally received bits and pieces in the mail, a few bars now and then that didn't seem to match up. One day he got a tape with four pieces, and he was trying to choreograph those. He finally threw up his hands. All the Ballet Theatre people were in the rehearsal studio and Ailey was hot to go, but he was completely frustrated because he didn't have the music. He flipped. He went clean out of his mind. He hurled the whole thing—notebooks, tapes and all—up against the mirror and yelled, "Fuck it, I can't work like this."

At that precise moment the door opened and in walked Duke in his white cashmere coat surrounded by his entourage. The whole room stopped. In fact, it fell to its knees. Ailey told me later that what he wanted to scream was, "Where's the music?" Instead they went outside and sat and talked. Ailey told Duke he couldn't work without the whole score. Duke said to Alvin, "Listen, if you'd stop worrying about this music and do more choreography, we'd be a whole lot better off."

The show, needless to say, did go on. The program for the Lincoln Center premiere billed the ballet as "Seven Dances from a Work in Progress Entitled *The River*." With one exception, the movements that were *not* performed were the ones that arrived too late: "The Falls," recorded by the big band only seventeen days before the premiere without the benefit of a piano preview; "The Neo-Hip-Hot Cool Kiddies Community," a mere sketch (less than two minutes) recorded by the big band the same day as "The Falls"; and "Her Majesty the Sea," just ten days before the premiere. There remains one anomaly: the movement called "The Run" was available on time in both the piano sketch and the big band sketch (in the Playlist); its omission may represent an esthetic choice by Ailey because its peculiar (though winsome) march rhythm offers little balletic scope.

There can be no doubt that it was Ailey's choreography chores that were the sticking point. Collier orchestrated "The Falls" in time for the premiere, but Ailey could not choreograph it in time. He integrated it into subsequent performances of the ballet. There may have been more orchestrations that were omitted for lack of choreography. Looking back years later, Collier said, "I don't know how many [movements] were written," that is, orchestrated. Only "The Falls" survived, to be added in later performances.

## "A Cohesive, Elegant Work of Art"

Maybe it was the backstage tension that Ellington provoked that gave *The River* its creative glow. "*The River* was an enormous and immediate popular and critical success," Dunning (1996, 258) says. "Balletomanes got to see their favorite dancers let down their hair. Critics had the opportunity to write poetically of the ceaseless, easy flow of rivers and this one in particular. And Alvin could be proud that he had successfully bridged the gap between ballet and modern dance." Ailey's choreography is described and discussed by Thomas DeFrantz (2004, 149–55), an aspect that will necessarily be underplayed here but is highly recommended for listeners who want a fuller appreciation.

The critical reception at the premiere is well documented by John Franceschina (2001, 162–64). It was reviewed positively—and prominently—in the New York dailies and *Newsweek*. Clive Barnes, in the *New York Times*, praised its "blend of classical ballet, modern dance and jazz movement, a most rewarding hybrid." Barnes noted, "The piece is not finished. But it is a delight. It is the most considerable piece from Mr. Ellington since his *Black, Brown and Beige Suite* [sic]; it is quite lovely. And Mr. Ailey has never previously created with such power and force for a classic troupe." He added, "The separate parts could not be shifted around or omitted. . . . What there was provided its own satisfactions," a point that will certainly strike home for those listeners (myself among them) who came to *The River* innocent of its backstory, hearing it simply as a completed suite of music. Franceschina (164) sums up its reception as "an immediate popular and critical success . . . in which Alvin Ailey bridges the gap between modern dance and classical ballet," and he points out that it "became a staple of the American Ballet Theatre's repertoire."

When the critics' raves came in, Ailey's frustrations quickly dissipated. He acknowledged the power of his collaboration with Ellington by performing *The River* frequently in the next decade and twice revising its choreography. Ailey's astute reviewer, Thomas DeFrantz, compared it favorably to Ailey's masterpiece: "In terms of length and ambition, the work rivaled *Revelations* with its tiers of casting and as a sustained suite that gathered power cumulatively." Ailey died in 1989 at age fifty-nine, but his choreography for *The River* lives on as a feature for many dance companies.

For the rest of his professional life, Ailey occasionally choreographed other Ellington compositions. He performed an athletic solo to Ellington's "Reflections in D," a piano trio recorded in 1953. A television tribute called *Ailey Celebrates Ellington* on CBS Festival of Lively Arts for Young People in November 1974, six months after Ellington's death, included his dances set to Ellington's "The Mooche," a 1928 composition, and a "shimmering"

*Night Creature*, a 1963 symphony that is recognized as "one of Alvin's wittiest and most ravishingly pretty dances." These collaborations were obviously less stressful for Ailey because he started with the music safely in hand. "Reflections in D" and *Night Creature* remain chief attractions for the Ailey corps in perpetuity.

### *The River*—Music in Motion

For each of the seven movements of *The River* in the following discussion, I cite Ellington's prose description from his narrative in *Music Is My Mistress* (201–2). Ellington may have intended his description as a program note for the premiere or perhaps as a narration for a concert version, but it was never used. It is useful because it provides another clue to Ellington's original conception. For each movement, I then consider Ellington's music in whatever renditions he has left us.

**The Spring** Ellington says, "*The River* starts as The Spring, which is like a newborn baby. He's in his cradle . . . spouting, spinning, wiggling, gurgling, making faces, reaching for his nipple or bottle, turning, tossing, and tinkling all over the place."

In Ellington's conception, the spring is no artesian gush but a minimal, barely visible trickle of water. It opens the ballet almost in silence. Ron Collier describes Ellington's piano sketch, his first draft of the movement, as "noodling," and Ellington uses the word "tinkling" in his description. According to Collier, Ellington gave a tape of his piano noodling to organist Wild Bill Davis and asked him to transcribe it. Davis was traveling with the orchestra at the time and playing organ in the ensemble as well as contributing a few charts. Writing out Ellington's piano sketch was obviously not to Wild Bill's taste because what Collier received, he said, was "just melodies, no chords, no bar lines." He also received the tape, and Collier retranscribed it, putting in the bar lines, and then sending it to the rehearsal pianist at the American Ballet Theatre. The sparse melody may explain why Ellington's second sketch of the movement was not arranged for the band, as all the others were, but played on piano with bass accompaniment. Moreover, it is brief (more than a minute shorter than either the piano sketch or the symphonic score). Ellington was apparently working from Davis's transcription but Ailey and Collier were working from Collier's fuller version. As a result, in this case, the piano/bass sketch, lyrical though it is, is an impoverished reflection of the other two versions.

Collier's orchestration rightly begins with noodling but it is noodling of a different order. Collier said, wryly, "I can't start off with bassoon because Stravinsky did that in *Rite of Spring*, so I start off with French horn." And the French horn, somber and mysterious, almost motionless at first, adds color to the tinkling opening and then carries the music into the accelerando as the spring gathers momentum. The quiescent opening makes a clever adaptation of Ellington's conception of the spring as birth, and it is easy for listeners to imagine the slow stirring of the dancers on the darkened stage with the slow stirring of the music in the first half of the three-minute movement until it comes fully alive with a handsome melody and recedes gracefully.

**The Meander**, the movement that followed "The Spring," was characterized by Ellington as "rolling around from one side to the other . . . up and down, back and forth." The rest of Ellington's description mixes metaphors and empurples the prose, but these few phrases capture the indecisive motion of meandering.

The music of "The Meander" meanders from a swaying motion at the start to a lonely flute solo and then momentarily resounds with rich jazz-like chords before quieting with woodwinds, lonely again at the faded ending. Its caprices were undoubtedly intended to provide Ailey with shapeshifting choreographic possibilities but, as Dunning (256) notes, "this quick-darting *Meander*" ended as an "unemotional, almost abstract . . . dance." For listeners as apparently for Ailey, the music of this movement is the least defined—or, put positively, the most meandering. Ellington's big band sketch (5:08) doubles the length of the piano sketch (2:26) without noticeably adding color or spice to it. Collier's orchestration, wisely, takes the shorter option (3:57), but judging by Dunning's critique of Ailey's choreography, even that was perhaps too long.

**Giggling Rapids**, also known as **"Grap"** (following an unexplained practice in which Ellington gave four-letter nicknames to many of his compositions starting in the 1960s). The meandering river comes to a rough, rocky expanse that, Ellington says, "races and runs and dances and skips and trips . . . until exhausted."

The tempo rises and stays up for this lively, fetching movement. Ellington's piano version is a delight in its own right, a jazz waltz that he plays with great panache. The big band version is played with similar gusto, opening with Ellington's piano accompanied by bass, and then gaining depth as the band enters playing rich countermelodies around the piano/bass motif. The arrangement is intricate and deft (and deserves to be played by other bands).

Collier's symphonic score retains the constant bass motif but assigns Ellington's piano melody mainly to the woodwinds with countermelodies played by brass and other instrumental groupings. The latter half of Collier's score has the feel of a bouncy Broadway arrangement, eminently danceable but perhaps less Ellingtonian than it might have been. All three versions are lively and vivacious. All three giggle in their own ways.

**The Lake**, Ellington says, "is beautiful and serene. It is all horizontal lines that offer up unrippled reflections. There it is, in all its beauty, God-made and untouched, until people come—people who are God-made and terribly touched by the beauty of the lake. They, in their admiration for it, begin to discover new facets of compatibility in each other, and as a romantic viewpoint develops, they indulge themselves."

This movement glows with the romantic impetus that Ellington's words express, with long melodic lines and languid sensuality. It is the centerpiece of the ballet, as the fourth of seven movements. It is also the longest movement and the most lyrical. Ironically, it came into being at the point at which Ellington appears to have been losing interest in the project. We can infer this from the production gap that follows this movement, as Ellington takes ever longer to produce the music so urgently needed by the others.

Ellington's waning interest can also be inferred from Collier's recollection. "He gave me one piece, it was called 'Lake,' and it was up in his room," Collier said. "I had dinner at his place. [He handed me] just a little piece of sheet music, single-line chord changes, and he said, 'This is a *pas de deux*, two dancers.' I said, 'What would you like me to do with it?' He says, 'Well, you know what to do with it.'" Collier was dumbfounded. He said, "You know, it's almost seven minutes long on the tape but that's all the instructions: 'You know what to do with it,'" Collier said, "so I went home and it sat on the briefcase." A few days later, he got a call from Ellington telling him that the band would be recording "Lake" the next day. Collier stayed up all night writing the arrangement, "doing it for a small orchestra," with the help of Joe Benjamin, Ellington's bass player who also served as his copyist.

Judging by the three versions, Collier must have had the symphonic score of "The Lake" underway when he carried out the rush job on the band arrangement. Both the big band arrangement and the symphony score double the length of Ellington's piano solo. They are rich expansions of the piano sketch, and the ballet music mirrors the big band arrangement more faithfully than any of the other sketches. Ellington obviously knew exactly what would happen when he told Collier that he knew what to do with it. His expansion of Ellington's piano sketch perfectly sustains its lush romanticism, and indeed elaborates it to make this breathtaking centerpiece.

DeFrantz calls "The Lake" "a rich adagio," and he describes how Ailey's choreography of the *pas de deux* complements the music (149–50): "Ellington's score . . . develops a two-part melodic theme set in alternating minor and major modes. Ailey's choreography develops this binary as a tension between romantic partners. A shirtless man enters suddenly from the side of the stage. The woman becomes wary, discarding her lyrical freedom to move with sharpened precision, retreating from his pursuit. He reaches her and manipulates her into a series of awkward, sharply angled positions. Eventually she surrenders to his advances to dance with, rather than against, him. Her acquiescence is timed to a melodic swell and release into a major mode articulation of the musical theme."

Ellington's music is heartfelt and moving, as is the dance it inspired. If Ellington's enthusiasm for *The River* was waning at this point, as seems evident, he should have been grateful to see that Collier's was not. "The Lake" forms an expansive, showstopping still point at the heart of the ballet.

**The Falls**, Ellington writes, "always looks the same at the top and always sounds the same at the bottom. You can always hear the voice of the spirit that has gone over the falls and into the whirlpool, yelling and reaching back up the falls to regain the place of serenity that is the lake."

The calm of the lake spills into a rollicking, bombastic waterfall. Ellington did not attempt a piano version of this movement, presumably because he would have needed at least three hands to create its dissonances. In the studio with his big band, he added a fifth trumpet and a battery of percussionists (timpani, glockenspiel, and xylophone/marimba). Whitney Balliett, jazz critic of the *New Yorker*, was present at its recording and, in his special way, provides an evocative account of the music (2002, 334): It "turned out to be unlike anything I had heard Ellington do. But then," he says, "nothing new of his is quite like anything he has done before. The section passages . . . are brief but dense and booting, there are solo parts by Paul Gonsalves, and there are heavy, dissonant full-band chords. All of this is done against the furious *rat-a-tat* of the snare, the glockenspiel, and the timpani. It is exciting, tight crescendo music, and it reminded me of early Stravinsky, except that it was unmistakably a jazz composition." It is, like so many of the band sketches, music that stands up to repeated hearings, and it surely merits a niche in the repertoire of adventurous contemporary jazz bands.

The symphonic movement, the latecomer of the ballet, retains the percussive undertow of snare and timpani. It transfers the raunchy tenor saxophone of the jazz band to wind ensembles in the orchestra, and the effect is much more dulcet and perhaps a letdown to anyone who knows Ellington's big band version. In the ballet setting, Collier's relatively civil transposition of Ellington's "heavy, dissonant" original undoubtedly sounds bombastic enough.

**Vortex**, also known as **The Whirlpool**, captures the precipitous motion that Ellington describes simply: "Then he goes over the falls and down into the whirlpool, the vortex of violence."

One of the drawbacks for people listening to the score rather than watching the ballet is that "The Falls" and "Vortex," coming side by side, place the two most sonically similar movements together in a single stretch. Rhythm dominates "Vortex," as it does "The Falls." For both big band sketches, Ellington bolstered his rhythm section by adding percussionists (and, for both, he did not attempt a piano sketch).

Ailey apparently saw their similarity as a potential problem as well. It was not an issue for him at the premiere because "The Falls" was not yet prepared. (Ellington's band arrangement of "The Falls" was recorded five days after "Vortex," the margin of difference, apparently, between inclusion and exclusion.) In subsequent performances when "The Falls" was added, Ailey made them visually distinctive by choreographing the first dance for a four-man ensemble and the second for a solo woman. De Frantz (2004, 151) describes them: "Ellington's spare *Vortex* features percussive outbursts against an incessant snare drum roll. Ailey's choreography matches the angular oscillations of the score with a virtuosic woman's solo designed to test the balance and rhythmic ability of its dancer. . . . The virtuosic demands of *Falls* offer the male counterpart to *Vortex* in a pure dance variation for four men. . . . [I]t is explicitly concerned with the technical rendering of densely ordered virtuosic feats." The dense percussion of both movements required extraordinary athleticism from the dancers (leading DeFrantz to use the word "virtuosic" three times in his description).

Listening to the score without the advantage of Ailey's visual contrasts in the gender of the dancers, and of course the costumes, the lighting, and the motion confront one with the aural similarity. Undoubtedly it is that similarity that persuades many symphonic performances to omit "The Falls."

**Riba**, (pronounced "ribba"), also known as **The River** and **Mainstream**. Ellington writes: "From the whirlpool we get into the main train of . . . the river, which gallops sprightly and, as it passes several inlets, broadens and loses some of its adolescence. Becoming ever more mature, even noble, it establishes a majestic wave of monumental cool as it moves on with rhythmic authority."

"Riba" is the most directly jazz-rooted piece in the suite, and indeed it has a mainstream jazz pedigree. It is based on a simple riff-based blues number by Mercer Ellington called "Taffy Twist." In his autobiography, Mercer wrote (1978, 173), "I take some credit for the section known as 'Mainstream,' or 'Riba,' which was borrowed directly from one of my compositions. All in the family, you might say!" If he had not said so, it might have escaped notice. "Taffy Twist" was privately recorded by Ellington's orchestra in 1962 and obscurely released a quarter of a century later in England on a compilation of stockpile recordings (in the Playlist). For the ballet, Ellington adapted his son's undulating riff, based on a repetitive dance rhythm that was a late 1950s craze called "The Twist." In Ellington's reinterpretation, the bumptious rhythm becomes the musical counterpart of the free-flowing current of the rambling river. Mercer's original jazz version was mainly a peg for hanging improvised solos on. Ellington's big-band arrangement for *The River* preserves the swing of the repeated riff and enriches it with shifting layers of harmony. His big band "Riba" is a textured, greatly enriched "Taffy Twist."

For Collier, arranging the textures of "Riba" with the resources available in the large orchestra must have been a joyful exercise, and it comes through in the music. He unleashes the full complement of orchestral devices to convey the flowing motion. For Ailey, choreographing this movement—one of the longest at almost four minutes—proved impossible in the few days he had after the music reached him. Collier's orchestration was prepared, and presumably, it was the inherent appeal of the jazzy score that led Ailey to keep it in the ballet at the premiere by the extraordinary measure of sending the principal dancer and budding choreographer Denis Nahat onto the stage to improvise a solo. "To his horror, Nahat watched as the others bounce out into the wings when their choreography was done," Dunning (1996, 257) says. "He waved bravely as they left, and discovered that, alone onstage, he was being followed by the spotlight. He sashayed slowly to the back, trying to fill up the endless-seeming music with dance that might look as if Alvin had made it." His performance was enthusiastically received and drew a laugh when, at the last note, he made a gesture of resignation and hurried off the stage.

Ailey's choreography, when he got around to it a few days after the premiere, also played heavily on the comic. "*Riba* (*Mainstream*) demands that the dancers 'play black' in a jokey parody of Cotton Club routines," DeFrantz says. "Mining a tradition of derisive dance as parody, *Riba* signifies on stereotypical modes of public black performance suggested by Ellington's hard-swinging twelve-bar blues."

**Village of the Virgins**, the last movement of *The River*, Ellington says, is a city at the river's mouth "whose riparian rights are most carefully preserved." If his verbal synopsis slights the city with its brevity, he more than makes up for it in his composition, which is a graceful, hymn-like rhapsody that rises into a soaring crescendo.

Ellington opens the big-band sketch playing the twelve-bar hymn austerely on piano with bass accompaniment, and then he reiterates the melody in a stately succession of twelve-bar sequences by varied instrumental ensembles. The melody is played three times in rich and varied textures, each more graceful than the last. After forty-eight bars, the orchestra plays a rising four-bar crescendo, and it then returns to the beautiful melody with still more varied textures. The melody is at once stately and spiritual, as spiritual as "Come Sunday" from *Black, Brown and Beige* but incomparably lush in its instrumental texture. The arrangement embellishes it in sumptuous variations. It is one of Ellington's most beautiful melodies.

Faithfully following Ellington's lead, Ron Collier's orchestration gives full respect to the hymn-like melody, varying the orchestral textures in its reiterations and replacing the third repeat with a variation that in Ellington's big band sketch (as I hear it) originates not in his written melody but in one of the lyrical improvisations on the melody. The orchestral structure is *AAB*, with the variant leading into the four-bar crescendo like an invocation. As the endpoint of the ballet, on its final iteration, the orchestra swells and ends in a climactic cadenza that palpably cues the audience to rise to its feet in homage to the audio-visual feast that Ellington and Ailey have provided. It is a glorious, uplifting finale—life-affirming and in its own dignified way, perhaps, "a heavenly anticipation of rebirth."

## The Score on Its Own

Like the ballet, Ellington's music for *The River* has taken on a life of its own in the symphonic version. Of the three distinct instrumental takes, the symphonic version was the last written and the first made public. Both the piano sketches and the band sketches were released posthumously among the treasures of the stockpile, the vast cache of private recordings that Ellington amassed in the 1950s and 1960s (Chambers 2015, 2016).

Ellington's symphonic score, in Ron Collier's orchestration, has been recorded by several orchestras. In the Playlist, I show entries for CJRT Symphony Orchestra (1974, cond. Ron Collier [7 mvts, 30:34], the definitive recording that unfortunately awaits release) and also the Detroit Symphony

Orchestra (1993, cond. Neeme Järvi. Chandos Records [7 mvts, 26:50]); Collier gave the Detroit recording his imprimatur as "a really beautiful recording."[25] Both renditions leave out "The Falls," as did the Lincoln Center premiere. Some symphonic versions are even more selective in the movements they play, no doubt representing a trend by cultural institutions in the internet age to keep the music short in hopes of holding the attention of screen-schooled audiences.

The Schirmer website (in the Playlist) lists thirty-one leases of the symphonic score in the decade from 2005 to 2015, the most recent tally, by orchestras in Australia, Austria, Canada, Croatia, England, France, Germany, Switzerland, and fourteen states of the United States from Washington and Wyoming to Massachusetts and North Carolina. In their program, Symphony Silicon Valley (2014) notes that "Duke Ellington's music demonstrated that the divergent idioms of jazz and classical music could merge into a cohesive, elegant work of art."

## The Duke and *The River*

While the symphonic suite has carved out a space for itself in various parts of the world, scrutinized by conductors and musicologists in matters of tempo and voicing, Ellington's piano sketches and big band sketches have received little attention from musicians, even though they flow directly out of what the whole world recognizes as his natural idiom. The neglect started with Ellington himself, who slotted only one of them into his nightly routines: he recorded "Grap (The Giggling Rapids)" in a New York studio in a version that annotator Bjarne Busk contends "is considerably better performed than the earlier issued version," that is, than the sketch that Ailey worked from (in the Playlist). There were no commercial releases of the music in Ellington's lifetime. The band sketches came out of the stockpile thirteen years after Ellington's death, and the piano sketches a whopping thirty-one years after. They were totally unexpected, even to aficionados, genuine revelations, as were most pieces in the stockpile.

If Duke Ellington treated the sketches as ephemera, in the end, he slighted the ballet and its symphonic score as well. When the ballet had its well-publicized debut at the anniversary gala of the American Ballet Theatre at Lincoln Center in New York on June 25, 1970, Ellington was 700 miles

---

25. An online version by the Warsaw Symphony Orchestra (1977, conducted by Wojciech Rajski, with Mercer Ellington and a big band) https://www.youtube.com/watch?v=C2KR_5TS2Ks toys with the score. Mercer reverses the order of the last movements, playing "Riba" (based on his old riff) last, after "Village of the Virgins," and adds jazz solos to them.

away in Chicago. What business kept him away? He was playing yet another one-nighter in yet another venue, this one at the Grant Park Music Shell in the Chicago Loop. It is a sobering indication of Ellington's priorities that he chose to spend that evening beaming at the small crowd on the hardwood benches around the bandshell while his band played "Take the 'A' Train" for the six-thousandth time (literally; at least 200 times a year for thirty years) rather than, tuxedoed at Lincoln Center, graciously accepting the bouquet of roses after the triumphal premiere of his brand-new ballet.

A possible rationale, though Ellington never said so, was the omission of "Her Majesty the Sea." It may have stung, given his investment in the rebirth theme. In that, he was not blameless, of course. Not only did he submit the music too late, but, as I hear it, Ellington's haste at the end may have led him to invest this movement with considerably less majesty than was necessary for his lofty purpose. For the audience at the premiere and indeed for generations of audiences since, knowing only what *The River* includes and neither knowing nor caring about what might have been, we can only rejoice that the de facto ending, "Village of the Virgins," makes a graceful, rhapsodic, and altogether uplifting finale.

More likely, his neglect of the premiere was simply by choice. At this stage, he seemed to be in thrall to the endless round of one-nighters in theaters, arenas, old cinemas, high-school gyms, and even bandshells. As Luther Henderson said, "He would never leave his band to work on a show" or apparently to attend the premiere of a masterpiece.

Indeed, in the three healthful years that remained for him, Ellington never saw the ballet performed, and he probably never heard the symphonic score played. Collier sent him a tape of the seventy-fifth birthday concert (April 29, 1974) in Toronto, at which he conducted *The River* and another late symphony, *Celebration*, but Ellington was hospitalized and Collier said, "I don't know whether he ever heard it." Ailey made no secret of his disappointment (Dunning 308).

## "A Great Artist's Sketchbooks"

It is a rare privilege, perhaps unprecedented, to have two or sometimes three renditions of a composition and see it evolve from a piano solo to a fourteen-piece band to a symphony orchestra. And it is a stroke of luck beyond imagining that each rendition is listenable in its own right and brings its own distinct pleasures. As Stanley Dance (1987), who saw to the release of the big band sketches together with Mercer Ellington, said, "None of these were intended for release, but today they are the equivalent of a great artist's sketchbooks, and as such are presented here."

When we listen to *The River* in any of its three forms, the faintly harrowing backstory counts for nothing. Duke Ellington's hyperactive schedule, as if he were trying to slow the relentless turning of the Earth, his taunting of the people he so depended on—giving a token to one and saying, "You know what to do with it," handing scraps to another and saying, "We'd be better off if you would do more choreography"—if these incidents count for anything, it is to increase our wonder in what is accomplished. What appear to us to be Duke Ellington's distractions, his idiosyncratic priorities, his bizarre daily regimen, his sensitivities, and his insensitivities—well, they were not that different in his seventy-first year, when *The River* came into being, than at any other time in his long creative life. What we are left with, when all is said and done, is a glorious sequence of music, rich in texture and mood and especially in movement.

## Acknowledgments

Ted O'Reilly provided me with the studio-quality recording of Duke Ellington's 75th Birthday Concert with Ron Collier conducting *The River* and *Celebration*. John Hornsby provided me with the tape recording of Ron Collier's reminiscences at the Duke Ellington Conference in 1996. I presented a version of this material, with music, at the Ellington Conference 2021, under the auspices of the Duke Ellington Society of Sweden managed by Ulf Lundin. https://ellington.se/2021/07/14/ellington-2021-jack-chambers/.

## Playlist

(Recordings cited in order of appearance in the chapter)

"The Spring" 3:20 New York, May 11, 1970. *The Piano Player* (Storyville CD [2005]). Duke Ellington solo piano.

"The Spring" 2:26 Chicago, May 25, 1970. *The Private Collection: The Suites*, Vol. 5. (SAJA Records [1987]). Duke Ellington p with overdubbed grace notes in middle section, Joe Benjamin b.

"The Spring" 3:32 Toronto, April 29, 1974. Unissued. CJRT Orchestra conducted by Ron Collier. "Spring" 3:00. Detroit, October 3, 1992. Detroit Symphony Orchestra conducted by Neeme Järvi. Chandos American Series (Chandos Digital 1993).

"The Run" 2:46 New York, May 11, 1970. *The Piano Player* (Storyville CD [2005]). Duke Ellington solo piano.

"The Run" 2:34 Chicago, May 25, 1970. *The Private Collection: The Suites*, Vol. 5. (SAJA Records [1987]). Cat Anderson, Cootie Williams, Mercer Ellington, Fred Stone tp, Chuck Connors, Booty Wood, Julian Priester tb, Russell Procope as, cl, Norris Turney fl, Harold Ashby ts, cl, Paul Gonsalves ts, Harry Carney bs, cl, Duke Ellington p, Wild Bill Davis org, Joe Benjamin b, Rufus Jones d.

"The Run" was not included in *The River* and is not orchestrated.

"The Meander" 2:36 New York, May 11, 1970. *The Piano Player* (Storyville CD [2005]). Duke Ellington solo piano.

"The Meander" 5:08 Chicago, May 25, 1970. *The Private Collection: The Suites*, Vol. 5. (SAJA Records [1987]). Band personnel as for "The Run" above.

"The Meander" 4:01 Toronto, April 29, 1974. Unissued. CJRT Orchestra conducted by Ron Collier. "Meander" 3:57. Detroit, October 3, 1992. Detroit Symphony Orchestra conducted by Neeme Järvi. Chandos American Series (Chandos Digital 1993).

"Grap" (= "The Giggling Rapids") 2:48. May 11, 1970. *The Piano Player* (Storyville CD [2005]). Duke Ellington solo piano.

"The Giggling Rapids" 4:19 Chicago, May 25, 1970. *The Private Collection: The Suites*, Vol. 5. (SAJA Records [1987]). Band personnel as for "The Run" above.

"The Giggling Rapids" 3:17 Toronto, April 29, 1974. Unissued. CJRT Orchestra conducted by Ron Collier. "Giggling Rapids" 2:55. Detroit, October 3, 1992. Detroit Symphony Orchestra conducted by Neeme Järvi. Chandos American Series (Chandos Digital 1993).

"The Lake" 3:36 New York, May 11, 1970. *The Piano Player* (Storyville CD [2005]). Duke Ellington solo piano.

"The Lake" 6:53 Chicago, May 25, 1970. *The Private Collection: The Suites*, vol. 5. (SAJA Records [1987]). Band personnel as for "The Run" above.

"The Lake" 7:58 Toronto, April 29, 1974. Unissued. CJRT Orchestra conducted by Ron Collier. "Lake" 6:51. Detroit, October 3, 1992. Detroit Symphony Orchestra conducted by Neeme Järvi. Chandos American Series (Chandos Digital 1993).

"The Falls" 2:59 New York, June 8, 1970. *The Private Collection: The Suites*, Vol. 5. (SAJA Records [1987]). Dave Burns, Cat Anderson, Cootie Williams, Al Rubin, Fred Stone tp, Chuck Connors, Booty Wood, Cliff Heathers tb, Russell Procope as, cl, Norris Turney fl, Harold Ashby ts, cl, Paul Gonsalves ts, Harry Carney bs, cl, Duke Ellington p, Wild Bill Davis org, Joe Benjamin b, Rufus Jones d, Elaine Jones timpani, Walter Rosenberger glockenspiel, David Fitz marimba and xylophone.

"The Falls" not included in Toronto (1974) or Detroit (1993). Issued "Falls" 3:14 Louisville, Kentucky 1983. *Suite from The River* (First Edition Records 1983). The Louisville Orchestra, conducted by Akiro Endo.

"The Whirlpool" (= "Vortex") 3:23 New York, June 3, 1970. *The Private Collection: The Suites*, Vol. 5. (SAJA Records [1987]). Cat Anderson, Cootie Williams, Al Rubin, Fred Stone tp, Chuck Connors, Booty Wood, Julian Priester tb, Russell Procope as, cl, Norris Turney fl, Harold Ashby ts, cl, Paul Gonsalves ts, Harry Carney bs, cl, Duke

Ellington p, Wild Bill Davis org, Joe Benjamin b, Rufus Jones d, Elaine Jones timpani, Walter Rosenberger glockenspiel, David Fitz marimba and xylophone.

"Vortex" 2:27 Toronto, April 29, 1974. Unissued. CJRT Orchestra conducted by Ron Collier. "Vortex" 2:13. Detroit, October 3, 1992. Detroit Symphony Orchestra conducted by Neeme Järvi. Chandos American Series (Chandos Digital 1993),

"Taffy Twist" 5:49 (Mercer Ellington) New York, June 6, 1962. *The Feeling of Jazz* Black Lion CD [1988]). Cat Anderson, Bill Berry, Harold Baker, Ray Nance tp, Lawrence Brown, Chuck Connors, Leon Cox tb, Jimmy Hamilton cl, ts, Russell Procope as, Johnny Hodges as, Paul Gonsalves ts, Harry Carney cl, bs, Duke Ellington p, Aaron Bell b, Sam Woodyard d. Solos: Ray Nance, Jimmy Hamilton ts.

"The River" (= "Riba" or "Mainstream") 3:55 New York, June 3, 1970. *The Private Collection: The Suites*, Vol. 5. (SAJA Records [1987]). Cat Anderson, Cootie Williams, Al Rubin, Fred Stone tp, Chuck Connors, Booty Wood, Julian Priester tb, Russell Procope as, cl, Norris Turney fl, Harold Ashby ts, cl, Paul Gonsalves ts, Harry Carney bs, cl, Duke Ellington p, Wild Bill Davis org, Joe Benjamin b, Rufus Jones d.

"Riba" (= "The River") 3:50 Toronto, April 29, 1974. Unissued. CJRT Orchestra conducted by Ron Collier. "Riba" 3:18. Detroit, October 3, 1992. Detroit Symphony Orchestra conducted by Neeme Järvi. Chandos American Series (Chandos Digital 1993),

"Stud" (= "The Neo-Hip-Hop Cool Kiddies Community") 2:25 New York, May 11, 1970. *The Piano Player* (Storyville CD [2005]). Duke Ellington solo piano.

"The Neo-Hip-Hop Cool Kiddies Community" (= "Stud") 1:46 New York, June 3, 1970. *The Private Collection: The Suites*, Vol. 5. (SAJA Records [1987]). Band personnel as for "The River" above.

"The Neo-Hip-Hop Cool Kiddies Community" was not included in *The River* and is not orchestrated.

"Her Majesty the Sea" 2:35 (also called "The Mother Her Majesty the Sea") New York, June 15, 1970. *The Private Collection: The Suites*, Vol. 5. (SAJA Records [1987]). Cat Anderson, Cootie Williams, Mercer Ellington, Fred Stone tp, Chuck Connors, Booty Wood, Julian Priester tb, Russell Procope as, cl, Norris Turney fl, Harold Ashby ts, cl, Paul Gonsalves ts, Harry Carney bs, cl, Duke Ellington p, Wild Bill Davis org, Joe Benjamin b, Rufus Jones d.

"Village of the Virgins" 5:09 New York, June 15, 1970. *The Private Collection: The Suites*, Vol. 5. (SAJA Records [1987]). Band personnel as for "Her Majesty the Sea."

"Village of the Virgins" 5:38 Toronto, April 29, 1974. Unissued. CJRT Orchestra conducted by Ron Collier. "Village Virgins" 4:21. Detroit, October 3, 1992. Detroit Symphony Orchestra conducted by Neeme Järvi. Chandos American Series (Chandos Digital 1993).

"Grap (The Giggling Rapids)" 3:11 National Recording Studio, New York April 28, 1971, *Togo Brava Suite* (Storyville CD [2001]). Cootie Williams, Eddie Preston, Money Johnson, Mercer Ellington tp, Booty Wood, Malcolm Taylor, Chuck Connors tb, Harold Minerve, Norris Turney, Harold Ashby, Paul Gonsalves, Harry Carney reeds; Duke Ellington p, Joe Benjamin b, Rufus Jones d..

Chapter 11

# The Missing Last Act of an American Composer

> It is time we paid our respects to a man who has spent his life reducing the violence and chaos of American life to artistic order. I have no idea where we shall all be a hundred years from now, but if there is a classical music in which the American experience has finally discovered the voice of its own complexity, it will owe much of its direction to the achievements of Edward Kennedy Ellington.
> —RALPH ELLISON (1986, 86)

It is safe to say that the music of Duke Ellington, notwithstanding its ingenuity, astounding variety, independence of mind and spirit, and mastery of form and function—all the luminosity celebrated in this book and dozens of others—has not found a secure niche in the musical firmament. The breach was noticed by a few attentive souls in his lifetime, and by a few who revered him and wondered why their reverence was not more widely shared. Barney Bigard, Ellington's clarinet soloist from 1928 to 1942, lamented it in the years following Ellington's death but held out hope for future generations. "Do you know till this day he has never had all the credit that he deserves," he wrote (1986), and then he added, "Like all other great artists. They have to be dead a hundred years before the world will really know their worth."

To some extent, its neglect seems to emanate from the composer himself. He was a diffident advocate, for all his eloquence, and a timorous exhibitor of his extended compositions.

It became a phobia in the end, a tragic flaw, perhaps a kind of sociopathy. It caused the composer to enshroud a significant dimension of his accomplishment. "Sociopathy" is probably too strong a word if it conjures up some debilitating obsession. *Weltschmerz* is better, as a kind of apathy that obviates what seems a reasonable social expectation. A kind of malaise when some action is expected.

We see it, for instance, in the Shakespeare suite *Such Sweet Thunder*. The twelve brilliant movements amounted simply to that—twelve brilliant movements. They exist in a cluster, without internal organization of any kind. On the three occasions when they were played together, that is, as a suite, they were played in a different order each time, apparently randomly. Each movement is dazzling, but the suite lacks the cumulative effect it might have had by giving them cohesion.

Wondering why the suite was left *un*suited, so to speak, raises a further, more unsettling, question: Why bother organizing them if they are never going to be played together? Ever. And that question taps into the flaw that especially dogged the last hyperactive years of Duke Ellington's career but was visible, to anyone who was watching critically, years earlier—the repression of artistic ambition.

### "No Desire to Take His Orchestra off the Circuit"

The problem was noticed by a few critical observers in Ellington's lifetime. In 1971, jazz historian Martin Williams, putting Ellington's final decades in perspective, concluded, "Most Americans, including most American musical academicians, if they really know of him at all, think of Ellington, the popular song writer. . . . They are less likely to know the instrumental compositions from which these sometimes simplified ditties were derived. And the great Ellington . . . remains largely unknown territory. Yet it is these works that make him a great American composer" (1989, 236). As we shall see, Benny Green, the astute British critic, also rued the critical fade-out of Ellington's ambitions and had the temerity to confront Ellington with it. A few observers whose view was broader than the jazz scene saw it, including Alvin Ailey, the great dancer/choreographer who collaborated with Ellington on *The River*, and Norman Granz, the impresario who presented Ellington's concerts all over Europe. Most jazz writers, dazzled by the public persona of the man as he plied his seemingly endless rounds of one-nighters, looked no further.

Ironically, Albert Murray, a great booster of Ellington's music, saw the problem but not its gravity. Murray (1976, 182) wrote:

There are those who even as they used to declare Duke Ellington to be the greatest of American composers immediately began wringing their hands and shaking their heads over what struck them as being the cruel state of affairs that forced him to spend most of his time on the road with his orchestra playing in nightclubs, ballrooms, and theaters. The fact that Duke Ellington had already become Ellington the Composer by writing music for such places long before his first Carnegie Hall concert seems to have escaped them at such moments, as did the fact that as important as formal concerts came to be to Ellington, he never expressed any desire to take his orchestra off the circuit.

Murray's unnamed critics are certainly right in lamenting the fading away of the musician he aptly names "Ellington the Composer," but remiss in saying he was "forced" to spend his days and nights on the road. The real cause for the "wringing of hands and shaking of heads" is Ellington's avoidance of those "formal concerts." For more than a decade, from at least 1960 to the end, Ellington assiduously avoided occasions that might have celebrated his place among "the greatest of American composers." That choice was not foisted upon him but chosen by him, and he stuck with it even toward the end when he seemed to take less pleasure in his time on the road. The smile often seemed pasted on, as his son remarked, and the bonhomie with audiences seldom radiated genuine sincerity. Though Ellington apparently basked in the instant applause that greeted the opening strains of "Take the 'A' Train," he glided about the stage for as much as half an hour while the band played a medley of melodies that were older than most of the people in the audience. He gratified the spruced-up suburbanites who had given up an evening of television for his concert by bringing on Money Johnson to mimic Louis Armstrong's famous vocal on "Hello, Dolly!" or Nell Brookshire swinging her hips as she belted out "Rocks in My Bed." In the end, he presided over this variety show to the exclusion of almost everything else, consoling himself with the idea that he was indulging the audience's nostalgia, though by then the nostalgia was probably more imagined than real for most members of the audience. He provided just enough music to keep the knowledgeable fans (and perhaps the musicians) from revolting.

Granted, you might say, a man has to make a living. But does it have to be an "easy" living? He did so to the exclusion of "formal concerts," that is, occasions that might have shone a spotlight on Ellington as a composer of suites and other extended works. They were now, to Murray's regret and many other boosters, past history.

## One-Night Stands

Even when opportunities arose that might have drawn forth loftier ambitions, Ellington did not exploit them. In 1965, he accepted an invitation to appear as guest soloist with the Boston Pops Orchestra at Tanglewood (in the Playlist). Apart from two pieces from his incidental music for performances of *Timon of Athens* at the Stratford Shakespeare Festival, the repertoire was decidedly unambitious, as he played piano while his most familiar big band tunes ("Caravan," "Satin Doll," and nine others) were recited in supper club arrangements concocted not by Ellington or Strayhorn but by a staff arranger supplied by the host.

The matchless harmonies and bold imagination that raised his stature among contemporary bandleaders and songwriters exist abundantly on record. So do the extended works that solidify his stature as composer, though less abundantly. In 1963, he recorded five of those compositions with symphony orchestras in Stockholm, Hamburg, and Paris (in the Playlist). In 1970, he recorded three of his compositions with the Cincinnati Symphony, which included a definitive exhibit of his piano virtuosity on Luther Henderson's orchestration of *New World A-Comin'*. They were effectively one-night stands, set down in recording studios and not in concert halls. After the extended works in the 1930s that whetted his ambitions as composer and the output spurred by his Carnegie concerts from 1943 to 1948, he settled into the role of composer of multipart suites crafted for the talents of his bandmembers and executed by them with consummate skill. They too became one-night stands, played as suites in the recording studio, and otherwise ignored except for a tune or two inserted into the nightly selection of older pieces. For his most knowledgeable fans, the insertion of a relatively new piece added a welcome dash of color to the proceedings.

The orchestral works of his final years had considerable flair, though they came into being with the dedicated assistance of willing and able arrangers—the magnificent ballet *The River*, orchestrated by Ron Collier in 1970; *Celebration*, for the Jacksonville, Florida, centennial, also by Collier, in 1972; *Three Black Kings*, orchestrated by Luther Henderson in 1973; and *Black, Brown and Beige Suite*, orchestrated by Maurice Peress in 1973. Peress, an adventurous conductor and an eloquent advocate of Ellington's extended works (2004), led the American Composer's Orchestra in his orchestration of *Black, Brown and Beige Suite* and Luther Henderson's orchestration of *Three Black Kings*, both completed in Ellington's final days, as well as *New World A-Comin'* and *(A Tone Parallel to) Harlem* (in the Playlist). The sad truth is that, apart from *Celebration*, Ellington apparently never heard any of them performed. Perhaps his stamina was fading at the time, but mainly his priorities lay elsewhere.

The symphonic adaptations cited above were high points, undeniably, but they are not necessarily keys to his stature as composer. Almost all his symphonic works came into being first in jazz band versions. The *Tone Parallel to Harlem*, brilliant as it is in the symphonic version, is a masterpiece in its jazz band version. Obviously, it is not alone. The suites—from *Liberian Suite* in 1947 to *Togo Brave Suite* in 1971—exist only in band arrangements. The clandestine *Queen's Suite*, composed in 1959 for Queen Elizabeth II, never played in public and unheard by anyone until 1976 when the recording was released posthumously, would have made a regal feast of pastoral jazz—idyllic jazz—if it had been presented in a concert setting. Two of his Hollywood scores, as we have seen, seemed preordained for an afterlife as suites—as, say, *Suite Anatomy* (surely a title Ellington would have relished) from *Anatomy of a Murder* and as *Paris Blues Suite*. The components are there, in abundance, awaiting the composer's crowning touch. Forever.

If Ellington had aspired to make his mark as Ellington the Composer, the gala concerts celebrating his gifts would have required both a jazz band and a symphonic corps—uniquely, probably, among "serious" composers and his marque, surely, in that company.

### The "Moron" at the Palais de Chaillot

Most observers would probably date Ellington's phobia for putting his extended works on display to 1956 when he premiered the *Festival Suite* at the Newport Jazz Festival. On the occasion, he was visibly quaking in fear about its reception. Perhaps that was the tipping point, but there were portents of it much earlier.

One of them Ellington told on himself. In his memoir (*MiMM* 188), he seemingly takes delight in describing what objective readers might see as his humiliating capitulation to an importunate spectator during the band's tour of Europe in 1950. During a concert at the Palais de Chaillot in Paris, Ellington writes,

> [W]e encountered a very, very knowing audience. . . . This was the first time the band had been in Europe since 1939, and the Paris jazz enthusiasts are very knowledgeable. . . . They had not heard all the stuff we had written year after year, from the beginning in 1943, when we had started writing a long work each year up to this time. So I was

showing off with the band, and we were playing *The Liberian Suite*. At the end of one of the movements, or somewhere along the line, a fine young man came strolling down the aisle and up to the stage.

"Mr. Ellington," he said, "we came here to hear Ellington. This is not Ellington!"

With that, of course, we had to tear up all the programs and go back to before 1939, to "Black and Tan Fantasy" and that kind of thing.

This little episode, tossed off by Ellington some twenty years after the fact with what some might see—as Ellington himself apparently saw—as humility, seems tragic. Ellington's response is no less than a betrayal of his vocation. This, from the man who once told a reporter, "We could've gone on for 50 years playing the old things . . . but it's a form of condescension, the worst of all artistic offences" (Cohen 2010, 511). Here, he is committing what he himself declared as the worst of all artistic offenses. Generations of readers must have wished for a show of rectitude. More appropriately, Ellington could have told the young man that the music he was playing was "indeed Ellington!" and, with a smile, bid him good luck in catching up. Or more in keeping with his pacifist style, he might have thanked the young man for his concern and carried on playing the program as scheduled.

The tragedy is all the more bitter when we learn that Ellington totally misunderstood the young man's mission. Boris Vian, the novelist and jazz trumpet player and a *truly* knowledgeable Ellington enthusiast, was in attendance that night at the Palais de Chaillot, covering the concert for a national newspaper, and his report provided a totally different take on the incident. Vian was merely reporting the incident; he had no way of knowing Ellington's perspective on it, because Ellington's account came out decades after Vian's newspaper article. As an eyewitness fully conversant with the language and culture, Vian saw that the protest was not about Ellington's "new" music at all but was simply the carping of a disgruntled trad purist, at that time a very vocal minority in the jazz world. The clarion call of the trad purists was sounded by the French critic, Hugues Panassié, in 1942 (59), who decreed that jazz, "already spoiled by an excess of instrumental virtuosity, finally lost all its purity with the disappearance of the great New Orleans musicians"; the demise, in Panassié's chronology, "began after 1930."

It was a viewpoint that neither Boris Vian nor Ellington could countenance. Vian was, in fact, entranced by Ellington's new music. He had heard the *Liberian Suite* the night before at a concert in Le Havre, and he was moved by it. "As I hear the *Liberian Suite* for the second time, I once again consider it to be by far the most interesting part of the concert," says Vian. "It is one of the 'serious' works by Ellington, and it is beautiful music."

Vian had an equally direct opinion about the young protester. He saw Ellington's "fine young man" as a "moron," a judgment with which all Ellington enthusiasts would surely concur. "A moron in the room finds a way to protest," Vian wrote, and then he revealed the benighted source of his protest.[26] "Of course this music doesn't sound like King Oliver, but no one except him obviously has come here to listen to King Oliver." As a working jazz musician, Vian's view of the "knowing audience" is also at odds with Ellington's. "It's unfortunate to witness that the French public is always the most rude on earth when attending jazz concerts," he says. Ellington's decision to revert to his old hits pained him and presumably all the other truly knowledgeable Paris jazz enthusiasts that night: "Obviously, of course the people who came to listen to twenty [sic] musicians playing a lot of great arrangements were more than a little disappointed."

One of the happier implications of this incident is the evidence that in 1950, Ellington was still willing to play his extended compositions at his concerts. He was, he says, partway through the five-movement *Liberian Suite*, only three years old at the time, when the young man aired his complaint. He had played the suite the night before, Vian says, to considerable acclaim. So Ellington had firsthand evidence that the French audiences were receptive.

Perhaps it was the obdurate young Frenchman who quashed Ellington's ambition to play the suites in their entirety, that is, as suites, for all time. He obviously contributed to it. But he was not the first reactionary to chide Ellington for giving him more music than he deserved. And he would not be the last.

### Breaking the Three-Minute Barrier

In 1931, Duke Ellington composed *Creole Rhapsody*, an extended form that took up two sides of a disk in the 78 rpm technology of the day. The work was more openly experimental than anything he had written before, an adventurous attempt at balancing two forms that occur in standard jazz formats, an eight-bar sequence (Theme A) and a twelve-bar blues sequence (Theme B). The

---

26. The translation of "Duke Ellington au Palais de Chaillot" is by Leïla Olivesi with her gracious permission.

experimental nature of the piece came clear not only in its extended length but in a second recording, five months after the first, when Ellington expanded it by adding further thematic variations.[27] (Both versions are in the Playlist; for a tabular comparison of the two, see Howland [2009, 170].)

Formally, *Creole Rhapsody* introduces each theme in turn and invites instrumentalists to embellish it. Theme A is played by the ensemble three times (twenty-four bars) and is then given over to variations by Barney Bigard on clarinet, Johnny Hodges on alto saxophone, and Cootie Williams on trumpet. The horn variations are capped by a piano solo, a striking variation on the theme, by Ellington. (The longer, second recording adds a dance-tempo sequence on muted trumpet by Arthur Whetsol at the end of Part 1.) Theme B, the blues, is then introduced and expanded in instrumental solos by Bigard and Williams. Another piano interlude by Ellington brings the themes together, as he opens his solo with Theme A and modulates to Theme B. The themes then meld into more subtle interplay and become more covert with intricate orchestral figures (identified by Howland as Theme C with variations $C^1$, $C^2$, and $C^3$).

*Creole Rhapsody* is a delight, notwithstanding the need to hear it with fades imposed by 1930s technology. Its uncommon length—six and a half minutes on the first recording, eight and a half on the second—seems to have escaped the notice of the American jazz critics who came down hard on Ellington a few years later for breaking through their self-ordained time limits with *Reminiscing in Tempo* in 1935 (four parts, twelve minutes) and the multipart *Black, Brown and Beige* in 1943. Maybe it was the novelty that saved it from the ire of the critics—maybe they saw *Creole Rhapsody* as a passing fancy, something that Ellington had to get out of his system. Or maybe it was easy to ignore in 1931, surrounded as it was by gems like "Mood Indigo" and "Rockin' in Rhythm" among his 'regular-length' records.

Unnoticed at the time—and since, for that matter—the British critics applauded Ellington's ambitions in *Creole Rhapsody*. Spike Hughes, who would soon join the vitriolic Americans in his contempt for *Reminiscing in Tempo*, praised *Creole Rhapsody* as "the first classic of modern dance music" in which "the individual player is, for the first time, completely subservient to the personality of the composer." Charles Fox, who reported Hughes's appraisal, agreed wholeheartedly and pointed out that "Hughes realized

---

27. The longer second version may actually be the original that was truncated to fit on two ten-inch Brunswicks in the first recording, whereas Victor later allowed Ellington two twelve-inch disks for the full version. Commentators find it hard to choose between them. I prefer the second recording because of its fantasia sequence featuring trumpeter Arthur Whetsol in Part 1 that is missing from the earlier version and a more polished solo by Cootie Williams in Part 2.

that here was a composition which took jazz an important step forward" (Fox 1959, 123–24). Some years later, as we shall see, Benny Green, the jazz reviewer for the *Observer* and *Punch*, would also extol its virtues. It is surely no coincidence that it was the British critics, innocent of the caste structure of American society, who lauded Ellington's ambitions on *Creole Rhapsody*. It was the American critics who would, as Harvey Cohen put it, impose "strict limitations on Ellington's and all African-American musicians' growth and artistic freedom" (2010, 79).

### "Who the Hell Wants to Dance in Carnegie Hall?"

As Mark Tucker says in his introduction to what he calls the "debate in jazz," the length of *Creole Rhapsody* "had caused grumbling in some quarters" (1993, 118), but it was largely ignored by the American critics. It was Ellington's further ambitions in fusing disparate themes into extended concert-length compositions that generated vituperation and a volume of commentary, some in defense but most in opposition, often scathing. Of all the commentators, the critic who left a scar on Duke Ellington and succeeded, albeit tacitly, in curtailing his grandest aspirations was John Hammond.

Hammond wielded considerable influence in the jazz world from a young age. He was a scion of the Vanderbilts on his mother's side, conspicuous among the Manhattan elite. In that august company, he was a rebel. Active in the Young Communist League (though apparently not in the Communist Party, according to his testimony before the Un-American Activities inquisition in the 1940s), he lent his voice to causes involving racial and ethnic prejudice. His other preoccupation, and the source of his influence in the music world, was combing backstreet clubs and juke joints searching for marketable musical talent. He was good at it, as shown by the conspicuous claim that he "discovered" Billie Holiday, Count Basie, Benny Goodman, Teddy Wilson, Aretha Franklin, Bob Dylan, and Bruce Springsteen. He had a hand in getting musicians recording contracts through his association with Columbia Records. It was an association that profited the company and Hammond and gave welcome exposure to the musicians.

In what became a stereotype in corporate success in the music business, Hammond assumed his prowess as talent-scout-cum-producer entitled him to dictate to his protégés on matters involving bandmembers, stage presentations, and recording sessions. The musicians felt a sense of obligation to Hammond, but his advice did not always sit well with them. Duke Ellington was not a protégé of Hammond's—Hammond was wending his way through a sequence of exclusive boys' schools when Ellington was taking giant strides as a Harlem bandleader and composer—but that did not stop Hammond from trying to dictate terms to him. Ellington was not a musician who took kindly to managerial dictates. He had fired longtime manager Irving Mills in 1939, and though he never cited Mills's persistent interventions in the music among the reasons for the split, his musicians had no qualms about complaining about it. It is a matter of record that Mills added his name to the credit line of numerous Ellington compositions and took a healthy share of the royalties and the publishing rights.

Hammond's animosity may have had its roots in Ellington's disdain for his advice. Leonard Feather, who was working for Ellington as his business manager, recounted an incident between them on Ellington's first contract with Columbia Records. Hammond had already advised Ellington, Feather says, "to get him to make certain changes" in the musicians he had hired; he particularly objected to hiring technically adroit players in the band. His advice had fallen on deaf ears, of course. "The climax came one day in the Columbia recording studios when Duke was making 'Serenade to Sweden,'" Feather wrote (1943, 174). "John Hammond, who was working for Columbia at the time, was supervising the recording, and at one point he told Duke that one of the soloists was departing too far from the melody and that Duke should have him keep it straight."

"Duke fixed Hammond with a cool grin and said, 'John you're getting more and more like Irving Mills every day.'"

"According to those who were in the studio at the time," Feather added, "John never quite got over that."

The incident in the Columbia Studio took place in 1939, midway between Hammond's two well-publicized attacks on what he saw as Ellington's overweening ambitions. In 1935, in the fallout from *Reminiscing in Tempo*, he published "The Tragedy of Duke Ellington, the Black Prince of Jazz" in the *Brooklyn Eagle*. He railed against Ellington's attempts at moving beyond the "simplicity and charm" that Hammond saw as his African American birthright. His ambitions, in Hammond's view, were nurtured by the misguided praise of critics outside the jazz world, among them European classical composers (1935, 119–20). "Confronted with the undiscriminating praise of critics like Constant Lambert," he wrote, "he felt it necessary to go out and prove that he could write really important music, far removed from the simplicity and charm of his earlier tunes. . . . His newer stuff bears superficial resemblance to Debussy and Delius." Hammond's observation about the 'European' elements was equally valid for "Mood Indigo" or even the earlier "Creole Love Call," among other "tunes" that Hammond presumably approved. And if the resemblance to the French composers was, as Hammond said, "superficial," it was simply because Ellington had never listened to those French composers but discovered the rich harmonies through repeated, almost incessant, composing and arranging for his skilled musicians in all kinds of musical contexts.

Eight years later, in 1943, in the fallout from *Black, Brown and Beige* at the first Carnegie Hall concert, Hammond published a broadside called "Is the Duke deserting jazz?" "It was unfortunate that Duke saw fit to tamper with the blues form in order to produce music of greater 'significance,'" said Hammond. As he saw it, those ambitions led Ellington to add technically facile players such as trombonist Lawrence Brown and clarinetist Jimmy Hamilton for the sole purpose of playing his newly "significant" music. Hammond (1943, 172–73) wrote, "He has introduced complex harmonies solely for effect and has experimented with material farther and farther away from dance music." Hammond's critique then becomes fixated on what he saw as the abandonment of dance rhythms. He ends his piece with this lament: "The conclusion that one can draw from this [Carnegie Hall] concert is that Duke is dissatisfied with dance music as a medium for expression and is trying to achieve something of greater significance."

Looking back on the debate decades later, Cohen (2010, 589fn) notes, "The large amount of financially and artistically successful danceable Ellington orchestra recordings of the 1930s and '40s make Hammond's grousings seem almost humorous." In the heat of the moment, Leonard Feather (1943, 175) chimed in with this over-the-top rebuttal: "Who the hell wants to dance in Carnegie Hall? And what does Hammond know about music for dancing, since he doesn't even dance?" Feather may have succeeded in trivializing Hammond's claims, but he might have been better off pointing out that *Black, Brown and Beige* and *Reminiscing in Tempo* are in fact constructed around the dance rhythms of the Swing Era, which were probably never as broadly defined (and practiced) at any other time in history, running the gamut from foxtrots to jitterbugging, with waltzes, jive, and all manner of Latin American dance music in between.

## Longing for the Ersatz Jungle

Hammond's complaints were basically just one more bellow from the nostalgia boom that reared up in the 1930s. Though he spoke from a loftier height and clothed his contempt in fancier words, he was just one more voice in the chorus that eventually included Boris Vian's "moron" at Palais de Chaillot. For many listeners nurtured by the music of the Cotton Club days, any departure from it signaled impurity. The movement gained momentum in the late forties when trad lovers staked a claim to authenticity that the new generation, the beboppers, defiled, giving rise to a heated debate described, in the polemics of the day, as the moldy figs defending their turf against the upstart hepcats. One of Ellington's discographers, Dick Bakker, ended his first volume in 1933—"so collectors who are only collecting up to vintage 1931 or 1933 will not have too many 'unnecessary pages' to buy" (1977, 3). He was accommodating fans who subscribed to Panassié's chronology. There were, naturally, throwback bands doing what they could to indulge their predilection for the earliest sounds coming up the Mississippi. "The jazz world," as Benny Green said, "has always been too ready to equate technical crudities with sincerity" (1973, 145).

Hammond and the other reactionaries soon discovered they had steered themselves into a cul-de-sac as jazz took a decisive turn in the direction of "complex harmonies." Hammond's miscalculation becomes glaringly obvious when we put the spotlight on his ominous prediction about Ellington in 1935 (120): "He and his music are definitely losing favor with a once idolatrous public," he wrote. "And unless there are definite changes very soon he will be in a very precarious position." Hammond was a spectator in the next forty years while Ellington made changes, all right, but certainly not in any direction that Hammond might have seconded, and he and his music maintained its favor, withstanding the vagaries of the music business, for the rest of his days.

In the end, Hammond conceded the point. In his autobiography years later, he devotes six pages to his spat with Ellington, which was by then some thirty years in the past. Ellington had been dead two years, and Hammond's criticisms were ancient history. His recounting of that squabble is, predictably, tedious. He feels the need to include it, he says, as a kind of duty (1977, 132). "I know I have puzzled or annoyed Duke's many admirers by my criticisms of his band and his music," and he adds, "The reasons for my reservations about Duke should be discussed, even if they are more revealing of me than of him."

That, dear reader, is about as close to an apology as you are likely to get from a Vanderbilt who spent a lot of energy, as his antagonist would gleefully point out, on lost causes.

## Trauma at Newport

Though Ellington never saw Hammond's quasi-apology, he would probably not have taken any solace from it. It was too vague, too circumspect. Ellington, for all his bonhomie, was deeply hurt by the grudging acceptance of his longer works in the general press, and he was especially stung by John

Hammond's persistent cavils. Hammond was, after all, an insider whose considerable clout went beyond club bookings and record contracts and now extended to the growing success of jazz festivals—he served on the board of the Newport Jazz Festival as an associate of the tobacco-rich Lorillards, its founders and sponsors, in Newport, Rhode Island ("stuffy old Newport, that bastion of entrenched wealth," he called it in his autobiography, 335). Hammond would become Ellington's *bête noire*, and for the rest of his days Ellington would go to considerable lengths to avoid crossing paths with him.

The evidence, typically covert, shows in numerous avoidance strategies. Ellington left the Columbia/Brunswick/Vocalion label for RCA Victor in 1940 because (according to Morton 2008, 22) the new owner, CBS, hired Hammond to run the jazz division. When George Avakian, a dedicated Ellington booster, joined Columbia Records as producer a few years later, he offered enticements to Ellington in hopes of bringing him back to the label, but Ellington resisted until 1947 and signed up only after receiving assurances that Hammond had left the company (Cohen 2010, 281). That Columbia contract covered a relatively flat period in Ellington's development (1947–52), but a subsequent contract with Capitol Records (1953–55) documented a period of growing vigor fueled by bright new soloists. Avakian foresaw Ellington's revitalization and brought him back to Columbia on very favorable terms.

Heretofore unrecognized is Hammond's role in the whiff of decay that surrounded Ellington's final years on this Columbia contract. Fatefully, Avakian left Columbia soon after Ellington's new contract came into effect. He produced Ellington's bestselling Newport album in 1956, and the impetus from that bestselling album combined with Ellington's reborn ambitions proliferated into a series of brilliant works until 1960, in one of Ellington's creative plateaus. Then, unexpectedly, the creativity tailed off in the final years of the Columbia contract with a string of decidedly unambitious works (a simulated dance date made up of old chestnuts, a jazzed-up score of a mediocre Broadway musical, and a recitation of French *chansons*). Ellington's best album from these last years is arguably the contract-defying *Johnny Hodges with Billy Strayhorn and the Orchestra*, made for Verve Records, not Columbia, with Ellington supposedly absent, though his fingerprints are all over it.

What happened? The only hint that Ellington offered was that he was displeased with the Columbia hierarchy for refusing to fund an album of his symphonic works.[28] The probable reason, though it went unnoticed at

---

28. Ellington signed a contract with Reprise Records and immediately recorded *The Symphonic Ellington* (January and February 1963) with symphony orchestras in Paris, Hamburg, Stockholm, and Milan (in the Playlist), thus filling the void that his Columbia bosses had forced.

the time, was that John Hammond had rejoined Columbia in 1959. Whether or not Hammond had a hand in vetoing the symphonic album, it was indisputably a decision that he would have applauded. And his presence, either in the studio or in the corridors at Columbia, was a specter that Ellington obsessively needed to avoid.

Firsthand evidence of Ellington's obsession with Hammond comes from Avakian, who witnessed his anxiety about his performance at Newport in 1956 (as told to Harvey Cohen 2010, 322). Leading up to the concert, Ellington had fretted because it included his three-part *Newport Festival Suite* (twenty minutes). The suite was underrehearsed, as Ellington's longer works often were, because of his deadline-defying regimen. The tensions were exacerbated because John Hammond, as a director of the festival, was lurking in the wings. Avakian, who was courting Ellington for Columbia at the time, was intimately involved with the preparations for the Newport concert, which he would record for Columbia, and had a close-up view. He recalled it vividly years later:

> Duke was very worried that if he couldn't get a good performance of the suite, it would be a career disaster for him for various reasons. . . . [H]e said it on the telephone [on the Friday before the concert], the words are quite memorable, he said, "Look, we've got to be ready to do something to protect this composition because I can't afford to not have it come out, I can't afford [it] to come out in a bad version, and the guys are simply not prepared."

And then Avakian reveals the obsession underlying his anxiety:

> He was nervous about any performances of long works. . . . He was actually traumatized, I would say—because he was so tired, as he said, of "having the John Hammonds of the world tell me I should stick to three-minute songs."

So John Hammond was the bogeyman, but in Ellington's mind he had become hydra-headed. The real monster was, as he told Avakian, *all* "the John Hammonds of the world."

## "Perversely Casual about His More Extended Works"

The depth of the wound shows most clearly in what Ellington ignored. Among the neglected works is *Creole Rhapsody*, the first of his extended works as a relatively youthful composer (he was thirty-one). Benny Green was one of the latter-day reviewers who lamented its neglect, and it led him to pose the question to Ellington that laid bare his phobia about performing his ambitious works.

One of promoter Norman Granz's unsung achievements was employing Green as annotator-in-residence for the copious outpourings from Pablo Records, Granz's fourth and final foray into the record business. Green's reputation as a jazz reviewer was mainly known in England until Granz gave him the international platform with Pablo. A tenor saxophone player born in Leeds, England, Green's reviews in British journals were prized for their brevity and wit, and for their breezy grasp of the dynamics and foibles of the jazz subculture. And they often displayed needle-sharp acerbity. (In reviewing the besotted Ray Charles's road show, for example, he observed, "While the voice croaks on, Charles maintains an incessant barrage of rolling piano chords which distil into concise melodic phrases only once or twice in an evening, giving a tantalising glimpse of the jazz pianist who lies half-buried under an inflated reputation.") Acerbity is not prominent in Green's liner notes for Pablo Records, either because Granz was looking over his shoulder or, more likely, because Green knew as well as anyone that acerbity was never a property of the liner note genre. He wrote dozens of liner notes for Pablo, perhaps a hundred or so in the 1970s and 1980s while the label lasted, and though the records he was annotating were often jam sessions, that is, spontaneous get-togethers with rudimentary planning, albeit with top-flight musicians, he almost always found an interesting angle to pursue. His notes were often the prize in the package.

One of the most challenging, or so it seemed, was an amorphous Granz concoction called *The Greatest Jazz Concert in the World*. The proceedings, occupying three hours and twenty minutes, are not a concert but a potpourri of concerts with a baffling assembly of talents built around Oscar Peterson, Duke Ellington, Ella Fitzgerald, and, uh, T-Bone Walker, a Texas blues shouter and guitarist. Ellington is generously represented with a little more than two hours of music, some of them with Fitzgerald, and in the idiosyncratic Granz mélange, occasionally with Peterson, Benny Carter, and Zoot Sims sitting in alongside his regular soloists.

Green, charged with filling a fourteen-page booklet (in the pocket-size three-CD release that came thirteen years after the four-LP box), rambles along in a tone well suited to the rambling music. At one point, he drifts into a digression on Duke Ellington that is absolutely revelatory (1975, 5):

> One time I asked him if he had ever considered giving a concert of his own music as one might present an evening of say Brahms or Delius, playing from top to bottom *Such Sweet Thunder*, *Liberian Suite* and *Suite Thursday*.

Ellington's reply baffled Green, as it surely did everyone who read it:

> He told me he doubted if audiences would really want that, but I told him he was underrating himself. He laughed at that, and then insisted he couldn't recall the main theme of *Creole Rhapsody*, an early 1930s work of startling prescience, and regrettably neglected in the last forty years, not least by Ellington himself. Whether or not he was just pretending about *Creole Rhapsody*, it is certainly true that Ellington was perversely casual about his more ambitious works.

From that, Green draws the obvious conclusion:

> [H]e regarded his actual concert appearances as something divorced from Ellington the writer of extended works. . . . [O]nce he stepped onto the concert stage, Ellington also stepped into a different persona and saw himself not so much as a composer as an entertainer.

Though Ellington never did revive *Creole Rhapsody*, Green's inquiry may have led him to go back and sample its considerable charms; in 1960, he revisited one of its themes under the title "Creole Blues" in a haunting version that features Lawrence Brown's trombone accompanied only by piano and bass (in the Playlist), and in 1969, his soundtrack for the movie *Change of Mind* prominently featured "Neo-Creole," a piece based loosely on two themes from *Creole Rhapsody*. As it happened, both "Creole Blues" and "Neo-Creole" suffered the same fate as their progenitor: they too were never played publicly, let alone merged into an updated take on *Creole Rhapsody*, as Green and many others might have hoped.

## "The Great Ellington ... Remains Largely Unknown Territory"

The problem goes beyond a career choice that favored entertainment over art, as Green knows. The ambitions that blossomed with *Creole Rhapsody* in 1931 flourished in the next decade and a half. But at every turn—or so it must have seemed to Ellington—he met opposition not only from symphonic mavens who could be dismissed because (as Mercer Ellington once said) they "don't know the language of jazz and don't understand what is being said," but also from inside, from "the John Hammonds of the world." If Ellington's manner and his bearing and his eloquence shielded him from the most brutal abuses, he nevertheless "felt the draft," as the sage tenor saxophonist Lester Young put it (Porter 1985, 1). "Racial discrimination was a frequent indignity Ellington had to face," Hasse (1993, 151) notes, try as he might to ignore it.

The advances he made by dint of his unbridled creativity were often shadowed by countermeasures. He presented concerts in Carnegie Hall as had his patron and predecessor Paul Whiteman the decade before him, but some members of the general arts press that had been so receptive to Whiteman damned him with faint praise or admonished him for his ambitions. While he was smarting from attacks on his early extended works, he could hardly fail to notice the uncritical accolades lobbed at George Gershwin, a Broadway songwriter suddenly gaining plaudits for his symphonic airs, including a Black opera that "borrowed," as Ellington said with unguarded candor (1935/1936, 114), "from everyone from Liszt to Dickie Wells' kazoo band." Ellington presented a moving elegy for President Franklin Roosevelt on his regularly scheduled radio hour in 1945 to universal acclaim, but his offer of an elegiac concert for President John F. Kennedy in 1963, whose assassination abruptly ended his tour of the Middle East for the US State Department, was vetoed as "inappropriate." His attempts at mounting Broadway shows were thwarted repeatedly, but after his death, a straightforward revue featuring his music, *Sophisticated Ladies*, ran for two years on Broadway and toured widely.

Though he kept on composing extended works, as we have seen, they were now commissioned, and thus paid for in advance, rather than self-initiated, as were *Creole Rhapsody*, *Black, Brown and Beige*, *New World A-Comin'*, and other early works. Once they were composed, he shied away from putting them on public display. When the commissioning group premiered his work, whether a motion picture soundtrack, symphony, or ballet, he was otherwise engaged and skipped the show.

At some point, apparently in the fallow period that coincided with his second Columbia contract in 1947–52, he must have decided that putting the extended compositions on public display was simply demeaning, ego-deflating, and (as George Avakian put it) traumatizing. He put an end to the Carnegie Hall showcases in 1948 with the excuse that "by 1950 everybody was giving concerts, and even a concert at Carnegie Hall no longer had the same prestige that it had in 1943" (*MiMM* 190). Eloquent though it seems, his rationale does not withstand scrutiny; his concerts there had become annual cultural occasions, playing to full houses with distinguished audiences and receiving notices in the daily press and other outlets. For Ellington, they may also have brought with them the threat of critical trauma. If he once saw that as an occupational hazard, it was now hardening into a phobia.

By contrast, the good old one-nighters brought him into contact with hundreds of beaming faces. The audience was across the footlights, but that was close enough for them to get the message: "The boys in the band want you to know that we do love you madly." And close enough for them to return the love. And the nightly performances diverted the spotlight onto his superb instrumentalists. As Benny Green (1975, 5) put it in his notes accompanying *The Greatest Jazz Concert in the World*:

> [I]t is certainly true that Ellington was perversely casual about his more ambitious works, and once you examine the items in this typical jazz concert program you begin to see what it was that seduced him away from the comparative formalities of his longer works. In this [Pablo] album, the orchestra plays a succession of pieces where, at least ostensibly, the performer is more important than the theme he is playing. . . . The evening is devoted to individual instrumental ability.

As time went by, the concerts became increasingly formulaic. The medley sequence with snippets of familiar old hits took up more space. Even the inner circle disliked it: "[W]hen Strayhorn was around, he would admonish him constantly about the medley," Mercer Ellington admitted (1978, 167). Though Ellington said it was played to placate the old couples in the audience who had courted to "I Got It Bad (and That Ain't Good)," he played the medley at jazz festivals and showcase events where audiences were expecting—and entitled to—more challenging fare. The travel was often exhausting—and never-ending—and the concerts were easy by comparison.

The first time Ellington's phobia intruded was many years before. In 1933, on the inaugural European tour, the English journal *Melody Maker* arranged a "Musicians Concert" so the Ellington orchestra could be heard in their undiluted glory, away from the music-hall ambience of the Palladium performances they were playing nightly with singers and tap dancers among the diversions. Ellington started the concert in good form—including

*Creole Rhapsody,* in a rare public airing. Fatefully, at some point in the first set, Ellington detected snickers in the audience when Tricky Sam Nanton unleashed his toilet-plunger solo, and it unnerved him. When he came on stage for the second set, he had watered down the playlist with pop tunes and novelty numbers. The British aficionados who made up the core of the audience were rightfully appalled. The poet Laurie Lee complained, "I had always considered Ellington the prophet of a new art, but on Sunday, I found a prophet who continually debased himself" (quoted by Jewell 1972, 54). Revered though Ellington was by a public that knew his music intimately from his records, this audience would not tolerate such pandering, and the outcry was tumultuous.

Their indignation obviously did not move Ellington, at least not for long. He became more apprehensive as time went by. His response to the young man at Palais de Chaillot seventeen years later was rooted in the same base instinct. And seventeen years after that came the trauma that had him quaking over *Festival Suite* at the Newport Jazz Festival. Those are the occasions that made it into the public record. So, of course, was the decades-long medley exercise, pandering to the nostalgia of old fans, perhaps always a constituency more imagined than real. And so was the obsessive scurrying from one-nighter to one-nighter, from one easily won standing ovation to another, until, quite literally, death forced him to stop.

## What Is Lost?

It was surely a failure of artistic integrity, a loss of courage, the avoidance of pain. Except for the few occasions when it became public, the pain was largely his secret—a pain whose torments rose up in the depth of the night, when the hangers-on had departed and the ghosts sauntered into the dim-lit room. It was a pain that could be masked in the light of day, though even that became more difficult as time went by. His son Mercer, his daily companion for the last twenty years when he served as trumpeter in the orchestra and its manager, was one of the few who got close enough to see it. "As the days went on, the smile turned into a grimace, there wasn't any sincerity there at all, it was just like he was onstage and the people would just more or less have to accept him on those grounds" (Nicholson 1999, 403).

Ironically, accolades for Ellington as a great American composer were still occasionally proclaimed even as he shunned the composer role in his public life.

Supposing he had found the resolve to stage occasional "Evenings with Duke Ellington," perhaps billed as, say, "An Evening with Duke Ellington and

His Famous Orchestra with Members of the Gotham Symphony Orchestra." Sponsors would surely have lined up to present him at Town Hall or the Lincoln Center or (why not?) Carnegie Hall. It would be, as Benny Green put it, "a concert of his own music as one might present an evening of say Brahms or Delius." One of Green's suggestions for the repertoire, for instance, is the Shakespeare suite "top to bottom." As we have seen, among the freakish lacunae of the Shakespeare suite in the form he left it to us, it does not have a definable top or bottom. Surely if it had been granted a celebratory—and richly deserved—presentation at "An Evening with Duke Ellington," the composer would have been obliged—or, better, inspired—to impose order on the movements, to give them a top and a bottom, and inevitably, a middle.

Similarly with the *Queen's Suite*, a pastoral feast in six parts (in the Playlist), it might have been given shape in a recital by opening with the Maestro spotlit at the grand piano as he glides into "The Single Petal of a Rose" and then segueing into "Sunset and the Mocking Bird," with its opening piano trills and sparse bass accompaniment, the continuity from Ellington's piano solo to the trilled introduction seamless (though not sequenced that way as it has come down to us). And the stage lights come up as the orchestra sounds the bucolic theme. And so on, finally, climactically, to the rousing kaleidoscope of "Northern Lights." And of course Ellington's spoken introduction to each of the parts is already available, as if he were picturing exactly this scenario as he worked out the idyllic movements in his solitary composing hours as the sun rose.

Perhaps there would be space for a world premiere of sorts, say, *Suite Anatomy*, assembled for just such an occasion. Anyone who has seen Ellington sidle up to the microphone in one of the countless online music clips (or of course anyone in the vanishing breed who saw him do it in person) can picture the scene as it might happen on "An Evening with Duke Ellington." Tuxedoed and elegant, in the first half of the evening, with his band behind him but not yet buttressed by the symphony players as they will be in the second half, Ellington comes to the microphone smiling modestly:

> And now, ladies and gentlemen, we would like to present a new suite based on our Academy Award–winning soundtrack for the film *Anatomy of a Murder*. We call it *Suite Anatomy*, and we open with the movement called "Polly's Theme," based on the main character in the picture, a lawyer named Paul Biegler, who seems like a happy-go-lucky fly-fishing country boy, but we discover he is really the smartest man in the movie. And Polly's character is based on a real man, Michigan Supreme Court Justice John Voelker, a vital presence

in the town of Ishpeming, Michigan, where we spent many happy weeks making this movie.

And so on, as preamble to the three-part suite with Ellington's incisive portraits of Polly and of Flirtibird, climaxed by the jittery drama of the bass-rich *Anatomy* theme.

Not that the evening would be devoted to Ellington's suites and extended works. What better way to send the crowd into the intermission than a railroad trilogy? Opening with "Choo-Choo (Gotta Hurry Home)" (1924), played by six musicians from the band emulating—but not imitating—the original Washingtonians, followed by the dynamic "Daybreak Express" (1933), and then capping it off with "Happy-Go-Lucky Local" (1946, but in the ebullient 1954 arrangement). Not a medley, but the full-length, three-piece diorama, sending the crowd (and the musicians) rocking into the break with the night train strain still resonating.

And while we are imagining what might have been, consider the fateful Pulitzer Prize debacle of 1965. The jury recommended Ellington for a special life-work award. The jury's recommendation was rejected by the advisory board without further explanation (Hasse 1993, 355–56). As a result, two of three jury members resigned, which made public what had until then been a confidential debate in the senior common room at Columbia University. The public outcry was immediate and vituperative. The rejection was seen as "a narrow-minded judgment by a narrow-minded group of men."

If it was embarrassing for the Pulitzer board, it must have been soul-crushing for Ellington, then sixty-six years old. As usual, he put up the brave front with his widely quoted *bon mot*: "Fate is being kind to me. Fate doesn't want me to be famous too young."[29] That was Duke Ellington in the light of day, cracking wise with a wry grin. Surely, in the depth of the night, the hoary old demons came thicker and faster. Now the John Hammonds of the world were showing their fangs. Time does not always heal. He could break the solitude with late-night telephone calls to friends and acquaintances in Hollywood or Paris or New York, but even phone calls to indulgent friends in inconvenient time zones could not last the night.

While we are thinking about what might have been, consider this: would the Pulitzer advisory board have come to the same soul-crushing decision

---

29. Ellington had previously used the *bon mot* ironically, more than a year earlier, in an interview with Max Jones in *Melody Maker* (February 1, 1964). Ellington expressed his disappointment in the cancellation of the final weeks of his State Department tour of the Middle East due to the assassination of President Kennedy. "I guess fate is being kind to me, as always," he said. "It doesn't want me to become too famous too young." (Thanks to Brian Priestley for pointing out the chronology.)

if the city had recently hosted "An Evening with Duke Ellington and His Famous Orchestra with Members of the Gotham Symphony Orchestra" at Lincoln Center? If the *Times* had run a review, and impresarios had been competing to make it a week-long event, and an annual one at that? Maybe it would not have required so auspicious a showcase for the Pulitzer committee to get it right. Maybe it would have sufficed if Ellington regularly played *New World A-Comin'* or *Night Creature* in their entirety at full length and garbed in their Ducal harmonies by the well-rested, well-rehearsed band or if he had devoted a segment of his concerts in one or two seasons to the complete Shakespeare suite or to the complete *Far East Suite*. Perhaps it would have sufficed if the nostalgia of the medley was replaced by a full-blooded revival of *Creole Rhapsody*. That is, if he had allotted some conspicuous space to Ellington the Composer.

## Smiling Put-Ons and Put-Downs

With a kind of perverse pleasure that characterized so much of Duke Ellington's style, you had to seek out the evidence of Ellington the Composer. Nothing was ever presented as hard-won, as something worth fighting for. The Shakespeare suite came about because, Ellington claimed, "as the jive boys say, Shakespeare was down, which means that he is dug by the craziest of cats" (Rasky 1957). From that description, one would hardly guess that he and Strayhorn had spent most of a year reading the works and consulting with Shakespeare scholars in America and England. "Mood Indigo," perhaps the most sensuous melody in the Great American Songbook, was reduced in Ellington's narrative to a schoolgirl's crush on a little boy who walked by her window. Serious discussions, he once said, "merely stink up the joint." He presented himself as musically semi-literate ("As far as anyone teaching me, there was too many rules and regulations, and I just couldn't be shackled into that"), but composer/educator Walter van de Leur (2017, 166), a perspicacious student of the 310 cubic feet of scores and other archival materials in the Smithsonian collection, says, simply, "Ellington not only *could* work like his European classical colleagues, he most often *did*." The haunting melody of "Solitude," he claimed, was scribbled on an envelope while he was leaning against a studio wall, waiting for another band to move out. Asked about presenting an evening of his own music, he laughed and pretended he couldn't remember how *Creole Rhapsody* went. His impeccable piano technique had been displayed on countless occasions by the 1960s, but when Max Jones asked if he would include material from his recent *Piano in the Foreground* album on his forthcoming British tour, he dismissed the idea by saying, "If I'm going to do anything like that, I'll have to start practicing" (Jones 1964, 5). He made it easy for casual fans—and reviewers—to underestimate his dedication and his talent.

These smiling put-downs and put-ons appear to mask a deep-seated fear of sounding self-involved. An ancient Japanese maxim from the isolationist Edo period says that the nail that sticks up is the one that gets hammered down. Despite all his years in the public eye, Ellington seems to have had a subconscious yen for that self-annihilating, initiative-throttling maxim. Somehow, he managed to hide in public places. Don George said, "Duke would stand up in front of an audience and talk and talk and talk, so people got the impression they really knew Duke, but that was the biggest smoke screen and the most effective one of all, because the more he talked, the less he said" (1981, 150). Irving Townsend, looking back on five highly productive years as Ellington's producer at Columbia Records, said, "Few men so eloquently 'wordy' have ever revealed so little of themselves to the world as did Duke Ellington. As some men hide behind public silence, he hid behind public phrases to build the walls around him ever higher" (1975).

Alvin Ailey lamented his shying away from gala occasions. Like Martin Williams, he rued the fact that "[t]he public knows him only by his pop pieces" (Dunning 1996, 309–10). In his preparations for the weeklong festival *Ailey Celebrates Ellington*, he declared, "Duke Ellington deserves that kind of tribute," implying that Ellington had neglected to provide it for himself.

One commentator who saw how destructive this diffidence was and said so out loud, was Norman Granz. "All I can think of is that, to the very end, he made sure he left nothing behind that would let people know the real Duke Ellington," Granz told Patricia Willard in 1989 (Hershorn 2011, 8–9). "That's the only conclusion you can come to. He really worked out a theory: let my music speak for me." What were the consequences? Granz saw that clearly too, and he draws the melancholy conclusion: "He really missed his last act."

## What Remains?

Ellington presents a great paradox, working tirelessly for fifty years on material for public presentation while gainsaying its worth and, in his final decades, shying away from culturally auspicious occasions for presenting it. What was lost by Ellington's suppression of Ellington the Composer? The music is all there, abundantly so. In his lifetime, Ellington's shrinking from occasions when he might have exhibited his longer works in gala settings undoubtedly allowed some cultural mavens to discount his *bona fides* as an

American composer. Undoubtedly, it cost him the Pulitzer Prize in music. Those were mere blips in the cultural landscape. He was, after all, hailed in his lifetime as an American composer by critics more influential than the men on the Pulitzer advisory board.

Because the music is all there, it might fall to enterprising younger musicians, gifted ones, to mount "An Evening with Duke Ellington," though obviously it will no longer include "his famous orchestra." The repertoire might, however, include the Shakespeare suite, organized "top to bottom." Perhaps it is too much to hope for "new" Ellingtonia such as *Suite Anatomy*, though the components are all there, awaiting an inspired, perhaps intrepid, collaborator. With or without *Suite Anatomy*, there is enough Ellingtonia to fill many evenings. Naysayers may bemoan the absence of Duke Ellington himself, tuxedoed and beaming as he stalks the proscenium. They should look harder. He will be there, as he always is, whenever his music is played.

He may yet get his final act.

## Playlist

(Recordings cited in order of appearance in the chapter)

*The Duke at Tanglewood.* Tanglewood Music Center, Lenox, Massachusetts, July 28, 1965. Duke Ellington Live and Rare. (Bluebird CD2 [2002]). Duke Ellington p, John Lamb b, Louie Bellson d, with Boston Pops Orchestra, Arthur Fiedler cond, Richard Hayman arr. "Caravan" 4:31, "Mood Indigo" 2:51, "The Mooche" 3:18, "I Let a Song Go out of My Heart" 2:44, "I'm Beginning to See the Light" 2:37, "Do Nothin' Till You Hear From Me" 2:39, "Sophisticated Lady" 3:21, "Timon of Athens March" 3:09, "Solitude" 3:00, "I Got It Bad (and That Ain't Good)" 4:12, "Satin Doll" 2:33, "Love Scene (from *Timon of Athens*)" 2:24, "Single Petal of a Rose" 2:41.

*The Symphonic Ellington.* Paris, January 31, 1963; Sundbyberg, Sweden, February 8, 1963; Hamburg, Germany, February 14, 1963; Milan, Italy, February 21, 1963. Originally Reprise Records, CD Discovery Records (1992). Cat Anderson, Ray Burrowes, Cootie Williams tp, Ray Nance cornet, violin, Lawrence Brown, Buster Cooper, Chuck Connors tb, Russell Procope, Johnny Hodges, Paul Gonsalves, Jimmy Hamilton, Harry Carney reeds, Duke Ellington p, Ernie Shepard b, Sam Woodyard d.
- *Night Creature*, first movement ("Blind Bug") 3:59 and second movement ("Stalking Monster") 7:48 with Stockholm Symphony; third movement ("Dazzling Creature") 3:58 with Paris Symphony.
- *Non-Violent Integration* 5:24 with Hamburg Symphony.
- *LaScala , She Too Pretty to Be Blue* 6:11 with La Scala Orchestra, Milan. Solos (dubbed later) Cootie Williams, Lawrence Brown, Russell Procope, Paul Gonsalves.
- [*A Tone Parallel to*] *Harlem* 14:01 with Paris Symphony.

American Composers Orchestra conducted by Maurice Peress. *Four Symphonic Works by Duke Ellington.* New York, RCA Studio C, June 27, 1988. Musical Heritage Society CD (1989).
- *Black, Brown and Beige Suite* 18:04. Orchestrated Maurice Peress. Solo: Frank Wess as
- *Three Black Kings/Les Trois Rois Noirs* 19:11. Orchestrated Luther Henderson. Solo: Jimmy Heath ts, ss.
- *New World A-Comin'* 13:47. Orchestrated Maurice Peress. Solo: Sir Roland Hanna p
- [*A Tone Parallel to*] *Harlem* 15:23. Orchestrated Luther Henderson and Maurice Peress. Solos: Jon Faddis tp, Bill Easley cl, Ron Carter b, Butch Miles d.

Duke Ellington, *Orchestral Works.* May 28, 1970, Cincinnati, Ohio. MCA Classics CD (1989). Duke Ellington, p, with Cincinnati Symphony Orchestra cond, Erich Kunzel. Ellington comp, symphonic scores Luther Henderson.
- *New World A-Comin'* 11:14
- [*A Tone Parallel to*] *Harlem* 14:12
- *The Golden Broom and the Green Apple*: Stanza 1: The Golden Broom 10:16, Stanza 2: The Green Apple 4:27, Stanza 3: The Handsome Traffic Policeman 5:57.

*The Queen's Suite.* New York, February 25, April 1, and April 14, 1959. *The Ellington Suites* (orig Pablo Records 1976, OJJCD 1991). Harold Baker, Clark Terry, Cat Anderson, Ray Nance tp, Britt Woodman, Quentin Jackson, John Sanders tb, Johnny Hodges, Russell Procope, Jimmy Hamilton, Paul Gonsalves, Harry Carney reeds, Duke Ellington p, Jimmy Woode b, Jimmy Johnson d.
- "Sunset and the Mocking Bird" 3:44, "Lightning Bugs and Frogs" 2:47, "Le Sucrier Velours" 2:40, "Northern Lights" 3:30, "The Single Petal of a Rose" 4:03 (piano/bass duet), "Apes and Peacocks" 3:00.

*Creole Rhapsody*, Part 1 3:07, Part 2 3:18. New York, January 20, 1931. *Early Ellington: Complete Brunswick and Vocalion 1926–1931* (GRP Records 3CD [1994]). Cootie Williams, Arthur Whetsol, Freddy Jenkins tp, Joe Nanton, Juan Tizol tb, Barney Bigard, Johnny Hodges, Harry Carney reeds, Duke Ellington p, Fed Guy gtr, Wellman Braud b, Sonny Greer d. Solos, Part 1: Ellington, Bigard, Williams, Hodges (obbligato). Part 2: Ellington, Williams, Williams/Bigard, Greer.

*Creole Rhapsody*, Part 1 (4:05), Part 2 (4:23). Camden, NJ, June 11, 1931. *Early Ellington 1927–1934* (Bluebird CD [1989]). Personnel as above. Solos, Part 1: Ellington, Bigard, Williams, Ellington, Whetsol (muted). Part 2: Ellington, Hodges, Bigard (chalumeau), Williams/Bigard.

"Creole Blues" 2:30. Hollywood, California, July 14, 1960. *Duke Ellington at the Bal Masque*, bonus tracks (orig. 1979 LP *Unknown Session*) (Essential Jazz Classics [CD 2011]) Lawrence Brown tb, Duke Ellington p, Aaron Bell b.

"Neo-Creole" 3:52 New York, June 20, 1969. *Up in Duke's Workshop* (Pablo [OJC CD 1979]). Cootie Williams, Willie Cook, Mercer Ellington, Money Johnson tp, Lawrence Brown, Benny Green, Chuck Connors tb, Johnny Hodges, Russell Procope, Norris Turney, Paul Gonsalves, Harold Ashby, Harry Carney reeds, Duke Ellington p, Victor Gaskin, Paul Kondziela b, Rufus Jones d. Solos: Ashby ts, Turney as.

# Works Cited

Ailey, Alvin, with A. Peter Bailey. 1995. *Revelations: The Autobiography of Alvin Ailey.* New York: Birch Lane Press.

Appel, Alfred Jr. 2002. *Jazz Modernism from Ellington and Armstrong to Matisse and Joyce.* New Haven, Conn: Yale University Press.

Armstrong, Louis. 1999. *In His Own Words: Selected Writings.* Edited with an Introduction by Thomas Brothers. New York: Oxford University Press.

Bakker, Dick M 1977 *Duke Ellington on Microgroove, Vol. 1: 1923–1936.* Alphen von de Rijn, Holland: Micrography.

Balliett, Whitney. 2002. *Collected Works,* New York: St. Martin's Griffin.

Balliett, Whitney. 1988. "Selfishness is essential." Originally *New Yorker.* In *Collected Works: A Journal of Jazz 1954–2001.* 2002. New York: St. Martin's Griffin. 521–25.

Balliett, Whitney. 1962. *Dinosaurs in the Morning.* New York: Lippincott.

Bamberger, Rob. 2000. Liner notes to Duke Ellington, *The Treasury Shows,* Vol. 1 (includes *FDR Memorial Broadcast*]. Denmark: D.E.T.S.

Bellerby, Vic. 1962. "Duke Ellington," In *The Art of Jazz,* ed. Martin T. Williams. The Jazz Book Club. London: Cassell & Co. 139–59.

Bernhart, Milt. 1996. "Milt, Murray and the Maestro." Excerpt from a talk Bernhart presented to the West Surrey Big Band Society, England, May 29, 1996, in Newsletter of the Duke Ellington Society, chapter 40, Toronto. November 2005 (*TDES Archive*).

Berry, Bill. 1999. Liner notes to *Such Sweet Thunder.* Columbia Legacy (stereo CD reissue). 13–16.

Bigard, Barney. 1986. *With Louis and the Duke: The Autobiography of a Jazz Clarinetist.* Ed. Barry Martyn. Oxford, UK, and New York: Oxford University Press.

Boyer, Richard O. 1944. "The Hot Bach." *The New Yorker.* June 24, July 1, and July 8. Reprinted in *The Duke Ellington Reader,* ed. Mark Tucker. New York and Oxford: Oxford University Press, 1995. 214–45.

Brown, Carrie Moea. 2006. "Kathryn Wimp's [a.k.a. Kay Davis's] Musical Journey with Duke Ellington." *Inside Shorefront* 7 (Spring). 9–15. http://shorefrontlegacy.org/Shorefront_Links/Publications_files/Vol 7 No 3 2006.pdf (accessed January 2021).

Burlingame, Jon. 2016. Liner notes to *Assault on a Queen, Music by Duke Ellington* (soundtrack recording). Dragons Domain Records CD (2016).

Bushell, Garvin, as told to Mark Tucker. 1990. *Jazz from the Beginning.* Ann Arbor: University of Michigan Press.

Chambers, Jack. 2016. "Duke Ellington's stockpile: The posthumous heritage." *IAJRC Journal* (Spring): 30–38.

Chambers, Jack. 2015. "Duke Ellington's Parallel Universe: The Stockpile." *Blue Light* 22 (Spring). 7–16.

Chambers, Jack. 2005. "Bardland: Shakespeare in Ellington's world." *Coda* 319 (March/April 2005): 10–17, 38. Reprinted DEMS Bulletin 05/1 (April–July 2005): www.depanorama.net/dems/051f.htm (scroll down to 1–43).

Chambers, Jack. 2001. "Sweet as Bear Meat: The Paradox of Johnny Hodges." *Coda* 298 (July/August). 16–20. https://chambers.artsci.utoronto.ca/hodges.html.

Chang, Rachel. 2021. "How Mahalia Jackson sparked Martin Luther King Jr.'s 'I Have a Dream' Speech." https://www.biography.com/musicians/mahalia-jackson-i-have-a-dream-influence (accessed October 25, 2023).

Chapman, Con. 2019. *Rabbit's Blues: The Life and Music of Johnny Hodges*. New York: Oxford University Press.

Clark, Lisa M. 2017. *Synchrony of the Sublime: A Performer's Guide to Duke Ellington's Wordless Melodies for Soprano*. Thesis in Musical Arts, University of Kentucky. https://uknowledge.uky.edu/music_etds/87 (accessed September 20, 2023).

Cohen, Harvey G. 2010. *Duke Ellington's America*. Chicago, London: University of Chicago Press.

Collier, Ron. 1996. "Working with Duke Ellington." Talk at Ellington '96: The Duke Ellington Conference. Park Plaza ballroom, Toronto. June 19–23.

Coss, Bill. 1962. "Billy Strayhorn Interviewed." *DownBeat*. In *The Duke Ellington Reader*, ed. Mark Tucker. New York: Oxford University Press. 498–503.

Crouch, Stanley. 1988. "On *Such Sweet Thunder*, *Suite Thursday*, and *Anatomy of a Murder*." Program note for Lincoln Center Jazz Orchestra. Reprinted in *The Duke Ellington Reader*, ed. Mark Tucker. New York and Oxford: Oxford University Press, 1995. 439–45.

Cullen, Jack. 1962. "Ellington on the Air in Vancouver." In *The Duke Ellington Reader*, ed. Mark Tucker. New York: Oxford University Press. 338–41.

Dance, Stanley. 1995. Liner notes to *The Far East Suite: Special Mix*. Bluebird CD.

Dance, Stanley. 1987. Liner notes to Duke Ellington, *Private Collection*, Vol. 5. *The Suites 1968, 1970*. WEA International CD.

Dance, Stanley. 1979. Liner notes to *Up in Duke's Workshop*. Pablo Records (Original Jazz Classics CD [1991]).

Dance, Stanley. 1975. Liner notes to *The Afro-Eurasian Eclipse*. Fantasy Records (Original Jazz Classics CD [1991]).

Dance, Stanley. 1974. *The World of Swing: An Oral History of Big Band Jazz*. New York: Da Capo Press reprint 2001.

Dance, Stanley. 1974a. Liner notes to *Second Sacred Concert*. Prestige Records (Fantasy CD [1990]).

Dance, Stanley. 1970. *The World of Duke Ellington*. London: Macmillan.

Dance, Stanley. 1969. Liner notes to Ray Nance, *Body and Soul*. New York, May 1969. (Solid State Records, Mighty Quinn CD [2006]).

Dance, Stanley. 1967. Liner notes to Duke Ellington, *The Far East Suite*. Bluebird CD (1995).

Dance, Stanley. 1962. Liner notes to *Duke Ellington & John Coltrane*. Impulse! MCAD-39103 (CD 1988).

Darrell, R. D. 1927–1931. "Criticism in the Phonograph Monthly Review 1927–1931." Excerpted by Mark Tucker. In *The Duke Ellington Reader*, ed. Mark Tucker. New York: Oxford University Press. 33–40.

Darrell, R. D. 1932. "Black Beauty." *Disques* III: 152–61. Reprinted in *The Duke Ellington Reader*, ed. Mark Tucker. New York: Oxford University Press. 57–65.

DeFrantz, Thomas F. 2004. *Dancing Revelations: Alvin Ailey's Embodiment of African American Culture*. New York: Oxford University Press.

Dobbins, Bill. 2017. "'Nobody Was Looking': The Unparalleled Jazz Piano Legacy of Duke Ellington." In *Duke Ellington Studies*, ed. John Howland. Cambridge, UK: Cambridge University Press. 108–56.

Dunning, Jennifer. 1996. *Alvin Ailey: A Life in Dance*. Reading, MA: Addison-Wesley.

Dyer, Geoff. 1996. *But Beautiful: A Book About Jazz*. New York: North Point Press.

Ellington, Duke. 1964. "Orientations." *Musical Journal* (March 1964). "Press Conference in Calcutta 1963." Reprinted in Stanley Dance, *The World of Duke Ellington*. 1971. London: Macmillan. 14–22.

Ellington, Duke. 1959. "Open-End Interview & Special Musical Platter [sic] with Duke Ellington." Interview transcribed in liner notes for *Anatomy of a Murder*. Columbia CD (1999). 29–33.

Ellington, Duke. 1939. "Situation Between the Critics and Musicians is Laughable—Ellington." *DownBeat* (April 1939). Reprinted in *The Duke Ellington Reader*, ed. Mark Tucker. New York and Oxford: Oxford University Press, 1995. 136–37.

Ellington, Duke. 1935/1936. "Ellington on Gershwin's *Porgy and Bess* . . .". In *The Duke Ellington Reader*, ed. Mark Tucker. New York: Oxford University Press, 1995. 114–17.

Ellington, Duke. 1931. "The Duke Steps Out." Reprinted in *The Duke Ellington Reader*, ed. Mark Tucker. New York and Oxford: Oxford University Press, 1995. 46–50.

Ellington, Edward Kennedy. 1973. *Music is My Mistress*. New York: Doubleday.

Ellington, Mercer, with Stanley Dance. 1978. *Duke Ellington in Person: An Intimate Memoir*. Boston: Houghton Mifflin.

Ellison, Ralph. 1986. "Homage to Duke Ellington on His Birthday." In *Living with Music: Ralph Ellison's Jazz Writings*. Edited with an Introduction by Robert G. O'Meally. New York: The Modern Library. 2001. 77–86.

Ellison, Ralph. 1945. "Richard Wright's Blues." In *Living with Music: Ralph Ellison's Jazz Writings*. Edited with an Introduction by Robert G. O'Meally. New York: The Modern Library. 2001. 101–19.

Enstice, Wayne, and Janis Stockhouse. 2004. *Jazz Women: Conversations with Twenty-One Musicians*. Bloomington: Indiana University Press.

Feather, Leonard. 1943. A rebuttal of Hammond. *Jazz* 18 (May 1943). Reprinted in *The Duke Ellington Reader*, ed. Mark Tucker. New York and Oxford: Oxford University Press, 1995. 173–75.

Feather, Leonard. 1964. "Blindfold test: Miles Davis." Reprinted in Bill, Kirchner, ed., *A Miles Davis Reader*. Washington: Smithsonian. 131.

Feather, Leonard. 1977. Liner notes in *Duke Ellington Carnegie Hall Concert January 1943*. Prestige 2CD.

Fox, Charles. 1959. "Duke Ellington in the Nineteen-Thirties," In *The Art of Jazz*, ed. Martin T. Williams. Reprinted by The Jazz Book Club, 1962. London: Cassell & Co. 123–38.

Franceschina, John. 2001. *Duke Ellington's Music for the Theatre*. Jefferson, NC: McFarland & Co.

Frazier, George F. Jr. 1933. "Music and Radio" (column). *Playhouse Magazine*. Cited by Harvey G. Cohen (2010) *Duke Ellington's America*. University of Chicago Press.

Friedwald, Will. 1999. Liner notes to *Blue Rose*. Columbia CD.

Friedwald, Will. 2014. "Sing a Song of Ellington, Or the Accidental Songwriter." In *The Cambridge Companion to Duke Ellington*, ed. Edward Green. Cambridge, UK: Cambridge University Press. 228–44.

Gabbard, Krin. 1996. *Jammin' at the Margins: Jazz and the American Cinema*. Chicago: University of Chicago Press.

Gavin, James. 2009. *Stormy Weather: The Life of Lena Horne*. New York: Atria Books.

George, Don. 1981. *Sweet Man: The Real Duke Ellington*. New York: Putnam's Sons.

Giddins, Gary. 1991. "Duke Ellington (Part 1: The Poker Game)." *Visions of Jazz: The First Century*. New York, Oxford: Oxford University Press. 102–17.

Gioia, Ted. 2012. *The Jazz Standards: A Guide to the Repertoire*. New York: Oxford University Press.

Gleason, Ralph J. 1975. *Celebrating the Duke. and Louis, Bessie, Billie, Bird, Carmen, Miles, Dizzy, and Other Heroes*. Boston: Atlantic-Little, Brown.

Graham Mingus, Sue. 2002. *Tonight at Noon: A Love Story*. New York: Pantheon Books.

Green, Benny. 1975. Liner notes to *The Greatest Jazz Concert in the World*. Pablo Records (reprinted in Pablo 3CD [1989]).

Green, Benny. 1973. *Drums in My Ears*. London: Davis-Poynter Limited.

Hajdu, David. 1996. *Lush Life: A Biography of Billy Strayhorn*. New York: Farrar Strauss & Giroux.

Hamilton, Jimmy. 1991. Interview in Duke Ellington Archive, Smithsonian Institution. March 1991.

Hammond, John, with Irving Townsend. 1977. *John Hammond on Record: An Autobiography*. Harmondsworth, UK, and New York: Penguin Books.

Hammond, John. 1943. "Is the Duke Deserting Jazz?" *Jazz* 18 (March 1943). Reprinted in *The Duke Ellington Reader*, ed. Mark Tucker. New York: Oxford University Press. 171–73.

Hammond, John. 1935. "The Tragedy of Duke Ellington, the Black Prince of Jazz." Brooklyn Eagle (Nov 1935). Reprinted in *The Duke Ellington Reader*, ed. Mark Tucker. New York and Oxford: Oxford University Press, 1995. 118–20.

Harman, Carter (unsigned). 1956. "Mood Indigo & Beyond." *Time* (cover story). August 20. Reproduced in *Annual Review of Jazz Studies* 6 (1993): 54–64.

Harrison, G. B. 1939. *Introducing Shakespeare*. Harmondsworth, UK: Pelican

Hasse, John Edward. 1993. *Beyond Category: The Life and Genius of Duke Ellington*. Washington: Smithsonian.

Haufman, Bo. 2021. "Louis Metcalf: A Forgotten Ellingtonian." *Bulletin of the Duke Ellington Society of Sweden* (February). 4–7.

Hedman, Frank. 1987. Liner notes to Alice Babs with Duke Ellington and Nils Lindberg, *Faraway Star*. Bluebell CD.

Henken, John. 2007. "About the piece 'Suite from The River.'" Los Angeles Philharmonic Association. < http://www.laphil.com/philpedia/musicdb/pieces/3822/the-river-suite> (accessed May 2015).

Hentoff, Nat. 1976. *Jazz Is*. New York: A Ridge Press Book/Random House.

Hershorn, Tad. 2011. *Norman Granz: The Man Who Used Jazz for Justice*. Berkeley, CA: University of California Press.

Howland, John. 2009. *Ellington Uptown: Duke Ellington, James P. Johnson, and the Birth of Concert Jazz*. Ann Arbor: University of Michigan Press.

Iverson, Ethan. 2017. Interview with Nicholas Payton. https://ethaniverson.com/interview-with-nicholas-payton/ (accessed April 2017).

Jack, Gordon. 2004. *Fifties Jazz Talk: An Oral Perspective*. Lanham, Maryland: The Scarecrow Press.

Jackson, Mahalia. 1969. *Movin' on Up*. New York: Avon Books.

Jackson, Travis A. 2002. "Jazz as musical practice." In *The Cambridge Companion to Jazz*, ed. Mervyn Cooke and David Horn. Cambridge and New York: Cambridge University Press. 83–95.

Jewell, Derek. 1977. *Duke: A Portrait of Duke Ellington*. New York: W.W. Norton.

Jewell, Derek. 1972. Liner notes to *The English Concert*. Original LP notes reprinted in BGO Records (CD 1999).

Jones, Max. 1964. "They're Trying to Make Me a Piano Player: I'll Have to Start Practising." *Melody Maker* (February 1, 1974).

Kelley, Robin D. G. 2009. *Thelonious Monk: The Life and Times of an American Original*. New York: Free Press.

King, Martin Luther. 1964. Letter to Mahalia Jackson, January 10, 1964. In Tom Reney 2019. "MLK, Mahalia Jackson, Duke Ellington and the Freedom Movement." httpswww.nepm.org/jazz-world/2019-01-21//mlk-mahalia-jackson-duke-ellington-and-the-freedom-movement (accessed July 2025).

Lambert, Eddie. 1998. *Duke Ellington: A Listener's Guide*. New York: Scarecrow Press.

Lasker, Steven. 1991. Liner notes to *Duke Ellington and His Cotton Club Orchestra: Jungle Nights in Harlem 1927–1932*. Bluebird CD.

Lawrence, A. H. 2001. *Duke Ellington and His World*. New York: Routledge.

Lees, Gene. 2000. *Arranging the Score: Portraits of the Great Arrangers*. London and New York: Cassell.

Levin, Matt. 2020. "A Masterpiece of Disharmony." *Paris Review* (December), Blog Archive. https://www.theparisreview.org/blog/2020/12/01/a-masterpiece-of-disharmony (accessed December 2020).

Lewis, Mike. 2009. Liner notes to Duke Ellington, *Live in Warsaw*. EU: Gambit Records.

Marsalis, Wynton. 1999. "Music by Duke Ellington." Liner notes for *Anatomy of a Murder*. Columbia CD. 11–16.

McDonough, John. 1969. "Reminiscing in Tempo: Guitarist Freddy Guy's Ellington Memories." *DownBeat*, April 17, 1969. Reprinted in DESS Bulletin (November 2021).

McLuhan, Marshall. 1964. *Understanding Media: The Extensions of Man*: Cambridge, Mass: MIT Press.

Miller, Paul Eduard. 1942. "Ivie Joined the Duke for Four Weeks, Stays with Band for Twelve Years." *DownBeat* (July 15, 1942). Reprinted in *The Duke Ellington Reader*, ed. Mark Tucker. New York: Oxford University Press. 458–60.

Morgenstern, Dan. 2004. *Living with Jazz: A Reader Edited by Sheldon Meyer*. New York: Pantheon Books

Morgenstern, Dan. 2014. "Ellington in the 1960s and 1970s: Triumph and Tragedy." In *Cambridge Companion to Duke Ellington*, ed. Edward Green. Cambridge, UK: Cambridge University Press.

Morton, John Fass. 2008. *Backstory in Blue: Ellington at Newport '56*. New Brunswick, NJ: Rutgers University Press.

Murray, Albert. 1976. *Stomping the Blues*. New York: Random House, Vintage Books (1982 reprint).

Murray, Albert. 1996. *The Blue Devils of Nada*. New York: Vintage International.

Nicholson, Stuart. 1999. *A Portrait of Duke Ellington: Reminiscing in Tempo*. London: Sidgwick & Jackson.

O'Meally, Robert. 1991. *Lady Day: The Many Faces of Billie Holiday*. New York: Arcade Publishing.

Orgel, Jeremy. 2021. "Louis Metcalf Interviewed." *Bulletin of the Duke Ellington Society of Sweden* (February).

Palmer, Robert. 1968. "Billy Strayhorn and Duke Ellington . . . a wide-ranging, omnivorous musical sensibility." Liner notes to *. . . And His Mother Called Him Bill*. RCA Victor (Bluebird CD [1987]).

Panassié, Hugues. 1942. *The Real Jazz*. Translated by Anne Sorelle Williams, adapted for American publication by Charles Edward Smith. New York: Smith and Durrell.

Peress, Maurice. 2004. *Dvořák to Duke Ellington: A Conductor Explores America's Music and Its African American Roots*. New York: Oxford University Press.

Piazza, Tom. 1988. "Black and Tan Fantasy." Reprinted in Piazza, *Blues Up and Down: Jazz in Our Time*. New York: St. Martin's Griffin. 1997. 50–61.

Porter, Lewis. 2023 "Ellington-Strayhorn: World Premiere of Such Sweet Thunder!" Playback with Lewis Porter (October 7, 2023). https://lewisporter.substack.com/ (accessed November 2023).

Porter, Lewis. 1985. *Lester Young*. Boston: Twayne Music Series.

Priestley, Brian. 2014. "Ellington Abroad." In *The Cambridge Companion to Duke Ellington*, ed. Edward Green. Cambridge, UK: Cambridge University Press. 55–66.

Rasky, Harry interview, ca. April 29, 1957, New York City. Broadcast CBC radio May 15, 1957.

Ross, Alex. 2018. "Beauty in the Void." *New Yorker* (October 29). 61–65.

Ruff, Willie. 1991. *A Call to Assembly: An American Success Story*. New York: Viking Penguin.

Schiff, David. 2012. *The Ellington Century*. Berkeley, CA: University of California Press.

Schiff, David. 2017. "The Moor's Revenge: The Politics of *Such Sweet Thunder*." In *Duke Ellington Studies*, ed. John Howland. Cambridge, UK: Cambridge University Press. 177–96.

## WORKS CITED

Schirmer Music Sales Classical, "Edward K. (Duke) Ellington, The River (1970). http://www.musicsalesclassical.com/composer/work/27671 (accessed September 29, 2016).

Schuller, Gunther. 1989. *The Swing Era: The Development of Jazz 1930–1945*. New York: Oxford University Press.

Seale, Archie. 1935. "The Cotton Club, the Aristocrat of Harlem." *New York Age*.

Shapiro, Nat, and Nat Hentoff, eds. 1955. *Hear Me Talkin' to Ya: The Story of Jazz as Told by the Men Who Made It*. New York: Rinehart.

Shih, Hsio Wen. 1959. "The Spread of Jazz and the Big Bands." In *Jazz: New Perspectives on the History of Jazz*, ed. Nat Hentoff and Albert J. McCarthy. New York: Holt Rinehart and Winston, DaCapo paperback 1975. 171–87.

Singer, Barry. 2000. "Luther Henderson: Bridging the Worlds of Broadway and Jazz, Outside the Limelight." *New York Times* (September 24). https://www.nytimes.com/2000/09/24/arts/music-bridging-the-worlds-of-broadway-and-jazz-outside-the-limelight.html (accessed November 2020).

Slome, Stanley. n.d. "The River." Newsletter of the Duke Ellington Society, Southern California chapter. http://ellingtonweb.ca/Slome-River.htm (accessed April 13, 2013).

Smith, Bob interview, Georgian Towers Hotel, Vancouver. Broadcast on "Hot Air," CBC radio (Vancouver), November 1, 1962.

Smith, Willie "the Lion," with George Hoefer. 1964. *Music on My Mind: The Memoirs of an American Pianist*. New York: Doubleday.

Stewart, Rex. 1972. *Jazz Masters of the Thirties*. New York: Macmillan.

Stratemann, Klaus. 1992. *Duke Ellington Day by Day and Film by Film*. Copenhagen: JazzMedia Aps.

Symphony Silicon Valley. 2014. Program notes on "Orchestral Suite from the ballet *The River*." <https://www.symphonysiliconvalley.org/concerts.php?pagecontID=56&showID=57c> (accessed September 2016).

Talese, Gay. 1966. "Frank Sinatra Has a Cold." *Esquire*. Reprinted in *The Frank Sinatra Reader*, ed. Steven Petkov and Leonard Mustazza. 1995. New York: Oxford University Press. 99–129.

Taylor, Duval. 2019. *Zora and Langston: A Story of Friendship and Betrayal*. New York: W. W. Norton.

Townsend, Irving. 1975. "Ellington in Private." *The Atlantic Monthly* (May 1975). http://www.theatlantic.com/unbound/jazz/townsend.htm (accessed February 25, 2003).

Townsend, Irving. 1960. "When Duke Records." Reprinted in *The Duke Ellington Reader*, ed. Mark Tucker. New York: Oxford University Press, 1995. 319–24.

Townsend, Irving. 1958. Liner notes to *Black, Brown and Beige*. Columbia Records. Reprinted in Columbia Legacy CD (1999).

Townsend, Irving. 1957. Liner notes to *Such Sweet Thunder*. Columbia Records. Reprinted in Columbia Legacy CD (1999).

Townsend, Irving. 1956. Liner notes to Rosemary Clooney and Duke Ellington and His Orchestra, *Blue Rose*. Columbia Records (reprinted on CD 1999).

Tucker, Mark. 1993. Introduction to John Hammond, "The Tragedy of Duke Ellington." In *The Duke Ellington Reader*, ed. Mark Tucker. New York: Oxford University Press. 118.

Tucker, Mark. 1991. *Ellington: The Early Years*. Oxford, UK: The Bayou Press.

Tucker, Mark. 1986. Liner notes to Duke Ellington, *The Blanton–Webster Band*. Bluebird 3CD.

Tucker, Mark. 1954. Liner notes to Duke Ellington, *Piano Reflections*. Capitol CD (1992).

Udkoff, Bob, interviewed by Stuart Nicholson. 1999. *A Portrait of Duke Ellington: Reminiscing in Tempo*. London; Pen Books. 326.

Ulanov, Barry. 1946. *Duke Ellington*. New York: Creative Age Press.

Unidentified interviewer. 1945. "Why Duke Ellington Avoided Music Schools." *PM* (newsmagazine). Reprinted in *The Duke Ellington Reader*, ed. Mark Tucker. New York: Oxford University Press, 1995. 252–55.

Van de Leur, Walter. 2017. "'People Wrap Their Lunches in Them': Duke Ellington and His Written Music Manuscripts." In *Duke Ellington Studies*, ed. John Howland. Cambridge, UK: Cambridge University Press. 157–76.

Van de Leur, Walter. 2002. *Something to Live For: The Music of Billy Strayhorn*. Oxford, UK: Oxford University Press

Van de Leur, Walter. 1996. Liner notes to *Portrait of a Silk Thread: Newly Discovered Works of Billy Strayhorn*. The Dutch Jazz Orchestra. (Kokopelli Records).

Vian, Boris. 1950. "Duke Ellington au Palais de Chaillot." Translated by Leïla Olivesi. Quoted in her presentation "Ellington Medleys," at Duke Ellington 2022 conference (April 25, 2022). https://ellington.se/ellington-meetings/ellington-2022/presentations/leila-olivesi-2/ (accessed May 11, 2022).

Voce, Steve. 1993. Obituary: Adelaide Hall. *The Independent*. https://www.independent.co.uk/news/people/obituary-adelaide-hall-1502902.html (accessed February 2019).

Westin, Martin, and Lars Westin. 2018. "Rolf Ericson Interview." *Duke Ellington Society of Sweden*, Bulletin 3. August 2018. 9–14. English translation from original Swedish in *OrkesterJournalen* (May 1994).

Whittaker, Byng. 1965. *The Duke*. CBC-TV broadcast (59:27). Recorded September 2 and 3, 1964, broadcast March 2, 1965. Toronto, CBC Studio, 354 Jarvis Street.

Wilder, Alec. 1972. *American Popular Song: The Great Innovators 1900–1950*, ed. with Introduction by James T. Maher. New York: Oxford University Press.

Willard, Patricia. 2004. Liner notes to Duke Ellington, *Piano in the Foreground*. Columbia Legacy CD. 9–11.

Williams, Martin. 1989. *Jazz in Its Time*. New York, Oxford: Oxford University Press.

Wilson, John S. 1963. "Busy Duke Likes It That Way." *New York Times*, August 7.

Woideck, Carl. 2017. "Authentic Synthetic Hybrid: Ellington's Concepts of Africa and Its Music." In *Duke Ellington Studies*, ed. John Howland. Cambridge, UK: Cambridge University Press. 224–64.

Zolotow, Maurice. 1977. *Billy Wilder in Hollywood*. New York: Putnam.

## Index of People and Places

Academy Awards (American Academy of Motion Pictures), 138, 149, 228
African Americans, 7, 13, 16, 20, 30, 92, 157, 189
African Republic of Togo. *See* Togolese Republic
Afro-Eurasians, 158–72
Ager, Milton, 140
Ahlert, Fred, 88
Ailey, Alvin, 5n, 188–206, 190n, 231
*Ailey Celebrates Ellington 1976* (TV special), 189, 197–98, 231
Allen, Geri, 52
*All's Well That Ends Well*, 180
Alvin Ailey American Dance Theater, 188, 197
American Ballet Theatre, 188, 190, 195, 204
American Composers' Orchestra, 212
American Federation of Musicians (AFM), 95
*American Popular Song: The Great Innovators 1900–1950*, 88
Amman, 157
*Anatomy of a Murder* (movie), 138, 147–54, 228–29
Anderson, Cat, 35, 37, 182
Anderson, Ivie, 73, 88, 91–94, 110
Anderson, Marian, 4
Angelou, Maya, 175
Ankara, 157
*Antony and Cleopatra*, 127–28
Apollo theater, 190n
Appel, Alfred, Jr., 101
Arlen, Harold, 88, 92, 93
Armstrong, Louis, 10, 70, 101, 142, 144–45, 154, 211

*Ascenseur pour L'Echafaud* (movie), 137
Ashby, Harold, 161, 164
*Assault on a Queen* (movie), 138, 139, 140–41
Athens, 171
Atlantic City, 170
Auckland, 171
Australia, 161, 204
Austria, 204
Austronesia, 160
Avakian, George, 221, 222–24, 226

Babs, Alice, 82–85, 110
baby boom, 89–90
Bach, Johann Sebastian, 112, 161
Baghdad, 157
Baker, Dorothy, 90
Baker, Harold "Shorty," 119, 153–54
Bakker, Dick, 222
Balliett, Whitney, 127, 191, 201
Baltimore, 59, 75
Bamberger, Rob, 77
Barclay Studios, 143
"Bardland: Shakespeare in Ellington's World," 186
Barnes, Clive, 197
Barris, Harry, 73
Barron's Club, 6
*Bartlett's Quotations*, 178
Basie, William "Count," 34, 49, 144, 217
Basin Street East, 103
Bearden, Romare, 4
Beethoven, Ludwig van, 113
*Beggar's Holiday*, 143
*Beggar's Opera*, 143
Beiderbecke, Bix, 43
Beirut, 170

Bell, Aaron, 44, 59, 63, 125
*Belle of the Nineties* (movie), 136
Bellerby, Vic, 10, 28
Bellevue Asylum, 55
Benin, 161
Benjamin, Joe, 163, 168, 199
Benjamin, Sathima Bea, 101
Berklee College of Music, 59, 64
Berlin, Irving, 88
Bernhart, Milt, 145
Berry, Bill, 180
Beyoncé, 98n
Bigard, Barney, 9, 15, 72, 209, 216
Birdland, 178
Birmingham, 168, 169
*Black and Tan* (movie), 136
Blake, Eubie, 4, 70
Blanton, Jimmie, 14, 46–48, 122
Blanton-Webster Band, 14, 15, 126
Block, Harry, 7
Bloom, Rube, 88
Bluebird Records, 63, 120
Blue Four, 43
Bojangles (= Bill Robinson), 4, 154
*Bolero*, 190
Bombay, 157
bossa nova, 168
Boston, 118
Boston Pops Orchestra, 212
Bowie, Steve, 69n, 85
Boyer, Richard O., 12, 14, 25, 37–38, 99–100
Brahms, Johannes, 69, 224, 228
Bricktop (= Ada Beatrice Louise Virginia Smith), 4, 6
Bridgers, Aaron, 146
Briggs, Bunny, 79n
Bristol, 165
Britain, 53
Bronze Buckaroo, 97
*Brooklyn Eagle*, 218
Brookshire, Nell, 211
Brown, Carrie Moea, 68, 74–75
Brown, James, 36
Brown, Lawrence, 9, 77–79, 92, 97, 139, 146, 219

Brown, Les, 90
Brown, Ray, 36
Bruckner, Anton, 69
Brunswick Records, 216n, 221
Buckingham Palace, 53
*Bundle of Blues* (movie), 92–93, 136
Burlingame, Jon, 140
Bushel, Garvin, 7
Busk, Bjarne, 204

*Cabin in the Sky* (movie), 136
Caesar, Julius, 183
Café Society, 81
Cairo, 76n
Calcutta, 36, 170
Cambridge University, 43
*Camille* (movie), 137
Canada, 205
Canadian Broadcasting Corporation (CBC), 60, 64
Capitol Palace, The, 6
Capitol Records, 34, 35, 37, 49n, 105, 150, 221
Capitol Transcription, 33, 35, 124
Capote, Truman, 147
*Carmen Jones* (movie), 148
Carmichael, Hoagy, 90, 112
Carnegie Hall, 33, 48, 49, 68, 74, 75, 77–78, 104–5, 122, 212, 219, 225, 228
Carney, Harry, 11, 18, 30, 35, 63, 70, 74, 152, 159, 164, 165, 168, 180, 183
Carroll, Diahan, 143, 144, 154
Carter, Benny, 223
Caruso, Enrico, 89
Cathedral Church of St. John the Divine, 84
CBS Festival of Lively Arts for Young People, 196
Celley, Al, 17
Cendrars, Blaise, 174
Century of Negro Progress Exposition, 96, 189–90
Ceylon, 157
Chambers, Jack, 203
Chandos Records, 204
*Change of Mind* (movie), 138–40, 154
Chapman, Con, 117, 131

Charlap, Bill, 52
Charles, Ray, 223
Chase, Lucia, 188–89, 193, 194
*Check and Double Check* (movie), 73, 136
Chicago, 30, 32, 91, 92, 94, 100, 106, 205
China, 171
Christie, Agatha, 18n
Cincinnati Symphony Orchestra, 49, 212
Civic Auditorium, 75
Civic Opera House, 33, 75
CJRT Symphony Orchestra, 203, 206
Clark, Lisa M., 69n, 85
Cleopatra, 180
Clooney, Rosemary, 81–82, 107, 110, 123, 125, 126
Cocoanut Grove, 73
Cogdell, Josephine, 3
Cohen, Harvey G., 17, 30, 38, 76n, 91, 217, 219, 221, 222, 224
Cole, Honi, 79n
Cole, Nat "King," 73, 90, 105
Collier, Ron, 191–95, 197–206, 212
Collins, Judy, 175
Colombo, 157
Coltrane, John, 55, 57
Columbia Records, 37, 53, 54, 59, 81, 107, 108, 121, 144, 146, 177, 178, 184, 185, 217, 218, 221–23, 221n, 225
Columbia University, 61, 112, 229
Communist Party, 217
Concord Records, 82
*Conjure-Man Dies, The*, 18n
Conover, Willis, 58
Conte, Richard, 140
Cook, Willie, 126, 164
Cooke, Alistair, 43
Cootie Williams and His Rug Cutters, 11
Copland, Aaron, 69
Cornell, Joe (Cornell Smelser), 144n
Cornell University, 75
Coss, Bill, 98, 119
Cotton Club, The, 6–9, 11, 12, 13, 15, 25, 30, 44, 70, 72, 91, 92, 112, 140, 163, 170, 202, 219
Coventry Cathedral, 169

Cox, Marion, 79n
Creamer, Henry, 4
Crosby, Bing, 73, 81, 89
Crouch, Stanley, 150
Crowther, Bosley, 145
Cullen, Countee, 4
Cullen, Jack, 73, 80

Dakar, 166, 168, 171
Dallas, 157
Damascus, 157, 171
Dance, Stanley, 25n, 33, 47, 49n, 53, 57, 84, 118, 122, 130, 132, 139, 159, 163, 165, 178, 190, 206–7
Darrell, R. D., 29, 45, 68–70, 71, 85, 109–10
Davis, Kay, 68, 73–80, 82, 94, 98, 104–5, 110
Davis, Miles, 55, 56, 113, 137
Davis, Wild Bill, 118, 197
Day, Doris, 90
Debussy, Claude, 51–52, 54, 69, 104, 161, 218
DeFrantz, Thomas F., 196, 201, 202
De Lange, Eddie, 96, 100–101, 102
Delius, Frederick, 69, 112, 218, 224, 228
Denmark, 181
Denny, Reginald, 140
Detroit Symphony Orchestra, 203–4
Diamond, Leslie and family, 53
Dobbins, Bill, 35
Dorsey, Tommy, 91
Douglas, Aaron, 4
Douglas, Alan, 55
Douglas, Kirk, 90
*Down Beat*, 76, 145, 148
Drake, 98n
Drake, Alfred, 143
Du Bois, W. E. B., 4
*Duke, The* (TV documentary), 60, 64
Duke Ellington Fellows (Yale), 57
Duke Ellington Music Society (DEMS), 186
Duke Ellington Society of Sweden (DESS), 206
Duke Ellington Society New York (DESNY), 61
Dunning, Jennifer, 194, 196, 198, 202
Dutch Jazz Orchestra, 103

Dyer, Geoff, 31, 157
Dylan, Bob, 27, 217

Eckstine, Billy, 89
Ellington, Daisy Kennedy (mother), 6, 24–25, 37, 52–53
Ellington, Edward Kennedy "Duke:" "aristocrat of Harlem," 6–8; arrival in Harlem, 3–5; Billy Strayhorn disciple and peer, 4, 26, 31–33, 51, 63, 81–82, 97–98, 102–5, 116–17, 119–21, 142, 158–59; and civil rights, 16–17, 19, 143, 157–58; composing methods and styles, 10–13, 17, 35, 37, 107–8, 158–59, 169–70, 179, 182–83; daily regimen, 193–94, 206; itineraries with band, 29–30, 62, 75, 76–77, 92, 129, 157, 161, 166, 190, 206, 228; "jungle music," 9, 122–23, 163, 219–20; metamorphs/adapting minor pieces into showcases, 83n, 128–29, 202; mother's presence and influence, 6, 24–25, 37, 52–53; in motion pictures, 29, 32, 92, 135–55; as pianist, 35, 44–64; rebirth at Newport 1956, 78n, 127, 177; reluctance to display or develop concert pieces, 147, 153–54, 185–86, 210–13, 219–31; Sacred Concerts, 62, 84–85, 106, 165, 169, 191; the stockpile/privately recorded sessions, 53, 204, 205–6; train travel and train music, 24–38
Ellington, Marie (vocalist), 73, 94, 105
Ellington, Mercer (son), 31, 36, 38, 47, 53, 72–73, 96, 98, 99, 107, 114, 118, 143, 148–49, 166, 190, 191, 204n, 205, 226, 227; as composer, 26, 29, 76, 78, 116–17, 202
Ellington, Ruth (sister), 31, 116, 117
Ellison, Ralph, 4, 209
Elizabeth II (queen), 53, 213
Emancipation Proclamation, 4, 96
England, 204
Englewood Cliffs, 121
Enstice, Wayne, 107
Ericson, Rolf, 118
Evans, Bill, 52

Evanston, Illinois, 74
"Evening with Duke Ellington and His Famous Orchestra and Members of the Gotham Symphony Orchestra, An," 227–30, 232
*Exodus* (movie), 148

Far East, 160
Fargo, North Dakota, 119
Fauser, Jessie, 5
Feather, Leonard, 56, 218, 219
Ferguson, Otis, 42
Fields, Dorothy, 7, 8
Fischer, Doug, 58
Fisher, Rudolph, 18, 18n
Fitzgerald, Ella, 90, 95, 101, 223
Flamingo Club, 98
Flender, Harold, 143
Foreman, Carl, 90
Forrest, Jimmy, 35–36
Fox, Charles, 122, 216–17
France, 204
Franceschina, John, 196
Franciosa, Anthony, 140
Franklin, Aretha, 217
Frazier, George F., 20
Friedwald, Will, 82, 88, 94, 96, 101, 102

Gabbard, Krin, 136, 148, 153
Gare St. Lazare, 143, 144, 146
Garrison Junior High School, 178
Garvey, Marcus, 4
Gavin, James, 92, 99
Gay, John, 143
Gazzara, Ben, 148
George, Don, 33, 95, 96, 126, 178, 194–95, 231
George V (king), 174
Germany, 204
Gershwin, George, 88, 225
Ghana, 161
Giddins, Gary, 29
Gillespie, John Birks "Dizzy," 57
Gioia, Ted, 104
Gleason, Ralph J., 27, 135, 142, 149, 171

# INDEX: PEOPLE AND PLACES

Global Village, 160–61
Gonsalves, Paul, 78n, 126, 127, 142, 146, 151, 152, 164, 165, 180, 184n, 200
Goodman, Benny, 12, 34, 91, 217
Gospel of Matthew, 109
Grace Cathedral, 106, 169, 191
Graham Mingus, Sue, 57
Grammy Awards (National Academy of Recordings Arts and Sciences), 138, 149
Grand Terrace, 91, 92
Grant, Kathryn, 148
Grant Park Music Shell, 205
Granz, Norman, 36, 126, 140, 212, 223, 231
Great Depression, 16
Green, Benny, 49, 57, 210, 220, 223–25, 226, 228
Greer, Sonny, 28, 30, 31, 46–47, 71–73, 91–92, 142
Grouya, Ted, 97
Guy, Fred, 25

Hajdu, David, 16, 31, 102–3, 116, 118, 122, 128, 178
Hall, Adelaide, 70–71, 72, 74, 75, 76, 79, 80, 85, 110
Hamburg, 212, 221n
*Hamilton* (musical), 91n
Hamilton, Jimmy, 35, 37, 77–79, 128, 129, 146, 151, 159, 164–65, 168, 181, 183, 219
Hamlet, 154, 181–82
Hammond, John, 122, 217–22
Hampton, Lionel, 34
Handel, George Frideric, 194
Hanna, Roland, 33
Hardwick, Otto, 6, 11, 28, 70
Harlem Renaissance, The, 3, 15, 20, 136, 171
Harman, Carter, 177
Harrison, G. B., 179
Harrison, Max, 137–38
Hasse, John Edward, 18, 19, 29, 30, 75, 95, 150, 225, 229
Hawaii, 161
Hawkins, Coleman, 55, 139
Hawkins, Erskine, 31n

Hayes, Cleo, 92
Hedman, Frank, 83, 84
Heifetz, Jascha, 7
Hemingway, Ernest, 17, 17n
Henderson, Fletcher, 112
Henderson, Luther, 49, 191–92, 206, 212
Henken, John, 194
Hentoff, Nat, 30, 50
*Here Come the Girls* (movie), 81
Hershorn, Tad, 231
Hines, Earl, 91
Hippolyta, Queen, 179
Hit Parade, 91
Hodges, Edith Cue, 118, 126
Hodges, Johnny, 35, 48, 84, 114–32, 139, 141, 146, 147, 152–53, 161, 164, 170, 181, 216; as composer/co-composer, 114, 125–26, 139; return to band in 1955, 125–27, 133
Hoefsmit, Sjef, 186
Holiday, Billie, 101–2, 217
Hollywood, 135–36, 140, 142, 148, 149, 157, 164, 213
Holman, Bill, 150
Homer, 115–16
Hong Kong, 161
Hope, Bob, 81
Horne, Lena, 99, 136
Hornsby, John, 64, 206
Howard University, 58
Howland, John, 75, 216
Hughes, Langston, 3, 4, 5
Hughes, Patrick Cairns "Spike," 216–17
Hunter, Alberta (Alberta Prime), 71
Hurston, Zora Neale, 4

Iago, 180
Île de France, 17
Impulse! Records, 55
India, 171
Indonesia, 161
Ink Spots, 95
Iron Curtain, 160
Isfahan, Persia (Iran), 130

Ishpeming, 151, 229
"Is the Duke Deserting Jazz?," 219
Italian Renaissance, 3
Iverson, Ethan, 119–20, 128
Ivie's Chicken Shack, 94

Jack, Gordon, 164
Jackson, Mahalia, 106–10, 154
Jackson, Quentin "Butter," 180, 183
Jackson, Rudy, 70
Jackson, Travis, 54
Jacksonville, 212
James, Harry, 90, 95
Japan, 37, 161, 164, 171, 231
Järvi, Neeme, 204
Jeffries, Herb, 30, 97–98
Jewell, Derek, 31, 132, 168, 227
Johnny Hodges and His Orchestra, 120, 121
*Johnny Hodges with Billy Strayhorn and the Orchestra* (CD), 121
Johnson, Jack, 4
Johnson, James P., 4, 44, 45, 61
Johnson, James Weldon, 5
Johnson, Jimmy, 148
Johnson, Money, 211
Jones, Jimmy, 121
Jones, Max, 229n, 230
Jones, Philly Joe, 142
Jones, Rufus, 163, 168
Jordan, Taft, 125
Juan-les-Pins, 168

Kabul, 157
Katz, Dick, 36
Kelley, Robin D. G., 12
Kemp, Chubby, 79n
Kennedy, John F., 76n, 157, 229n
Kenny, Nick, 9–10
Kenton, Stan, 105, 113, 145
Kentucky Club, 91
Kern, Jerome, 88
Kessel, Barney, 145
King, Martin Luther, 107, 154
*Kiss Me Kate*, 184

Koehler, Ted, 92, 93
K-pop, 168

Lady Macbeth, 181
Lamb, John, 168
Lambert, Constant, 112, 218
Lambert, Eddie, 61n, 70, 72, 163, 168
Larkin, Philip, 174
Lasker, Steven, 8
La Touche, John, 143
Lawrence, A. H., 10, 14, 53
Lee, Laurie, 227
Lee, Peggy, 90, 149–50, 151
Leeds Festival, 53
Lees, Gene, 51
Legrand, Michel, 137
*Les Liaisons Dangereuses* (movie), 137
Lester, Seelig, 139
Levant, Oscar, 49
Levin, Matt, 55
Lewis, John, 98, 137
Lewis, Mike, 164, 166
*Lift to the Scaffold* (movie), 137
Lincoln, Abraham, 4
Lincoln Center for the Performing Arts, 195, 204–5, 228, 230
Lincoln Center Jazz Orchestra, 150
Lisi, Verna, 140, 141, 154
Liszt, Franz, 225
Ljubljana, 171
London, 71, 171
London, Julie, 89
London Palladium, 76, 226
*Lonely Planet, The*, 162
Longfellow, Henry Wadsworth, 79
Loomer, Martin, 20
Lorillards, 221
"Lotus Eaters" (Tennyson poem), 53, 115
Lucey, Lawrence, 25n
Lunceford, Jimmy, 61n
Lundin, Ulf, 206

*Macbeth*, 181
MacDonald, Ramsay, 174

## INDEX: PEOPLE AND PLACES

Madras, 157
Mahler, Gustav, 69
Malaysia, 161
Malle, Louis, 137
Manhattan, 61
*Man with the Golden Arm, The* (movie), 148
Marco Polo Hotel, 166
Marie's Cave, 143, 144, 146
Marsalis, Wynton, 113, 150, 153
Massachusetts, 204
Marshall, Wendell, 51
Mathieu, Bill, 37
Maxwell, Jimmy, 51
Mayes, Wendell, 147
McEachern, Murray, 142, 145, 146, 147
McDonough, John, 25
McHugh, Jimmy, 7, 8
McKinney's Cotton Pickers, 43
McLuhan, Marshall, 160–61, 171
*Melody Maker*, 126, 226, 229n
*Merchant of Venice, The*, 176
Metcalf, Louis, 72, 73
Metropolitan Opera House, 17, 75
Miami Beach, 166
Middle East, 76n, 157, 158, 160, 225, 229n
*Midsummer Night's Dream, A*, 180–81
Milan, 221n
Miley, Bubber, 10, 45, 70, 80, 93
Miller, Glenn, 31n, 34
Miller, Paul Eduard, 88
Mills, Florence, 45, 154
Mills, Irving, 30, 218
Mingus, Charles, 54–57
Mingus, Sue Graham, 57
Minnelli, Vincente, 137
Miranda, Lin-Manuel, 91n
Miss Boston (English teacher), 178
Modern Jazz Quartet, 98
Monaco, 171
Monk, Thelonious, 12, 57, 88, 137, 137n
Monteverdi, Claudio, 113
*Moon Is Blue* (movie), 148
Morgenstern, Dan, 123
Morton, Jelly Roll, 88, 106

Mulligan, Gerry, 123
*Murder at the Vanities* (movie), 136
Murphy, Dudley, 137
Murray, Albert, 24, 26, 32, 210–11
Museum of Modern Art (MOMA), 58, 59
Musicraft Records, 33–34, 35
Myanmar, 161

Nahat, Denis, 202
Nance, Ray, 18, 32–33, 74, 76, 79, 80, 107, 148, 151, 152, 181
Nanton, Joe "Tricky Sam," 10, 15, 74, 93, 227
National Association for the Advancement of Colored People (NAACP), 17, 19
NBC Symphony Orchestra, 17
Near East, 157, 160
Negro Arts Festival, 160, 166–68
Nemo, Harry, 96
New Delhi, 157
Newman, Paul, 142, 143, 144, 145
New Orleans, 20, 70, 106, 147, 214
Newport Jazz Festival, 78n, 83, 107, 127, 177, 180, 221, 227
*Newsweek*, 196
*New York Daily Mirror*, 9
*New Yorker*, 14, 126, 200
*New York Post*, 76n
*New York Times*, 145, 186, 196, 230
*New York Tribune*, 29
New Zealand, 161
Nicholson, Stuart, 4, 30, 36, 46, 55, 56, 91–92, 126, 142, 149, 227
Nielsen, Leslie, 139
North Carolina, 204
Northover, Jim, 20, 64
Northwestern University, 74
Norton, June, 79n
*No Sun in Venice* (movie), 137

*Observer, The*, 217
Oceania, 160
O'Connell, Arthur, 148
*Odyssey, The*, 115–16
Ohno, Ted, 154

Oliver, King, 70, 106, 215
Olivesi, Leïla, 215n
O'Meally, Robert, 101–2
Open-End Interview, 151
O'Reilly, Ted, 206
Orgel, Jeremy, 72, 73
ORTF (*Office de radiodiffusion-télevision francaise*), 59–60, 63, 64, 167
*Othello*, 180, 183
*Ottawa Citizen*, 58

Pablo Records, 223–24, 226
Palais de Chaillot, 213–15, 219, 227
Palmer, Robert, 131
Panassié, Hugues, 214, 220
Papa Ibra Tall, 167
Paradise Theater, Detroit, 94
Paramount Pictures, 92, 140
Paris, 13, 32, 104, 142, 171, 212, 213–15, 221n, 229
*Paris Blues* (movie), 32, 138, 142–47
Parks, Bernice, 143
Parish, Mitchell, 69
Pastor, Tony, 81
Patterson, Tom, 178, 186
Peress, Maurice, 5, 212
Perkins, Michael, 151, 154, 169
Peterson, Oscar, 36, 223
Pettiford, Oscar, 35
*Phonograph Monthly Review*, 9, 45, 69
Piazza, Tom, 150–51
Pie Eye (Duke Ellington character), 148
P.I. Five, 148
Poitier, Sidney, 142, 143, 144, 154
Popeye (comic strip), 116
Porter, Cole, 88, 183
Porter, Lewis, 184n, 225
Power, Tyrone, 137
Prague, 170
Preminger, Otto, 148
Previn, Andre, 113, 137
Priestley, Brian, 229n
Prime, Alberta (Alberta Hunter), 71
Prince, Georgie, 79n
Procope, Russell, 35, 84, 161, 164, 168, 183

Puck, 181
Pulitzer Prize, 229–31, 232
*Punch*, 217

Queen Elizabeth Hall, 71
*Queen Mary*, 140

Rajski, Wojciech, 204n
Rasky, Harry, 178–79, 186, 230
Ravel, Maurice, 29, 190
Razaf, Andy, 4
RCA Victor, 95, 120, 221
Red Hot Peppers, 43
Redman, Don, 112
reggae, 168
Remick, Lee, 148, 152–53, 154
Reprise Records, 55, 83, 221n
Rhythm Boys, 73
*Richard II*, 181
Ringle, Dave, 27
Rinker, Al, 73
Roach, Max, 54–56, 61, 142
Roberts, Luckey, 45
Robinson, Bill "Bojangles," 4, 154
Robeson, Paul, 4, 69, 137
Roche, Betty, 94, 95
Rodgers, Richard, 88
Rome, 171
*Romeo and Juliet*, 127–29, 181
Roosevelt, Franklin D., 75–76, 225
Ross, Alex, 52
Royal Canadian Air Force (RCAF), 58
Rubinstein, Arthur, 49
Ruff, Willie, 57n
Rugolo, Pete, 105
Russell, Bob, 96

Sagittarius Productions, 139
*Sait-On Jamais* (movie), 137
Salle Pleyel, 42
Sanders, John, 126, 180
San Francisco, 106
*San Francisco Chronicle*, 171
Savoy Ballroom, 12
Schaap, Phil, 151

Schiff, David, 54, 180
Schirmer Music Sales Classical, 204
Schoenberg, Arnold, 113
Schuller, Gunther, 6, 29, 113
Scott, George C., 148
Seale, Archie, 7–8, 20
Sears, Al, 117
Senegal, 100, 160, 166–67, 170
Senghor, Léopold Sédar, 100
Serling, Rod, 140
Shafer, Bob, 27
Shakespeare, William, 42, 127–28, 176–79
Shank, Bud, 141, 164–65
Shapiro, Nat, 10
Sherman Hotel, 94
Sherrill, Joya, 73, 94–96, 110
Shih, Hsio Wen, 9
*Shuffle Along* (musical revue), 70
Simone, Nina, 101
Sims, Zoot, 223
Sinatra, Frank, 89, 90, 140–41
Singapore, 161, 171
Singer, Berry, 191–92
Sissle, Noble, 4, 70
Sloane, Carol, 107
Slome, Stanley, 190
Smiles, Harry, 146
Smith, Ada Beatrice Louise Virginia (Bricktop), 4, 6
Smith, Bessie, 106–7
Smith, Bob, 177, 183, 186
Smith, Willie "The Lion," 6, 45, 51, 61, 106
Snowden, Elmer, 6, 27, 28
Socé, Ousmane, 42
Sonny and the Deacons, 72
Sousa, John Philip, 69
South America, 160
Stevens, Robert, 139
Stewart, James, 148, 151–52, 154
Stewart, Rex, 99
Still, William Grant, 4
St. Jacques, Raymond, 139, 154
St. John the Divine, 84
St. Louis, 30
Stockholm, 83, 171, 212, 221n

Stokowski, Leopold, 7
Storyville Records, 96, 161
St. Patrick's Catherdral, 170
St. Peter's Lutheran Church, 33, 62
Stratemann, Klaus, 136, 139, 142, 144, 148
Stratford Shakespearean Festival, 61, 177, 185–86, 212
Stravinsky, Igor, 29, 69, 200
Strayhorn, Billy, 16, 37, 61, 94, 142, 212, 226; as composer/arranger, 5, 31–33, 81–82, 97–98, 103–5, 114–32, 128n, 159, 177–78; death, 33, 63–64, 130–31; joining the band, 102–3, 116–17
Sunrise Records, 124
Sweden, 83–84
Swift, Taylor, 98n
Swing Era, 12, 31, 50, 94, 122, 221
Switzerland, 205
Sydney, 171
Symphony Hall, 75
*Symphony in Black* (movie), 136
Symphony Silicon Valley, 204

Talbot, Irving, 140
Talese, Gay, 141
*Taming of the Shrew, The*, 183
Tanglewood Music Center, 212
Tatum, Art, 52
Taylor, Billy (string bass), 47
Taylor, Billy (piano), 33
Taylor, Tuval, 3
Tempo Music, Inc., 117
Tennyson, Alfred Lord, 53, 115
Terrasson, Jacky, 52
Terry, Clark, 57, 126, 181
Texas, 30
Thigpen, Ed, 36
*Timon of Athens*, 61, 212
Tin Pan Alley, 68, 69
Togolese Republic, 161–62
Tokyo, 171
Toronto, 192, 194
Toronto Duke Ellington Society, Chapter 40 (TDES), 20, 64
Toscanini, Arturo, 17

Town Hall, 184, 184n, 185, 228
Townsend, Irving, 81, 108, 178, 180, 181, 185, 231
"Tragedy of Duke Ellington, the Black Prince of Jazz, The," 218
Travis, Dempsey, 98
Travis Air Force Base, 158
Treasury Show broadcasts, 76, 95, 124
Trent, Jo, 7, 69, 72
Truman, Harry S., 19
Truman, Margaret, 19
Trumbauer, Frank, 43
Trumbo, Dalton, 148
Tucker, Bobby, 101
Tucker, Mark, 15, 24, 26–27, 28, 37, 51, 69, 217
Turney, Norris, 162–3, 164–66
Tynan, John, 145, 148

Udkoff, Bob, 117
Ulanov, Barry, 24–25, 30, 117
Un-American Activities inquisition, 217
*Understanding Media*, 160
University of New Mexico, 98
United Artists, 143
Uplands Air Force Base, Ottawa, 58
US Naval Academy, 8
US State Department, 129, 157–58, 225, 229n

Vadim, Roger, 137
Vallee, Rudy, 72
Van Cleave, Nathan, 140
Vancouver, 193
van de Leur, Walter, 97–98, 103, 123, 128, 128n, 130, 230
Van Gelder, Rudy, 121
*Variety*, 8, 76, 148–49
Vaughan, Sarah, 89, 101
Venice, 171
Verve Records, 36, 121
Vian, Boris, 174, 214–15, 219
Vienna, 171
Vocalian Records, 221

Voce, Steve, 71
Vodery, Will, 4, 6
Voelker, John D., Michigan Supreme Court Justice, 147, 152, 228–29
Voice of America (VOA), 58

Walker, T-Bone, 223
Warren, Earl, 31n
Warsaw, 168, 171
Warsaw Symphony Orchestra, 204n
Washingtonians, 6, 27–28, 71–72, 91, 189, 229
Waters, Ethel, 5, 92
Webb, Chick, 91
Webster, Ben, 14
Welles, Orson, 137
Wells, Dicky, 225
West, Mae, 136, 137
Westin, Lars, 159
Westin, Martin, 159
Westinghouse High School, 116
Westminster Abbey, 191
Whetsol, Arthur, 9, 216, 216n
Whiston, Richard, 139
White, Walter, 5
*White Christmas* (movie), 81
Whiteman, Paul, 75, 225
Whitney Museum, 61–62
Whittacker, Byng, 60, 64
Wilder, Alec, 88
Wilder, Billy, 137
Willard, Patricia, 44, 231
Williams, Bert, 5
Williams, Cootie, 9, 10–13, 15, 32, 48, 72, 80, 96, 139, 216, 216n
Williams, Martin, 210, 231
Williams, Mary Lou, 45
Wilson, Gerald, 37
Wilson, John S., 84, 186
Wilson, Teddy, 52, 217
Woideck, Carl, 100, 166–67
Wood, Mitchell "Booty," 164
Woode, Jimmy, 126, 148, 151, 183
Wooding, Sam, 7

Woodman, Britt, 180, 183
Woodward, Joanne, 143, 145, 146
Woodyard, Sam, 59, 125, 126, 163, 168, 183
Wordsworth, William, 17n
Wurlitzer keyboard, 191
Wyoming, 204

Yale University, 57, 57n
Yeats, William Butler, 89
Young, Lester, 225
Young Communist League, 217
*Young Man With a Horn* (movie), 90–91

Zolotow, Maurice, 137

# Index of Compositions and Songs

9:20 Special, 31n
23rd Psalm, 107

Accordion Joe, 144n
Afrique, 162–63
*Afro-Eurasian Eclipse* (CD), 160–63
All Too Soon, 50
Almost Cried, 153
Amour Amour, 62
*Anatomy of a Murder* (CD), 108, 149, 150, 215
Anatomy of a Murder (Main Title), 151, 153
Anatomy Theme (= "the bass theme"), 129, 149, 151, 153
*And His Mother Called Him Bill* (CD), 63, 131
A-Oodie-Oobie, 114
*Assault on a Queen* (CD), 141
Autumnal Suite, 146, 147, 154

Ballade for Very Tired and Very Sad Lotus Eaters, 114–15, 122, 125
Battle Royal, 144, 145
*Beautiful Indians, The*, 33
Beautiful Woman Walks Well, 140, 141, 154
Bird of Paradise, 61, 61n, 62
Birmingham Breakdown, 8
*Black, Brown and Beige* (CD), 5. 95, 105–6, 196, 203, 219, 225
*Black, Brown and Beige Suite*, 212
Black and Tan Fantasy, 7, 8, 42, 46, 62, 70, 163
Black Beauty, 45, 59, 70, 154
Black Butterfly, 139
Blessings on the Night, 140

Blood Count, 130–31
Bluebird of Delhi (Mynah), 159, 166
Blue Cloud (= Blood Count), 130
Blue Light, 99
Blue Mood, 12, 13
Blue Pepper (Far East of the Blues), 170
Blue Rose, 82
*Blue Rose* (CD), 81–83, 123
Blues, 47
Blues, The, 95
Bojangles, 47, 154
Bolero, 190
Boogie Stop Shuffle, 56
Botch-A-Me, 81, 82
Boys from Harlem, The, 10–11
Brown Berries (= Harlem River Quiver), 8

Caravan, 55, 56, 61, 62, 214
Carolina Shout, 44, 61
*Celebration*, 205, 206, 212
Charlotte Russe (= Lotus Blossom), 124
*Chinoiserie*, 160–61
*Chocolate Kiddies* (musical revue), 7
Choo Choo (Gotta Hurry Home), 26–28, 69, 229
Choo Choo Blues, 27
Choo Choo Charlie, 27
Circle of Fourths, 180, 184n, 185
C-Jam Blues, 62
Claire de Lune, 52
Clementine, 132
Come Easter, 169
Come On-a My House, 81
Come Sunday, 59, 83, 106–10, 169, 203

Concerto for Cootie, 11n, 48
*Concerto for Piano and Percussion*, 116
Confab with Rab, 114
Cootie's Concerto, 11n
Cop Out, 184n, 185
Creole Blues, 224
Creole Love Call, 68, 70–71, 74, 75, 76, 79–80, 85, 218
*Creole Rhapsody*, 139, 217, 225, 227, 230
Crescendo in Blue, 77–78, 127

Dance No. 2 (from *Liberian Suite*), 170
Dancers in Love, 50, 62, 99
Daybreak Express, 28–29, 31, 33, 170, 229
Day Dream, 120–22, 123, 124, 127, 132
December Blue, 50
*Deep South Suite, The*, 33
Depk, 159, 159n
Didn't It Rain, Children, 107
Diminuendo in Blue and Crescendo in Blue, 77–78, 127
Do Nothin' Till You Hear From Me, 11n
Don't Hurt Yourself, 98n
Drop Me Off at Harlem, 9–10
*Duke Ellington Meets Count Basie* (CD), 144
*Duke Plays Ellington, The* (= *Piano Reflections*) (CD), 50
*Duke's in Bed* (CD), 114–15

East St. Louis Toodle-Oo, 8, 46, 70
Echoes of Harlem, 11–13
Edward the First, 139
Elf, 130
*Ellington at Newport* (CD), 81, 177, 221
*Ellington '55* (CD), 34
Emotionless, 98n

Falls, The, 195, 200–201, 204
*Far East Suite, The* (CD), 129–30, 158, 230
*Feeling of Jazz, The* (CD), 202
*Festival Suite* (*Newport Festival Suite*), 222
Five O' Clock Whistle, 93
Flamingo, 97–98
Flaming Sword, The, 119

Fleurette Africaine, 56, 61
Flirtibird, 150, 154, 229
*Flirtibird Theme*, 151, 152–53, 231
Flower Is a Lovesome Thing, A, 115, 124
Flying Home, 34
Freakish Lights (= Blood Count), 130
*Freedom Now!* (CD), 55
Freight Train Blues, 27

Get Yourself a New Broom, 93
Giggling Rapids (GRAP), 198–99, 204
God Bless America, 119
Grand Finale, The, 151
GRAP (= Giggling Rapids), 198–99, 204
*Greatest Jazz Concert in the World, The* (CD), 223–24, 226

Half the Fun, 128, 128n, 132, 180, 185
Happy as the Day Is Long, 93
Happy Birthday, 83
Happy-Go-Lucky-Local, 33–37, 229
Harlem Air Shaft, 14–16, 170
Harlem Flat Blues, 13–14
*Harlem/Harlem Suite*. See *Tone Parallel to Harlem, A*
Harlem River Quiver (Brown Berries), 8
Haupe, 152, 154
Heaven, 84
Hello, Dolly!, 211
Her Majesty the Sea, 190, 193, 195, 205
Hero to Zero, 152
Hora Decubitus, 57, 57n

I Cover the Waterfront, 32
I Got It Bad (and That Ain't Good), 226
I'm Beginning to See the Light, 94–95
I'm Gonna Go Fishin', 149–50
In My Solitude. See Solitude
In the Beginning God, 169
In the Mood, 34
Intimacy of the Blues, The, 132
Intimate Interlude, 165
In Triplicate, 165
Isfahan, 83n, 129–30

It Don't Mean a Thing (If It Ain't Got That Swing), 93–94, 99

Jack the Bear, 47, 48
Janet, 59
Jeep's Blues, 48, 127
*Johnny Hodges with Billy Strayhorn and the Orchestra* (CD), 221
John Sanders' Blues, 62
*Joya Sherill Sings Duke* (CD), 96
Jungle Nights in Harlem, 9, 163

Kinda Dukish, 44, 50, 59
Ko-Ko, 47

Lady Mac, 180, 181, 185
Lake, The, 191, 199–200
La Mer, 194
La Plus Belle Africaine, 168–70
Le Sucrier Velours, 62
*Liberian Suite*, 170, 214, 215, 224
Lightnin', 28
Little African Flower, 61
Little Max, A, 55
*Live at the Whitney* (CD), 62–63
Lonely Again (= Lush Life), 103
Lots o' Fingers, 45–46
Lotus Blossom, 62, 63–64, 124–25
Low Key Lightly, 152
Lush Life, 74, 102–5, 105n

Madness in Great Ones, 181–82, 185
Mainstream. *See* Riba
Main Title (Anatomy of a Murder), 151, 153
Mama Bahama, 141
Mama Bahama Islander, 141
Mambo Italiano, 81
Meander, The, 198
Meditation, 62
Melancholia, 50, 51, 52, 59, 61, 99
Midnight Indigo, 152
*Midnight in Paris* (CD), 146
Minnehaha, 78–79
Mkis. *See* Soul-Soothing Beach
*Money Jungle* (CD), 54–57

Money Jungle (composition), 55
Mooche, The, 45, 70, 163, 170, 196
Mood Indigo, 29, 62, 68, 69, 93, 94, 96, 119, 145, 218, 230
Moody (= Serenade to Sweden), 83
Moon Mist, 76, 78
Mother Her Majesty the Sea, The (Her Majesty the Sea), 190, 193, 195, 205
Mr. J.B. Blues, 47
Multi-Colored Blue (= Ultra Violet; Violet Blue), 124
Mural From Two Perspectives, A, 62
*My People* (musical revue), 96, 99, 189–90, 190n

Neo-Creole, 139, 224
Neo-Hip-Hop Kiddies Community, The, 195
*Newport Festival Suite*, 222, 227
New World A-Comin', 48–49, 58, 62, 169, 212, 225, 230
*New York Concert* (CD), 61
Night Creature, 196–97, 230
Night in Harlem, A, 8
Night Shepherd, The, 62
Night Train, 35–37, 229
*Night Train* (CD), 36
Nite, 147
Northern Lights, 228

Oh! How I Love My Darling, 72
On a Turquoise Cloud, 78–79, 79n
One O'Clock Jump, 34
Open-End Interview, 151

Paris Blues, 60, 143, 145–47
*Paris Blues Suite*, 147, 153, 213
Parlor Social De Luxe, 71
Passion Flower, 50, 115, 120–22, 123, 125, 126, 127
*Piano in the Background* (CD), 37
*Piano in the Foreground* (CD), 59, 125
*Piano Reflections* (CD), 50, 51, 52–53, 54, 59, 61, 99
Pitter Panther Patter, 47–48
Plucked Again, 47

*Polly Theme*, 151–52, 228–30
Poor Pilgrim of Sorrow (A City Called Heaven), 76
Prelude to a Kiss, 50
Pretty Girl, 128
Pretty Little Girl, 128–29

*Queen's Suite, The*, 53, 61, 62, 213, 228

Railroad Blues, 27
Railroad Man, 27
Raising the Rent, 93
Reflections in D, 50, 51, 51n, 59, 61, 99, 196–97
Reminiscing in Tempo, 52–53, 216, 219
Retrospection, 50, 99
*Revelations* (dance), 188, 196
Riba (The River; Mainstream), 83n, 201–2, 204n
Rite of Spring, 198
River, The. *See* Riba
*River, The* (ballet suite), 188–206, 212
Rockin' in Rhythm, 44, 98–99, 170, 216
Rocks in My Bed, 211
Round about Midnight (Round Midnight), 12
Run, The, 195

Sacred Concerts, 62, 84–85, 106, 165, 169, 191
Satin Doll, 49n, 59, 61, 62, 68, 150, 212
Sepia Panorama, 47
Serenade to Sweden, 83–84, 83n
Shakespeare suite (= *Such Sweet Thunder*), 108, 176–87, 230, 232
She Walks Well (= Beautiful Woman Walks Well), 141
Shortenin' Bread, 34
Single Petal of a Rose, The, 53–54, 61, 228
Skillipoop, 61
Sloppy Joe, 72
Soda Fountain Rag, 46, 62
Solitude, 93, 99–102, 230
*Solos, Duets and Trios* (CD), 46
Something to Live For, 102–3
Sonnet for Caesar, 183, 184, 185

Sonnet for Hank Cinq, 183, 184, 185
Sonnet for Sister Kate, 183, 184, 185
Sonnet in Search of a Moor, 183, 184, 185
*Sophisticated Ladies* (musical revue), 225
Soul Flute, 165
Soul-Soothing Beach, 62, 162, 163
Spring, The, 191, 198–99
Star-Crossed Lovers, The, 83n, 128–29, 128n, 131, 181, 185
Strange Fruit, 101
Stompin' at the Savoy, 34
Stormy Weather, 92–93
Such Sweet Thunder (composition), 179–80, 185
*Such Sweet Thunder* (suite and CD), 108, 128n, 176–87, 212, 226. *See also* Shakespeare suite
*Suite Anatomy*, 153–54, 213, 228–29, 232
*Suite Thursday*, 224
Sunset and the Mocking Bird, 228
Swampy River, 45
Sweet as Bear Meat, 115
Sweet Georgia Brown, 25n
*Symphonic Ellington, The* (CD), 221n

Taffy Twist, 202
Take the 'A' Train, 5, 31–33, 61, 83, 104, 114, 116–17, 142, 145–46, 205, 211
Telecasters, The, 180, 185
Tell Me It's the Truth, 169
That's the Blues Old Man, 35
This Ole House, 81
Three Black Kings, 212
Three Little Words, 73
Tiger Rag, 25n, 29
*Timon of Athens Suite*, 61, 212
*Togo Brava Suite* (CD), 62, 161–63, 165, 213
Tone Parallel to Harlem, A, 5, 14, 16–19, 214–15
Tonk, 61
Toto (Afrique), 162–63
Transblucency (A Blue Fog You Can Almost See Through), 77–79
T.T.G.T., 84–85
Tuxedo Junction, 31n

Twist, The, 202

Ultra Violet (= Violet Blue; Multi-Colored Blue), 115, 124
Up and Down, Up and Down (I Will Lead Them Up and Down), 128n, 180–81, 185
Upper and Outest, 153

Very Special, 56
Village of the Virgins, 191, 203, 204n, 205
Violet Blue (= Ultra Violet; Multi-Colored Blue), 115, 124
Vortex, The (The Whirlpool), 201

Wanderlust, 139, 154
Warm Valley, 56, 59, 119–20, 132
*Water Music*, 194
Way Early Subtone, 153
We Are Never Ever Getting Back Together, 98n
What Good Am I Without You, 139
Wig Wise, 56
Work Song, 107–8

Yankee Doodle, 32

## About the Author

Photo by Hans Goebl

**Jack Chambers** is professor of linguistics at University of Toronto. His jazz writings include the prizewinning biography *Milestones: The Music and Times of Miles Davis* and *Bouncin' with Bartok: The Incomplete Works of Richard Twardzik*.

Printed in the United States
by Baker & Taylor Publisher Services